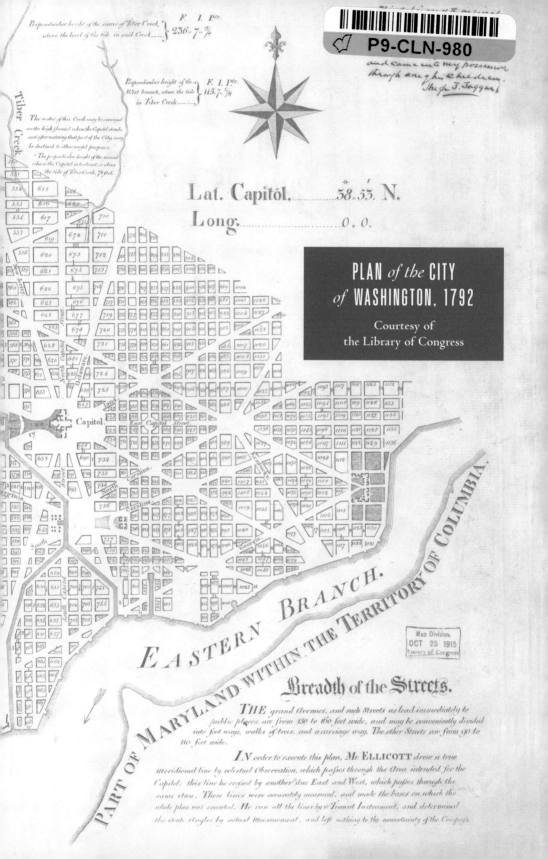

Perpendicular height of the source of Tiber Creek, above the level of the tide in said Creek. F. I. P.ts 236. 7. 5/4

Perpendicular height of the West branch, above the tide in Tiber Creek. F. I. P.ts 113. 7. 5/8

and came into my possession through one of his children. Thos. J. Jaggar

The water of this Creek may be conveyed on the high ground where the Capitol stands, and after watering that part of the City, may be destined to other useful purposes.

The perpendicular height of the ground where the Capitol is to stand, is above the tide of Tiber Creek, 78 feet.

Lat. Capitol.............. 38.53. N.

Long.............. 0, 0.

PLAN *of the* CITY *of* WASHINGTON, 1792

Courtesy of
the Library of Congress

Tiber Creek

Capitol

East Capitol Street.

EASTERN BRANCH.

PART OF MARYLAND WITHIN THE TERRITORY OF COLUMBIA.

Breadth of the Streets.

THE grand avenues, and such Streets as lead immediately to public places, are from 130 to 160 feet wide, and may be conveniently divided into foot ways, walks of trees, and a carriage way. The other Streets are from 90 to 110 feet wide.

IN order to execute this plan, Mr. ELLICOTT drew a true meridional line by celestial Observation, which passes through the Area intended for the Capitol: this line he crossed by another due East and West, which passes through the same Area. These lines were accurately measured, and made the bases on which the whole plan was executed. He ran all the lines by a Transit Instrument, and determined the acute angles by actual Measurement, and left nothing to the uncertainty of the Compass.

SECRETS *of* THE LOST SYMBOL

SECRETS

of

THE

LOST SYMBOL

The Unauthorized Guide
to the Mysteries Behind
The Da Vinci Code Sequel

by Dan Burstein *and* Arne de Keijzer

SENIOR CONTRIBUTING EDITOR
David A. Shugarts

CONTRIBUTING EDITORS
Lou Aronica and Paul Berger

WILLIAM MORROW
An Imprint of HarperCollins*Publishers*

HarperCollins books may be purchased for educational, business, or sales promotional use. For information please write: Special Markets Department, HarperCollins Publishers, 10 East 53rd Street, New York, NY 10022.

FIRST EDITION

Library of Congress Cataloging-in-Publication Data has been applied for.

ISBN 978-0-06-196495-4

10 11 12 13 14 RRD/OV 10 9 8 7 6 5 4 3 2 1

For Julie,
Who, for thirty-nine years, has been both my Aphrodite and
my Athena . . . and will always be so . . .

And for David,
Already so accomplished and so far down the road
of his unique hero's journey . . .

—Dan Burstein

For "D,"
A great and gentle man, sorely missed . . .

And, as ever, for Helen, and Hannah,
warvb loza ddd sysssrt fua xhe wagvet xr ql lika

—Arne de Keijzer

Contents

Chapter One
INTELLECTUAL ALCHEMY

Chapter Two
HISTORY, MYSTERY, AND MASONS

Chapter Three
SECRET KNOWLEDGE

Chapter Four
SCIENCE, FAITH, AND THE BIRTH OF A NATION

Chapter Five
MAN MEETS GOD, AND GOD MEETS MAN

Chapter Six
YE ARE NEW AGE GODS

Chapter Seven
MYSTERY CITY ON THE HILL

Chapter Eight
INTO THE KRYPTIC . . . ART, SYMBOLS, AND CODES

Chapter Nine
DIVINING DAN BROWN

Chapter Ten
BROWNIAN LOGIC

Editor's Note

Secrets of The Lost Symbol: The Unauthorized Guide to the Mysteries Behind The Da Vinci Code Sequel follows the same format as the earlier books in our *Secrets* series, *Secrets of the Code*, *Secrets of Angels & Demons*, and *Secrets of Mary Magdalene*.

Once again we have sought to provide a comprehensive reader's guide to a fascinating and complex novel by carefully gathering original writing, extensive interviews with experts, and excerpts from books, publications, and Web sites. We are again intrigued by Dan Brown's technique of weaving rich and historically important ideas into the heart of his action/adventure story. At the same time, Brown's blending of real sources with the fictional needs of his plot sets off the question, what is fact and what is fiction in *The Lost Symbol*? We have taken on the task of answering that question, exploring further the realm of history and ideas, and analyzing the plot points and devices used by the author.

We have taken care to distinguish our editors' voices from the authors' contributions by setting our introductory comments in bold. The text that follows is in the original voice of the author or interviewee. The attribution "by the Editors" means it was an original contribution by one of our contributing editors but written in the collective "voice" of the book. All material is copyrighted by Squibnocket Partners LLC unless otherwise indicated in the copyright notice that can be found at the bottom of the first page of the contribution.

Working with such a wide range of source materials, we have tended to regularize spelling and naming conventions in our own work, while leaving undisturbed the original spellings and conventions that appear in works that are excerpted here. For example, some experts refer to the Albrecht Dürer etching used to provide a major clue to Robert Langdon as *Melencolia I*—the intentionally misspelled name Dürer himself gave it; others spell it more expectedly as *Melancholia*. We have tended to standardize on the former, which is also the spelling used by Dan Brown.

References to chapter numbers and cover artwork of *The Lost Symbol*—often abbreviated as *TLS*—refer to the U.S. edition published in September 2009. References to Dan Brown's other works are sometimes shorthanded as *DVC (The Da Vinci Code)* and *A&D (Angels & Demons)*.

In giving readers a quick taste of the ideas and writings of a great many experts, we have inevitably had to leave things out we would have otherwise liked to use. We want to thank all the authors, interviewees, publishers, and experts who have so generously made their thoughts and materials available to us. In return, we urge our readers to buy the books written by our experts (often cited in our introductions as well as in the contributors section) and pursue the multitude of ideas referred to within these pages in their original sources.

Introduction

by Dan Burstein

At precisely 3:01 A.M. Eastern Daylight Time on September 15, 2009, my Kindle sprang to life soundlessly, unobtrusively. Two minutes later, it had downloaded Dan Brown's new novel, *The Lost Symbol*. A few minutes after that, I was busy using the Kindle's search function to ascertain if this was the book I had long thought it might be. I had a list and I started checking off the items . . . Freemasons? Check. Masonic rituals? Check. Washington, D.C.? Check.

Washington Monument ✔
George Washington ✔
Benjamin Franklin ✔
Alchemy ✔
Isaac Newton ✔
Albrecht Dürer ✔
Rosicrucians ✔
Francis Bacon ✔
Invisible College ✔
Capitol Rotunda ✔
The Apotheosis of Washington painting ✔
Hermes Trismegistus ✔

House of the Temple headquarters of Scottish Rite Masons ✔

Albert Pike ✔

James Smithson and the Smithsonian ✔

King Solomon and his temple ✔

The "widow's son" ✔

Thomas Jefferson ✔

Deism ✔

Egypt, Greece, Sumer ✔

Kabbalah, Zohar, Old Testament, Gnostics, Buddhists, Hindus ✔

Compasses, squares, magic squares, skulls, cornerstones, pyramids, pantheons, hieroglyphics, Zoroaster, codes, *Kryptos,* Pythagoras, Heraclitus, Revelation, Apocalypse ✔

So yes, this was, indeed, the book I had been expecting for more than five years . . . and now, in the late days of summer 2009, it was finally here.

My journey into the meaning of *The Lost Symbol* (*TLS*)—and the archaeology of this book that you now hold in your hands—actually originated one night nearly seven years ago. Like many others, I came across *The Da Vinci Code* in the summer of 2003 when it dominated the bestseller lists. It was by a seemingly unknown author named Dan Brown. It sat by my bedside along with dozens of other unread books and all the other things typical of the competition for mind share in the complex, chaotic, information-intense world in which we all live.

Then one day I picked up *The Da Vinci Code* and started reading. I read all night, fascinated. I literally couldn't put it down. This kind of absorption in a book was an experience I used to have frequently in my younger years, but not so often in this season of my life, as I was then turning fifty. At one point, as I read the provocative assertion that there was a woman in Leonardo da Vinci's *The Last Supper*—and that the woman was Mary Magdalene—I got out of bed and pulled the art books down from our library shelves. I looked at the Leonardo painting that I had encountered, of course, hundreds of times previously. Yes, it really did look like a woman seated next to Jesus!

By morning, when I had finished the book, I was as intellectually challenged as I had been by any book I had read in a long time. I wanted to know what was true and what was not, what was fact and what was fiction. As soon as my local Barnes & Noble opened, I was there, sipping latte and rummaging through scores of books that had been mentioned or alluded to in *The Da Vinci Code*. I left the store with hundreds of dollars' worth of books and went home to absorb this material.

Fast forward a few months into 2004. My writing partner, Arne de Keijzer, and I had put together a massive project, including more than fifty writers, editors, and world-class experts on subjects that ranged from theology to art history, Gnostic gospels and alternative scriptures to codes and cryptography. We deployed this team to develop a breakthrough book, *Secrets of the Code*: *The Unauthorized Guide to the Mysteries Behind The Da Vinci Code*, which was published in April 2004. *Secrets of the Code* immediately became a bestseller in its own right. As it rose into the top ten on the *New York Times* bestseller list (eventually reaching number seven—not bad for a book about another book), I found myself suddenly, and quite surprisingly, in demand all over America and the world as an expert on all things *Da Vinci Code* and Dan Brown.

We had developed some fascinating insights into *The Da Vinci Code* and had become experts ourselves on all of the ideas and arguments that swirled through the vortex of debate and discussion about Dan Brown's novel. For the next two years, with the public's fascination with *The Da Vinci Code* seemingly insatiable, I was interviewed by hundreds of TV shows, newspapers, magazines, and Web sites, and invited to speak to religious groups that ranged from the 92nd Street Y in New York (Jewish) to the Pope John Paul II Museum in Washington (Catholic), from retirement homes to high schools, from community colleges to the Ivy Leagues, from New Age spas to Rotary Clubs and Kiwanis, from medical conventions to movie theaters, from public libraries to corporate meetings.

Regardless of what audiences thought of *The Da Vinci Code*—some loved it, some hated it, some enjoyed it as a good potboiler, some took it way too seriously as either gospel truth or diabolic heresy—I found a torrent of ideas and interest. Programs ran way longer than expected, people wanted to stay after the event was over, and many, many people who had never gone to an author event in their lives wanted to talk, explore, and discuss it into the night.

Secrets of the Code went on to become the world's bestselling guidebook to *The Da Vinci Code (DVC)*. It was translated into more than thirty languages and appeared on more than a dozen global bestseller lists. Eventually, we would create additional titles in the *Secrets* series, including a guidebook to *Angels & Demons*, the 2000 novel that reads like a rough draft for *The Da Vinci Code*, for which Dan Brown first created the Robert Langdon character, and an anthology of fascinating new thinking about the woman at the center of the *DVC* phenomenon, *Secrets of Mary Magdalene*.

Our team made many discoveries in the course of researching *Secrets of the Code*. We learned about an eighteen-hundred-year-old carpet fragment that may offer the oldest depiction now extant of Mary Magdalene. We got early information about the world-shaking (and highly credible) discoveries having to do with the long lost Gospel of Judas, one of the most theologically/philosophically important of the Gnostic gospels. It had resurfaced and was being authenticated and studied—even though it wouldn't be published for another two years. We heard a marvelous tale (although it turned out to be a nineteenth-century hoax) about the "Jewish Da Vinci Code"—involving the lost golden menorah from the Temple of Solomon, supposedly hidden in the Tiber River in Rome. We were among the first to hear a piece of music based on musical notes decoded from symbolic writing in Scotland's Rosslyn Chapel—a fifteenth-century chapel to which thousands of visitors had been flocking since reading about it in *DVC*.

But the most tantalizing of all our discoveries was the one made by our investigative reporter, David A. Shugarts. (Dave contributed several wonderful commentaries to *Secrets of the Code*, and has done it again for *Secrets of The Lost Symbol*). With Dave's help, we cracked the code that had been discovered in the form of slightly bolded randomized letters on *The Da Vinci Code* jacket flaps. Strung together, these letters spelled out the enigmatic question, "**Is there no help for the widow's son?**" We would soon come to understand that this is a very important coded message in the history of Freemasonry. It refers back to the murder of Hiram Abiff, the legendary master builder of King Solomon's Temple, who some see as either the first Mason or at least the archetype for future Masons. "Is there no help for the widow's son?" has, for at least the last several centuries, been a distress call from a Mason in need to his brother Masons. From the research we did around this discovery, we felt confident enough to issue a press release in 2004 predicting that Dan Brown's next book would be about Freemasons and would be set in Washington, D.C.

Very shortly thereafter, Dan Brown and his publisher confirmed that yes, indeed, Brown's next book, then thought to be titled *The Solomon Key*, would again feature Robert Langdon, would be set in Washington, and would feature a plot set against the backdrop of the history of Freemasonry in America—exactly as we had predicted.

Soon, Arne de Keijzer and I would be having coffee and bagels and looking at six volumes of dossiers Dave Shugarts had compiled in his attempt to "reverse-engineer" the mind of Dan Brown. If we believed Dan Brown's next book would be about Freemasons and would be set in our nation's capital, what aspects of history, religion, and philosophy would likely prove interesting? What artworks? What elements of science? Symbols? Codes? Could we imagine, before Dan Brown even wrote a word of this sure-to-be blockbusting *DVC* sequel, what its contents might be? We adopted this bold experiment and set Shugarts off on the path that would become the 2005 book, *Secrets of the Widow's Son*—a book by David Shugarts, with an introduction by me, that was, for all intents and purposes, a book about a bestseller that hadn't been written yet (and wouldn't be published until *TLS* almost five years later).

How could we have been so sure of where Dan Brown would go in a book he hadn't yet written? We had a certain advantage in this inquiry for two reasons. First, we had already spent two years reverse-engineering the ingredients that went into the intellectual stew of *The Da Vinci Code* and *Angels & Demons*. Where Dan Brown had found some books on the Gnostic gospels, for example, and pulled some interesting ideas out of them, we had gone to the world's leading experts—people like Elaine

Pagels, James Robinson, and Bart Ehrman—and interviewed them at length. We had come across the strange brew of legend and lore known as *Holy Blood, Holy Grail* and used an excerpt from it in *Secrets of the Code,* with permission from its authors. In my 2004 introductory note to that excerpt, I had written, *"Holy Blood, Holy Grail* is the book that 'started it all.' Reading the book, one can almost see the places where Dan Brown might have highlighted something or put a Post-it on it, and said, 'Aha! I've got to use that!' "

I referred to *Holy Blood, Holy Grail* as the "Ur-text for *The Da Vinci Code,"* but noted that it was a book of significantly questionable veracity, and saluted Brown for weaving some of its purported nonfiction elements into his work of *fiction.* As it turned out, in writing those words, I had forecast a) the plagiarism lawsuit that the authors of *Holy Blood, Holy Grail* would bring against Brown two years later (unfair and without merit, in my opinion—with the London court that heard the case eventually upholding Brown's innocence and the judge, amazingly, issuing part of his opinion in code); b) I had managed to foresee the evidence that the other side would try to argue in support of their claim of plagiarism (court depositions showed that Dan Brown and his wife, Blythe, had indeed marked up and highlighted passages of *Holy Blood, Holy Grail* as part of their research on *The Da Vinci Code,* just as I suggested); and c) I had outlined the case-winning defense: Brown was writing fiction, and using bits of what was alleged to be nonfiction from the other authors, only to create a more interesting fictional plot.

In short, we were developing a good track record, validated by subsequent events, in understanding how the mind of Dan Brown works.

As it turned out, we were right to encourage Shugarts to write *Secrets of the Widow's Son.* His work cracking Dan Brown's codes was so amazingly good and predictive that, five years before *The Lost Symbol* was even published, we had guessed that Dan Brown might utilize all the items mentioned at the beginning of this introduction. More than that: Dave went so far as to guess that Brown might use artworks by Albrecht Dürer. Amazing enough that he would be right about that. But not just any Dürer: Dave specifically suggested Brown would be interested in Dürer's

Melencolia I, with its magic square contained within the image. And sure enough, five years later, Dürer's *Melencolia I* turns up as a critical ingredient in Robert Langdon's solution of the riddle of the Masonic pyramid in *The Lost Symbol.* Dave didn't just say "I think Brown will want to use the National Cathedral in his plot" (which of course Brown did in *TLS*), Dave specifically mentioned the detail of the Darth Vader grotesque on the facade of the National Cathedral as likely to attract Brown's attention. Five years later, my wife and I are on our own impromptu tour of Washington, D.C., in the wake of the publication of *TLS*, and I find myself looking up at Darth Vader at the National Cathedral, and am genuinely amazed myself that Dave correctly predicted that this small detail would show up in *The Lost Symbol.*

I had a similar experience in the Capitol Rotunda standing under its massive dome in the fall of 2009, right after reading *The Lost Symbol.* Great stories about the Capitol abound, so if you knew or at least believed Brown would write a thriller set in D.C., you could make a relatively easy and successful guess that the Capitol building itself might be involved. In fact, it turned out to be so important to *TLS*, that it is in the very center of the book's cover image. And the central action of the book begins and ends in the Rotunda. But to envision specifically the use Brown would make of Brumidi's *Apotheosis of Washington* fresco painted into the top of the domed ceiling in the Rotunda—which lawmakers and tourists alike generally walk by and ignore because you have to stop and crane your head and neck up to see it—this was again nothing short of amazing.

Freemasonry is a body of thought and an approach to the world that relies very heavily on a wide variety of historical experiences and allusions, images and symbols, myths and rituals. Once you succeed at pulling back the veil and becoming an insider to this body of thought, the connections become electrifying and dazzling. Since the Freemasons themselves choose to connect their experience to so many other historical movements of learning, knowledge, spiritualism, and mysticism, and to express so much of their cosmology in potent symbolic form, ascending the winding staircase into this world is a lot like playing the grand master version of the Kevin Bacon game. Everything is connected to everything else by a thousand threads. Egyptian pyramid builders to Pythagoras to King Solomon to Jesus to Gnostics to Knights Templar to Francis Bacon to Isaac Newton to George Washington. All of this can be interpreted as a continuous, interconnected story. Indeed—that's the point: the inter-connectedness of everything.

For an author like Dan Brown, and a protagonist like Robert Langdon (and his Freemason/noetic coheroes in *TLS*, the Solomon siblings), this is a wondrous world to choose for a thriller. This is a novel of ideas. And that's the joy (and sometimes the frustration) of doing a book like this about one of Dan Brown's books. The appearance of the "Hand of the Mysteries" at the opening of *The Lost Symbol* indicates that Robert Lang-don has been "invited" on a life-changing journey. We, too, as readers, have been given an invitation to think about some of the most profound ideas in the history of civilization and to engage in some of the most pro-found debates of both our recent and our ancient heritage.

Chapter
ONE

INTELLECTUAL ALCHEMY

EXPLORING THE COMPLEX COSMOS OF *THE LOST SYMBOL*

by Dan Burstein

Time is a river . . . and books are boats. Many volumes start down that stream, only to be wrecked and lost beyond recall in its sands. Only a few, a very few, endure the testings of time and live to bless the ages following.

—*The Lost Symbol*, based on language taken from Masonic writings

Is *The Lost Symbol* one of those books that will stand the test of time? Probably not. In the nearly three millennia history of written books, few works of popular culture, with a handful of exceptions such as Shakespeare's, have achieved centuries of endurance and longevity. But Dan Brown's *The Lost Symbol* may, in retrospect, be a different kind of enduring achievement. It may provide future historians and anthropologists one of the best renderings, in one volume, of humankind's early twenty-first-century thoughts, debates, and inarticulate pointings at currently inexpressible ideas about some of the biggest questions, mysteries, and challenges of human existence.

Set in Washington, D.C., *The Lost Symbol* ironically and quixotically ignores virtually all the pressing issues of contemporary Washington. *The*

Lost Symbol is essentially unconcerned with wars, health care, economic stimulus, or other items on this version of Washington's "big questions." Instead, its agenda looks more like this:

Is there a God?

Is God an exterior force or is God interior to all of us?

Is there a soul? If there is, what happens to it when we die?

Why are we here?

What if there is no God, no prime mover of any kind? How will we know? How should we live in such a world?

What is our purpose in the universe?

What happens after we die?

Can all the world's religions and spiritual systems be read essentially as one large vision of humanity's quest for connections to the larger universe?

Is there a physicality to the "mind," the "soul," and human thoughts that can be focused, shaped, and turned into energy, causation, and change in the external material world?

Do the latest advances in physics, cosmology, biology, and neuroscience mirror our ancient philosophical, mythic, and religious ideas about who we are and what the universe is?

Did ancient philosophers, Renaissance alchemists and mystics, and even America's Founding Fathers have insights into the process of humanity coming to harness its inherent power?

When the ghoulish severed hand of Peter Solomon turns up in the Capitol Rotunda, Dan Brown is using one of the hundreds of symbolic/metaphorical tricks that he will use throughout the novel, drawn from his grab bag of the last several thousand years of mystery writings he has researched. The evil Mal'akh is using the symbol of the "Hand of the Mysteries" to invite Robert Langdon to become a pawn in Mal'akh's own deadly game—his personal quest to discover the meaning of the "Ancient Mysteries" and the "Lost Word."

Langdon will go on a classic "hero's journey" during the cold, twelve-hour January night on which the book is set. This is his own elaborate ritual quest and rite of initiation and passage. We, as readers, are invited onto a simultaneous, parallel journey. Ours is a journey that will touch, albeit only superficially, on some deep ideas and theories about the most compelling questions of human existence. Whether or not one agrees with the ideas as presented on this tour, even the most rudimentary exegesis of *The Lost Symbol* suggests a whole series of extraordinary and thought-provoking discussion topics.

In the penultimate moments of *TLS*, Robert Langdon and Katherine Solomon are lying on their backs, gazing up at the magnificent mythic fresco, *The Apotheosis of Washington*, that fills the top of the Capitol Dome, "two kids, shoulder to shoulder," contemplating the meaning of life, after their heroic night of revelatory adventure. Langdon remembers his teenage years, canoeing out into the lake at night, gazing at the stars, and thinking about "stuff like this." Like the teenage Langdon, we all did this at some point in our lives. So, too, did people in all societies from prehistory to the ancient Egyptians, Babylonians, Greeks, biblical-era Jews and Christians, Romans, gnostics in the desert, medieval alchemists, Renaissance humanists, Galileo, Newton, and even Benjamin Franklin. (Franklin was known for his "lunatic society" walks on moonlit nights with fellow big thinkers discussing the big questions.)

Almost all children do art and music when they are young, then stop doing these activities somewhere along the line. Similarly, most of us once spent some moments of our lives reflecting on the "big questions." Typically, this was in our adolescence or young adulthood. But as we grow older, most of us cease to focus on weighty matters like these. Weighed down by the pressures of daily life, having come to believe whatever we have come to believe through our life experiences, and convinced (by our usually less than successful attempts to think for too long or too deeply on these matters). We generally conclude that there are no satisfactory answers to the bigger existential questions and simply continue on life's journey. Just as we no longer sing or paint as regularly as we did when we were children, most of us stop asking ourselves questions like: What existed before the Big Bang?

Except for a handful of us who are cosmologists, physicists, philosophers, or theologians by profession, or another handful of us who have decided to make the quest for these answers an integral part of our personal lives, most of us have religious beliefs or gut feelings about these questions, but we don't spend much time actively contemplating them.

And that's what so interesting about *The Lost Symbol*. In the form of an extremely accessible pop fiction book—a fast-paced beach read, an airplane page-turner, whatever you want to call it—we have the opportunity to revisit these questions. Whether Brown's presentation of them is right or wrong is almost immaterial. The process of wrestling with the questions can be extremely thought-provoking and can allow any of us to engage in our own way, at whatever level of depth we choose to pursue.

Of course it's easy to dismiss *The Lost Symbol* as not particularly meaningful. It is a novel, like Dan Brown's previous works, in which clunky clichés, impossible plot points, purple prose, awkward sentences, over-italicization, and vast oversimplifications of complex ideas are the rules, not the exceptions. I am an unabashed Dan Brown fan—but I am also the first to howl at his frequently awful lines of dialogue, glaring factual errors, and the one-dimensionality of his characters. We need to bear in mind at all times that *TLS* is a work of *fiction* (this time, as opposed to *The Da Vinci Code*, Dan Brown put the words "a novel" right on the cover to remind us of this obvious fact). It may or may not be your idea of great fiction. But I will argue that it is interesting, intriguing, and, at the end of the day, important fiction.

We live in a society that is less and less inclined to engage in long-form debate or to read substantial book-length nonfiction. True literary fiction is also disappearing and, frankly, there is a poverty of ideas in much of what passes for literary fiction today. *The Lost Symbol* may be a beach read, but underneath the sand, it is a novel of ideas. That's why we have created *Secrets of The Lost Symbol:* a book to explore those ideas. The exploration that starts here is not only based on my own thoughts and those of my colleague, Arne de Keijzer and our *Secrets* team, but even more so on the wisdom of the many world-class thinkers and experts whose views are reflected throughout this volume. And if our mission here is successful, you will have the raw materials to extend your own ideas and interests in a multiplicity of directions.

OF FREEMASONS AND DEISTS: AMERICA WAS FOUNDED AS AN INCLUSIVE NATION

The agenda of *The Lost Symbol* is nearly as vast as attempting to explore the universe and the whole of human history of ideas. So let's begin with just a handful of the novel's bigger ideas and themes.

"America wasn't founded a Christian country. It became a Christian country." This crisp statement made by Dan Brown in an interview with NBC's Matt Lauer sums up the purpose of dozens of references, historical anecdotes, and arguments that are one of the major leitmotifs of *TLS*. In the last thirty years of American history, our society has come under the sway of a powerful modern myth that would have us believe America's Founding Fathers were animated by a Christian fundamentalist worldview similar to that of today's religious right. In fact, just the opposite is the historical case, according to *TLS*.

The reason Brown dwells on the importance of Freemasonry to the early American experience is because Freemasonry is a cohesive body of philosophical thought that recognizes a generalized God concept but rejects a specific definition of God and faith. In Brown's rendition (which is undoubtedly overidealized), Freemasonry emphasizes tolerance, respect for many religious traditions, and diversity of belief. It focuses on morality, progress, personal development, intellectual enlightenment, and communitarian values, but not on specific religious belief. The Freemasons draw inspiration from the wisdom of the ages and from thinkers and writings from many cultures, both sacred and secular. *TLS* reminds us that in the

Scottish Rite Freemasonry's Washington, D.C., headquarters—the so-called House of the Temple, where both the opening and climactic scenes of *TLS* take place—the Old Testament, New Testament, and Koran sit together on the altar table.

George Washington, Benjamin Franklin, John Hancock, Paul Revere, and numerous other leading architects of American democracy were Freemasons. The secret passwords exchanged among Freemasons to establish bonds with one another played a major role in at least one decisive moment of our nation's history. On the very day of Paul Revere's famous ride, he was taken into custody by a British police captain. When it was established that both men were brother Masons, the policeman released Revere, who went on to make his famous ride for freedom and against British tyranny.

At least nine signers of the Declaration of Independence were Freemasons. Many of the early presidents were Freemasons (including Washington, Monroe, and Jackson). Numerous leading lights of the European Enlightenment were Freemasons, from Voltaire to Diderot. Concepts, phrases, and symbols flowed freely from the philosophical world of Masonic thought of the late eighteenth and early nineteenth centuries into the documents, decisions, debates, laws, art, and architecture of the new American nation. George Washington was sworn in for his first term on the Bible from the nearby Masonic lodge; he famously led a Masonic procession in his Masonic apron and regalia while presiding over a Masonic ritual to lay the cornerstone of the Capitol.

Benjamin Franklin and the French philosopher Voltaire, two of the greatest minds of the transatlantic Enlightenment, met together in the Parisian *Loge des Neuf Soeurs* (the Lodge of the Nine Sisters). Indeed, Franklin helped initiate Voltaire into this storied French Masonic lodge. As early as elementary school we learn about the great support the American Revolution received from the French general Lafayette. But what we aren't told in school is what may have helped Washington and Lafayette, despite language barriers and a huge difference in age, bond immediately and work in such close alignment for the success of the American cause. They were motivated, of course, by the common goal of opposing the British. But they were also brother Masons, able to understand and trust each other because they saw the world from similar viewpoints. Even today, a heroic statue of Lafayette stands directly in front of the White House, testament to Washington and Lafayette's shared belief in liberty, equality, and, perhaps especially notably, fraternity. Many of the foreigners who joined the American cause were also Freemasons, including Baron von Steuben, the Prussian military expert who is credited with helping Washington shape up his ragtag army, as well as with writing the first training manual for the American troops.

Thomas Jefferson, while not a Freemason, was philosophically a deist. Freemasonry and deism are cousins of sorts. Deists typically believe in a supreme being, but one that created the world in an architectural sense and doesn't continue to intervene in human affairs. For deists, there is not much need for organized religion. God is not a miracle worker on earth. *TLS* reminds us of the Jefferson Bible, which, unfortunately, gets all too little attention in what we know and learn about Thomas Jefferson in school. This great thinker and founder of American democracy, the man who wrote most of the inspiring words of the Declaration of Independence, also made his own "edit" of the Bible. He removed references to the virgin birth, the resurrection, and other miracles and supernatural phenomena he found irrelevant to the moral wisdom of biblical teachings, which he sought to emphasize.

The beliefs of Freemasons and deists are not in necessary contradiction with Christian beliefs. Most of the Founding Fathers, including all of the figures mentioned above, undoubtedly considered themselves Christians. Yet these pioneers of the American experience believed deeply in the separation of church and state. These were not just words to them. This was a fundamental principle. They also believed in learning from all sources of valuable knowledge and were generally well versed not only in the Old and New Testaments, but in Greek and Roman classics, and sixteenth- and seventeenth-century philosophical works today considered obscure and borderline "pagan," such as those of Francis Bacon, one of the more intriguing characters from history referenced by Dan Brown in *TLS*.

True to the "inclusiveness" of Freemasonry that Brown promotes in *TLS*, the intellectual history of the Masons right up to the present day draws from deep wellsprings into the ancient beliefs, myths, rituals, systems of thought, signs, symbols, as well as the Judeo-Christian tradition and a wide variety of Eastern religions and civilizations. Like a cosmic intellectual grab bag, Freemasonry includes bodies of ideas from geometry to alchemy, Gnosticism to quantum physics. It includes schools of philosophical thought from the pre-Socratics to the Knights Templar, the Renaissance humanists, and the scientific, political, literary, and musical geniuses of the Enlightenment

Christianity is not in contradiction with Freemasonry. The reverse is true as well. However, there is a clear difference in emphasis between the open, tolerant, exploratory Freemason/deist worldview of the late eighteenth century, and the more fixed, specific, rigorous religious vision of Christianity some would like to project (incorrectly) backward on to the America of the Founding Fathers. One of Dan Brown's contributions to contemporary political discussion is to show why it just won't work to picture the Founding Fathers as evangelical Christians in order to legitimize and justify attempts to superimpose such a worldview on American society today and in the future. It won't work because it isn't true. "In God we trust" was first used on coins in 1864; "under God" was not added to the Pledge of Allegiance until 1954. Jefferson, Washington, and Franklin tended to speak sparingly of "Providence," "Divine Providence," the "Creator," and other such euphemisms. They almost never invoked "God," or "Jesus."

Dan Brown tells us he is not a Mason himself. But there is no mystery about his feelings on why Freemasonry epitomizes values he identifies with personally. As he wrote in a letter to a Freemason group after publication of *TLS*:

In a world where men do battle over whose definition of God is most accurate, I cannot adequately express the deep respect and admiration I feel toward an organization in which men of differing faiths are able to "break bread together" in a bond of brotherhood, friendship, and camaraderie. Please accept my humble thanks for the noble example you set for humankind. It is my sincere hope that the Masonic community recognizes *The Lost Symbol* for what it truly is . . . an earnest attempt to reverentially explore the history and beauty of Masonic Philosophy.

The Lost Symbol is a shout from the rooftops. Brown is saying that "the real America" is the America of Washington, Franklin, and Jefferson, of Freemasons and deists. It is the America of the open mind and the insatiable desire for knowledge of every type. The America open to all comers and all ideas and all traditions. The America where church and state are separate, shades of belief or nonbelief are personal choices, and no religious dogma prevents innovative minds from freely expressing themselves or advancing themselves through life.

FREEMASONS: THEATER DIRECTORS OF DEMOCRACY

Whether or not they have any actual linkage to ancient pyramid or temple builders, Freemasons have studied and assumed that heritage. Thus, it is no surprise that some of the most recognizable, appealing, and influential public buildings have been created by Masons or those influenced by Masonic styles. Robert Mills, the architect of the world's most famous obelisk—the Washington Monument—was keenly aware of the importance of Egyptian civilization and its symbols to George Washington and the Masonic heritage the Monument was honoring. (Masons were among the chief fund-raisers for the Washington Monument!) Gustave Eiffel, the designer of the Eiffel Tower in Paris—a different kind of obelisk—was a Mason. Both the Washington Monument and the Eiffel Tower make symbolic statements about humankind's aspirations to touch the heavens. Both suggest the soaring nature of their societies. Both have fabulous interplay with light, sunsets, moonrises, and the stars. Both were considered oddities when they were first built but have now become enduring classics, emblematic of and central to their cities. The ambition of both monuments is relentless. Both had to be built against the odds of financial battles, political infighting, and aesthetic criticism. When the Washington Monument was finished in 1885, it became the tallest building in the world at 555 feet. Its completion forever put an end to centuries of cityscapes dominated by cathedrals and religious buildings. Just four years later, the Eiffel Tower almost doubled the Washington Monument's height, rising 1,063 feet at its completion in 1889.

If Pierre l'Enfant, the designer of Washington's street plan (who came to America with Lafayette), was not a Mason, he was certainly very closely involved with Freemasonry and had a great appreciation for the Masonic geometry of ovals, ellipses, squares, and circles. He worked closely with George Washington, who was himself a land surveyor and urban planner by training, on the layout of this new city, this "Athens on the Potomac." Renwick, the architect of the Smithsonian "castle" building, may have been inspired by Templar and Freemason castle redoubts in Europe, including Rosslyn Chapel of *Da Vinci Code* fame.

Several composers of some of our most uplifting music were Freemasons—people like Mozart, Haydn, and Elgar, the composer of *Pomp and Circumstance*, today's nearly universal American music for graduations and other rites of passage. As lifelong students of ritual, rite, and symbolic presentation, the Freemasons are like theater directors to our world, and it should be no surprise that they play a disproportionately large role at certain key moments in our history.

MYSTICAL TRADITION IS OUR "THIRD CULTURE"

From its opening pages to its last, *The Lost Symbol* is an argument for the nonlinear, not-necessarily-rationalist, magical-mystical-spiritual tendency in human thought to be recognized as a major force in shaping the development of civilization. We learn in school that the Renaissance was triggered by Europe's rediscovery, during the Crusades, of classical knowledge of mathematics, philosophy, and the arts held in the great repositories of knowledge in Byzantium and the Mideast. But no high school teacher ever adds that Crusaders, Templars, and travelers also brought back the mystical teachings and "secret knowledge" of the neo-Platonists, whose writings had dominated the Library of Alexandria. If you want to know about the impact of Hermes Trismegistus on the Renaissance, you'd better get an occult/esoteric book, because you won't find these exotic mystical ideas in our mainstream texts.

We learn about the great rationalist minds of Isaac Newton, Thomas Jefferson, and Benjamin Franklin, without ever being told of Jefferson's interest in Bacon and the Rosicrucians, or Franklin's interest in astrology and Freemasonry. As for Newton, we all learn the tale about the apple falling. But most of us never learn that he spent the majority of his capacious waking hours not on the laws of motion, but on alchemical experiments, searching for the lost wisdom of ancient civilizations, attempting to reimagine the Temple of Solomon, and otherwise decoding the meaning of Scripture.

Some of us may wish to think of America as born in the spirit of Christian fundamentalism, and some of us may wish to think of America as born in a pure, rationalist, *Federalist Papers*–type celebration of democratic theory. But the reality is messier and more complicated that either pole of the debate would suggest. As novelist and *Time* magazine reviewer Lev Grossman said of *TLS*, "What he did for Christianity in *Angels & Demons* and *The Da Vinci Code*, Brown is now trying to do for America: reclaim its richness, its darkness, its weirdness. It's probably a quixotic effort, but it is nevertheless touchingly valiant . . . Our history is as sick and weird as anybody's! There's signal in the noise, order in the chaos! It just takes a degree from a nonexistent Harvard department to see it."

One of the great experts on the evolution of the "mystery traditions" over the last two thousand years is Joscelyn Godwin. Godwin, a professor of music at Colgate, is about as close as we will ever see to a real-life Robert Langdon. Think about this quick tour of the ancient mysteries he provides in his 2007 book, *The Golden Thread: The Ageless Wisdom of the Western Mystery Traditions*:

After the Roman Empire, Hermeticism . . . expanded to include alchemy and the occult sciences (divination, astrology, magic, etc.). All three Abrahamic religions (Judaism, Christianity, Islam) found a place for it, although sometimes a grudging one . . . In the Renaissance era, the Hermetic philosophy served as neutral ground for Protestants and Catholics alike. Alchemy and the other occult sciences to which it provided the intellectual underpinning flourished as never before.

Because it is essentially a cosmological and practical teaching, rather than a theology, Hermeticism can coexist with any religion . . . Its historical record is innocent of intolerance and bloodshed, its way of life one of science, contemplation, and self-refinement . . .

Freemasonry, which arose in its present form in the seventeenth and eighteenth centuries, was the most lasting creation of the Hermetic tradition in the West . . .

After demonstrating the connective tissue that runs intellectually from Plato and Pythagoras through to the alchemists, the Rosicrucians, the Freemasons, and the American Founding Fathers, Godwin considers the "Philosopher's Dilemma": should the enlightened person, who has access to the cosmological secrets, work for the betterment of the world? Or is the world such a lost cause that such a person should work only for his own ability to obtain immortality? As theologian Deirdre Good suggests in chapter 5, the religion of Dan Brown may sound universal, inclusive, ecumenical. But if it separates people into their own self-development pods, focused only on their own self-improvement, it cannot harness the collective energy necessary to change the world for the better.

Godwin quotes Madame Blavatsky, the founder of the nineteenth-century Theosophy movement as saying, "The *permanent* preservation of a personal identity beyond death is a very rare achievement, accomplished only by those who wrest her secrets from Nature, and control their own super-material development . . . [It is] accomplished only by adepts and sorcerers—the one class having acquired the supreme secret knowledge by holy methods, and with benevolent motives, the other having acquired it by unholy methods, and for base motives." This is the origins of Dan Brown's Mal'akh. To obtain genuine immortality, the adept must have forged, during life, a "radiant body." (This, of course, is what Mal'akh has been trying to do with his fitness regimen, his tattoos, self-castration, etc.) But he also needs access to the "supreme secret knowledge," and for that he must use the "unholy methods" of taking Peter hostage and entrapping Robert Langdon and conniving to obtain their help in his quest.

HARRY POTTER, ROBERT LANGDON, AND THE PHILOSOPHER'S STONE

The fiction bestseller lists in the first decade of the twenty-first century have been dominated by two book series—J. K. Rowling's and Dan Brown's—each involving a very likable everyman sort of character (Harry Potter, Robert Langdon) who has to enter a world of mystery, magic, myth, alchemy, and ancient crafts, and use intelligence (mostly) and physical skills (only occasionally) to do battle with the darkest of evil forces. Although Harry Potter is widely perceived as being for teens, and Robert Langdon for adults, there is an interesting crossover in the audiences. *The Da Vinci Code* proved to be one of the first adult novels many high school students read a few years ago, and a huge following exists among adults for Harry Potter. Both book series have captured the attention of global audiences and both have generated very successful mass-market films.

The books even involve a few of the *same* characters. Dr. Abaddon in *TLS* and Apollyon in *Harry Potter*, are Hebrew and Greek versions of the same word for destruction and serve as names for malevolent characters. Nicolas Flamel, a French alchemist, is said to have been a friend of Dumbledore's in *Harry Potter*. Meanwhile, in *DVC*, Flamel is said to have been a fourteenth-century Grand Master of the Priory of Sion. Although Flamel is a real historic personage, the references to him in both books are fictional.

The first Harry Potter book had to have its American title changed from *Harry Potter and the Philosopher's Stone* to *Harry Potter and the Sorcerer's Stone* because the U.S. publisher thought American teenagers wouldn't know what the philosopher's stone was. Now both Harry Potter and Robert Langdon, as well as their fans and readers, know plenty about the search for the power of alchemical transformation that lies at the heart of the concept of the "philosopher's stone." Interestingly, the philosopher's stone is most often associated with alchemists' frenzied efforts to turn base metals into gold. But many alchemists, and Flamel in particular, also believed that the philosopher's stone could be used to render a person immortal. Spiritual riches—rather than gold and material riches—and the search for the immortal soul in particular, lie at the heart of *The Lost Symbol*.

OUR JOURNEY IS COMPLEX AND LAYERED WITH SYMBOLS AND METAPHORS

Following in the footsteps of Kabbalists, neo-Platonists, and all kinds of mystery writers, everything in *The Lost Symbol* is "overdetermined." Almost every plot point, character name, symbol, historic reference, number, and artwork has multiple meanings and interpretations. Consider these elements and aspects of *TLS*:

The Entire Book Is Structured to Take Robert Langdon and the Reader Through a Rite of Initiation, a "Hero's Journey"

Key events and scenes draw from the degrees and rituals of Masonry. In this way, *TLS* is similar to Mozart's *Magic Flute*, among other Masonic works that have the structure of initiation rites built into them. *TLS* is also structured like an archetypal "hero's journey," as described by thinkers like Carl Gustav Jung and Joseph Campbell. (In terms of the Zeitgeist it is notable that Jung's long unpublished personal diary of his own dreams, nightmares, and primal thoughts, known as *The Red Book*, which touches on many of the same issues as *TLS*, is being published for the first time in the same season that has brought Dan Brown's new novel.)

The greatest of all hero's journeys in Western civilization is Homer's *Odyssey* (replicated structurally by James Joyce in his masterpiece of modernism, *Ulysses*). Throughout *TLS*, Brown weaves symbolic references to specific Masonic initiation rites, as well as more general hero's journeys. It's not always clear which is which. *TLS* opens with a specific Masonic initiation ceremony, where Mal'akh, in bad faith, is initiated by his own father (unbeknownst to Peter Solomon) into the 33° ritual of Scottish Rite Freemasons. The story moves chapter by chapter through various classical elements of mythic initiation rites: the quest to find lost objects (the Lost Word, the Lost Symbol), the intellectual puzzling over the meaning of symbols, the painful moral choices between loyalty to one's word and to one's friends (whether Robert should betray Peter's secret in order to help save him), the heroic battle with adversaries (Mal'akh), the need to defeat skeptics (Sato), the near-death experience (Total Liquid Ventilation Tank), the appearance of resurrection/rebirth/coming back to life (especially important, since mock death and resurrection are part of Masonic ritual), the return of the lost objects (the pyramid, Peter's ring), the epiphany of discovery (Robert and Peter at the top of the Washington Monument), the journey home (back to the Capitol Dome, where Robert and Katherine are reunited like Odysseus and Penelope at the end of *The Odyssey*), and the arrival in the light (sunrise over the Washington Monument), a suitable ending, since "enlightenment" is the ultimate destination of Freemason ritual.

Some steps along the rite of passage seem odd, until you put them in the context of the initiation structure: When Robert Langdon (and Dan Brown, by proxy) is greeted in chapter 1 of *TLS* by Pam, the passenger services representative in the Dulles Airport private air terminal, he finds her dismissing his last book (i.e., *The Da Vinci Code*) as if the Harvard symbologist had written nothing more than an intentionally salacious bestseller. Referring to Langdon's book about "the sacred feminine and the church," Pam says, "What a delicious scandal that one caused! You do enjoy putting the fox in the henhouse!" She then tweaks him for wearing his "uniform" of Harris Tweed jacket and khakis, deriding his customary turtleneck as hopelessly "outdated."

Here Brown is poking a bit of fun at himself, his own wardrobe, and his own books. But it is not just self-deprecation for the sake of warming the hearts of the readers. Looked at in terms of the initiation process, the banter with Pam is a studied scene in preordeal humiliation. Langdon is taking the first steps on the journey of this night, with the outside world mocking his appearance and reminding him that, Harvard professor or not, he is an ordinary mortal. Although Pam's comments are trivial, she is playing the role of the critic stripping the warrior of his clothing. Only the rest of the evening will tell if he has what it takes to be the wise warrior he will need to be to save Peter and Katherine and learn the secrets of the Ancient Mysteries.

When Pam tells Langdon how much her book group enjoyed the last scandalous romp, Langdon replies, "Scandal wasn't really my intention." This is Dan Brown telling us that he has high hopes for *TLS*. It isn't just another thriller. It actually means something important to him, and he hopes people will understand his true intentions. Intentionality itself will become an important theme much later in *TLS* when we learn of Katherine Solomon's "noetic science" experiments.

Another Structural Tool of TLS *Is Specific Coded and Hidden Messages*

The book jacket of the American hardcover edition of *TLS* contains a variety of embedded codes, several of which have now been deciphered. (For more on codes and clues, see chapter 8, "The Summer of the Clues"). Here, I will comment on three codes that have been decrypted and one slightly hidden message:

POPES PANTHEON

This decrypted phrase is mainly a reference to John Russell Pope, the Freemason architect who designed many important buildings, including the 1915 Scottish Rite headquarters in Washington, better known as the House of the Temple. It is a pantheon of sorts in that it includes symbols and allusions to several different religious traditions. By using "Pope's Pantheon," Brown is probably also pointing to other buildings and ideas as well. For example, the Jefferson Memorial was also designed by John Russell Pope and was clearly inspired architecturally by the shape of the Pantheon in Rome, as well as the Panthéon in Paris.

as religious monuments in great cities throughout the ages have served the purpose of connecting people to their past and extolled certain virtues and values, the designers of Washington and its monuments wanted to have the same visual and philosophical impact, connecting Americans to the heroic past accomplishments of the mortal men (and in more recent years, women) who built America.

ALL GREAT TRUTHS BEGIN AS BLASPHEMIES

Dan Brown is a defender of heretics. He believes that, just as Jesus was at first anathema to the Roman Empire, so later, when Christianity was adopted as Rome's state religion, the Christian state became just as zealous in crushing heretical voices as the pagan emperors had been.

Brown reminds us that many of the basic ideas of science were initially censored by religious authorities as heresy, including principles like heliocentrism that we know today to be scientific facts. He further tells us that the Dark Ages arose when Christendom decided to wall itself off from the wisdom of ancient knowledge-based cultures of pagan Egyptians, Greeks, and Romans, and declare much of this past wisdom to be heresy. Europe found its way to the light again only when this ancient wisdom was rediscovered. Rearmed with the ancient wisdom, the Renaissance could emerge and flourish, and lead, within the short space of three centuries, to the Enlightenment, democracy, and the Industrial Revolution.

The reason Freemasons gathered in secret was not fundamentally to practice weird rites or to conspire in a morally negative sense. Instead, they were conspiring in a morally positive sense. They were creating the body of ideas and beliefs that would lead to revolutionary notions of liberty and eventually to overthrowing a world dominated by monarchy and clergy and replacing it with the *novus ordo seclorum* referred to on the great seal of the United States—a new *secular* and democratic order.

In Brownian cosmology, the breaking away of America from England and the commitment to truths Americans would come to hold as self-evident (that all men are created equal; that they are endowed, not by a specific God, but by their much more abstract "creator," with inalienable rights to life, liberty, and the pursuit of happiness) are also indicators that the blasphemers and the declaimers of the traditional order need to be tolerated, heard, encouraged, and ultimately welcomed.

Of course not every unpopular, unconventional, or heretical idea will prove to be correct. Just because the majority of the scientific community today criticizes the research methodology of the noetic scientists, it does not follow that the scientific community is wrong. Brown goes overboard in claiming noetics as a science and in reading far too much into the limited data that has today been gathered by people doing this kind of research. Noetics is absolutely fascinating as a metaphor, and is willing to contemplate some daringly innovative ideas. But only time will tell whether it is truly promising as a scientific direction for understanding the universe and the place of the human mind and human thought within it.

YOUR MIND IS THE KEY

The Lost Symbol argues for a worldview in which the human mind is the most powerful force on earth and the most concentrated expression of divinity we can know. Throughout its pages, we are told that all the great philosophers, teachers, and "adepts" emphasized that anything is possible through the human mind. Access to the great thoughts that can be thought, the great artworks that can be created, the great words that can be written, the great inventions that can be generated, the great dreams that can be dreamed, all come from the human mind.

Speaking through the thoughts of Peter Solomon, *TLS* asserts that "Freemasonry, like Noetic Science and the Ancient Mysteries, revered the untapped potential of the human mind, and many of Masonry's symbols related to human physiology . . . *The mind sits like a golden capstone atop the physical body.*" The mind is the real "Philosopher's Stone" that has been sought by the alchemists throughout the ages. *"Through the staircase of the spine"* (the spine has thirty-three vertebrae at birth—there's that unique number so important to Masons again), *"energy ascends and descends, circulating, connecting the heavenly mind to the physical body . . . The body is indeed a temple.* The human science that Masons revered was the ancient understanding of how to use that temple for its most potent and noble purpose." Langdon calls the Ancient Mysteries "a kind of instruction manual for harnessing the latent power of the human mind . . . a recipe for personal apotheosis." He also says, "The human mind was the only technology the ancients had at their disposal. The early philosophers studied it relentlessly." To which Katherine replies, "Yes! The ancient texts are obsessed with the power of the human mind. The [Indian] Vedas describe the flow of mind energy. The [Gnostic] *Pistis Sophia* describes universal consciousness. The *Zohar* [Jewish/Hebraic mystical texts] explores the nature of mind spirit. The Shamanic texts predict Einstein's 'remote influence' in terms of healing at a distance. . . ."

One message of *TLS* is that the human mind is the ultimate creative and divine force, and that we need to free the human mind from its remaining shackles to move to the next era of enlightenment. But that message is tempered by another one. The human mind is also capable of thinking evil and destructive thoughts. Mal'akh is the character in the story most devoted to learning the ancient secrets and practicing the ancient arts. Yet he has crossed the line and is willing to kill or destroy as needed to achieve his own personal apotheosis. The example of Mal'akh applies to science and technology as well. The alchemists who were trying to transform matter in the hopes of turning base metals into gold have been superseded by the scientists who *succeeded* in transforming matter by creating nuclear fission. With their success, the world now has the dangerous power of atomic weapons. Dan Brown is correctly concerned and even a bit cautionary about his new heroes among the noeticists. If they are successful in proving that matter outside the body can be transformed through human thought, or that it is possible to intervene in other minds and bodies at a distance, such success would have its own obvious perils. But Brown is an optimist. He believes we are heading into a new enlightenment not a new dark age. And the golden treasure to fund that enlightenment, the source of energy and the power of the wisdom are not really "buried out there." As it turns out, it's buried in here; hidden in plain sight. It is the unseen human mind within the body.

AS ABOVE SO BELOW

This well-known mystical aphorism is not in a coded message like the prior three references. It's just a bit hard to see. On the back of the U.S. hardcover edition, "As above" is in the demi-arc band at the top of the back cover; "so below" is upside down in the demi-arc at the bottom. This remarkably powerful and long-lived four-word phrase is most often attributed to Hermes Trismegistus, who in turn derived it from the mythical "emerald tablet." The phtase is thought in the annals of Medieval and Renaissance mystics to be definitional as to the relationship of man to god, earth to universe, material world to spiritual world. It also appears prominently in astrological studies of the same time period. *TLS* quotes "As above, so below" explicitly seven different times. What's more, if you look at the scenes staged in the book by Dan Brown, you find multiple conceptual reenactments of the relationship between "above" and "below." Thus, at the beginning of the book, Peter's severed hand in the Capitol Rotunda is pointing up to the image of Washington's apotheosis above, reflecting Mal'akh's own misguided desire for personal apotheosis. At the end of the book, Robert and Katherine are sharing their big thoughts about the mind and the universe while staring up at the *Apotheosis of Washington* fresco. The episode in which Peter Solomon leads Robert Langdon on the trip up and down the Washington Monument is its own mini spiritual journey to demonstrate the alleged truth that the "Lost Word" is buried at the bottom of a long descending staircase. But along the way, we learn that the obelisk architectural form connects the sun to the earth and that the staircase is a metaphor for Jacob's ladder to the heavens and for the spine connecting brain to body.

"As above, so below" can be read, along with the other decoded proverbs from the cover, as another way of stating the same humanistic principle that runs throughout *TLS:* What really matters is the world we live in. And the world we live in, as well as our minds and our selves, are no different—for good or ill—than the divine world religions imagine reside in the heavens. We are not fundamentally sinners, we are fundamentally divine. All the powers we ascribe to gods exist on earth among humankind. Everything we are usually told to believe is holy, sacred, and ideal can also be interpreted as profane, secular, and real.

A BRIEF HISTORY OF PHILO OF ALEXANDRIA

A character of considerable importance, in my view, to understanding *The Lost Symbol* is not among the dozens of philosophers, mystics, and adepts mentioned in Brown's voluminous inventory. He is Philo of Alexandria, and his lifespan is generally cited as between 20 B.C.E. and 50 C.E. He is associated with some of the earliest efforts to read traditional Scripture nonliterally, and to look for the hidden meanings, numerology systems, and codes within the sacred texts. Philo believed there was a Bible within the Bible, a body of knowledge and wisdom designed for those seekers who wanted more than normal meanings. *TLS* references this view numerous times. Peter reminds Robert that Corinthians tells us the biblical parables have two levels of meaning, "milk for babes and meat for men," where the "*milk* is a watered-down reading for infantile minds, and the *meat* is the true message, accessible only to mature minds." Peter quotes the Gospel of John as saying "I will speak to you in parable . . . and use dark sayings" and quotes Psalm 78 as avowing, "I will open my mouth in parable and utter dark sayings of old." All this talk of dark sayings causes Langdon to remember that "dark" in this context means hidden and shadowed, not evil. Age of Wonder poet William Blake wrote: "Both read the Bible day and night, / But thou read'st black where I read white."

Philo made a protoscience of finding the hidden, shadowy, dark meanings in the Bible. Just a small tasting of Philo's premises for finding clues in biblical texts that tell the careful reader that a nonliteral meaning is about to be disclosed:

- Look for the repetition of a phrase.
- Look for an apparently superfluous expression.

- Look for an entirely different meaning by a different combination of the words, disregarding the ordinarily accepted division of the sentence into phrases and clauses.
- A play on words can signal a deeper meaning.
- If something is omitted that by all reason should be there, it means something.
- References to numbers and quantities are important. Numbers aren't just numbers, but mean something particular.
- Interpret words according to their numerical value (Hebrew letters each have a numerical value; thus words are the sum of the letters within them). One word with the same total numerical value can be used as a clue to point to another word of similar numerical value.

Dan Brown knows these forensic tools of Philo's—and the many other mystics who have used similar methods to discern various Bible codes. In his love of puzzles, anagrams, and cryptic phrases, Brown constantly signals us to understand that these codes are the creation of mortal men—like Benjamin Franklin and Albrecht Dürer—not the divine work of a God who wanted to leave us a coded message about how we are supposed to worship him.

THE LOST SYMBOL CAN BE READ AS A CODED MESSAGE

Narrowly speaking, there are specific coded messages in the text. For example, the "Thread #" that appears on page 475, in reference to a Web chat room where CIA employees are discussing the meaning of the *Kryptos* statue, is given as 2456282.5. Elonka Dunin, a contributor to this book (see chapter 8), one of the world's leading experts on *Kryptos*, and the real-life near anagram of *TLS* character Nola Kaye, tells me that the thread number is "obviously intended to mean the Julian date, December 21, 2012, which ties in to the 2012 reference in the same chapter." Here *TLS* is referencing the growing media hype imagined in the novel by Peter Solomon over the interpretation of the Mayan calendar's prediction of the end of the world on that date in 2012. Solomon sees no reason to believe the world is actually going to end, and knows that those who are worried are misinterpreting the meaning of the symbols and the texts. Although it only gets only passing mention here, the Mayan calendar prediction could well figure in Dan Brown's *next* book.

In any event, Elonka Dunin's decoding of a seemingly haphazard number in the text, 2456282.5, seems to be a case in point of Philo's approach to dissecting sacred texts.

Much has been made by reviewers of Dan Brown's "bad writing" in *The Lost Symbol*. And it may just be a case of horrendously bad writing in many places. There are any number of wickedly funny and biting critiques of Brown out there, but my personal favorite is to be found in blogger Maureen Johnson's online guide to *The Lost Symbol* at http://maureenjohnson.blogspot.com/. Johnson expresses every moment of outrage over the plot and the text that I felt when reading *TLS*—and much more. She calls Mal'akh the "hardest working bad guy in literatire," and parodies Brown's amazing list of evil feats he performs—in one night, all by himself, with no henchmen, coconspirators, or posse to provide even minor assistance. Plus she brilliantly satirizes Brown by reading some of his short, staccato passages as if they were modernist poems and comparing them to similar passages from T. S. Eliot, William Carlos Williams, and Walt Whitman.

In chapter 10, our own investigative reporter, Dave Shugarts, writes another tour de force critiquing Dan Brown's errors of fact, geography, technology, anatomy, and much else. But my guess is that the story behind the bad writing, plot flaws, and factual errors may be more complicated.

Why all the use of italics? There are italicized words on most pages of *TLS* and the sentences in italics often offer no special reason as to why they should be italicized. The reviewers have had a field-day parodying Brown's overuse of italics, often randomly *italicizing words and sentences in their own reviews to demonstrate the apparent absurdity of this technique.* But following Philo's guidance, my bet is the italics are telling us something in one coded way or another.

And what's up with all the repetition? Why is "hell"—as in Robert Langdon's oft-uttered, *"What the hell?"*—used almost fifty times? Philosopher Glenn Erickson, a longtime student of the neo-Platonists, including Philo, tells us in chapter 3 that the phrase "Franklin Square" appears fifty-five times in the novel, and further that "fifty-five is the sum of the numbers on any side of any such pyramid with *Dürer's* magic square at its base." What's more, says Erickson, "the 'magic constant' (the sum repeated in the rows, columns, and diagonals) in a normal six-by-six magic square is III, the same number of times the sequence 'Washington' appears in the novel."

Erickson goes on in chapter 3 to highlight the possibility that every character in *TLS* may correspond to a character in the Tarot deck, and to show us how a number of specific situations in the book are scripted to look like scenes from Tarot cards. Tarot, of course, has long been looked to by all kinds of mystics as containing coded messages of ancient wisdom. It was a favorite subject of Manly P. Hall, the best-known twentieth-century aggregator of ancient wisdom, whose *Secret Teachings of All Ages* Brown invokes in an epigram to launch *The Lost Symbol*, quoting him again five hundred pages later to conclude the book. Almost all the mystical names, theories, and ideas mentioned in *TLS* are also referenced in Hall's *Secret Teachings of All Ages*. (For more on Hall, see Mitch Horowitz's interview in chapter 4, describing Hall's role within the long tradition of the occult in America.)

Call me credulous. But I believe that most, and possibly all, of the odd scenes that strike critics as simple cases of bad writing (or bad editing by Brown's Doubleday editor, Jason Kaufman, who makes his now de rigueur appearance in *TLS* as Jonas Faukman) are structured around specific symbolic content. Katherine Solomon and Robert Langdon end up in the kitchen of Cathedral College, part of the National Cathedral complex, because Katherine gets the brilliant idea to boil the pyramid in order to see if it gives up its secrets. As Sato deadpans later, "You *boiled* the pyramid?"

The boiling of the pyramid gives Robert and Katherine a few minutes to act out a sweet domestic bit of comic relief, although it is hard to believe they are actually joking about the difference between a lobster pot and a pasta pot at a time like this, let alone thinking about fine dining experiences with celebrity chef Daniel Boulud. They also get the chance to talk about the little-known temperature system devised by Isaac Newton, well before Fahrenheit and Celsius overtook the scale. And what was the boiling point of water in the Newton Scale? Thirty-three degrees, of course, which gives Katherine and Robert the chance to go mano a mano over how much each of them knows about Newton and the importance of the number thirty-three to Pythagorians, Rosicrucians, Freemasons, and other mystics. We learn that Jesus is said to have been thirty-three when crucified, that he is said to have accomplished thirty-three miracles, and that God's name is mentioned thirty-three times in Genesis. It has apparently dawned on Katherine that the previous clue, *All is revealed at the thirty-third degree*, which Langdon had previously thought to have something to do with the highest rank in Masonry, should really be read as instructions to heat the pyramid to thirty-three degrees in the Newton Scale in order to learn the next clue. ("All," it turns out, is never revealed in these games of clue hunting, or the game would be over.)

The bottom line: She boils the pyramid! And she gets results! Using boiling water as an agent of *transformation* (again, one of the big themes of *TLS*), and, after arguing about the difference between luminescence and incandescence, this magical pyramid begins to glow with previously invisible letters that now spell out "Eight Franklin Square."

I believe at the heart of this scene, according to some structurally scripted language—Tarot, myth, religious pilgrimage, whatever script Brown is using here—he had to work in a ritual boiling of water. He finally came up with this madcap scene, and, while he was at it, he helped himself to the opportunity to engage in a game of speed–Trivial Pursuit over the number thirty-three.

Remember Philo, who calls upon us to be on the lookout for omissions, and think about the passage where Langdon heads into the bowels of the Senate to find Peter Solomon's Masonic Chamber of Reflection, replete with all its symbols of mortality and death. On the way down, Langdon thinks to himself that he is on a *"journey to the center of the Earth."* A little melodramatic for a few floors of an elevator ride, although we know Langdon doesn't like elevators, gets claustrophobic in them, and has apparently had a childhood trauma in the Eiffel Tower's elevator. Of course the italicized phrase is actually a reference to Jules Verne's novel of the same name, even if Verne is not mentioned. Verne is thought by many to have been a disciple of Rosicrucian thought, and so the "omission" is another way of pointing at Rosicrucianism. (The Eiffel Tower's excellent restaurant, high above the ground, is also named for Jules Verne.)

Speaking of the Eiffel Tower, United Technologies wonders if their corporation somehow fits into a Dan Brown code. According to the *Hartford Courant*, "No one around here is sure why, but *The Da Vinci Code* author Dan Brown has some kind of fascination with United Technologies. Before you barely turn a page in his new thriller, *The Lost Symbol*, two UTC companies, Otis Elevator and Pratt & Whitney, are part of the story. 'We called Doubleday because we are curious,' said UTC spokesman Peter Murphy. Brown's novel opens with an 'Otis elevator climbing the south pillar of the Eiffel Tower' and, a few paragraphs later, main character Robert Langdon awakens in a corporate jet where 'the dual Pratt & Whitney engines hummed evenly.'" Murphy thinks this is most likely simply a reflection of the ubiquity of his company's products, but with Dan Brown, we just never know. It would be a mistake to assume these are random well-known corporate names selected without a conscious purpose.

On a recent tour of the George Washington Masonic National Memorial in Alexandria, Virginia, I entered the elevator that takes visitors to the rooms dedicated to re-creating the Temple of Solomon, a Templar church, and other wonders and curiosities inside this 1920s-era building, which is designed to honor George Washington's life as a Mason, and to physically resemble an artist's impression of the great Lighthouse at Alexandria (Egypt, not Virginia).

The first thing the guide said on entering the elevator was that it was built by the Otis elevator company. As he went on to explain the engineering marvel behind this particular set of dual elevators that incline at inward angles toward each other rather than moving straight up and down vertically, I felt I was re-experiencing the early pages of *The Lost Symbol*, where for no apparent reason, one encounters the Otis elevator at the Eiffel Tower.

The tour guide was an interesting fellow. From him I learned that Dan Brown had spent a full day here several years earlier, researching Washington's Masonic beliefs and engagements. Members of the staff had read *TLS* as soon as it came out, and found themselves happy that their institution was mentioned in the book, as well as relieved that their precisely 333-foot-tall tower had not been used by Brown as a venue for a murder. They also felt that Brown had generally treated Freemasonry with reverence, respect, and accuracy. But they were ultimately disappointed that their building figured only as a diversion and didn't even get an actual visit from Robert Langdon in the book.

In an oddly eerie moment, it turned out I was visiting this intriguing place on the exact day of Yom Kippur, the Jewish Day of Atonement. Dan Brown likes to call atonement, "at-one-ment," making a wordplay that works only in modern English, not in the original Hebrew from which it comes. Nevertheless, it's a good try at a humanist view that says our sins against our fellow man are the most important ones. We might all be well served by using the meditative process called for on the Day of Atonement to think of ways to bring all of us—all peoples, all religions—together.

Inside the George Washington National Masonic Memorial there is a replica of parts of the Temple of Solomon, and we looked at a display that sought to capture the Ark of the Covenant in the interior of the Holy of Holies. Scripture suggests the Holy of Holies was opened only by the high priest once a year, on the Day of Atonement. Even for a completely secular person such as myself, standing in front of a somewhat dusty, old-fashioned museum replica, I felt the psychological power of being privy to secrets, of gaining access to the most sacred knowledge and experience.

On the walls of this particular room, there were some Hebrew words written, and the guide explained that they had to do with the name of God, which, as most Old Testament readers know, is never pronounced out loud. There is a deep intellectual river running through the history of

Freemasonry (not to mention Judaism itself, as well as Kabbalah and various mystical trends), that is focused on the name of God as one of those bits of powerful secret knowledge that creates centuries-long searches for lost words and lost symbols. It is said that God told his name to Moses at the burning bush, and it is believed by some mystics that Solomon too knew this name of God and used that knowledge to summon angels and spirits. Those who read Hebrew in modern temple prayers all know not to pronounce out loud the name that is spelled out by the Hebrew letters for God, but to pronounce one of several euphemisms instead. In any event, the guide explained that the writing on the walls was intentionally imperfect in order not to cross the line over things that should not be written or said.

He volunteered that he thought Dan Brown's mistakes were a bit like that as well—that is, mistakes by intention. Again, I thought of Philo: where we find a mistake in *The Lost Symbol*—and there are many—could it be a portal to take us to a different level of the code?

WHAT'S IN A NAME? IDENTITY, HISTORY, MYTH, CONTEXT, CONNOTATION.

The character names within *TLS*, and the characters themselves, form their own kind of coded, metaphoric, allusive ballet. You can certainly get at least one or two additional levels of meaning from *TLS* by deconstructing what went into their selections.

Robert Langdon, of course, is back from two prior novels. He was first used in *Angels & Demons*, where Brown also introduced a series of "ambigrams" (artistically calligraphed words that can be read upside down as well as right side up). The ambigrams were each important to the plot development of *A&D*. While the novel tried to make much of the secrets of ambigrams as a kind of coded language used by the Illuminati, the fact is that, as an art form, they are very twentieth century. Their leading designer is John Langdon, who happened to be a friend of Dan Brown's father, and who agreed to design the ambigrams for *A&D*. Another John Langdon was an American revolutionary, a member of the Continental Congress, a signer of the Constitution, one of the first senators from Dan Brown's home state of New Hampshire, and later governor of New Hampshire. Surprise, surprise: he was also a Freemason. Yet another Langdon, Samuel Langdon, was a real-life president of Harvard, and his tenure extended through most of the American Revolution. He helped Washington set up headquarters on the Harvard campus after the battles of Lexington and Concord. Robert Langdon no doubt knows that history of his Harvard forebear.

Mal'akh is a transliteration into roman characters of the Hebrew word for angel. So we begin our tour of this pathological villain by understanding that he has given himself a name that means "angel." We learn through his rambling monologues that he sees no difference between angels and fallen angels. This is an allusion to Lucifer/Satan, who, in some accounts is considered a "fallen angel." It may also be an allusion to the recent scholarship that has been done on the long-missing Gnostic Gospel of Judas, which emerged as accessible and in translation in the years between *DVC* and *TLS*.

During his days on his Greek island after escape from his Turkish jail, Mal'akh first called himself Andros, a reference to his androgynous sexual status (he will later castrate himself in his search for purity). Mal'akh has escaped from jail under unusual circumstances. This mirrors the experience of Silas in *DVC*, as well as the experience of Silas, the fellow traveler of Paul's in Acts:16. Like Silas in *DVC*, Mal'akh eventually becomes a fanatic and a murderer. Both men engage in ritual "mortification of the flesh" (originally recommended by Saint Paul). Silas does this through his self-flagellation and his spiked cilice belt; Mal'akh through self-tattooing and ultimately self-castrating. While in Greece, he reads John Milton's *Paradise Lost*, and becomes fascinated with what Mal'akh calls "the great fallen angel . . . the warrior demon who fought against the light . . . the valiant one . . . the angel called Moloch." In frightening lines of poetry, Milton tells the story of the demon Moloch, a "horrid king besmear'd with blood of human sacrifice and parents tears," who deceives King Solomon into building a temple to him adjacent to Solomon's great temple to God. Moloch was a Canaanite god, contemporary with the early days of Jewish religion, who demanded not just human sacrifice but particularly the sacrifice of children. Milton notes in the poem that the cries of the children were drowned out by the playing of drums and timbrels (tambourines). We will learn in *TLS* that Peter Solomon failed to understand the plight of his son Zachary (now Mal'akh) in the Turkish jail.

King Solomon may have been induced by one of his wives to build an altar to Moloch, not realizing that child sacrifice would be required to appease this god. Thus, the Moloch story leads us leads us right to Solomon, Peter Solomon.

Peter Solomon: The name most obviously brings together two of the most important figures in Christianity and Judaism. First is Peter, the leader of the Apostles, the "rock" upon which Jesus built his church according to the Gospel of Matthew (petros meaning "rock" in Greek), the first Pope, the arbiter of who gets into Heaven.

As for Solomon, he is, of course, the great King of the Jews, and the builder of the first great temple, and known throughout the Middle East of that time period for both his wisdom and his wealth. In a flashback scene in *TLS*, Peter Solomon forces his son Zachary to make a choice between wisdom and wealth, even though the biblical King Solomon is said to have had both. (For an interesting commentary on this dilemma, see our interview with Rabbi Kula in chapter 5). In both Kings and Chronicles, it is said that when Solomon started on his temple-building project, he sent for Hiram Abiff, a "widow's son" and master builder to help. Some Freemasons identify Hiram as, in effect, the first Freemason, and his murder by some of his workers in the course of building the Temple as the "primal moment" reenacted in Freemason rituals of death and rebirth. In the nonbiblical mystical tradition, Solomon is known not just as a wise and wealthy king, but as a magus, a magician/alchemist type, with incredible powers of sorcery and conjuring. For several years, the book that became *The Lost Symbol* was said to be titled *The Solomon Key*. (Some critics, notably Janet Maslin in the *New York Times*, have argued that *The Solomon Key* is actually a much more compelling title for this book—and I agree). Solomon's powers as a magus are commemorated in a mystical book, *The Key of Solomon* (in Latin *Clavis Salomonis* or *Clavicula Salomonis*), a grimoire, or book on magic, attributed to King Solomon, but most probably written during the early part of the Italian Renaissance. In addition, there is a seventeenth-century grimoire known as *The Lesser Key of Solomon*. This version of "the Solomon Key" is cited in Manly P. Hall's *Secret Teachings of All Ages,* among many other ideas about Solomon that have obviously seeped into *TLS.*

Solomon is central to alchemy, since it was thought that he had access to the "philosopher's stone" and the techniques and incantations for transforming base metals into gold and for summoning demons and spirits to do his bidding. Isaac Newton spent years trying to use the clues in the Bible to draw up a detailed map showing what the original Temple of Solomon must have looked like. You can see Newton's drawings in his *Chronology of Ancient Kingdoms.*

In *TLS,* Peter Solomon is said to be brilliantly wise, enormously wealthy, and a respected 33° Mason, who has a day job as "secretary" of the Smithsonian. In this particular role, Brown may have had two influences. One might be James Smithson himself, the endower of the Smithsonian. Smithson was a brilliant chemist, perhaps an alchemist, perhaps a Freemason, and a very wealthy man. He left instructions in his will that, on the death of his last relative, his fortune should go "to the United States of America, to found at Washington, an establishment for the increase and diffusion of knowledge among men." He gave these explicit instructions even though at the time of his death, he had never even set foot in America, and it was not at all common in those days for wealthy individuals to endow institutions for science and the diffusion of knowledge.

Peter Solomon may also draw from the persona of Andrew Mellon, the industrialist, financial genius, treasury secretary, Freemason, and philanthropist. Mellon was a kind of modern alchemist, first with his investments in coking technology that turned what was essentially industrial waste into valuable products, and then with his creation of financial wealth more generally. As a philanthropist, he seeded the creation of the National Gallery in Washington with masterworks from his own art collection and $10 million in cash. John Russell Pope, the architect and fellow Freemason who designed the House of the Temple and the Jefferson Memorial (aka "Pope's Pantheon" in Brownian code), designed the National Gallery. Moreover, the Mellon family remained closely involved with the National Gallery for the next six decades, with Andrew Mellon's son Paul (who apparently was never faced with the choice of wealth or wisdom, and ended up with both) serving as the National Gallery's first president in 1938 and continuing various involvements until his death in 1999.

There is one more level of Solomonic allusion important to mention here. Francis Bacon pops up seven times by name in *TLS* and more without specific mention. He was the subject of some of the more intriguing official clues offered up by Dan Brown and his publisher before *TLS* appeared. Bacon was a brilliant philosopher, and Bacon historians and researchers have seen him as the real Shakespeare, the brains behind the King James Bible, the founder of Rosicrucianism, and much else. Thomas Jefferson was a Bacon devotee, and Bacon's image is used in the Library of Congress to connote the wise philosopher and brilliant writer. Just a generation ago, Bacon was much more widely known in America than he is today. Daphne du Maurier's biography of Bacon, *The Winding Stair,* was a 1976 bestseller.

Early in *The Lost Symbol,* Dan Brown refers to the Royal Society of London and its forerunner, "The Invisible College," and the great minds that maintained "secret wisdom" there. According to Brown, one of those minds belonged to Francis Bacon. When the action heats up in the novel, Robert Langdon, making his escape from the Library of Congress, passes the Folger Shakespeare Library, which he notes houses "Francis Bacon's *New Atlantis,* the utopian vision on which the American forefathers had allegedly modeled a new world based on ancient knowledge."

Bacon's *New Atlantis* was published in 1627, right after his death. The novel tells the story of the imaginary Pacific island of Bensalem and the government-run scientific institution there, where advanced experiments of wide-ranging scope are conducted on all manner of nature and human interaction with nature. *New Atlantis* makes a strong case for humans (rather than God) being in control of humanity's future, It posits a utopian vision of a world where scientific exploration leads to a flourishing of the human condition. Some of the experiments described sound a bit like Katherine Solomon's research into noetics; the scope of the work done in this research institute at the heart of Bacon's *New Atlantis* sounds a bit like the Smithsonian Museum Support Center. So what is this temple of scientific experiment—this world-class center of learning in the middle of this utopian society—known as in Bacon's story? "Salomon's House."

Katherine Solomon: In *TLS*, Dan Brown has continued the tradition he established in his prior books (including not just *DVC* and *A&D*, but *Digital Fortress* and *Deception Point* as well) of having a female lead who is both brilliant in some deeply technical way, as well as physically beautiful. There is usually a familial relationship between the beautiful, brilliant woman and the old wise man who has been murdered (or in this case has had his hand severed and is being held hostage). In *A&D*, Vittoria is a "bio-entanglement" physicist who got pressed into action together with Robert Langdon after her adoptive father was murdered. In *DVC*, Sophie is a top code breaker drawn into working with Langdon after the murder of the grandfather who had raised her. And here, in *TLS*, Katherine is the world's leading noetic scientist, doing breakthrough research that will allegedly change the world's understanding of human thought and the human mind. She is also the sister of Peter Solomon, who appears to have been murdered at the outset, but we later learn is still alive suffering "only" a severed hand. This time, Katherine is a bit older—fifty—than the beautiful/brilliant late-twentysomethings and early-thirtysomethings who inhabited this role in prior books. For the first time, Langdon is working with a female lead who is older than he is. This calls to mind the age gap between Dan Brown and his wife, Blythe, who is known to be very interested in noetics, just like Katherine Solomon. It should be noted that Blythe was also very interested in the "sacred feminine," Gnosticism, Mary Magdalene, the legend of the bloodline, and the other topics that inspired *DVC*. She is clearly Dan Brown's research partner. She is so important to his work that some analysts view her as a major intellectual and creative force in the partnership, with Dan as the master storyteller of the page-turner format.

Katherine is also probably an allusion to Saint Catherine of Alexandria, also known as Saint Catherine of the wheel, who is legendary in the Alexandrian time period for her beauty and her brilliance. Condemned to death for the crime of converting Alexandrians to Christianity, her personal strength was so great that she broke the torture wheel that was supposed to break her, and in the end, had to be beheaded instead.

If the *TLS* characters correspond to the Tarot deck, then Katherine may likely be connected to either the fourth or tenth trump. A correspondence to the tenth trump, the "wheel of fortune" card, would emphasize the connection of Katherine Solomon to St. Catherine of the wheel. The card usually depicts a female goddess of "fortuna," which can mean both fate and financial fortune.

The fourth trump, the "Popess," recalls the medieval legend of the female Pope Joan. Dan Brown mentioned this particular Tarot card in *DVC*, in a passage where we learned that heroine Sophie Neveu used to play Tarot games with her grandfather, the esteemed Saunière. This card is also known in many decks as the high priestess. A Wikipedia search tells us that "in the Rider-Waite-Smith Tarot deck, upon which many modern decks are based, The High Priestess is seated between the white and black pillars—'J' and 'B' for Jachin and Boaz—of the mystic Temple of Solomon. The veil of the Temple is behind her." In addition to the general Solomonic connotation suggested by this card, and on top of the emphasis throughout Freemasonry on those particular Temple of Solomon pillars, Jachin and Boaz, there is another connection made here with the depiction on the Tarot card of the temple "veil."

This word *veil* and the concept behind it resounds loudly in the final pages of *TLS*. Here, Katherine Solomon and Robert Langdon debate whether the traditional message of the Bible allows for the interpretation that the temple is within each person, or whether the temple is, of necessity, a physical place for worshipping an exterior God. Robert Langdon says he thinks the Bible is clear: the temple is to be a two-part physical structure, including an outer Holy Place and an inner sanctuary, the "Holy of Holies." These two structures are to be separated by a "veil." But Katherine turns this literal reading of the Bible around on Robert and argues for the theory of personal apotheosis and divinity that she shares with her brother, Peter (and her nephew, Mal'akh). She tells Robert that the human brain is composed of two parts—an outer "dura matter" and an inner "pia matter," and that these two parts are "separated by the arachnoid—a *veil* of weblike tissue."

Katherine is also the first major character in a Langdon novel to be clearly drawn, at least in significant part, from a real-life person. Except in her case, it's not one but two people whose work bears a striking resemblance to Katherine's research—Lynne McTaggart and Marilyn Mandala Schlitz, both of whom are contributors to this book. Of course Dan Brown has fast-forwarded the noetic research in *TLS* to a place where Katherine Solomon can claim she has established irrefutable, conclusive evidence and proof of her ideas. However, back in the real world, McTaggart and Schlitz, while highly confident of the separate research directions they are going in, would, I think, acknowledge that there is still a long way to go to prove their theories fully and to understand the experimental results they have seen.

Warren Bellamy: Freemason, close friend of Peter Solomon's, holder of the exalted title of the Architect of the Capitol, and keeper of the keys to all the Capitol's secrets. The part of Warren Bellamy in *TLS* is written, as more than one reviewer has noted, as custom-made to be played by a distinguished African-American actor like Morgan Freeman.

The name Bellamy is first and foremost a wink on Dan Brown's part at his origins as a thriller writer. After graduating from Amherst, Dan Brown first tried to make it as a musician and a composer. As he tells his own story, he was on vacation in Tahiti during this period of his life and he picked up a Sidney Sheldon thriller, *The Doomsday Conspiracy*. After racing through it, he concluded that he, too, could use his talents to write thrillers like that. Soon thereafter, he was at work on what would become *Digital Fortress*, a novel that established many of the patterns we find later in *A&D, DVC,* and *TLS*. The lead character in *Doomsday Conspiracy,* by the way, is named Bellamy.

That's a humorous nod to his past, but there's more to Bellamy than that. Reverend Francis Bellamy, a Freemason, Christian socialist, and Baptist minister, is one of the famous Bellamys in American history. He wrote the original Pledge of Allegiance in 1892. It was written to glorify the flag and the American ideal in the midst of the great movement to celebrate the four-hundredth anniversary of Columbus's voyage, epitomized by the famous Columbian Exhibition in Chicago.

Francis Bellamy had a much more famous cousin, the utopian socialist Edward Bellamy. Edward, also a Freemason, is the author of *Looking Backward*, published in 1888. One of the most influential books of its day, the utopia pictured by Bellamy in *Looking Backward* owed much to the ideals of democracy and brotherhood he had learned in his Freemason lodge. One more detail not likely to have eluded Brown: while most famous for the Masonic-infused *Looking Backward*, Edward Bellamy wrote a more obscure short story in biblical parable language and form, designed to critique the failings of the robber baron capitalism he saw all around him. The title was "The Parable of the Water Tank." Langdon, of course, is going to have a near-death experience in Mal'akh's water tank.

Warren Bellamy and Katherine Solomon as a pair: Dan Brown uses Katherine Solomon and Warren Bellamy in an unarticulated subplot. Brown knows that one of the most obvious weak links in Freemasonry's claim to openness, tolerance, and inclusiveness is the fact that the vast majority of Masonic lodges do not admit women and are specifically designed as fraternities of men. Moreover, he is aware of the historic fact that Albert Pike, the nineteenth-century Scottish Rite Freemason leader credited with codifying and spreading the gospel of modern Masonry, was a Confederate general (the only Confederate leader honored with a statue in today's Washington, D.C.). Any discussion of Pike inevitably triggers the historic rumors that he may have been in involved in some way with the founding of the Ku Klux Klan. The fact that many African Americans have been Freemasons, and that there is a historically African-American group of Masonic lodges (the Prince Hall movement), doesn't fully defuse the suggestion of racism. Brown skips the logical argument that other American institutions we respect and revere today (and heroes like Thomas Jefferson himself) were less than modern in their thinking about gender and race—so it's no surprise that Freemasonry may have suffered from the same historic biases. He vaults to the next step and creates the characters of Katherine Solomon and Warren Bellamy to make his point. Bellamy couldn't be more distinguished. He is the Architect of the Capitol and close friend of Peter Solomon's. As a leading African-American Freemason, his persona seems designed to obviate any wonder about racism among the Masons. As for Katherine, she actually says toward the end of the book that Peter "initiated" (the word is a very specific choice) her into his secret philosophical and mystical knowledge of Freemasonry years ago. Peter and Katherine have a platonic brother/sister love for each other and each other's minds. So, too, it is said, did Albert Pike have a very special relationship with his friend Vinnie Ream. He spent the better part of two decades meeting with Vinnie regularly and exchanging letters with her, as he sought to bring her, a woman, into the intellectual world of Freemasonry. Brown shorthands the argument that Freemasonry really is inclusive through the personas and characters of Katherine Solomon and Warren Bellamy.

Christopher Abaddon: This is the identity assumed by Mal'akh for his life in the outside world. He uses this name in his first encounters with Katherine when he is posing as Peter Solomon's psychiatrist. "Christopher" suggests Malakh's Christlike aspirations—for personal apotheosis, martyrdom, and resurrection in a heavenly world. His surname, "Abaddon," connotes "place of destruction" or "the destroyer," in Hebrew. In the Book of Revelation, Abaddon is the angel of the Abyss, the bottomless pit, and possibly another way to refer to the Antichrist. Mal'akh embodies all of this evil, and his basement laboratory is indeed a place of death and destruction. The word *abyss* is mentioned multiple times in *TLS*, especially as Robert Langdon sinks into the near-death abyss of Mal'akh's "liquid breathing" tank. Indeed, the 1989 movie *The Abyss* is recalled as one of the first depictions of total liquid ventilation.

Inoue Sato, the female CIA official of Japanese ancestry, has been roundly criticized by reviewers as one of the most inexplicable and annoying characters in recent fiction. What inspired Dan Brown to invent this character with this set of attributes is far from clear. Sato is an extremely common Japanese name. But there is one notable Sato of recent stature who might have come across Brown's radar screen: Mikio Sato. Although male, this Sato has done path-breaking work in mathematical physics. He is known especially for his work on something known as the FBI Transform, which has nothing to do with the Federal Bureau of Investigation, but is named after the mathematical physicists who developed it. However, one can imagine Brown being attracted to a scientific undertaking called FBI— for its resonance to the fact that longtime twentieth-century FBI boss J. Edgar Hoover was a Freemason, and Sato, although she works for the CIA, is carrying out what should decidedly be the FBI's work on American soil. Brown may also like the second part of the FBI Transform, since the theme of transformation is such a continuous subtext of *TLS*.

Sato's work, meanwhile, sounds like it would fit right in with Brown's vision of noetics and ancient wisdom being new again: those experts who understand Mikio Sato's work say that "it relies on an old idea in the Orient that phenomena in the real world are shadowed by phenomena in an imaginary world which lie outside the real world but infinitely close to it." Sato is seen by some as the modern inheritor of Newton and Leibniz, both of whom have roles in *TLS*.

BIG THEMES: LOSS, SACRIFICE, MORTALITY, MELANCHOLY, DEATH, TRANSFORMATION, REBIRTH.

The Lost Symbol is an extremely ambitious novel. In addition to big philosophical issues from five thousand years of civilized history, it also attempts to wrap in several of the major literary themes that have captured novelists and storytellers throughout the ages. Dan Brown is working against some long odds here, as he tries to comment on issues that have been tackled in history by many great novelists, and specifically the great novelists who have been Masons. *Faust*, Goethe's central work, occupied the great German writer for six decades. The completed book, published only after Goethe's death in 1832, deals with deep questions about the soul, man's search for happiness and satisfaction, and the meaning of life. *Faust* is a psychological novel before there was psychology; it is a political novel that rings with the spirit of Freemasonry; it is a religious novel that deals with good, evil, God, and the devil. It may have been based on a German legend about a medieval alchemist. In many ways, *The Lost Symbol* is another retelling of the *Faust* story, obviously not as brilliant as Goethe's, but addressing similar issues of life and death, of science, magic, and religion, and of trying to obtain the immortality of the soul through methods both holy and unholy.

The Da Vinci Code was Dan Brown's novel about birth and life. It features the sacred nature of sex (*hieros gamos*, in Greek) and of femininity in early religions. The theme of the sacred feminine runs throughout the book. Mary Magdalene is the star of the story. The plotline emphasizes the secret of the marriage of Jesus and Mary and the presumed bloodline they engendered through their children.

The Lost Symbol is Dan Brown's book about loss and death. It opens with the sentence "The secret is how to die." It is filled with imagery of death. Consider, for example, the Masonic "Chamber of Reflection" in the secret Senate basement, where we find a scene complete with skulls, grim reaper scythes, and other death imagery, all designed to focus the Mason's mind on his mortality and on making the most of his brief life on earth. The climactic scene of the book takes place in the House of the Temple, which in actuality is stylized not on the Temple of Solomon, but the mausoleum at Halicarnassus—an ancient wonder of the world devoted to housing the dead. The ancient philosophers Brown references were interested in the immortality of the soul; Katherine is doing research on what happens to the soul after death; Mal'akh is trying to immortalize his soul through mystical means and ritual death.

The problem of loss is ever present in *TLS*. We moderns have lost the ancient knowledge and need to get it back. The lost pyramid, the Lost Word, the reference to Milton's *Paradise Lost*, are all emphasizing the deeper knowledge we have lost in the course of modernity's progress. The descendants of King Solomon have lost their temple. Books have been lost in wars and fires. The cornerstone of the Washington Monument has been lost. In this book whose very title emphasizes the theme of loss, Peter has lost his son and Zachary has lost his father. Although Katherine is an important character, this is a very male-oriented book, based on a story about the Freemasons, a virtually all-male fraternal order. It is also about fathers and sons.

The story brings to the forefront the biblical story of the Akedah—the binding of Isaac and his aborted sacrifice by Abraham (Genesis 22: 1–19). One of the most troubling of all Bible stories, the Akedah episode has engendered long-standing debates about what kind of God would ask a father to sacrifice his son, and what the meaning and intent of Bible writers and editors may have been in this passage. Mal'akh is perversely seeking to re-create every detail of this frightening, terrifying, profoundly disturbing story from Genesis, with the desired goal of having his own father, Peter, forced to sacrifice him like Isaac, and thereby release his soul from his earthly bindings. Like the maniacally meticulous Matthew Weiner on the set of TV's *Mad Men*, Dan Brown has worked to an amazing level of detail in re-creating this tableau from Genesis. Consider just this one small example. In Jewish study circles, where every detail of the Torah is parsed to an infinite degree, it is not always seen as completely clear what happens to Isaac when the angel stays Abraham's hand and gives Isaac his reprieve from being sacrificed. We learn that Abraham sacrificed a ram instead. We also learn that Abraham came back down the mountain, but Genesis does not specifically say Isaac descended the mountain with him. (The mountain in question is believed in biblical tradition to be the same Mount Moriah where King Solomon would later build his temple, and which today is home to the sacred Muslim site the Dome of the Rock.)

In *The Lost Symbol*, once Peter Solomon understands that Mal'akh is, in fact, his long lost son, and that his son is trying to force him to sacrifice him like Isaac, he resists and strikes the knife instead into the granite altar, whereupon the sacrificial scene is interrupted both by Robert Langdon rushing in to tackle Peter before he plunges the knife and by the CIA's black helicopter crashing into the skylight of the House of the Temple. (A black helicopter, which shadows Langdon on his search, is itself an allusion to a conspiracy theory about one world government taking over the country—see the interview with Michael Barkun in chapter 10.) Just as the angel stayed Abraham's hand, so Mal'akh is not killed by his father. However, the narrator paints a picture of Mal'akh writhing in pain from presumed injuries caused by the shattering jagged shards of glass from the broken skylight overhead. But is he really dead? When Katherine comes into the room, the narrator tells us she sees a "corpse" on the altar table. But the same narrator referred to Robert Langdon as a "corpse" only a few chapters earlier, when Mal'akh left him for dead in the water tank. So we don't know for a fact what has happened to Mal'akh, and there is no further mention of him in the book—just as there is no final mention of Isaac's whereabouts at the end of the Akedah scene in Genesis.

Dan Brown wants us to believe that Mal'akh has obtained the actual knife used in the Akedah on the antiquities black market for use in his own ritual sacrifice. Supposedly, this knife was "crafted over three thousand years ago from an iron meteorite" and has been through a succession of owners including "popes, Nazi mystics, European alchemists, and private collectors." This is sheer fiction on Brown's part.

If Mal'akh hasn't died, he has certainly had a near-death experience. In another clever twist, we hear Mal'akh's interior monologue describe his near-death experience as heading into darkness and "infinite terror" as he encounters the blackness of a "prehistoric beast" rearing up and "dark souls" confronting him. This would be the opposite of most accounts of near-death experiences studied by the real-life noetic scientists Brown cites. Many accounts report bright white shining light, the feeling of ascendancy, and sensations of serenity and happiness. Not surprisingly after the destructive havoc he has wreaked, Mal'akh is apparently headed the other way.

It isn't just Mal'akh who has a near-death experience (NDE). There are several other NDEs in *TLS*. Robert Langdon has one in the water tank, when he comes within seconds of expiring. Katherine, who studies NDEs professionally, has one when she nearly bleeds to death in the wake of Mal'akh's fiendish effort to turn her into a human hourglass with the blood draining slowly out of her.

In the course of these near-death experiences, we learn something interesting about Dan Brown and his thinking. As the narrator shares each person's near-death thoughts, it seems each one is more focused on their work and ideas that will be lost as a result of their death than thinking about their families, their loved ones, or their important personal memories from their lives. In real life, many people's final thoughts are about their loved ones. But these characters have no loved ones. Langdon is unmarried and childless, and, so far as we know, hasn't been on a date since he got to know about Vittoria Vetra's hatha yoga expertise in *Angels & Demons*. (Following the recipe for *DVC*, *TLS* has no sex and only the very mildest romantic energy between Langdon and Katherine.) Katherine is unmarried, with no mention ever made of a significant other. She is apparently childless as well. Peter's wife "never forgave him" for leaving Zachary to die in the Turkish prison, and their marriage is said to have fallen apart six months after Zachary's presumed death. (Like a Disney movie where the central character has no mother—think Aladdin, Peter Pan, Little Mermaid, etc.—Zachary/Mal'akh is essentially a motherless child.) It would be important to note here that Dan Brown has no child either, so perhaps this is simply how he thinks about the world. But I believe he is actually referencing some of the ideas in Goethe's *Faust* here. Faust, after all his travail, and all he has experienced, finds the moment of happiness he seeks in the free association of men and the collective work of the community—people he doesn't even know. Brown is suggesting something along those lines with the metaphor of the Freemasons and the never-ending search for knowledge.

Prior to the moment Faust finds his bliss, he is the prototype for the "dejected adept" in Dürer's *Melencolia I*. Take a look at the image. (By the way, it is a woman in the *Melencolia* image in the opinion of most art historians, including our contributor Diane Apostolos-Cappadona whose essay is in chapter 8. Brown is apparently so gun-shy of the criticism he received for arguing that Mary Magdalene was in *The Last Supper* that he doesn't even bother to mention that the central artwork of *TLS* is focused on a woman. Instead, he writes about the adept in the Dürer engraving in gender-neutral terms.)

The school of ancient mysteries' take on *Melencolia I* is that Dürer is reflecting the psychological pain of the adept who hoped to gain secret, sacred knowledge about the meaning of life and perhaps find a way to immortality, but has failed. The scientific and mathematical tools are all there. Several of them, like the compass and the "smooth ashlar" of the mystical polyhedron, are about to become standard symbols of Freemasonry in the two centuries after Dürer's life. But in spite of access to the proper tools and the right knowledge, the desired result has not occurred. The adept therefore is frustrated, sad, melancholic, perhaps like Faust, suicidal. There is even a dog in the image, reminiscent of the stray dog Faust brings home, who morphs into the soul-collecting devil.

The adept has been at this for a long time, but has not been able to figure out how to obtain physical immortality. Neither, we might note, have any of the ancient mystery school heroes of *TLS*. We, the readers, share the adept's frustration in our own lives. We can come close to real sacred knowledge about the meaning of life, we can find metaphors and symbols to approximate our ideas, but almost by definition we can never quite catch it, any more than we can travel faster than the speed of light. As it turns out, like so much else, the meaning of life is all about the journey. The fact that the desired result of the quest for higher knowledge is unobtainable should not stop us from trying to reach for it. But our happiness and fulfillment will come from the process, not the unobtainable end product.

TLS succeeds mightily in raising interesting questions and giving us enough to go on to trigger our own interior explorations should we be

Dürer's *Melencolia I* (1514).

so inclined. But it certainly doesn't offer much in the way of answers. Indeed, as we close page 509, having finished the final chapter (conveniently numbered 133), we aren't even sure what we've been looking for all this time: The lost pyramid? The lost symbol? The lost word? Nor are we sure what we've found: The Washington Monument (lost pyramid)? The circumpunct (lost symbol)? The Bible (lost word)? Is Dan Brown's most important book about preparing for our ultimate death . . . or about how to live our lives?

The Lost Symbol's focus on death is not pessimistic. Masons pay attention to death and reenact death scenes in order to increase the focus on the here and now. As much as *TLS* is about loss and sacrifice and death, it is also a novel about change and transformation. It references the alchemists' search for transformation, the mystics' search for transformation, the scientists' search for transformation. And it celebrates the American revolutionaries who, learning from the ancients in Greece and Rome, made one of the world's most important historical transformations, overturning centuries of government by kings and clergy and establishing the first modern government elected and run by ordinary mortal men.

Dan Brown's telling of *The Lost Symbol* story has apocalyptic overtones. All his books do. We live in those kind of times. But both Robert Langdon and Peter Solomon reassure us multiple times in the course of their night in Washington that the world is not really going to end in 2012 or any other time soon. Christian/Greek references to "apocalypse" mean only the end of the world *as we know it*, and therefore the potential for Revelation and with it, the beginning of a new and more wonderful world ahead, enriched by what will be re-membered from the ancient wisdom and re-called from the Lost Word. Rebirth and renaissance lie ahead. Perhaps even a new age of wonder.

At least that is Dan Brown's wish for humanity at the end of Robert Langdon's long night's journey through the mysteries of Washington.

Chapter
TWO

HISTORY,
MYSTERY,
AND MASONS

Dan Brown's Freemasonry

by Arturo de Hoyos, 33°, Grand Cross

In *The Lost Symbol*, Freemasonry is portrayed as a benign, benevolent order dedicated to facilitating one's journey toward "the light." It protects protagonist Robert Langdon and provides him with the clues that will lead him physically to the villain and metaphorically to his discovery of "the Word" and the truth that can reunite man with his severed spirituality. These are no small feats in the space of the twelve-hour story.

Before the novel was published, it was widely assumed that the Masons, with their love of secrecy and mysterious rituals, would get treated in *The Lost Symbol* in much the same way Dan Brown had portrayed the Illuminati in *Angels & Demons* and The Priory of Sion in *The Da Vinci Code*: as a shadow organization with shocking secrets to protect and great conspiracies to generate. Instead, Brown and his alter ego, Robert Langdon, seem not only intrigued with the Masons, but so admiring as to be about ready to join.

So who are these Masons? What is their history, and how are they organized? And despite his admiration of them, does the novelist portray the brotherhood and its rituals accurately? To find the answers to these and other questions we reached out to the man widely regarded as America's most authoritative scholar of Masonry: Grand Archivist and Grand Historian Arturo de Hoyos, a 33° Mason and holder of the Grand Cross of the Court of Honor in the Supreme Council of the Scottish Rite in America.

De Hoyos begins by tracing the roots and explaining the nature of Freemasonry. He then switches gears and addresses *The Lost Symbol* directly. While he finds the novel "respectful and inoffensive" on the whole, de Hoyos says that it is inaccurate and misleading in some places when it comes to the presentation of some of the finer points of Masonry.

Freemasonry is the world's oldest and largest fraternity, developed from the stonemason associations of the Middle Ages in Scotland and England. The word *freemason* is a contraction of *freestone mason*, meaning hewers of freestone, a fine-grained stone that could be carved equally well in any direction. In 1717 the first Masonic "Grand Lodge" (or governing body) was created in London, setting a model for fraternal development and self-governing organizational principles. Degrees were established as a type of initiatory ceremonial drama, using esoteric symbolism to teach life lessons in philosophy and morality.

During the mid-1700s many additional degrees were created and so-called haute-grade (high-degree) "Appendant" Masonry became popular. The most successful of these Appendant orders, in terms of membership, is the Ancient and Accepted Scottish Rite, which was founded in Charleston, South Carolina, on May 31, 1801. Its governing body today is called the Supreme Council, 33°. The Scottish Rite administers thirty-three degrees, the highest of which, the thirty-third, is given to only a few as an honor for faithful service, and to certain presiding officers. One need not be a stonemason anymore to join the fraternity. The governing rules state that membership requires only a belief in a Supreme Being, that one be of good moral character, and that one have a hope for a future state of existence. Freemasonry has no unique religious dogmas, and offers no plan of salvation. Indeed, religion and politics are not allowed to be discussed at lodge meetings.

The purpose for the ancient regalia (e.g., aprons, gloves), titles, rituals, and symbols, as well as the practical working tools (squares, compasses, etc.), is to teach life lessons in philosophy and morality that will help the Mason reach a higher degree and move closer to "the light" of self-improvement and moral perfection. It is not to protect themselves as a secret society.

In spite of what we know concerning Masonic origins, and how it was developed into a fraternity by skilled craftsmen in the seventeenth and eighteenth centuries in Scotland and England, there are advocates of a "romantic school" within the brotherhood who assert that ancient writings, legends, mythology, symbolism, and circumstantial evidence suggest much older origins, including Solomon's Temple, the ancient Egyptians, the mystery schools, the alchemists, Kabbalists, Rosicrucians, Knights Templar, and other arcane orders. In earlier times enthusiasts attributed the craft's origins to Noah, Nimrod, and even Adam, because of his fig-leaf apron.

For modern conspiracy theorists, however, it is of minor importance from whence Freemasonry comes, although it is of supreme importance whither it travels and what influence it allegedly exerts. Adolf Hitler, the Ayatollah Khomeini, and other dictators accepted the same anti-Masonic ravings as the conspiracy theorists who fear that the fraternity supports a one-world government known as the New World Order. Inevitably, they turn to forgeries, such as the *Protocols of the Elders of Zion*, or to hoaxes, such as the writings of "Léo Taxil," or to pseudoscholarly works like those of C. W. Leadbeater. Such works advocate fringe notions such as Jewish-Masonic conspiracies, Luciferianism, or alleged connections to the ancient mysteries rather than relying on the work of competent historians.

Dan Brown's Freemasonry dances near the perimeter of such notions. Mal'akh's Freemasonry is esoteric, and borders on being conspiratorial. The fraternity's true "principal tenets"—brotherly love, relief, and truth—are overshadowed by an obsession that rushes him toward a Kafkaesque metamorphosis he calls the "transformation." By discovering and using the ultimate Masonic secret, the "Lost Word," he seeks liberation

The Roman Pantheon is interesting to Dan Brown (who used it in *Angels & Demons*) for two reasons: First, like all pantheons in the ancient world, it is a temple to multiple gods, emphasizing Brown's point that all religions are essentially one. Second, the Roman Pantheon began as a pagan polytheistic shrine but was later repurposed as a Christian church.

In all his books, the novelist is reminding us that modern religions are built on a pastiche of ancient traditions. In *The Da Vinci Code*, for example, it is the pagan legend of the Persian sun god Mithras, which transmigrated into the Christian story of Jesus. (Mithras was born of a virgin birth, his birthday is around December 25, and he is said to have been resurrected three days after his death.) In *TLS*, it is the "god-eating rites of Holy Communion" in Christian worship, which Brown claims have their roots in primitive religious cults. The novelist seems to be saying: We may think Masonic rituals and symbols weird, but are Christian congregants not engaged in a parallel ancient rite when they symbolically drink the blood and eat the flesh of Jesus during Communion? The conclusion of this line of reasoning is cautionary humility. Those who believe they are following the word of the One True God are actually following nothing more than an edited collection of prior beliefs, myths, and practices. The corollary is to look for what has been edited out of the current tenets that were there at the beginning: the sacred feminine, for example, or potential for man to realize his own divinity.

The Panthéon in Paris also deserves mention here, because Jefferson knew and admired its history from his days as U.S. ambassador to France. This famous landmark in the fifth arrondissement of Paris was originally designed to be a Catholic church but was still under construction when the French Revolution occurred. The revolutionaries decided to repurpose it and turn it into perhaps the world's first temple to man. The "saints" who are honored in the Parisian Panthéon are thinkers, writers, scientists, and artists, all of them explicitly *not* religious figures.

It is no coincidence that Jefferson modeled his Monticello after a pantheon, and that the style inspired his Monument as well. Brown sees a similar impulse in the design and layout of Washington as a whole. Just from mortality. Also skirting the edge is the portrayal of Peter Solomon. True, his Freemasonry is benevolent and borders on the sacred, yet there are strong suggestions of political influence running like an undercurrent through Washington, D.C.'s halls of power. In general, however, Brown's presentation of Freemasonry—errors and all—is respectful and inoffensive.

Additionally, there are a number of more concrete elements to Dan Brown's interpretation of Masonic practices and symbols, where facts tend to lose themselves in the fiction of *The Lost Symbol*. Here is a sampling:

- The prologue of *TLS* describes a 33° initiation ritual as it is conferred upon Mal'akh in the Temple Room at the House of the Temple at 8:33 P.M. However, the 33° is neither conferred at the House of the Temple nor at night. It is regularly conferred mid-afternoon during biennial meetings (called "sessions") of the Supreme Council 33°, Southern Jurisdiction, held near the end of September or the beginning of October in odd years, and usually at a Scottish Rite building located at 2800 Sixteenth Street, N.W., about ten blocks north of the House of the Temple. Furthermore, Mal'akh is too young to receive the 33°. He is described by Dan Brown as thirty-four; the *Statutes of the Supreme Council* require that he be at least thirty-five years old. Although Mal'akh is dressed "as a master," and those present wear lambskin aprons, sashes, and white gloves, this is fiction, not fact. Initiates and attendees at 33° do not dress in aprons, sashes, or white gloves; a black tuxedo is sufficient.

- Peter Solomon is called the "Worshipful Master," but in reality the principal officer of the Supreme Council is the "Sovereign Grand Commander." During his reception of the 33°, Mal'akh reminds himself that "the secret is how to die." Although the importance of this phrase will escape most readers (including most American Masons), it occurs in many English rituals of the 33° Master Mason, during a part known as the "Exhortation of the Worshipful Master." In this brief discourse, Nature is said to prepare us for the closing hour of existence and "finally instructs you how to die"—a definition of philosophy shared by Plato (*Phaedo*, 67d) and Cicero (*De Contemnenda Morte*, 30).

- As a part of his 33° initiation, Mal'akh drinks wine from a human skull to seal his 33° oath. This has never been the practice within the mainstream of the Scottish Rite. It was the practice of a splinter group that called itself the Cerneau Scottish Rite, a pseudo-Masonic organization that competed with the Scottish Rite during the 1800s.

- The interpretations of some of the symbols are also errant. For example, the red symbol displayed prominently on the front cover of the American edition of the book represents the seal impression of Peter Solomon's 33° ring, which is thus described: "Its face bore the image of a double-headed phoenix holding a banner proclaiming ORDO AB CHAO, and its chest was emblazoned with the number 33." Its band, says the novelist, is engraved with the words "All is revealed at the 33°." In reality, the seal of the Supreme Council 33° actually uses a double-headed *eagle*. Furthermore, the double-headed eagle does not appear on the 33° ring at all. Rather, the 33° ring is simply a triple band of gold, which may or may not bear the number 33 within a triangle. The inner band of the 33° ring is engraved with the words DEUS MEUMQUE JUS (my God and my right), which is the motto of the degree. The motto ORDO AB CHAO is instead the motto of the Supreme Council 33°, not of the degree itself.

However, the phoenix does turn out to be a fitting symbol for Brown's story in a different way. The phoenix was a mythical bird that was reborn from its own ashes, and may represent the "transformation" that Mal'akh seeks. According to Adam McLean's *Hermetic Journal* No. 5 (1979), "The Phoenix completes this process of soul development. The Phoenix bird builds its nest which at the same time is its funeral pyre, and then setting it alight cremates itself. But it arises anew from the ashes transformed. Here we have captured the alchemist's experience of spiritualization. He has integrated his being so much, that he is no longer dependent upon his physical body as a foundation for his being."

- It may help the plot of *TLS*, but the "Lost Word" is not that mysterious. According to Masonic legend, King Solomon's Temple was built by three classes of craftsmen: apprentices, fellow crafts, and master masons. Each class was paid according to its skill, and each possessed a password that identified his class. All were under the direction of Hiram Abiff, who was a widow's son, of the tribe of Naphtali (see I Kings 7:14). Three rebellious fellow crafts, dissatisfied with their pay, tried to extort the "master's Word" from the chief architect, who refused to submit and died a martyr to his integrity.

  The word that Hiram Abiff refused to divulge became known as the "Lost Word." A variety of Masonic legends have grown up around this word—some of which depict it as a mere word, while others describe it as a symbol for philosophical truth. Robert Langdon's description of the Lost Word as "a single word, written in an arcane language that man could no longer decipher" is extreme and not Masonic. Neither does Freemasonry assert that the word possesses "hidden power," or that knowledge of it will make "the Ancient Mysteries . . . clear to you." And it is certainly never claimed that "when the Lost Word is written on the mind of man, he is then ready to receive unimaginable power." Such statements make great fiction, but are gross exaggerations. And yet, because Freemasonry *is* symbolic, there are people, including some Masons, who have made extravagant and outlandish claims about the Lost Word and its "hidden meaning" even when the official rituals do not.

- The Akedah knife is given an importance that it does not have in modern Masonry. The biblical story found in Genesis 22:1–19 of the binding of Isaac by Abraham (called the *akedah* in Hebrew) is briefly mentioned in some versions of Masonic ritual, but it is virtually unknown in the United States, and is not a part of the Scottish Rite rituals. This small mention is developed into a major theme when in chapter 119 it is declared that "the Akedah had always been sacred in Masonic ritual." Mal'akh believes that his own ritual killing will be the means of his transformation, something that is never taught in Freemasonry.

- The *ashlar* is explained to Robert Langdon by Dean Galloway, dean of the National Cathedral, as a shape venerated by Masons because "it is a three-dimensional representation of another symbol," which happens to be a cross when unfolded. In Symbolic Masonry there are actually two types of *ashlars:* one, a rough stone; the other, squared and dressed. According to Masonic ritual, "The rough *ashlar* represents man in his rude and imperfect state by nature; the perfect *ashlar* represents man in the state of perfection to which we all hope to arrive by means of a virtuous life and education, our own endeavors and the blessings of God." The stone that unfolds into a cross is known as the *cubic stone.*

- The description of the House of the Temple is fairly accurate, but errs in some points. For example, the Temple Room's square skylight is not an oculus (which would be round). Its green granite columns are not "monolithic" (they're each built of five sections). The back elevator does not open "in full view of the Temple Room"; it opens to the library, on the right side of the Grand Staircase, which leads to the Temple Room. One of the more interesting features of the building is that it actually *does* have two sealed burial vaults in which the remains of two former Grand Commanders of the Scottish Rite, Albert Pike (1809–91) and John Henry Cowles (1863–1954), are entombed.

- The term *Heredom* is not commonly used for the House of the Temple, as Robert Langdon would have it, although some Scottish Rite publications bear the word on the title page. I was mildly amused when I read the so-called encyclopedia entry for *Heredom* in chapter 114. The definition that appears there was actually co-authored by S. Brent Morris and myself for inclusion in the annual transactions of the Scottish Rite Research Society, a publication that happens to be entitled *Heredom*. Our definition does not appear in encyclopedias.

- Finally, in chapter 117 we learn that Mal'akh secretly videotaped his initiation as a 1° Entered Apprentice: "He was dressed in the garb of a medieval heretic being led to the gallows—noose around his neck, left pant leg rolled up to the knee, right sleeve rolled up to the elbow, and his shirt gaping open to reveal his bare chest." Dan Brown's description is actually borrowed from Christopher Knight and Robert Lomas, *The Hiram Key* (2001), an overly dramatic fiction; Masonic scholars dismiss the "medieval heretic" notion.

Mal'akh also manages to videotape a 33° initiation and in so doing captures the faces of prominent members, including two Supreme Court justices, the Speaker of the House, three prominent senators, and the secretary of homeland security. Langdon fears that if the video is uploaded onto the Internet it will "create chaos." He wonders what the leaders of foreign nations would think if they saw the ritual and concludes that "[t]he global outcry would be instantaneous and overwhelming." In today's world it is difficult to believe that the rituals described would upset "prominent leaders of Russia or the Islamic world," when they have actual human atrocities with which to contend.

It is true that the social fabric of America was once shaken by the revelation of Masonic rites. In 1826, it was alleged that William Morgan, of Batavia, New York, was "murdered by the Masons" for preparing an exposure of Masonic ritual. The public outcry dealt a severe blow to the fraternity. The event resulted in public exhibitions of Masonic ritual, and dozens of books revealing the "secrets" of Freemasonry were published. Most of the lodges in the United States ceased operating, and mass defections were commonplace, at least until about 1842. Yet, ironically, during the height of the "Morgan affair," a Mason was elected president of the United States! Andrew Jackson, the hero of the battle of New Orleans, president from 1829 to 1837, had served as Grand Master of Masons of Tennessee from 1822 to 1824, and remained a strong supporter of the fraternity.

These and other examples of what Dan Brown would undoubtedly call simple literary license should not detract from the many things that are reflected accurately about the Masonic tradition in *The Lost Symbol*. As Robert Langdon finds out in the course of his adventure, American Freemasonry provided the framework within which the Old World could evolve into the New with its promise of the free exchange of ideas, religious tolerance, ethical development, and the importance of a spiritual search for universal truth.

A Mason Reveals His "Journey to Light"

by Mark E. Koltko-Rivera

Who are the Masons? What are their symbols and values? Why did Brown choose to make Freemasonry central to his novel?

Mark Koltko-Rivera, Ph.D., a specialist in the psychology of religion, is a Master Mason, holding the third and highest degree in regular Freemasonry. Additionally, in the world of "high-degree" Freemasonry, he is (technically speaking) a Master of the Royal Secret, that is, a holder of the 32° within the Scottish Rite of Freemasonry (the oldest division of which—the Southern Jurisdiction of the USA—is actually headquartered in the House of the Temple featured in *The Lost Symbol*). Koltko-Rivera is also a member of the Masonic version of the Knights Templar in the York Rite of Freemasonry. He is one of a small group of authors and bloggers who have followed developments involving Dan Brown's *The Lost Symbol* for several years before it appeared in print. Here he begins by asking the question: What kind of journey does one undertake to become a Mason?

Every Mason undertakes his own ritual "journey to light," where each ceremony constitutes a "degree" of initiation. In basic Masonry, there are three such degrees, each named for a stage in the imagined professional development of a medieval stonemason: Entered Apprentice ("the first degree," written "1°"), Fellow Craft (2°), and Master Mason (3°). As part of the journey to light, there are ritual challenges and trials, the imparting of information and the testing of knowledge, and the presentation of symbolism and the interpretation thereof. Virtually everything in the ritual—the clothing, the actions, the words, the placement of the officers, even one's path around the lodge room—has symbolic significance.

Let's consider what Mal'akh, the villain of *The Lost Symbol*, would have undergone to become a Mason (a process Brown only hints at in the prologue). First, in an anteroom outside the actual lodge meeting room, the candidate is asked to declare, upon his honor, that he is prompted to enter Masonry because of a favorable view of the fraternity; that his desire is both to obtain knowledge and to be of service to his fellow man, and that he does so without any mercenary objectives. No doubt Mal'akh would have lied and said yes, as he did in the 33° ceremony in the prologue. Mal'akh had no intention of being of service to others; rather, his objective was to *block* human progress.

For ritual purposes, the lodge room is symbolically transformed into one portion or another of what the Bible holds as the most venerable of all ancient stone buildings: the temple built by King Solomon. At the lodge room's center is an altar, upon which sits a Volume of the Sacred Law (usually represented by a copy of the King James version of the Holy Bible). At this altar, the candidate takes upon himself the Obligation of the degree he is receiving. (Each candidate is entitled to have a Volume of the Sacred Law that is sacred to *him* on the altar at his Obligation.)

To what do Masons obligate themselves, by solemn oath, at each degree? Ethical injunctions regarding honesty, charity, benevolence, and the giving of aid and assistance are prominent. In addition, Masons swear that they will keep secret certain signs of recognition (such as passwords and hand grips) by which two men, otherwise strangers to each other, may confirm that each is a Mason. Masons do indeed bind themselves under oath to endure bloodcurdling penalties for transgressing these obligations—penalties, it should be understood, meted out by God, not other Masons.

Within each of the first three degrees of Freemasonry, the candidate encounters symbols, some of them tools of the stonemason trade that Masons have endowed with moral meanings. The morality taught here starts off with the very practical (for example, exhorting the Mason to allow time for charitable work and religious devotion), and moves on to encourage such interpersonal virtues as honesty, egalitarianism, and the need to put effort into the building of fellowship. Even the famous Masonic secrecy has a moral point: a man who cannot be trusted with little secrets (like a password or a grip) cannot be trusted with the greater secrets of life either; keep your word, Masonry says to its candidates (a test that Mal'akh fails spectacularly).

A man is never more of a Freemason than when he has received the third degree of initiation and become a Master Mason in a basic or "Blue" Lodge. However, from the earliest days of modern Masonry in early eighteenth-century Europe, other degrees of initiation have been developed to enhance the Masonic experience and provoke the Mason to further consider his intellectual, spiritual, and moral development. These are the province of so-called high-degree organizations, or Rites, which offer their ritual initiations only to Master Masons.

One such organization is the Scottish Rite, which offers numbered degrees from the 4°, Secret Master, to the 32°, Master (or Sublime Prince) of the Royal Secret. These involve exposure to various spiritual traditions and both mythic and historic events to teach yet more principles of morality and philosophy. A very few Scottish Rite Masons receive the final 33° as an honor—the honor that Mal'akh receives in the prologue to *The Lost Symbol*.

THE LOST WORD OF FREEMASONRY

One common mythic theme across the various Rites of Masonry is the search for the Lost Word. This is a legendary password connected with the building of the temple by Solomon—a password that, the candidate learns, has been lost through villainy.

Like so much else in Masonry, the Lost Word is a symbol that can be understood in several ways: as an especially sacred word; as a principle necessary for enlightenment; as a secret that cannot even be expressed in words; as the secret of human destiny. Knowing this about the Lost Word gives a special significance to the title of Dan Brown's novel *The Lost Symbol*, and special insight into the quest that drives much of the novel's plot.

The ritual structure of Freemasonry and the central importance of the Lost Word are illustrated in the very tattoos that cover Mal'akh's body (*TLS*, chapter 2). His feet are tattooed with a hawk's talons, perhaps symbolizing the ancient Hermetic mysteries from which some suppose Masonry sprang. Mal'akh's legs are tattooed with the pillars, Boaz and Jachin, that the Bible says were set up in front of the temple built by Solomon. One will see these pillars reproduced in every lodge room. Thus, Mal'akh's legs claim a progression from the ancient Hermetic mysteries to the mysteries of the Blue Lodge of Freemasonry.

Mal'akh's abdomen is tattooed with a decorated archway. Mal'akh refers here to the traditional completion of the Master Mason degree, in the Royal Arch degree of the York Rite (another high-degree organization).

Mal'akh's chest tattoo, while called a double-headed phoenix by Dan Brown, is the double-headed eagle on the seal of the Supreme Council of the Scottish Rite. (Readers of the American edition of *The Lost Symbol* see a version of this seal impressed in wax in the middle of the front-cover dust jacket.)

Every inch of Mal'akh's body is tattooed, except for a small circle at the very crown of his head. It is here that Mal'akh plans to tattoo the Lost Word of Freemasonry. Herein lies a profound contrast between Mal'akh and the honest Mason. In Freemasonry, the search for the Lost Word is part of an ongoing program to transcend the self in the service of humanity. For Mal'akh, who has entered the fraternity under false pretences, the search for the Lost Word is the centerpiece of his program to gain immense personal power. Mal'akh's intent is to use the Lost Word to achieve a kind of dark godhood in Hades: he sees the Lost Word as a Word of Power, a device that a practitioner of true magic would use to exercise power over the demons of the netherworld.

The search for the Lost Word is the MacGuffin that drives the plot of the entire novel. This search leads Mal'akh to kidnap, torture, and mutilate Peter Solomon. It is the reason Mal'akh deceitfully lures to Washington, D.C., the world-renowned symbologist and expert on esoteric lore, Robert Langdon, whose efforts to find the Lost Word for Mal'akh, and thereby rescue Peter Solomon, comprise the story of the novel.

The Lost Word of Freemasonry (at least as Dan Brown defines it) is also the key to understanding the novel's conclusion. As Mal'akh lays dying on the altar where he had falsely sworn his Masonic oath, he learns that the Word he has received is as fake as his journey through Freemasonry; having lied and murdered his way through his bogus journey to light, at the moment of his death Mal'akh feels himself hurtling into what it seems will be an eternity of darkness and terror.

As a counterbalance, Peter Solomon teaches Robert Langdon the nature of the true Word, as a symbol—the Lost Symbol of the novel's title—of the divine potential inherent in each human being. As the ignominious death of Mal'akh is the dramatic climax of the novel, so Robert Langdon's discovery of the true Lost Word and its meaning is its emotional and intellectual climax.

Why Dan Brown Focused on Freemasonry

Within the realm of Masonic values, we find the answer to a mystery, not *within* the novel, but rather *about* it: why did Brown choose to focus on Freemasonry?

By coincidence, the publication of *The Lost Symbol* on September 15, 2009, was followed three weeks later by the biennial session of the Supreme Council of the Southern Jurisdiction of the Scottish Rite. The Supreme Council invited Dan Brown to speak at this meeting. Having a heavy schedule of commitments, Brown sent in his place a letter (dated October 6) that addressed his authorial choices. Brown wrote, in part:

> In the past few weeks, . . . I have been repeatedly asked what attracted me to the Masons so strongly as to make it [i.e., Freemasonry] a central point of my new book. My reply is always the same: "In a world where

men do battle over whose definition of God is most accurate, I cannot adequately express the deep respect and admiration I feel toward an organization in which men of differing faiths are able to 'break bread together' in a bond of brotherhood, friendship, and camaraderie." Please accept my humble thanks for the noble example you set for humankind. It is my sincere hope that the Masonic community recognizes *The Lost Symbol* for what it truly is . . . an earnest attempt to reverentially explore the history and beauty of Masonic Philosophy.

This is why Dan Brown made Freemasonry central to *The Lost Symbol*. He admires the fact that Freemasonry encourages tolerance of religious differences, that Masonry fosters fellowship and even friendship across the lines drawn by different religious affiliations. (Questions about religious affiliation, and discussions of sectarian religion, are strictly prohibited in the lodges.) He expressed thanks for the "noble example" that he says Masonry sets "for humankind." By holding up this example, Dan Brown is trying to change the world—which is his ultimate objective as an author.

There is a very real sense in which Dan Brown's true vocation is that of a philosopher of religion. Each of his Langdon novels can be seen as an attempt to outline the characteristics of an improved approach to religion—Dan Brown's Religion 2.0, as it were. In *Angels & Demons*, Brown promotes the idea that religion and science need not be in conflict, that the best form of religion would recognize and even consecrate the discoveries of science. In *The Da Vinci Code*, Brown tries to reform conventional notions of God to create a point of entry for Western religion to celebrate the divine feminine. Now, in *The Lost Symbol*, Brown promotes the notion that a good religion reaches across denominational and sectarian boundaries to unite people of goodwill from all backgrounds, into a celebration of the divine potential within every human being.

What an ocean of blood we have seen over the last millennia, spilled in the name of religion. In this context, the tradition of religious toleration among Masons may be centuries old, but at the same time it is downright radical.

DEFINING FREEMASONRY[*]

by Mark A. Tabbert

The preceding essays conveyed the reaction of two learned Masons to *The Lost Symbol*. We now turn to Mark Tabbert of the George Washington Masonic National Memorial in Alexandria, Virginia, for an explanation of the Masonic movement as a whole.

In *American Freemasons*, Tabbert's authoritative history of Freemasonry, he traces the movement's evolving role in American society from the Founding Fathers through today. And along the way he emphasizes that although Masonic rituals may be secret, the benefits of Masonry to individual growth and the many examples of Masons' good deeds are highly visible and very beneficial to society as a whole. In service of that point, he quotes one of America's most famous Masons, Benjamin Franklin: "[T]he Freemasons, . . . are in general a very harmless sort of People, and have no principles or practices that are inconsistent with religion and good manners."

Here, Tabbert attempts to define just what it is that makes Masonry—the symbolism, the rituals, the secrecy, or the philosophy of helping a fellow man—and how Masonry has been perceived by others over the past three hundred years.

*Excerpted from *American Freemasons: Three Centuries of Building Communities* by Mark A. Tabbert. Copyright by the National Heritage Museum, Lexington, Massachusetts. Used with permission.

By speculative Masonry we learn to subdue the
passions, act upon the square, keep a tongue of good
report, maintain secrecy, and practise charity.
—*William Preston, 1772*

Freemasonry's rituals, symbols, and constitutions have led many Masons and non-Masons to attempt to define the craft. To the extent that it is a unique institution, it is not easily defined. Traditionally, Masons have defined the fraternity as "a peculiar system of morality, veiled in allegory and illustrated by symbols." While this is essentially true, it is more than a system. Freemasonry is an institution and a collection of distinct communities of men, and as such, it exists only when men voluntarily come together. The definition, therefore, has varied from Mason to Mason and lodge to lodge over the course of American history.

One basic way to view Freemasonry is to see it as a voluntary association akin to the Elks, Rotary, Boy Scouts, or other community club. Unlike these clubs, a prospective member cannot even attend a lodge meeting before seeking admission. Furthermore, he does not become a member until he takes upon himself various obligations. The importance of maintaining the obligations are emphasized by references to severe "ancient" penalties. He must first pass through a series of three initiation rituals before he is a full member. And in many jurisdictions, a man must prove he has memorized and understood the lessons and symbols of one degree before receiving the next.

Before the 1920s, Freemasonry was often called a "secret society." Since that time, this terminology has increasingly assumed sinister connotations, and Masons' new attempt to counter this definition and the conspiratorial image it conveys by referring to the fraternity as "a society with secrets." In fact, the society has not had secrets to hide since the 1720s, when its rituals were first exposed in London newspapers. As Benjamin Franklin, himself a leading Freemason in Philadelphia, commented in the 1730s, "Their grand secret is that they have no secret at all." The craft's origin, symbolism, purposes, and rituals still strike some people as "weird" and "spooky," despite the fact that there are lodges in nearly every town, tens of thousands of published books on the craft, millions of members, and a growing number of Internet sites. The feelings are largely due to a lack of response from the fraternity in the face of the overactive imagination of conspiracy theorists, the sensationalism of modern journalists, and the rigid views of certain well-meaning, but ill-informed, religiously minded individuals.

When scholars attempt to make sense of the fraternity, some dismiss Freemasonry as a patriarchal cult or "old boys" club, where hypocrisy and ambition overrule true fraternity or equality. Its rituals and symbolism are often mistakenly equated to the sophomoric pranks of college fraternities, and its membership is erroneously identified through such television characters as *The Honeymooners'* Ralph Cramden and Ed Norton. Other academics who have given the fraternity serious attention have discovered in Freemasonry sources for American gender, class, ethnicity, race, and intergenerational phenomena. Still others have sought ways to understand the genuine love and pride generations of American men have felt when they "meet upon the level, act upon the plumb, and part upon the square"—whether in the lodge or on the street. While these scholars have much to say about Freemasonry that is valuable, most of them are not members, have never attended a meeting, and have not actually witnessed the rituals performed. This limits their ability to fully understand the craft.

Since the 1730s, the Roman Catholic Church and certain Protestant denominations have, at various times, labeled Freemasonry dangerous. The craft's combination of prayer, initiation rituals, obligations, symbolism, morality, and charity has caused the Church to see the fraternity as a rival, parallel, or false religion. Some believe Freemasonry is a religion, because lodge meetings begin and end with a prayer, a holy book (in America most frequently the Bible) is open in the center of the lodge room during meetings, and a man swears to be good to his word by placing his hand on the holy book he holds sacred.

When challenged by these positions, Freemasonry replies that its use of the nonsectarian title "Grand Architecture of the Universe," for example, allows those of different faiths to come together in harmony. While each Mason must profess a belief in God, Freemasonry also believes that the relationship between the individual and God is personal, private, and sacred. *Anderson's Constitutions of 1723* charges members to "leave their particular opinions [on religion] to themselves" so that they will not have to suffer religious zealots or "stupid atheists." Masons stress that the fraternity only encourages men to be more devout in their chosen faith. These explanations do not diminish the spiritual dimensions of the fraternity nor do they prevent some men from professing that attending lodge meetings fulfills their spiritual needs.

American politicians, especially after the French Revolution and during the Napoleonic era, began to suspect and accuse the fraternity of conspiratorial tendencies. These attacks reached their most violent stage during the anti-Masonic hysteria of the 1820s and 1830s. Ever since, the idea of private groups of men bound together by rituals and oaths has troubled certain Americans and political leaders. Freemasonry has endeavored to rebut such attacks by pointing to not only the constitutional right of peaceable assembly but also *Anderson's Constitutions*, which forbids the discussion of politics in the lodge and charges brothers to be "peaceable subjects to the civil powers."

The fact that Freemasonry means different things to so many different people has been one of its greatest strengths. Its definitional elusiveness continues to attract new members while remaining the source of inspiration for its varied detractors and critics. Its supporters and critics notwithstanding, Freemasonry is an important part of many lives, entire families, and communities.

In the course of one lodge meeting, Freemasonry is a spiritual organization where the chaplain leads the brethren in prayer and asks for the blessing of deity. It is a guild when the master of the lodge teaches the new Mason the symbolic uses of stonemasons' tools. It becomes a school of instruction when the new brother learns about the importance of the seven liberal arts and sciences. At other moments, it is an amateur theater company when the ritual is performed. The lodge becomes a men's social club when meeting for dinner and fellowship. It becomes a charitable group when relief is provided to distressed brothers, their families, or the local community. It is also a business association when members with similar interests share ideas. The lodge resembles a family when fathers and sons, strangers and friends, bond as "brothers," and it is a community league when volunteers are needed for a project.

Yet at other times Freemasonry's constitutions, tenets, and symbolism have emanated from the lodge as Masons have carried the principles into their communities. Just as *Robert's Rules of Order* caused the birth of infinite committees, so Freemasonry sparked the creation of thousands of American voluntary organizations. Masons and non-Masons have adapted Masonic rituals and symbols to create new fraternities. These groups teach morality and inspire "brotherly love" within diverse communities, such as the B'nai B'rith did among Jewish-Americans, the Order of AHEPA did among Greek-Americans, and the Knights of Columbus did among the country's Roman Catholics. Other Masons used Masonic relief to develop mutual benefit associations and life insurance companies or to build hospitals, orphanages, and retirement homes, such as the Benevolent Protective Order of Elks. Still others, dropping the rituals and symbols, formed social, business, educational, and community service clubs, such as Lions International.

All these things cannot adequately explain why Freemasonry has spread around the world and found especially fertile soil in American society. But it does reveal the great desire of men like Harry Truman who join a Masonic lodge to improve themselves, care for one another, and build their communities. From an obscure past, a fraternity of millions of men has given billions of dollars and untold hours establishing, building, and adorning their lodges for the betterment of an unknown future.

Freemasonry is a symbol of man's search for wisdom, brotherhood, and charity. This universal search is ancient and is renewed every time a lodge of Masons initiates a new brother. Through rituals, symbols, and obligations, a volunteer becomes a part of a community as he begins his own individual search. Freemasonry refers to this as a journey in search of light.

ALBERT PIKE: THE GHOST IN *THE LOST SYMBOL* MACHINE?

by Warren Getler

Dan Brown loves to tease . . . with mysteries, puzzles, codes, ciphers, and all things esoteric. In *The Lost Symbol,* his big tease is about hidden Masonic treasure in America (and more specifically in Washington, D.C.). The implication throughout *TLS*'s five-hundred-plus pages is that this treasure is linked to Freemasonry, and, in particular, to the branch of Freemasonry known as the Scottish Rite. As readers of *TLS* know, Brown's indefatigable protagonist, Robert Langdon, discovers that the "treasure" is more allegorical, figurative, and spiritual than it is concealed monetary riches, such as gold, silver, and diamonds. This may have come as a disappointment to some who expected a bigger payoff.

As with Brown's approach in his previous works, things are not always as they appear. Could the author have been hinting at something tangible— real treasure tied to the Masons and secreted for some ill-defined larger purpose, perhaps spiritual? Such themes surface in no uncertain terms in the Disney *National Treasure* film series, with the second film, *National Treasure: Book of Secrets,* specifically linking the long-serving head of the Scottish Rite, Albert Pike, to the rumored treasure ultimately discovered out West by the film's lead character, Nicolas Cage's Benjamin Gates.

In *The Lost Symbol*, Albert Pike curiously gets but passing mention (his bust is noted as a feature in the Scottish Rite House of the Temple on Sixteenth Street, where Pike is interred and where much of the action in *TLS* takes place). Much of the book's girth revolves around the Scottish Rite—with its elaborate thirty-three degrees of initiation—yet there are very few words about the group's Sovereign Grand Commander who led it from 1859 to the time of his death in 1891.

This in itself is a bit of a mystery, since at the time Dan Brown and I met (in New York City in 2003 at an early *Da Vinci Code* event), he explicitly said that his next book would be about the former Scottish Rite leader. Brown mentioned that he was aware of my nonfiction book, *Rebel Gold*, which had just been published. When I mentioned Pike in conversation, he was a bit shocked and said, "I'm not sure I should read your book right now; my next book will be about Albert Pike." In many ways, he was true to his word. Pike, who singlehandedly brought the Scottish Rite into national and international prominence, looms in the background of much of *The Lost Symbol*, yet his name barely appears. It's the equivalent of writing a book about the Founding Fathers and not going into any details about George Washington other than to mention that he's buried at Mount Vernon. Brown notes as an aside that two bodies are buried inside the walls of the Scottish Rite House of the Temple . . . one of them, of course, being Albert Pike. To be sure, Albert Pike is deeply embedded in the House of the Temple. There's a whole, shrinelike museum room in honor of him, exhibiting his enormous library, his smoking pipes, and other fascinating memorabilia.

So why did Dan Brown choose to make this immensely mysterious and controversial historical figure, Albert Pike, little more than a footnote in *TLS*? Perhaps it has to do with the fact that Pike presents an inconvenient truth. Pike is just that: controversial. *The Lost Symbol* praises Freemasonry for its inclusiveness, particularly in the religious realm, but in the social realm, Pike, in his own words, and as head of the Scottish Rite, was not always inclusive. Or, perhaps it is simpler: maybe Dan Brown didn't want to cover territory already highlighted in the *National Treasure* films.

Although he did not turn out to be a major character in *TLS*, Pike is a major character in the history of Freemasonry. An imposing six-foot-three, three-hundred-pound bear of a man, Pike is a fascinating and, at the same time, divisive character for Masons and non-Masons alike.

A brilliant scholar, linguist, and lawyer, Pike was also a Confederate general and—according to recent research—may have led a subversive Confederate underground group, the Knights of the Golden Circle (KGC). Research I have been involved with over the last decade suggests that the KGC had direct ties to the Scottish Rite's Southern Jurisdiction, led by Pike during and after the Civil War. The research, put forward in the 2003 book I coauthored with Bob Brewer, *Rebel Gold: One Man's Quest to Crack the Code Behind the Secret Treasure of the Confederacy* (Simon & Schuster) points to the Knights of the Golden Circle as having buried large amounts of gold, silver, and weapons during and after the Civil War in the South and Southwest in a very sophisticated, geometric underground depository system. The initial reason for the burial of the riches was to fund the revival of the Confederacy in the event of the South's defeat. But later, this treasure grid morphed into something else, with generations of sentinel families asked to guard the hidden wealth and keep its locations secret.

As Bob Brewer and I suggested in *Rebel Gold*, the KGC systematically buried the treasure "under a masterful grid likely devised by Pike and others. The system employed complex ciphers, precision surveyor's techniques, cryptic Masonic-linked inscriptions on trees and rock faces, and a handful of bewilderingly coded maps." Our research revealed that the notorious bank and train robber of the post–Civil War era, Jesse James, a Mason, was the field commander of the Knights of the Golden Circle and may have controlled the KGC underground depository network in the American South and Southwest. But was it also true for Albert Pike, with his arcane knowledge of the Knights Templar/Rosicrucian sacred geometry, his extensive ties to the American South and West, and his behind-the-scenes influence in the corridors of power? Was he the dark genius behind what would have been a treasonous enterprise? Some anti-Masonic critics of Pike say that the former Confederate officer went on to become the Grand Dragon of the Ku Klux Klan. This charge has dogged Pike for the last century, but there is little specific, concrete evidence that has emerged to support the claim.

Perhaps because he was swept up in the lingering "unreconstructed" prejudicial sentiments of the times, Pike felt moved to write these words in 1868, three years after the South's surrender, in a newspaper editorial appearing in the *Memphis Daily Appeal*:

> The disenfranchised people of the South can find no protection for property or life except in secret association. We should unite every white man in the South, who is opposed to Negro suffrage, into one great Order of Southern Brotherhood with an organization . . . in which a few should execute the concentrated will of all, and whose very existence should be concealed from all its members.

When visitors come to Washington, D.C., to explore the key Masonic sites portrayed in *TLS*—places like the Scottish Rite House of the Temple and the George Washington Masonic National Memorial in nearby Alexandria, Virginia—they will now have a knowledge-based compass, thanks to Dan Brown, to navigate by. But author Brown, while generally treating the Scottish Rite Freemasons much better than other organizations that have been prominent in his prior books, left the road map itself full of mystery and ambiguity. Just as he wanted it, no doubt. Albert Pike, whose looming presence floats in the background of Robert Langdon's twelve-hour jaunt through D.C., once said: "The simplest thing in the universe involves the ultimate mystery of all." Now what might that be?

MOZART AND ELLINGTON, TOLSTOY AND KIPLING

Inside the Brotherhood of Famous Masons

by David D. Burstein

In the mid-twentieth century, when Masons in America claimed several times as many members as today (in a population half the size), they were arguably much less exotic and more widely known and understood than they are today. Moreover, the ideals and philosophy of Masonic movements over the years have attracted a disproportionate share of artists and creative minds. Put these two facets together, and you begin to see why there is such a body of Masonic lore running through our culture. We asked David D. Burstein, a twenty-one-year-old filmmaker and student of politics and new media, to look into Masonry's impact on our culture. Below is his report.

W e don't realize how much Freemasonry is all around us in our culture, hidden in plain sight, as Robert Langdon might say.

The influence of Masons and Masonic thinking on classical culture is powerful, although not widely understood. Just as most of us didn't learn that George Washington, Benjamin Franklin, and Paul Revere were all Freemasons (no matter how many high school classes we took on the

American Revolution), we are also unaware that many great cultural figures we study were Masons: Mozart, Tolstoy, Kipling, Oscar Wilde, Arthur Conan Doyle (the creator of the Sherlock Holmes series), poet Robert Burns, Goethe (author of *Faust*), the great Enlightenment-era philosopher Voltaire, and Mark Twain (although he appears to have had problems paying his dues), just to name a few. Mozart's *The Magic Flute* is an eighteenth-century Masonic allegory of initiation and mystical journey, although almost no one knows that fact; Edgar Allan Poe's famous "Cask of Amontillado," which many students read in middle school, is a biting nineteenth-century anti-Masonic allegory—but they don't tell you that in school.

It isn't only great creative minds of traditional literature and the arts from the eighteenth and nineteenth centuries who have been attracted to this unusual fraternity. As "high culture" moved into pop culture in the twentieth century, many figures from the entertainment world turned out to be members of Masonic lodges. There are the musicians and singers—people like Duke Ellington, Louis Armstrong, Irving Berlin, and Gene Autry. There are the movie moguls—Jack Warner, Cecil B. DeMille, and Billy Wilder. There are film stars like Harpo Marx, Burl Ives, Harold Lloyd, Roy Rogers, Red Skelton, Peter Sellers, and Jackie Mason. True to the premise of equality and tolerance espoused by Freemasonry, Jewish comedians, African-American jazz musicians, and other diverse groups have been attracted to the idea and the social network of the Masonic lodge.

Masonic themes and motifs have populated many films. *The Man Who Would Be King* (starring Sean Connery and Michael Caine) is based on a Masonic-themed story written by Rudyard Kipling, a passionate Freemason himself, and the first English-language winner of the Nobel Prize for literature. In the Kipling story, all the leading characters are Freemasons, and the plot includes the idea that ancient Masonic secrets had been handed down through generations of tribesmen in a remote part of Afghanistan since the days of Alexander the Great.

Fanciful treatment of Masonic legends is the hallmark of the intriguing but not very serious *National Treasure* series. Many people will recall the opening monologue of the original 2004 *National Treasure*, which is as mysterious and compelling as it is pseudohistorical:

> Charles Carroll was the last surviving signer of the Declaration of Independence. He was also a member of a secret society known as the Masons, people who knew about a secret treasure that had been fought over for centuries by tyrants, pharaohs, emperors, warlords. And then suddenly it vanished. It didn't reappear for more than a thousand years, when knights from the First Crusade discovered secret vaults beneath the Temple of Solomon. They brought the treasure back to Europe and took the name Knights Templar. Over the next century they smuggled it out of Europe and they formed a new brotherhood called the Freemasons . . . By the time of the American Revolution the treasure had been hidden again. By then the Masons included George Washington, Benjamin Franklin, Paul Revere . . .

Consider just a few other examples:

- In the 1965 Beatles movie *Help!*, Ringo Starr is asked to identify a Masonic ring, which he does correctly.
- "Heredom" appears to be an obscure Masonic code word known only to characters in *The Lost Symbol*. But Arnold Schwarzenegger references it in his appearance in the 1999 movie *The End of Days*.
- The plot of the 1990 *The Godfather: Part III* film centers around a set of fictional incidents mirroring the recent history of the so-called P2 Masonic Lodge and the Vatican.
- A Masonic Pyramid makes an appearance in the 1979 Peter Sellers movie *Being There*.

For all the references to Robert Langdon's famous Mickey Mouse watch, Dan Brown fails to mention in *The Lost Symbol* that Walt Disney is thought by many to have been at least associated with the Masons. This after Brown retold the tale of the "Priory of Sion" in *The Da Vinci Code*, alluding to the idea that Disney was one of the Priory's "grand masters."

Conspiracy theorists who persist in alleging a Masonic world conspiracy often accuse Walt Disney of being a Mason and of using his films to promote subliminal Masonic thinking. Most responsible research, however, seems to indicate that Disney was not actually a Freemason. He was a member of DeMolay, the Masonic youth organization named for Jacques de Molay, the Knights Templar grand master who would not give in to the powerful king of France and was burned at the stake as a heretic in 1314. Six centuries later, other American DeMolay members have included Bill Clinton, Buddy Ebsen, and John Wayne.

Walt Disney had such fond memories of his days as a youth member of DeMolay that he encouraged DeMolay to make Mickey Mouse an honorary member. During its early days, Disneyland apparently sponsored a Masonic club for its employees along with other recreational clubs like skiing and knitting. Additionally, a Disneyland private club restaurant was named Club 33, and while spokespeople insist there is no connection to the importance of the number 33 to Masons and the high-ranking 33° Mason title, it is an unexplained name for a club if it has no connection to Freemasonry.

Masons, always champions of progress and new technology, embraced film as a medium early on. There were explicitly Masonic films like *Bobby Bumps Starts a Lodge*, which even addressed the issue of racial equality in America—very pioneering for 1916. Countless modern films have subtle Masonic references. Some of these titles range from *Bad Boys II* to *Eyes Wide Shut*, Mel Gibson's *Conspiracy Theory* to *What's Eating Gilbert Grape?*

A not infrequent visual allusion in a film is to a Masonic hall or lodge in passing. Today, with many lodges struggling to stay afloat in the face of declining membership, they are often rented out for concerts, battles of the bands, and other local events. Many of us don't even notice or think about Masonic halls, but most of us pass by them all the time in our hometowns. Where I grew up in Connecticut we drive by a Masonic hall every time we go downtown. As with many Masonic halls, this one is not used primarily for Masonic activity today, but it still bears the name and still shows the compass and the square on the facade of the building—just another reminder of how deeply seated Masonic images are in our modern world.

Cartoons and comedies have also poked fun and satirized Freemasons and other fraternal orders for years. Some of it is good fun—simply showing how pervasive and ordinary these organizations were at one point in American life. In *The Flintstones*, Fred and Barney belong to the Loyal Order of Water Buffaloes Lodge No. 26. In *The Honeymooners*, Ralph and Ed belong to the International Order of Friendly Sons of the Raccoons. Stealing an idea from *ordo ab chao*, the Raccoons had their own Latin motto: *e pluribus raccoon*. Even *The Simpsons* have included Masonic subplots, such as the episode in which Homer joins a secret fraternity called the Stonecutters, an obvious reference to the presumed stonemason origins of Freemasonry.

Throughout *The Lost Symbol* Dan Brown makes reference to the Rosicrucians and their connections over the centuries to the Freemasons. To this day, historians are unsure if the Rosicrucians ever existed or were an elaborate intellectual hoax/allegory created by the brilliant Elizabethan-era polymath Francis Bacon. But once you have read *The Lost Symbol*, you will be in a better position to understand a rather bizarre scene in *Beat the Devil*, a 1953 film directed by John Huston (an influential Oscar-winning director and father of Anjelica Huston). *Beat the Devil* stars Humphrey Bogart. In the middle of the film, a man rushes in at a critical moment and delivers a speech to Bogart's character about the Rosicrucians and the international conspiracy they are organizing, confiding: "I am in a position to know. Secret information. The Rosicrucians, the great white brotherhood, the High Secret Orders, which have no faith . . . Faith and power, secret power, men who guard the trust from the deepest insides of the whatchamacalit. Mystic rulers all one club, chained together by one purpose, one idea, mankind's champions . . ."

Many of us, especially my generation, will be learning about Freemasons for the first time in the course of reading *The Lost Symbol*. Yet the fact is that most of us have seen or heard Masonic references in films, television, and books and usually don't even know it. For whatever else *The Lost Symbol* may be, it will be an eye-opener to many people about American history and about how the Masons have been involved for hundreds of years in the quest for knowledge, in preserving ancient wisdom, and in the encouragement of a more open, tolerant society. All of these themes have become part of the familiar fabric and archetypal nature of our popular culture and our world.

SEARCHING FOR MASONS IN THE CORRIDORS OF POWER*

by Eamon Javers

CHAPTER 1

The reporter walked into his office expecting a normal day at work: cup of coffee, call some sources, the usual routine.

But this wasn't going to be an ordinary day at all.

His editor had other ideas. Darker ideas.

The editor wanted an article on [Robert Langdon's] dramatic quest in and around Washington's most famous landmarks to find a secret hidden long ago by the Masons. But the editor was intrigued by a real-world question: how many present-day members of Congress are Freemasons? And is any member of Congress also a Knight Templar—a famous subgroup of Masons that traces its lineage to the medieval crusaders?

In a flash, the reporter realized he had spent years acquiring the skills needed to complete the quest to find the Freemasons on Capitol Hill—and finish it before the looming deadline.

---

* Reprinted with permission of *Politico*.

I am the only man in this cubicle who can write this story.

My God!

CHAPTER 2

The reporter turns to the same exotic and arcane research tool Langdon uses in the book: Google. There, he finds a clue.

A YouTube video shows a member of Congress accepting an award from his fellow Masons in 2008. It's Joe Wilson . . . He says he is a member of the Sinclair Lodge of West Columbia, South Carolina. "For over two hundred and fifty years, Masons have been a part of the fabric and leadership of the United States," Wilson says on the video. "The grand tradition of brotherhood is a reflection of the very framework this nation was founded upon."

No answers there, and Wilson's office declined to elaborate.

Next, the reporter dialed the number of Dick Fletcher, executive secretary of the Masonic Service Association, a sort of national clearinghouse for Masonic information. But Fletcher said Masons don't keep records of government officials who are members—and wouldn't release them if they did, for privacy reasons.

Deadline approaches. There were forces at work that no one could comprehend.

The reporter turned to an even more eminent figure, Senate historian Don Ritchie. But Ritchie said there's no list of Masons in Congress. Politicians have long been drawn to the group, he says, because of its grassroots political organizing power.

The reporter heard a chime and looked up at his computer screen in astonishment. An electronic message had appeared there, as if by magic.

These are words. And they're written in English, an ancient language I happen to speak.

It was an e-mail, from a hidden and well-placed source. And it contained a list of names of members of Congress. Hidden among them was the Knight Templar.

But which one was it?

CHAPTER 3

The reporter raced to the one place he knew he could find answers: the U.S. Capitol. Dashing into the building, he found the first of the names on his list—House Minority Whip Eric Cantor.

The Virginia Republican offered a few cryptic words as he ascended the grand House stairway just beneath an enormous painting of George Washington: "I joined the Masons about twenty years ago because my dad and uncle were members of a lodge down in Richmond," Cantor said as he climbed the stairs. "But I haven't participated in a long time. I'm just too busy."

The reporter quickly moved to a subterranean portal: the Senate subway. Soon enough, a figure emerges from the long tunnel. It's Montana Democratic senator Jon Tester. He, too, is a Mason.

"I really like the ceremony," he says. "That's what drew me to it." He says his father-in-law invited him to join the Masons in the mid-1980s. "A lot of our Founding Fathers were Masons. Maybe because they liked to be so rebellious and nonconformist."

Maybe Tester's fellow Mason Senator Chuck Grassley can offer enlightenment. The Iowa Republican says part of the appeal is the fraternity's egalitarian worldview. "There are Masons in every country, and in countries like Iran, where they are probably underground. Hitler didn't like Masons," Grassley said.

The reporter was beginning to panic. He still hadn't found the Knight Templar.

He vowed to press on.

CHAPTER 4

It was going to take an even more exalted personage to solve the mystery. The reporter dialed the phone number of Representative Howard Coble (Republican, North Carolina), a 33° Mason. "It's a real first-class organization," Coble says of Masonry. "If people conducted their lives along the way the Mason code is spelled out, there would be far fewer problems, far more solutions, and far less chaos," Coble says.

Ordo Ab Chao: Order out of chaos. He's alluding to the Masonic credo. Now we're getting somewhere.

The reporter presses for an explanation. Coble demurs. "I can't speak more openly than that," he said. "I don't want to get drummed out of the lodge."

He explains that his Masonic brothers have already been lenient with him—since he's too busy to get to meetings very often, he recently forgot the password to the lodge in North Carolina. A fellow Mason had to vouch for him.

"I'm proud to be a Mason," Coble said. "But I'm not proud of my attendance record."

CHAPTER 5

The reporter raced through the other congressional Masons on his list. Representative Denny Rehberg (Republican, Montana): recently injured in a boating accident, he doesn't respond to the reporter's summons. Representative Jeff Miller (Republican, Florida): unavailable. Senator Robert Byrd (Democrat, West Virginia): recently hospitalized.

The reporter stood in the opulently carpeted Speaker's lobby just off the House floor, peering through the glass doors into the chamber. There, he spotted the object of his pursuit.

It was so obvious. How could he not have known?

The Knight Templar was standing in the back of the House chamber, chatting amiably with his fellow Democrats.

This was it, the moment the reporter had been working for.

Representative Nick Rahall (Democrat, West Virginia) emerged, briefly, from the chamber. A genial sixty-year-old with bushy eyebrows, the diminutive Rahall didn't look anything like a medieval crusader. In fact, his family roots are in Lebanon, not Europe.

But Rahall is also a 33° Mason, who joined the secretive society about five years before he ran for Congress in 1976. "When I joined, there were a great deal of older individuals who helped me along the way and to whom I am deeply indebted to this day," he said.

Rahall said he achieved his thirty-third-degree status by two routes: through the Scottish Rite and through the York Rite, where he participated in the Commandery. That's the portion of the Freemason tradition that makes Rahall a Knight Templar.

And although he hadn't read the Dan Brown book, Rahall says he understands why the Masons attract so many conspiracy theories. "It's because, particularly in the early days, there were code words to get into the lodge, and everything was done by rituals," Rahall said. "The Masons themselves helped perpetuate the myth, knowing it was just that—a myth."

The reporter screwed up his courage to ask one final question.

So is there a global conspiracy?

"No."

But you wouldn't tell me if there was, would you?

"That's right," Rahall said with a smile.

Chuckling, the Knight Templar traveled back though the portal to the ancient floor of the House of Representatives.

Chapter

THREE

SECRET

KNOWLEDGE

THE ANCIENT MYSTERIES AND *THE LOST SYMBOL*

by Glenn W. Erickson

Glenn Erickson, professor of philosophy at the Universidade Federal do Rio Grande do Norte, in Brazil, has written extensively on the interstices of philosophy, mathematics, and the arts. In our prior books, *Secrets of the Code* and *Secrets of Angels & Demons,* he has contributed essays that look at these novels from the viewpoint of a philosopher. Given his specialized knowledge of the history of Tarot cards, the sacred geometry of the Neopythagoreans, and the cosmology of the Neoplatonists, we asked him to examine Dan Brown's use of the "Ancient Mysteries" in *TLS.* What he found is nothing short of amazing—direct parallels to the Tarot, as well as specific numbers, names, and images from *TLS* that allude to the mystery texts of the Book of Revelation and related medieval and Renaissance works.

The legend, as Langdon recalled, never exactly explained *what* was
supposed to be inside the Masonic Pyramid—whether it was ancient
texts, occult writings, scientific revelations, or something far more
mysterious—but the legend *did* say that the precious information
was ingeniously encoded . . . (*The Lost Symbol*, chapter 30)

At the heart of *The Lost Symbol* lies one main tendency in the mystical
tradition of Christian Europe, called in the novel "the Ancient Mysteries." In general, ancient mysteries are just anything old and intriguing,
but what Dan Brown means by the phrase, "the Ancient Mysteries," is
specifically the Christian counterpart to the Jewish mystical tradition of
Kabbalah. Like Kabbalah, the Ancient Mysteries involve a complex allegorical system, an array of signs composed at once of symbolic and
conceptual elements.

In *The Lost Symbol*, the Ancient Mysteries, or at least a symbolic map
to locating their documentation, has allegedly been hidden in a Masonic
Pyramid. The villain Mal'akh forces hero Robert Langdon to discover
the Pyramid and decipher the Mysteries so that he might possess the
Lost Word and attain apotheosis. However misleading they are, none of
the explanations Robert Langdon gives of the Ancient Mysteries and the
Masonic Pyramid are clearly false, which circumstance gives the character
of the Harvard professor a greater degree of verisimilitude than in *The Da
Vinci Code* or *Angels & Demons*.

In between the lines of the text, Dan Brown shows, however, that
he understands the Ancient Mysteries much better than even his hero.
While Langdon merely uses the Ancient Mysteries to solve a series of
puzzles, Brown writes them into the fabric of his text. Brown's third mystery thriller thus becomes the most cryptographic of all, because it is also
a mystery revelation. In order to better appreciate revelation according to
Dan Brown, I propose to share something of my own comprehension of
the Ancient Mysteries.

ORIGIN OF THE MYSTERIES

The Ancient Mysteries come down to modern times from four main sources. *First,* there is the Book of Revelation, or Apocalypse, the final book of the New Testament, written, it is generally believed, in the mid-second century of the Common Era. The fact that the Ancient Mysteries are available, though in disguised form, within the Book of Revelation, makes it one of the chief texts in the canon of Western literature. *Second,* there is an important commentary on the Book of Revelation by Joachim of Flora in the late twelfth century, which became the lodestar of Franciscan theology. *Third,* there are the original decks of Tarot cards developed by unknown artists in northern Italy during the early to middle fifteenth century. *Fourth,* there is the great Spanish novel *La Celestina,* written by Fernando de Rojas in the very late fifteenth century and to which Shakespeare's *Antony and Cleopatra* is evidently indebted. All four of these are Christian documents and display a fundamental command of the Ancient Mysteries.

The Ancient Mysteries have older antecedents. They were probably developed over the quarter millennium prior to the writing of the Book of Revelation in what is known as Alexandrian culture. This pre-Christian culture takes its name from the city of Alexandria, in Egypt, which, once founded by Alexander the Great, quickly grew to be the largest, wealthiest, and most cosmopolitan of all the Greek-speaking cities.

Among several intellectual tendencies, which are both characteristic of Alexandrian culture and present in the Book of Revelation, are these:

- the philological tradition of the library of Alexandria, represented (to us) by figures such as the poet Callimachus;
- Neoplatonic philosophy, represented by the *Enneads* of Plotinus;
- Neopythagorean mathematics as found in textbooks by Nichomachus of Gerasa and Theon of Smyrna;
- the allegorical biblical exegesis of Philo the Jew; and
- the kinds of astronomy and astrology represented, respectively, by Claudius Ptolemy and Macrobius.

NATURE OF THE MYSTERIES

Ancient Mysteries are *complex* signs in the sense that they have multiple conceptual and symbolic aspects. They are wholes that may involve a number of components, such as:

- a geometrical figure,
- a number (for their place in the series of Ancient Mysteries),
- a graphic image (based on the geometrical figure),
- a name (for the graphic image),
- an emblematic device (based on the graphic image),
- a name (for the emblem),
- a pictorial composition (utilizing the emblem or other reference), as in Tarot,
- a name (for the pictorial composition), and
- a literary passage (based on one or more of the above), something found in the twentieth century in T. S. Eliot, Italo Calvino, Sylvia Plath, and Mario Vargas Llosa, among others.

Any of these components might be used to make reference to an Ancient Mystery.

The Ancient Mysteries are defined in terms of the systematic relationships they have with one another. These systematic contexts, which may vary over time and with purpose, determine symbolic interpretations. Among the purposes to which the Ancient Mysteries have been put are saving souls, predicting the future, making magic, codifying messages, and telling stories.

The Ancient Mysteries have been seen as Forms (Platonism), Emanations (Neoplatonism), and the Language of Angels (Gnosticism). They also have multiple meanings and roles in Tarot: Ancient Keys, Major Arcana, Triumphs or Trumps, and Tarot cards more generally.

In *TLS*, note the abundance of keys (and doors) in the stretch of text between "Keys will be arriving any moment" (chapter 32) and "I now have my own set of keys" (chapter 37). Cards appear in various places, for example, "Mal'akh had played his cards artfully" (chapter 12) and "Katherine realized she had one final card to play" (chapter 47).

Geometrical Figures

The doctrine of the Ancient Mysteries begins with the idea that Divinity would manifest itself in the physical universe as the most beautiful of forms. This "Paragon of Beauty" turns out to be the simplest right-angle triangle and its height, where the ratios of its sides and height are expressible in whole number ratio. The hypotenuse of the triangle in question is twenty-five; the other two sides, fifteen and twenty. Its height of twelve, which splits the hypotenuse into segments of nine and sixteen, divides the triangle into two similar triangles.

The geometrical figures associated with the other twenty members in the series of Ancient Mysteries are produced by multiplying this figure by the counting numbers from two through twenty-one. Stated differently, each figure is bigger than the last one by the size of the first.

Matter

A Geometrical Figure as a whole is called "Trinity" because it is the union of three component triangles. The smallest component triangle is "Mother," the middle one is "Father," and the largest, which is formed when Father and Mother join, is the "Son."

The height of a Geometrical Figure, plus its hypotenuse, let us call "Matter"; the sum of the other two sides (or legs) "Spirit." The aspect that is most often named to refer to the Ancient Mysteries is Matter.

In the First Ancient Mystery, Matter is the hypotenuse of 25 plus the height of 12, making 37. One of the names by which Mal'akh goes by in the novel is Inmate 37 (chapter 57). Meanwhile, in chapter 15, it is said that "thirty-seven Random Event Generators" become less random.

The Third Ancient Mystery has its Matter as 3 times 37, making III, and comes into the Tarot as "III The Emperor." The sequence of letters "Washington" appears exactly III times in *The Lost Symbol*. This is ironic insofar as George Washington refused to be king, much less emperor. But *TLS* is filled with references to the Hebrew names for God, including "Lord," and to the artistic and philosophical apotheosis of Washington, so there are many connections to be made there. In any event, the patterns are clear enough: Brown is not picking numbers out of the air. There is method to his madness here.

The Matter of the Fifteenth Ancient Mystery is 15 times 37, or 555. In *TLS*, it is stated four times that there are 555 feet in the Washington Monument (chapters 1, 20, 128, 129). Fittingly, in one main version of Tarot, the Fifteenth Ancient key is named "The Tower."

The eighteenth of the Ancient Mysteries has a Spirit of 630 and a Matter of 666, which successive triangular numbers add up the square of 36, or 1,296, the Trinity of this Ancient Mystery. The Graphic Image produced by these polygons is the most magnificent of them all, producing the Eighteenth Ancient Key in Tarot, "The Sun." Revelation 13:18 names this Ancient Mystery through the number 666, calling it "the Number of the Beast," and using it to represent the planet Saturn.

Graphic Images

Graphic Images are made from seven polygons, which are made by arranging stones and which are called the "Seven Stars." The simplest of these is the equilateral triangle, and the other polygons are constructed from this triangle. The other Stars are the cube, the hexagon, the four-point star, the six-point star ("Seal of Solomon," "Star of David"), the eight-point star ("Nativity Star"), and the twelve-point star.

Each of the Seven Stars comes in different sizes, and they are used to represent the values of selected aspects of the Geometrical Figures. Two polygons are selected when available. The larger is the basic figure of the graphic image, and is constructed of white stones. The smaller polygon (or at least a design with the same numerical value) is placed inside the larger by substituting the white stones with black ones.

More than one graphic image may be produced from the same Geometrical Figure. The First Ancient Mystery has two Graphic Images, traditionally called the "Eyes of God." The Left Eye of God corresponds to the emblematic device called the Square and Compass, which is the symbol of Masonry. The Right Eye of God is the Graphic Image behind the emblems utilized in the Pictorial Composition of the First Ancient Key in Tarot, named The Bagatelle or The Magician. This Right Eye also produces the literary vignette in Revelation in which the Son of Man appears before John with seven stars in his right hand. One of these eyes appears on top of the unfinished pyramid on the one-dollar bill (chapter 75).

Serial Numbers

The number of an Ancient Mystery (or of an Ancient Key of Tarot) is the place of its Geometrical Figure in the series from one through twenty-one.

The room in the subbasement of the Capitol Building to which the clues send the seekers is "SBB13," the thirteenth office, as in "XIII Death" in Tarot, because the story being told is that of a descent to Hell (as in "Homer's *Odyssey*," mentioned in chapter 57). When Langdon asks whose office it is, the answer is "Nobody's" (chapter 28), just as the Graphic Image of the Ancient Mystery is empty because none of the aspects of its Geometrical Figure correspond to any of the Seven Stars.

Note as well another key reference here: "the coyly nicknamed explosive Key4" (chapter 58).

An Allegorical Veil

Once again, the pictorial artist enjoys a certain degree of latitude in the constructing of Graphic Images; the Book of Revelation, Tarot, and Rojas offer alternatives. In Revelation, the Twelfth Graphic Image suggests the emblem of the Bottomless Pit (in *TLS*, Brown plays with a variety of references to pits, especially a Vestal fire in the basement of the Capitol). But in Tarot tradition, a different treatment of the smaller polygon yields the Purse and Noose, which are, respectively, the evangelical and the martyrological emblems of Judas Iscariot, emblems not available to the author of Revelation.

In Tarot, these emblems are always employed within a more inclusive Pictorial Composition. In the Twelfth Ancient Key of Tarot, the Purse and Noose emblem appears as a man holding a purse of silver coins and hanging from a noose by a foot. To be hung upside down, called "baffling," was a torture for traitors such as Judas. Intriguingly, Officer Alfonso Nuñez is said to be "baffled" by Warren Bellamy (chapter 42). (Incidentally, Dan Brown reports hanging upside down with gravity boots whenever he has writer's block or needs to work out a plot point.)

The Matter of the Twelfth Ancient Mystery is 444. In the Twelfth of the Major Arcana of Tarot, "The Hanged Man," the man crosses his legs in a figure 4.

Dan Brown may allude to XII The Hanged Man when Mal'akh wears a noose in the Masonic initiation in the prologue. What is more, since the Twelfth Ancient Mystery is cosmologically the Moon (see next section), it makes sense for Mal'akh to be called a "lunatic" various times.

Brown has Mal'akh assume the pseudonym Abaddon, which is the Hebrew name for the Angel of the Bottomless Pit in the Book of Revelation. Mal'akh/Abaddon then places Robert Langdon in an "endless abyss" (chapter 108); Brown may well be alluding to the Bottomless Pit symbol from Revelation.

Cosmic Psaltery

The Ancient Mysteries have been arranged in different geometrical models to express the spatial and temporal dimensions of the universe. Joachim of Flora, for example, places the Ancient Mysteries in a diagram called the Cosmic Psaltery. Each of ten cosmic spheres (in some of which planets orbit) is expressed by two Ancient Mysteries, but the Eleventh Ancient Mystery represents the Earth as Center of the Cosmos. Thus the sphere of the Moon is represented by the Tenth and Twelfth Ancient Mysteries, that of Mercury by the ninth and the thirteenth, and so forth. Between each pair of Mysteries is stretched a chord of the psaltery, on which God the Father, Christ, or David plays the Music of the Spheres. This diagram was frequently reproduced in medieval manuscripts.

Dan Brown seems to grasp this scheme in *The Lost Symbol.* In the Tarot, "XI The Old Man" (or "The Hunchback") is followed by "XII The Hanged Man." And Dean Galloway's surname might be understood as on the way to the gallows, as it were, of the hanged man. He is described as "stooped" (chapter 82) like a hunchback, and called an "old man."

At one point Dean Galloway asks, "How many do you need to detain an old man?" (chapter 92). Whereupon Inoue Sato replies, "seven of us [. . .] including Robert Langdon, Katherine Solomon, and your Masonic brother Warren Bellamy." There are seven because there are seven planets that circle the Eleventh Ancient Mystery, interpreted cosmologically as the Earth, and perhaps because several characters in the novel, including those named, are symbolically associated with the planets. Finally, Galloway responds, "Thank heavens."

THE GAME IS AFOOT!

The Lost Symbol calls for the mystically inclined reader to participate in a treasure hunt for the Ancient Mysteries. If Brown has really developed his characters in terms of Tarot trumps, we should be able to guess who's who. Here are some guesses about fifteen trumps, listed according to the names and numbers given in a late-fifteenth-century sermon.

0 Fool	Zachary Solomon and all his other identities: Inmate 37, Andros Dareios, Mal'akh, Dr. Christopher Abaddon, Anthony Jelbart	
1 Bagatelle	Robert Langdon, Harvard symbologist	
2 Empress	Inoue Sato, director, CIA Office of Security	
3 Emperor	Trent Anderson, Capitol police chief	
4 Popess	Katherine Solomon, Noetic scientist	
5 Pope	Peter Solomon, Supreme Worshipful Master	
6 Temperance	Nola Kaye, CIA senior analyst	
7 Love	Trish Dunne and Mark Zoubianis, hackers	
8 Car	Omar Amirana, cabbie	

 9 Force   Hercules, mastiff

10 Wheel   Turner Simkins, CIA field operations leader

11 Hunchback   Colin Galloway, dean of Washington's National
Cathedral

12 Hanged Man   Alfonso Nuñez, Capitol security guard

13 Death   Rick Parrish, CIA security analyst

14 Devil   Warren Bellamy, Architect of the Capitol

15 Arrow   Washington Monument

THE MASONIC PYRAMID AND *THE LOST SYMBOL*

Given Dan Brown's fascination with magic squares, it might turn out that his take on the Masonic Pyramid is for it to be a stack of increasingly large magic squares or their simulacra, such as Dürer's four-by-four square and Franklin's eight-by-eight square. It bears noting that the sequences of letters "Franklin Square" appears 55 times in the novel, and that 55 is the sum of the numbers on any side of any such pyramid with Dürer's magic square at its base. What is more, the "magic constant" (the sum repeated in the rows, columns, and diagonals) in a normal six-by-six magic square is III, the same number of times the sequence "Washington" appears in the novel, and the sum of the numbers in such a square is 666. Perhaps these things are not coincidences, but clues to a Masonic Pyramid embedded in the novel.

The Masonic Pyramid might also be a stack of what we are calling the Geometrical Figures of the Ancient Mysteries. This pyramid is four-sided, not five-sided like those built in ancient Egypt, as well as lopsided, because none of the sides is equal. The Mason is supposed to climb the steps of the pyramid, as well as he might, toward enlightenment and apotheosis.

In Neopythagorean mathematics, any series like the Geometrical Figures of the Ancient Mysteries is thought to derive from a collapsed figure consisting of a single point. This simple unit expresses, through geometric allegory, the (divine or Platonic) One from which the emanations flow in Neoplatonism.

Thus there is one more Ancient Mystery than the Twenty-One. Its Geometrical Figure is a single white stone. In Tarot, the One appears as the (zero or unnumbered) card called The Fool, and later as the Joker of the deck of regular playing cards. If the Lost Symbol of the novel's title is this One, Dan Brown has found both the most succinct and most sublime of all MacGuffins for his thriller!

An elaboration of this last figure would be the circumpunct, which places the single white stone inside a circle that represents, say, the Emanation of the Logos from the One. This figure, according to *The Lost Symbol,* is the false solution to the question of the Lost Symbol, the one accepted by foolish Zachary Solomon. The true solution understands *word* for *symbol,* and for *word* the Word of God, the item "lost" being the Masonic Bible buried in the cornerstone of the Washington Monument. This monumental obelisk—being a rather tall, thin pyramid—is then the materialization of the Masonic Pyramid itself, surrounded by decorative circles that suggest the combination of the monument in the circle as the circumpunct. Yet with all this of true and false, we might profitably recall that God's Word *is* the Logos, and that none do aspire higher than *to be* the Fool of God.

A Quick Guide to
the Philosophers in
The Lost Symbol

by Glenn W. Erickson

In *The Lost Symbol* Dan Brown employs the notion of "philosopher" in a very broad, even popular, sense of someone who has an "intellectual or spiritual outlook" in his writings and pronouncements. Brown's emphasis is on ancient, early, mystical, Hermetic, Masonic, Rosicrucian, Eastern, and "unified human" philosophies. Several of his characters reflect different attitudes and roles in this discussion: hierophant Peter Solomon is credulous; sorceress Katherine Solomon is esoteric; theurgist Mal'akh is manic; exegete Dean Galloway is rationalist; psychopomp Warren Bellamy is cryptic; hermeneutist Robert Langdon is skeptical; and witch hunter Inoue Sato pragmatic. The lyrical voice of Dan Brown is syncretistic, nonliteralist, transformative, fuzzy, hyper—in short, twenty-first-century, all too twenty-first-century. Here are quick sketches of some of the philosophers mentioned in and relevant to *The Lost Symbol*.

Pythagoras (sixth century B.C.), Greek philosopher famous for the Pythagorean theorem, one of the first concepts every schoolchild learns in geometry. He taught that reality is fundamentally mathematical and founded a movement that involved attributing sacred properties to various aspects of geometry. At once a philosophical school, religious brotherhood, and political faction, Pythagoreanism was an ancient precursor to the Rosicrucian and Masonic Orders. Though Pythagoras left no written record of his work, his "writings" are mentioned in *TLS* (chapter I29). He is credited with the saying "Know thyself" (chapter I02); his followers, the Pythagoreans, for an emphasis on the number 33 (chapter 89), which becomes important in Freemasonry, as well as for ascribing special significance to the geometric symbol, the circumpunct (chapter 84).

Heraclitus the Obscure (ca 540–ca 480 B.C.), Greek philosopher who taught that everything is in a state of flux ("One cannot step into the same river twice") and that the unity of things lies in the balance between opposites. These are presumably some of "the mystical secrets of alchemy . . . encoded into [his] writings" (chapter I29). Known as the "weeping philosopher," his melancholy might be the prototype for Dürer's engraving *Melencolia I* that figures so prominently in *TLS*.

Socrates (469–399 B.C.), Greek philosopher who suffered martyrdom for his principles. He is known for Socratic optimism, the Socratic method, Socratic irony, and the universal definition. He is the principle character in his pupil Plato's Dialogues. In *TLS* we learn that Robert Langdon chose not to join the Masons for the same reason that Socrates did not participate in the Eleusinian mysteries, because it would prevent him from discussing certain matters openly with his students (chapter 24).

Plato (427–347 B.C.), Greek philosopher and central figure in Western literary and intellectual traditions who is remembered especially for Platonic love, Platonic forms, the myth of Atlantis, and the myth of the cave. His dialogues—in particular the "trilogy": *Republic, Timaeus,* and *Critias*—gave Western mysticism much of its direction and tone. Plato is mentioned in *TLS* for his writings on the "mind of the world" and the "gathering God" (chapter I33), and his followers, the Platonists, for seeing the body as a prison from which the soul escapes (chapter I07).

Plato's concept of mind, or *nous,* is the ultimate origin of the "noetic science" practiced by Katherine Solomon.

Hermes Trismegistus ("Thrice-great Hermes"), a Neoplatonic combination of the Greek god Hermes and the Egyptian god Thoth, is the traditional source of mystical and alchemical knowledge in the Greco-Egyptian or Hermetic tradition. He is the pseudonymous author of Hermetic literature, which is a collection of religious and philosophical writings, probably composed from the first to the third centuries A.D., but formerly thought to be of much greater antiquity. His writings are mentioned (chapters 102, 129), specifically the "Hermetic philosophy" of the Kybalion (chapter 15). Hermetic adages, such as "As above, so below" (chapters 9, 21, 26, 82, 85, 96) and "Know ye not that ye are gods?" (chapters 82, 102, 131) resound throughout *TLS.*

Saint John (first century A.D.) was the supposed author of the Gospel according to John, his Epistles, and the Book of Revelation, and was also known as the "beloved disciple" of Jesus. Critical scholarship now sees various persons combined in one, the last of which—the pseudonymous author of Revelation—dating to the mid-second century. In *TLS* Dean Galloway states that "nobody knows how to read" the Revelation of Saint John (chapter 84), and the Gospel of John is twice cited (chapters 131, 133). Elements of Revelation, such as the Seven Seals, the Four Horsemen of the Apocalypse, and the Angel of the Bottomless Pit, also appear in *TLS. Revelation* and the Greek equivalent, *apocalypse,* both mean "disclosure."

Saint Augustine (354–430 A.D.), an Algerian Berber philosopher and theologian; wrote *The Confessions,* the most influential autobiography of all time, about his conversion to orthodox Christianity. One Tarot trump, "The Lovers," commemorates this conversion, depicting Augustine's mother, Saint Monica, as the matchmaker between her son and the Holy Church. Dean Galloway, speaking with respect to the arrival of "a transformative moment of enlightenment," prefers Augustine's clarity—along with Bacon's, Newton's, and Einstein's—to the obscurity of the Revelation of Saint John (Chapter 84).

Moses de Leon (ca 1250–1305), Spanish mystic, supposedly composed (or redacted) the Zohar. A collection of allegorical commentaries on the Pentateuch, this "Book of Splendors" (chapters 15, 131) is the primary document of Kabbalah (chapters 23, 84, 96, 131), Jewish mystical "tradition" entering importantly into Masonic lore.

Albrecht Dürer (1471–1528), German engraver and painter, is, according to Robert Langdon, "the ultimate Renaissance mind—artist, philosopher, alchemist, *and* a lifelong student of the Ancient Mysteries" (chapter 68). Dürer's gnomic magic square in his *Melencolia I* (1514) is one main element in decoding the Masonic Pyramid, and his name appears more than forty times in the novel (chapters 68, 70, 82, 85, 106, 129).

Paracelsus (1490–1541), Swiss physician who fused alchemy, Neoplatonism, Kabbalah, and Gnosticism. *TLS* cites him as a Rosicrucian and an alchemist (chapters 85, 129), some having speculated that he was even Christian Rosenkreuz, supposed founder of the Rosicrucian Order.

Sir Francis Bacon (1561–1626), English philosopher and statesman, traditionally shares the distinction of founding modern philosophy with Descartes. Some claim he is the actual writer of the plays of William Shakespeare. Robert Langdon remembers him as a member of the Royal Society of London (aka the Invisible College) (chapter 30), as a member of the Rosicrucian Order, and as possibly its founder, Christian Rosenkreuz (chapter 85). Dean Galloway admires the clarity of his vision of a coming age of enlightenment (chapter 84), which is expressed in his utopian novel, *New Atlantis*, housed in Washington's Folger Shakespeare Library (chapter 73). Peter Solomon fancies that he was "hired by King James to literally create the authorized King James Bible" and "became so utterly convinced that the Bible contained cryptic meaning that he wrote in his *own* codes," citing Bacon's *Wisdom of the Ancients* (chapter 131); but few scholars believe Bacon had much of a role in crafting the King James Bible.

René Descartes (1596–1650), French philosopher and mathematician, founded modern philosophy and invented analytic geometry. His famous saying is "I think, therefore I am." In *TLS*, he appears in Robert Langdon's list of sixteenth- and seventeenth-century luminaries belonging to the Mystical Order Rosae Crucis, along with Elias Ashmole, Francis Bacon, John Dee, Robert Fludd, Gottfried Wilhelm Leibniz, Isaac Newton, Blaise Pascal, and Baruch Spinoza (chapter 85). Descartes' "secret notebook," written in code, and later decoded by Leibniz, is the subject of a fascinating book by one of this book's contributors, Amir Aczel.

Robert Boyle (1627–91), both alchemist and first modern chemist, is best known for Boyle's Law. A gentleman scientist, Boyle promoted Christianity energetically both in word and deed. Robert Langdon mentions him as an early member of the Invisible College whose fellow member Newton told him to keep silence about their research (chapter 30).

Sir Isaac Newton (1642–1727), English physicist and mathematician, arguably ranks as top all-time scientist. The lion's share of his writing, however, was invested in eccentric biblical hermeneutics, esoterica, and alchemy. Twentieth-century economist John Maynard Keynes reportedly said, "Newton was not the first of the Age of Reason. He was the last of the magicians." In *TLS*, Newton's name appears as the answer to an anagram, *Jeovah Sanctus Unus* (chapter 30), which is how he sometimes signed his name; in connection with his temperature scale (chapter 89), which took the revered Masonic number, 33 degrees, as the boiling point of water; and for a surfeit of biblical interpretation (chapter 131). Newton also had a prominent role in *The Da Vinci Code*, where it was alleged that he was one of the grand masters of the "Priory of Sion." It is clear Dan Brown is fascinated with Newton's multifaceted personal history as scientist, geometer, exegete, alchemist, and mystic.

Benjamin Franklin (1706–90), American scientist and statesman, was an honorary member of the Royal Society of London (chapter 30) for his demonstration that lightning and electricity are one and the same phenomenon. He also appears in *TLS* for being one of the Masonic conceiver/designers of Washington, D.C. (chapter 6), a great inventor (chapters 21, 133), a printer (chapter 126), and an American forefather concerned about the dangers of interpreting the Bible literally (chapter 131). Yet his prominence in the novel owes itself to his hobby of designing magic squares, and particularly to a variant, mentioned in his *Autobiography*, featuring "broken diagonals."

Thomas Jefferson (1743–1826), American political philosopher and statesman, drafted the Declaration of Independence. The third American president, he was accomplished in science, architecture, education, and the humanities. Jefferson is mentioned for many relevant aspects of his life and work. *TLS* highlights what is today the little-known Jefferson Bible (chapter 131). Originally titled *The Life and Morals of Jesus of Nazareth*, this unique Bible reflected Jefferson's personal philosophy of deism. The Jefferson version of the story is the four Gospels expurgated of "superstition" and miracles; for example, he edited out the Virgin birth and the Resurrection.

Manly Palmer Hall (1901–1990), Canadian-born mystic, who lived most of his life in the United States, is best known for his *The Secret Teachings of All Ages: An Encyclopedic Outline of Masonic, Hermetic, Qabbalistic and Rosicrucian Symbolical Philosophy* (1928). Hall was a prolific writer on ancient mysteries of all types and ended up becoming a Freemason. Dan Brown has spoken about Hall's influence on his own appreciation of mystical truth, and quotes this book in the novel's opening epigraph as well as at its end. In effect, Hall gets the first and last word; Langdon sums up the whole long journey with the words of this "philosopher" (chapter 133).

Secret Knowledge

Hiding in Plain Sight in the Infinite Universe

an interview with Ingrid Rowland

Ingrid Rowland, an American academic based in Rome, is a fascinating writer and thinker on Renaissance art and philosophy. A frequent contributor to *The New York Review of Books*, she has written biographies of Giordano Bruno, the great sixteenth-century scientist/mystic/philosopher, and Athanasius Kircher, one of the most important but least known thinkers of the Baroque era. The daughter of a Nobel Prize–winning chemist, Rowland has a unique humanist perspective on science and on the experiences of the alchemists and the Greek and Renaissance philosophers that went into laying the groundwork for the scientific revolution. Dan Burstein interviewed Rowland on a day when she had just finished reading *The Lost Symbol* in preparation for a review she was writing for *The New Republic*.

Your overall reaction to The Lost Symbol?

Dan Brown never anticipated that *The Da Vinci Code* would be as successful as it was, and that people would have taken it so seriously. Now, with *The Lost Symbol*, he has truly taken stock of the power he can muster through the written word. This is a better thriller as well as a more responsible book.

The concept of the so-called Ancient Mysteries imbues TLS. *What do you think that is a reference to, or metaphor for?*

The phrase "Ancient Mysteries" refers to a long-standing European tradition that held that the Egyptians had access to extraordinary sources of wisdom and power. Both ancient Greeks, like Plato, and the Hebrew Bible refer admiringly to ancient Egyptian wisdom, as does the apostle Paul. Europeans in the Renaissance believed that the Egyptians recorded their highest truths in hieroglyphic symbols in order to ensure that such powerful knowledge could never be abused by the superstitious masses. But the idea that only an elite few understand the way the world really works is much older even than ancient Egypt; it may well be part of human nature to think so. The Mysteries to which Dan Brown refers are a body of beliefs once shared, in the same basic form, by Renaissance humanists, modern Freemasons, the Rosicrucians, and others. In his new book, however, he carefully avoids describing these beliefs in much detail—unlike *The Da Vinci Code,* which borrowed heavily, and not always successfully, from a book called *Holy Blood, Holy Grail,* which traced the story of Mary Magdalene much as we read about it in Brown's novel. In *The Lost Symbol,* however, Brown simply mentions a few enigmatic ideas and names, developing them only enough to further the plot of his story rather than trying to explain them in depth. The most important result of this careful process of self-editing is much faster, more economical storytelling, and this capacity to fine-tune his own work is the sign that Brown is a real professional in his chosen field, which is the writing of thrillers.

You've written the definitive modern biography of Giordano Bruno, the sixteenth-century mystic, protoscientist, and cosmologist. In Angels & Demons, *Brown alluded to Bruno, saying that many "scientists" were burned at the stake. Bruno seems to be one of the only examples of that—someone who might actually qualify as a scientist who was burned at the stake for his heresy. Brown again alludes to Bruno, and others before and after him, in* TLS, *as one of the early thinkers who imagined not only a solar-centered universe, but a human-centered universe as well.*

Bruno's ideas about the infinite universe—both his cosmos made up of multiple worlds, that is, multiple solar systems, and his conviction that the boundless universe is entirely built of atoms—remain truly significant steps toward our present understanding of nature. Bruno's reputation has suffered because our histories of cosmology are so focused on technology that they often begin with Galileo's discoveries with the telescope. Hence it is easy to make a case for Galileo as a recognizably modern scientist, whereas Bruno is a more elusive, and in many ways a seemingly more old-fashioned, figure. He posed thought problems that could barely be confirmed by experiment and called himself a "natural philosopher" rather than a mathematician, although he did refer to his work as a "natural and physical discourse." In fact, of course, many modern scientists still make their pioneering discoveries by first posing thought problems, much as Bruno did, long before they can prove their intuitions by experimentation.

Bruno's philosophy aimed above all to improve the position of individual human beings as citizens of an inconceivably large universe. He believed that an accurate understanding of our position within the cosmos would improve our moral behavior as well as the clarity of our thought. He wrote that we should seek God within ourselves rather than outside, for each of us has our own spark of divinity in us; it is only a question of knowing where to look for that spark.

There are other figures in the history of science, philosophy, and mystical knowledge that Brown mentions or alludes to. What are your thoughts on Paracelsus? Pythagoras? Agrippa? Dürer?

Paracelsus is still the foremost precursor, in many ways, of modern medical practice despite the radical strangeness of most of his ideas, especially his ideas about religion. Paracelsus believed that by mixing chemicals together in the right way he could compensate for imbalances in the human body. We do the same thing when we take pills for what ails us, although we don't define the imbalance in terms of the four humors, or define the chemicals, as he did, in terms of mercury, sulfur, and salt. Yet his division of matter into these three substances was of fundamental importance to the future of chemical analysis.

He was an extremely successful medical practitioner, and a rather conservative one—but he was also a showman. Many of his claims now sound bombastic, but underpinning his bombast is a clear idea that the entire world is made up of elements and that the human body needs a balance of those elements. He also firmly believed that human ingenuity could find a way to restore that balance. We bear witness to the same beliefs whenever we take a vitamin pill.

Paracelsus was also interested in alchemy, the long-held belief that matter could be transformed, under certain circumstances, from one form into another. My father, a chemist, told me recently that the alchemists misjudged the energy level required to perform their operations—it needs the same level of energy as is used for splitting the atom. But philosophically, the transformations of matter imagined by Paracelsus and other alchemists make sense.

What about Pythagoras? He's mentioned five times in TLS.

Pythagoras was already a legendary figure by the time of Plato, in the fourth century B.C.—he probably lived about two centuries earlier than Plato. We have none of his own writings, only the legends about him and his theorem about right triangles (the square of the hypotenuse equals the sum of the squares of the legs). He believed that numbers had special qualities that were significant in themselves, whereas we tend to use numbers just as tools for calculation. Algebra, calculus, and even advanced arithmetical operations were beyond his scope. But I suspect that we are less far removed from Pythagoras and his number theory than we may like to think.

Years ago, my father and I attended a conference called "Scientist to Scientist," an attempt to encourage scientists from different disciplines to converse with one another. I was put in as the humanist outlier. The particle physicists' description of their work, with its four kinds of energy pointing toward a final unity, sounded strangely like the Pythagorean search for a transcendent One. And their idea that this final revelation would be fully available only to a few physicists sounded suspiciously like the Pythagoreans' secret sect of initiates. To be sure, the particle physicists asserted that they could never make their discoveries without a huge, expensive instrument, the superconducting supercollider, whereas Pythagoras made his observations about music and its relationship to numbers on the strings of a lyre. But the legacies of Pythagoras and Plato live on in the aesthetic standards that scientists use for their proofs, which must be "robust," "elegant," and tend toward simplicity. The idea is remarkably persistent, and a number of younger scientists recognize that fact—Brian Greene's *The Elegant Universe* is a good example.

Agrippa?

Agrippa is another one of those names we always encounter in connection with "occult philosophy," whether in *The Lost Symbol* or anywhere else that treats similar subject matter—Agrippa wrote a book called *On the Occult Philosophy*. In fact, I was thinking about the concept of the "occult" this morning, and realized that an easy way to make information occult and secret in earlier ages was simply to write it down.

Wait a minute—write things down to keep them secret?

Well, until the modern era, writing things down required knowing how to read in order to have access to that knowledge—a pretty good way to keep it hidden. Ironically, then, recording something in a book made it almost by definition secret and hidden. Agrippa's book *On the Occult Philosophy* was totally incomprehensible to most of his contemporaries, who were illiterate peasants. His readers, like many people, really enjoyed that air of secrecy, and the fact that their knowledge was withheld from most people.

Dürer?

I suspect that Dan Brown would love to be an art historian but hasn't quite figured out yet how to read art. His interpretations of Leonardo's *Last Supper* in *The Da Vinci Code* weren't really very sophisticated, and earned him a good deal of criticism. In *The Lost Symbol* he mentions Dürer's amazing engraving, *Melencolia I*, but he doesn't really give it the kind of formal analysis he attempted in *The Da Vinci Code*. All Brown needs for his immediate purpose is the magic square in the engraving's background, and rather than tackle the still-unsolved problem of *Melencolia*'s symbolism and call down legions of irate scholars, he keeps his story focused on the arithmetical problem posed by the magic square.

Again, I think we see a highly self-critical writer figuring out what he can and cannot do. He wants to get an enigmatic picture in there for atmosphere, but he realizes that he doesn't have to explain the enigma, but rather evoke it. So he does what he does best, which is to weave Dürer's *Melencolia I* into his thriller plot.

You have a couple of references in your Bruno book to Dürer and potential interconnections there.

Bruno was an Italian who spent a good deal of time in Germany, and Dürer was a German who spent time in Italy. There were some fascinating interchanges back and forth across the Alps in the sixteenth century. The Germans were more interested in mathematics and the more verbal aspects of learning, and the Italians developed a marvelous visual language to express some of the same ideas. Both Dürer and Bruno created systems of astonishing complexity: mental systems, visual systems, symbolic systems. And both believed that all these systems ultimately tied together. And despite Italy's dominance over the artistic culture of early modern Europe, Dürer's skill as an engraver and woodcut artist stood, and still stands, in a class by itself.

Any other concluding thoughts with The Lost Symbol *so fresh in your mind?*

Several things struck me about the book, all of them relating to the current Zeitgeist. I can't help feeling that Brown's choice of exposure on the Internet as his villain's most dire threat must be a commentary on his own runaway success—the runaway, incontrollable aspect of it. First, he set out to write an adventure story, and ended up becoming an oracle. Out of their context the details of *The Da Vinci Code* are as silly as the sight of prominent senators performing Masonic rituals. And having propelled hordes of tourists to Paris, Rome, and Rosslyn, he has sensibly decided in a time of economic crisis to send them all to see Washington instead—good for their budgets, good for Washington's need for income.

Second, Brown basically says that the secret to all of the secret lore actually lies right under our noses, and we all know what that secret is: live a moderate life. We all know what it takes to lose weight, to listen to other people, to hold in our tempers—only it is just plain hard work to be virtuous.

Interestingly, several of the new book's characters have every reason to be deeply resentful of the United States: Sato, a Japanese-American woman born in the Manzanar internment camp, and Bellamy, an African-American who is keenly aware of a point that Langdon also makes, that slaves did the hard and ironic job of lifting the statue of Freedom to the top of the Capitol Dome. And yet, these characters are all loyal servants of the United States and dedicated to its ideals, even when reality often falls short of those ideals.

Then, as if to reinforce the message of personal responsibility, we have villainy that comes from within human nature—no Russians, Nazis, or jihadists coming from outside, but instead the forces of bad or misdirected discipline that knock us out of balance. There is a strong biblical subtext: Peter Solomon is asked to reenact Abraham's sacrifice of Isaac, but this time there's no angel to grab his arm. Instead, this tormented father feels all his terrible, vengeful thoughts, but still drives the sacrificial knife into a table rather than into his son. In the end, this humanity, the humanity to which we all really aspire, prevails. And this ability to control our basest impulses is, to me, really the essence of civilization.

The plot of *The Lost Symbol* assumes some real social responsibility: this is admirable proof that Dan Brown has thought carefully about his success and its larger implications. *The Da Vinci Code* ended by assuring us that there are descendants of a Merovingian monarchy living among us—who really cares? *The Lost Symbol* concludes with the vision of a United States that might really live up to its founding principles. That is, a vision that makes a tremendous difference in many lives all over the world. The book tells us in addition that redemption comes not as deliverance from outside, but as the hard-won result of a constant struggle between our better and our baser natures.

This is the same message conveyed by the Ancient Mysteries, and it's a hard message to hear. *The Lost Symbol* is lost by our own actions; it happens every time we lose touch with the real purposes of life.

Isaac Newton

Physics, Alchemy, and the Search to Understand the "Mind of God"

an interview with Thomas Levenson

If Dan Brown were going to invent an ideal historical icon, that creation would read an awful lot like Sir Isaac Newton. Newton is best known as the father of modern physics, but he was also an alchemist and he was obsessed with the Bible and the true meaning of Scripture. Since he didn't have to invent him, Brown makes liberal use of this very real figure. *The Lost Symbol* includes twenty-six references to Newton, and, as Langdon fans know, Newton also figured prominently in *The Da Vinci Code*, with a climactic scene of that novel set in Newton's crypt in Westminster Abbey.

Brown invokes Newton to underscore many of his points about the connection between science and spirit. But how much of what he says about Newton adheres to history and how much did he bend for the convenience of his story? To find out, we spoke with Thomas Levenson, a professor at MIT who runs MIT's graduate program in science writing. He has made several documentary films about science, and he is the author of four books, including the recent *Newton and the Counterfeiter*, which chronicles a little-known episode in Newton's life when he served as Warden of His Majesty's Mint.

One of the central themes of The Lost Symbol *is that science and mysticism were once closely intertwined, that "hard science" drove out all semblance of spirit in the laboratory, and that a new science is reuniting the physical and the spiritual worlds. Do you see a dichotomy between Newton as a scientist and Newton as an alchemist?*

There's no dichotomy between science and alchemy in the way Newton pursued it. I don't think Newton had a mystical side in the way that twenty-first-century people think of mysticism or spirituality. He was someone who, to borrow a phrase from Stephen Hawking, wanted to "know the mind of God." It wasn't at all strange then to have deeply intellectual people thinking about things that looked like magic. This kind of exploration was just another way of trying to learn about the world. Robert Boyle, who many regard as one of the founders of modern chemistry, was an avid alchemist. John Locke was a great political philosopher, a voice for religious tolerance, and a theorist about money, and he, too, was an alchemist.

Alchemy was an inquiry into how change happens in nature. Alchemists in Newton's time wanted to understand chemical transformations. This had nothing to do with magic or mysticism. It would not have been inconsistent with his role as a scientist to pursue alchemical experiments.

You mentioned Boyle. In The Lost Symbol, *Dan Brown refers to Newton's letter to Boyle asking him to maintain "high silence" about their experiments because the world would consider them dangerous and inflammatory. What was the nature of the Newton-Boyle relationship? Did Newton really ask Boyle to maintain such a silence?*

Newton did write a letter suggesting that it was not a good idea for Boyle to talk about an alchemical sequence of experiments.

There is a long-standing, alchemical tradition of secrecy and coded communication. This has a quasireligious element, along with elements of a religious closed society, which of course makes it great fodder for conspiracy theories and blockbuster fiction. Newton didn't believe that alchemists should publish scientific papers because of the potential implications of their work. Boyle wanted to publish and create an exchange of information and Newton told him in this letter that it was dangerous to reveal these secrets.

If we put these alchemical experiments in a modern context, it makes one think of enriching uranium or growing diamonds in a laboratory. The alchemists obviously lacked the tools to create fissionable reactions and so forth, but was this what they were going for?

Yes and no. We now know today that we can transmute elements in the lab and that nature transmutes elements all the time. Stars start from hydrogen and helium and make the rest of the periodic table as they "burn"—through the process of nuclear fusion. When radioactive elements decay, they decay into other elements. We can make plutonium, which does not exist naturally. We can make Neptunium. We can make more than twenty elements above the naturally occurring ones. I think alchemists of Newton's day, and perhaps Newton himself, would have seen the line of descent that lies between what they were doing and this work. But I think Newton would have been concerned with the radical erosion of the idea that one might detect the presence of God in such transformative events.

In The Lost Symbol, *Dan Brown refers to "secret papers" discovered in 1936. Did such papers exist?*

They existed, but they weren't secret. Newton's papers were scattered somewhat after his death. In fact, individual letters are still turning up. But the bulk of his papers went to the Earl of Portsmouth. The papers that were sold at Sotheby's in 1936 were alchemical papers that had been held by the Earls of Portsmouth for a long time. Earlier, they had attempted to donate a number of papers to Cambridge University Library, but the university turned down the alchemical papers, deeming them to be of no scientific interest.

Could Newton have also been a Freemason? Dan Brown seems to think so, even though by all accounts Freemasonry didn't have any real organized presence until very close to the end of Newton's life.

I think this makes for great fiction. People have had fun with the notion of secret societies for a long time. The associations that novelists ascribe to Newton and other brilliant figures are either not in the right time frame historically or are so elusive that it's difficult to give them any credence. I suppose there is a chance that Newton was a Freemason, but I strongly doubt it. For one reason, there isn't any institutional record of Masonic lodges in England until Newton was in his late seventies. And for another reason, Newton kept a lot of records—private papers on all kinds of things that he kept out of the public eye, such as stuff about his religious and alchemical beliefs—but I've never seen any papers in Newton's hand mentioning any connection to Freemasonry. Newton's major association and involvement was with the Royal Society, which he presided over for the last quarter of his life. That role of his is extremely well known and well documented.

Brown refers to a 1704 Newton manuscript seeking to extract scientific information from the Bible. Brown claims that, over his lifetime, Newton wrote more than a million words about Scripture.

I haven't actually totaled up the amount Newton wrote on religion, but it would add up to many thousands of words. Newton's interest in this subject was enormous. He wrote a huge amount about religion—and he rewrote and rewrote. However, I don't think he was attempting to extract scientific truth from Scripture. I think he was attempting to use his kind of scientific reasoning to recover Scripture from its decayed state. He felt that there had been decisions made in some of the early church councils that undermined a true religion and he sought to fix this.

What he did say in print in the early eighteenth century was that the universe is "the sensorium of God"—and that God extends throughout creation, all powerful and fully aware of all that exists within His creation. That is Newton's science informing his religion and his interpretation of Scripture, not the other way around.

Chapter
FOUR

SCIENCE, FAITH, AND THE BIRTH OF A NATION

From the Ground Up

Kindred Spirits Invent the Modern World

an interview with Steven Johnson

The eighteenth century was an extraordinary age of great ideas and groundbreaking innovations. The great minds of this European Enlightenment—Voltaire, Priestley, Banks, Herschel, and many more—were exploring all areas of human knowledge at once: philosophy, political theory, chemistry, astronomy, physics, mathematics, medicine, and more. Radical new ideas emerged from a number of loosely organized social networks of alchemists, proto-scientists, and scientists, meeting in coffeehouses, taverns, and even Masonic lodges—anywhere they could escape the suspicious eyes of Church and State. Sometimes facing marginalization and persecution by this "old order," a number of leading intellectuals increasingly saw America as the future, a land where freedom of speech and expression were taking hold. Although Europe continued to see itself as the center of the Enlightenment, some visionary thinkers already understood that the energy for innovation was shifting to the New World. This history fuels Dan Brown's view of the Founding Fathers' self-knowledge about the intellectual revolution they were making. In their integration of politics, science, cosmology, and new approaches to religion and faith, and in the way they remained fascinated and informed by "ancient knowledge," the thinkers of the time become the perfect reference point for several of Robert Langdon's soliloquies.

Contemporary author and polymath Steven Johnson calls this late-eighteenth-century moment the era of "intellectual plate tectonics." The title of his most recent book captures it perfectly: *The Invention of Air: A Story of Science, Faith, Revolution, and the Birth of America.* In it, Johnson explores the way new ideas emerged and spread, and the environment that fostered their breakthroughs. Johnson is also known for his writing about a wide variety of intriguing twenty-first-century topics. His previous book is *Everything Bad Is Good for You: How Today's Popular Culture Is Actually Making Us Smarter.*

In this dialogue with Arne de Keijzer, Johnson shares his perspectives on Enlightenment ideas and their influence on the founding of America through the person of Joseph Priestley. Priestley was one of the most celebrated men of the era as a scientist (a leader in the discovery of oxygen), a religious figure (a minister who broke from the church of England to help found Unitarianism), and a political activist (he supported the French revolution). Priestley makes only a cameo appearance in *The Lost Symbol*, but, as Johnson makes clear, Priestley represents the ideal intellectual synthesis that is always in the background of Dan Brown's novel.

While Dan Brown doesn't really delve into it in the way he did the era of Galileo in Angels & Demons *and early Christianity in* The Da Vinci Code, *the Enlightenment is surely the stage for the ideas behind* The Lost Symbol. *What was it about the eighteenth century that made it so important and such a turning point in history?*

The scientific, social, and political principles of the modern world were, in many ways, invented in the eighteenth century: the experimental method, the U.S. Constitution, the first great wave of the industrial revolution in northern England. Along with those extraordinary developments there arose another critical way of thinking about the world: the idea that society was advancing up a steady and predictable ladder of progress. The Renaissance had unleashed its own revolutions in human understanding, but the governing idea during that period was cyclical: historical periods of clarity were quickly followed by periods of darkness. It wasn't until the eighteenth century that we started to assume that science and technology were going to continue to advance, perhaps at accelerating rates. This idea is one of Priestley's great legacies; it's a dominant theme in his first big book on the history of electricity, and it was one of the things that I think appealed to Franklin and Jefferson about him.

It strikes me that the great minds of the era flourished in part because of the free and open flow of their ideas, across all kinds of topics. And they did this in coffeehouses?

Priestley met Franklin in the London Coffeehouse, which is not a minor detail in the story because coffeehouses were the intellectual hub of eighteenth-century London. Franklin had a group of like-minded souls, called the Club of Honest Whigs, who gathered at the coffeehouse every two weeks and spent hours there abusing caffeine, nicotine, and alcohol, and eating immense quantities of food, all the while debating religious dissent, the new science of electricity, the American question, industrial engineering, and a thousand other topics. It was the cross-disciplinary nature of the coffeehouse space that made it such an engine of innovation during that period.

You clearly see Priestley as a man with a cornucopia of ideas.

Priestley was one of the great polymaths of the period. He did cutting-edge work in linguistics and physics (mostly focused on electricity). Along with Lavoisier, he helped usher in the age of modern chemistry and isolated oxygen for the first time. He discovered one of the founding principles of modern ecosystem science: plant respiration, the fact that the earth's "breathable" atmosphere is entirely created by plant life. He cofounded the Unitarian Church in England, and wrote some of the most controversial religious books of the age. And he had a hand in the American Revolution as well, both as one of the most ardent English supporters of the American cause during the war, and as a major figure in the Alien and Sedition [Acts] controversy after his move to America. It's almost impossible to imagine a comparable figure today: imagine if Al Gore were not only a former vice president, but also a pioneering climatologist who had helped found a new religious sect. Of course, Priestley's talents as a polymath were matched by Franklin and Jefferson, but that's one reason both men found Priestley such a kindred spirit.

Why was Priestley so intellectually drawn to the Founding Fathers?

The key thing to understand about Priestley and the American Founders—particularly Franklin and Jefferson—is that their intellectual worldview was profoundly connective in nature. They were constantly trying to detect or create links between different fields: they saw religion and science and political theory as a unified web, not a series of different disciplines with impenetrable walls between them. In a sense, academic disciplines hadn't been fully codified yet, and so it was much easier to be a generalist back then, to dabble in a dozen different fields and make interesting links of association between them.

Why did Priestley escape England and move to the United States?

Priestley's political and religious positions radicalized over the 1780s, and thanks to a number of controversial essays and sermons, he had become arguably the most hated man in England by the end of the decade. (His early support for the Americans didn't help, of course.) In 1791, an angry mob burned down his house during the notorious Birmingham riots, which ultimately sent him packing to the young United States, where he was greeted as a hero. In moving to the United States, Priestley inaugurated one of the great traditions of this country: he was our first great scientist exile, seeking out the intellectual freedom of this new country. Unfortunately, that freedom turned out to be somewhat overrated, at least in the short term. He had a falling out with his old friend John Adams during Adams's presidency and wrote several essays critical of the administration (and siding with Jefferson). Adams nearly had him deported during the Alien and Sedition [Acts] crisis. But when Jefferson was elected president, one of his first acts was to write a wonderful letter to Priestley that really captures how the Founders felt about him: "Science and honesty are replaced on their high ground, and you, my dear Sir, as their great apostle, are on its pinnacle. It is with heartfelt satisfaction that in the first moments of my public action, I can hail you with welcome to our land, tender to you the homage of its respect and esteem, cover you under the protection of those laws which were made for the wise and good like you."

Priestley's religious views also had an impact on the Founders, particularly Jefferson. Moreover, Priestley's ideas about the bond between science and religion would also fit in well with Robert Langdon's.

Priestley's story is a reminder of how iconoclastic the founders were in their social and religious values. Priestley had the single biggest impact on Jefferson's view of religion; in fact, Jefferson directly credited Priestley with keeping him, at least nominally, a Christian. Jefferson's debt to Priestley stems in large part from the fusion of science and religion that Priestley had concocted in his very unorthodox vision of what it meant to be a Christian. He believed in the message and morals of Jesus Christ, but he felt that this original story had been distorted by centuries of priests and religious scholars who had felt the need to add layers of superstition and magic to the story to make it more captivating to the masses. This meant that Jefferson and Priestley believed in the words of Jesus, but they did not believe, for instance, that Jesus was the son of God, or that he came back from the dead. When Jefferson read Priestley's writing, he was inspired to create the famous Jefferson Bible, which edits out all the supernatural elements and leaves only the core words of Christ himself. And of course, where religion was concerned, Franklin was even more of a nonbeliever. (Priestley remarked in his autobiography that he always wished he'd been able to convert Franklin to his maverick version of Christianity, but Franklin apparently never had time to read all the religious tracts that Priestley would send him.)

Today we talk about the pros and cons of the cult of the amateur . . . but weren't people like Priestley basically amateur scientists, amateur political thinkers, amateur theologians—and weren't they able to have an enormous impact?

The Enlightenment was really created from the ground up by amateurs. In part this was because the whole concept of a professional scientist hadn't quite yet been invented. And in part it was because most fields were so nascent that you could do pioneering work without going to grad school for six years. So many discoveries were right there at the surface, waiting to have the scientific method applied to them.

From your work on technology and pop culture, can you help us compare what life was like in the late eighteenth century, with all these amazing industrial and scientific breakthroughs, inventions, and new cultural trends unfolding, with our own times? Are there similarities? You also have a great interest in the confluence of technology, society, and culture in the present, as evident by your recent book, Everything Bad Is Good for You. *Do you see any parallels between the remarkably inventive world of the late-eighteenth century with the present day?*

I think there are some exciting commonalities between today and Priestley's time. The digital revolution has created a comparable sense of open exploration: a sense that the world is most certainly on the edge of radical change, and that science and technology are driving that change. And of course, we have our own culture of amateur engagement now, thanks to the blogosphere and other forms of democratic media. (Priestley would have loved Wikipedia, for instance.) But where I think we can learn from Priestley and the American Founders is in the space between science and religion. For the Founders, as intellectuals, one of their primary goals was to forge connections between those two worlds, to figure out a way to make their religious values compatible with the new insights of science. That pushed them into some unusual religious views (even by today's standards), but there was great integrity to that struggle. Today, I fear, too many people of faith have decided that their religious beliefs and the world of science cannot be usefully connected. On this front, at least, it's time we got back to our roots.

FRANKLIN, FREEMASONRY, AND AMERICAN DESTINY

an interview with Jack Fruchtman Jr.

Yes, Benjamin Franklin was a Freemason. He was also the publisher in 1730 of a set of Masonic rituals, a member of a Masonic lodge in Philadelphia as well as in London and Paris, and, of course, one of the most important Masons in the fraternity of founding brothers. These facts might easily lead to the assumption that Masonic beliefs had a major impact on our system of government—for better (as many Masons would have it) or worse (as conspiracy theorists claim).

But just how important was Freemasonry and its beliefs to Franklin? To find out we turned to Jack Fruchtman Jr., one of America's leading authorities on Franklin and the intellectual influences that shaped his broad-ranging thinking on politics, philosophy, religion, and science. Fruchtman, interviewed here by Arne de Keijzer, teaches at Towson University and is the author of *Atlantic Cousins: Benjamin Franklin and His Visionary Friends*.

Dan Brown places Franklin hip-deep into the stream of Freemasonry, implying that it had a profound impact on his political, philosophical, and religious beliefs, which in turn influenced the foundations of our country. Is Brown right?

Franklin was indeed a Mason, a member of the Philadelphia Masonic Lodge (St. John's) as well as the legendary Paris Loge des Neuf Soeurs (Lodge of Nine Sisters). But Freemasonry was no more important to Franklin than any other civic or social association, many of which he himself created: for example, his club of fellow leather-apron men (the Junto), the Philadelphia Militia and Fire Company, the Library Company of America, and so on. Freemasonry fits into the many religious, scientific, and pseudoscientific phenomena that permeated the eighteenth century, and Franklin was clearly part of this development, especially when it had to do with powerful, mystical, and unknown forces like gases and air, electricity, ballooning (with its seeming ability to defy gravity), and vegetative and animal "magnetism" (which today we might well call hypnotism). Franklin viewed Freemasonry positively for its spirit and basic nontraditional views of religion. But he also saw it as a means for him to succeed as a socially mobile, middle-class tradesman. It is accurate to conclude that he used Freemasonry as one of his many stepping stones for self-improvement and upward mobility.

Still, Franklin counted the leading scientists and intellectuals of the day among his friends, sometimes having long, "secret" discussions with them in Masonic lodges in Paris. Many of these men were fascinated by the same search to understand and unlock the Ancient Mysteries that pervade The Lost Symbol. *Many of Franklin's contemporaries and peers saw in Freemasonry a path to blend their interest in ancient knowledge with their political, scientific, and spiritual quests. Wouldn't all this have influenced his perspective?*

Among Franklin's leading personal characteristics was his vast curiosity. He was interested in just about anything and everything that he came across, from the effects of oil on water to the underlying meaning of the game of chess. We see this in all of his scientific experiments, but also in his interest in the occult and the Ancient Mysteries. His friends in France were keenly aware of the ramifications of those subjects as well, which is why Franklin was drawn to people like Jérôme Lalande and La Rochefoucauld d'Enville, among others. The conventional and historic Masonic organization is the lodge, which refers not so much to the physical structure, but to the association of similarly minded, focused members. A lodge is like a chapter or a branch, and the lodges he joined in Philadelphia and Paris were among the most prestigious. Lalande was a well-known astronomer, and La Rochefoucauld was one of the first members of the French aristocracy to join the Third Estate during the Revolution. However, I do not think Franklin had a special interest in the occult and other mysteries other than what drew his attention to them in the first place, namely his unquenchable curiosity in trying to understand the natural world.

While imagining himself about to drown in the confines of a water tank, Langdon hears a chant tumbling through the void "like the drone of voices in a medieval canticle: Apocalypsis . . . Franklin . . . Apocalypsis . . . Verbum . . . Apocalypsis." Can you imagine why Brown might have invoked Franklin in this scene?

I think Dan Brown was attempting to link Franklin and perhaps the founding of the American nation to Freemasonry and its rites, which is a link that need not be overstated. Franklin never envisioned his apotheosis along the lines Brown describes when he writes about George Washington as depicted on the ceiling in the Capitol Rotunda. Franklin believed in an afterlife, but it was a belief that had more in common with the views of Thomas Jefferson and Thomas Paine. Franklin was a deist, not a Christian. He did not have orthodox views about a personal God or of human salvation. Langdon, at this point in the novel, knew that the key to his search lay in Franklin's magic squares. It is thus unsurprising that he would conjure up Franklin in his reverie. I believe Brown was doing his utmost to persuade his readers to accept the idea that Franklin was far more involved than he actually was in the rites and rituals of Freemasonry. Brown has given Franklin's Freemasonry far too broad a reading, much like his overstatement that the CIA might be engaged in a large-scale investigation, complete with military components, on U.S. soil.

Mention Franklin and most of us immediately think of bits of history we know—Poor Richard's Almanack, a sometime scientist who flew a kite in a thunderstorm, an envoy to France, and, of course, a Founding Father. But we don't often think of him within the context of the history of ideas. Can you place him there for our readers?

Franklin stands at the front and center of the American Enlightenment with his openness about the idea of republican government as the guarantor of free speech, freedom of religion, and especially freedom of inquiry. This last item is key to all of his thinking and his writings: his scientific experiments and diplomatic experiences afforded him ways to investigate the nature of the universe and the nature of human beings in differing geographical and social contexts. Franklin believed that if people do not have the right to investigate just about every political, social, and scientific problem, there can never be a free society and the alternative will be a government that shutters the mind from all that is worth exploring.

Active in America, England, and France, Franklin was a world-renowned natural philosopher (or scientist, as we would call him today) and a world-class diplomat, first on behalf of his colony of Pennsylvania, then three others (Georgia, New Jersey, and Massachusetts). He ultimately became America's first formal diplomat when he represented the United States in France in 1776. He literally knew hundreds of people and many thousands knew him or knew of him. Many people read his works—whether published anonymously or under his own name—and he was almost universally admired and respected.

It is no wonder that he had such wide-ranging contacts. He met Voltaire, one of the great figures of the French Enlightenment, just before the great philosopher's death in 1778. He knew and corresponded with Joseph Banks, a fellow member of the Royal Society of London (the most prestigious scientific organization in Britain, to which Franklin was elected as a foreign member in 1756). He was Joseph Priestley's friend, but even more important, his mentor, instructing him in scientific matters and reviewing in advance Priestley's major contributions to the history of electricity and the understanding of vision and color. It was a natural outcome that Franklin, along with Thomas Jefferson and John Adams, designed the new Great Seal of the United States to include the date of independence and the eye of Providence (note: not God, but Providence). To be sure, the Great Seal of the United States possesses a measure of Freemason imagery that was prevalent at the time. But there are also purely secular and indigenous aspects of its imagery: American independence, American unity, American power, American destiny, and American originality.

Franklin was the model of the uniquely American self-made activist, intellectual, and investigator. Nothing escaped his inquisitiveness. He produced a large body of work that extols the great principles that underlie American civil liberties and civil rights. No individual thinker or writer is indispensable. But if there ever were a single individual who embodied the founding of America, that would, in my judgment, be Benjamin Franklin.

Masons, Skulls, and Secret Chambers

The Postrevolutionary Fraternity

by Steven C. Bullock

The history of the Freemasons is intertwined with the birth and the early decades of the American republic. It's a story so rich that, with hindsight, it seems almost impossible for Dan Brown to have based his first American-inspired Robert Langdon thriller on any other group.

Steven C. Bullock, associate professor of history at Worcester Polytechnic Institute, is a leading historian of Freemasonry and its connections to the American Revolution and the Founding Fathers. Here, he charts the evolution of Masonic rituals, of Masonry in America, and of the causes and consequences of anti-Masonic hysteria that helped to trigger Freemasonry's decline.

Almost two hundred years before Dan Brown's terrifying villain Mal'akh infiltrated the Masons, another man who would try to expose Masonic secrets was given a wine-filled skull and told "it's time." Shocked by the ghoulish gesture, he protested. Immediately, six brothers drew their swords and surrounded him. Only after a minister explained that this ritual was necessary to join the brotherhood did Avery Allyn drink the wine. The oath he swore on that day in the 1820s was even more chilling than Mal'akh's calling for the wine to become poison if he revealed Masonry's secrets: Allyn extended his vows to the afterlife. In case of such infidelity, he said, "the sins of the person whose skull this once was" should be added to his own on Judgment Day.

The ritual was shocking. It was meant to be. The ceremony was developed in America in the period after the Constitution was written, roughly between 1787 and 1827, a time when many Masons believed their fraternity was of enormous importance. After all, as the fictional Harvard professor Robert Langdon tells students every spring in his Occult Symbols course, in 1793 it was brother George Washington himself who laid the cornerstone of the United States Capitol. Over the next forty years, initiates drank wine from skulls and, as Peter Solomon would do in the Capitol, sat in Chambers of Reflection. The real history of these rituals, the Founders, and the revelation of their secrets is as fascinating as the thriller itself.

When Robert Langdon opens the door to the mysterious basement room within the Capitol, he is horrified to see "something staring back"— a skull. After recovering, he explains to his companions that the room is a "Chamber of Reflection," a place for peaceful introspection. His first reaction, however, is closer to the room's original intent.

The Chamber of Reflection was part of the same postrevolutionary Masonic ceremony that included drinking from skulls—and it, too, was meant to provoke a strong reaction. At the start of the ritual, which has its roots in the Knights Templar legends featured in *The Da Vinci Code*, the blindfolded initiate was brought into a room and told he would find the Bible. Instead, to his horror, he discovered skulls and bones. Literally face-to-face with death, initiates were meant to be so overwhelmed that they could easily accept the degree's important lessons.

The Chamber of Reflection was the first stop on a long ritual journey that lasted more than an hour. Playing the role of a Christian pilgrim, the candidate passed through a number of settings (and a seemingly endless series of Bible readings) before arriving in the Knights' secret retreat.

There he knelt at a triangular table bearing another awe-inspiring sight, a coffin lit by twelve candles, a skull and crossbones placed on top. He then received the skull whose wine would seal his promise to be faithful both to Christianity and Masonry.

But Masonic initiations were not thrills for their own sake, even if they inspired Shelley's creation of Frankenstein. Like other rituals created during those years, the Knights Templar ceremony took advantage of the current thinking about education and human psychology. A century before, the English philosopher John Locke (known today mostly for his political theories that helped justify the American Revolution) had demolished long-held beliefs that people were born with ideas already within them. Instead, he suggested, people learned through their senses. This idea was revolutionary, not least because it encouraged hope that changing people's environments could dramatically improve their lives. Eighteenth-century Enlightenment thinkers imagined the mind being marked by new experiences that, literally, in a term still used today, "made an impression." Masonic degree ceremonies, bringing together overwhelming scenes with high moral lessons, sought to reshape the candidate internally, much as Mal'akh had done externally with his head-to-toe tattoos.

But there was another reason that the postrevolutionary fraternity turned to such overwhelming experiences. The brothers were anxious for rituals that fit their high visions of Masonry. The colonial fraternity had been relatively limited. Lodges were found only in the cities, and were frequented primarily by the upper levels of society as a means to build solidarity among the elite and to emphasize their elevation above the common people. During the Revolutionary years, however, Masonry was transformed, becoming larger, more relevant, more complex, and more democratic as it adapted to the Enlightenment ideals of the new nation. Within a few years, the fraternity reached every part of the new nation. By the 1820s, almost five hundred lodges met in New York State alone. Merchants, professionals, and politicians flocked to Masonry, finding it an invaluable means of establishing local reputations and building cooperative networks. The expanded fraternity took on a broader cultural meaning as well, becoming a central symbol of a new nation that was also committed to education, fraternal equality, and nonsectarian religion. By symbolically laying the foundations of monuments, public buildings, and even churches in cornerstone ceremonies, Masonry proclaimed postrevolutionary America's highest ideals. While the Knights Templar ritual acknowledged the difficulty faced by young men struggling to establish themselves, it also promised that they, too, could join an inner circle reserved for the most meritorious.

Masonry first emerged as a fraternal order out of the older craft organizations in England during the early eighteenth century. But the new organization included many men who belonged to Britain's pioneering scientific organization, the Royal Society, and participated in the cultural contradictions that Brown highlights in its president, Sir Isaac Newton. Even as Newton was helping to create modern science, he also drew upon a tradition that celebrated ancient wisdom as a deeper knowledge that had become obscured by human forgetfulness. These two sides, enlightened order and ancient knowledge, became central to Masonry as well, providing it with a flexibility that would allow succeeding generations to reshape it to fit changing times. Enthusiastic brothers in the postrevolutionary years found the tradition of hidden wisdom irresistible. In reshaping the brief, unsystematic, and relatively haphazard rituals of their colonial brothers, they helped to create a series of "higher degrees" that promised new levels of knowledge, even the discovery of the lost Mason's Word that had formed the center of the primary degrees given in the lodge. In the Royal Arch ceremonies that became part of the system leading to the Knights Templar, this word was revealed to be nothing less than the secret name of God.

While *The Lost Symbol* captures some of this excitement, it is considerably more confused about the Founding Fathers who led the Revolution. This earlier generation had little interest in ideas of mystical knowledge. It is the case, as Peter Solomon pointed out to Langdon at the base of the Washington Monument, that Thomas Jefferson cut and pasted together his own version of the Gospels. But the ex-president was not seeking hidden realities revealed by mystic readings—quite the opposite. Jefferson believed that such metaphysical complexity was the root of the problem. Only by removing what he termed "nonsense" would the simple moral teachings of Jesus be revealed.

Jefferson was not a Mason, but many of the other leading figures of the Revolution were. Members included Benjamin Franklin and Paul Revere as well as John Hancock and George Washington, the two men who presided over the adoption of the Declaration of Independence and the Constitution, respectively. In all, one-third of the delegates who followed Washington in signing the Constitution belonged to the fraternity. For these men, coming of age before or during the Revolution, the fraternity symbolized an enlightened identity that helped to proclaim their social standing and their cosmopolitan connection with the centers of culture, not as a place to find mysterious wisdom.

The Lost Symbol similarly mythologizes Washington, D.C., following the current trend of casting a city designed according to Enlightenment principles as an embodiment of occult mysteries instead. To his credit, Langdon rightly rejects the fears of an eager undergraduate who traces satanic symbols and Masonic conspiracies in the street plans. But the professor is less sure-footed about Washington's layout, seeing it as organized around the Washington Monument rather than the Capitol and the White House. And he perpetuates an even more bizarre confusion about the September 1793 cornerstone laying for the United States Capitol. In Langdon's description, the event was planned around propitious astrological conditions available only between 11:15 A.M. and 12:30 P.M. on that day. In reality, the many demands of that day seem unlikely to have allowed for such careful attention to timing. The difficulties in Langdon's account extend to Masonry as well. He suggests that three brothers planned the key design elements of the city. He is correct at least about Washington's involvement. But Pierre L'Enfant, the first architect of the capital city, never seems to have become a Freemason. (Franklin was technically no longer a Freemason in 1793, since he had, by then, been dead for three years.)

Besides rituals and the Founders themselves, a third element from the new nation plays an important role in *The Lost Symbol*. One of the book's central mysteries is the continuing involvement of Inoue Sato, the director of the CIA's Office of Security, in seeking to track down Peter Solomon's kidnapper. Only later does Brown reveal that she is driven by a concern for national security. Her fears that Mal'akh would release his videotapes of Masonic rituals were so strong that the loss of the life of the head of the Smithsonian Institution seems small by comparison.

From one perspective, Sato's fear of this exposure looks almost laughable. Accounts of even the most arcane Masonic rituals are easily available on the Internet. And the tradition of these exposés is almost as old as the order itself. No sooner had Masons started organizing their fraternity than outsiders grew interested in what took place behind closed doors with a sword-wielding guard. Americans published thirty editions of such revelations in the generation after the American Revolution. Even Masons themselves used these volumes to help them memorize rituals.

Despite this long history of exposés, Sato's fears of a major crisis created by the exposure of Masonic secrets are not entirely far-fetched. Such a revelation actually took place soon after Avery Allyn had taken the skull to his lips in the mid-1820s. And it set off a series of events that reshaped the nation. By that time, the rituals for the older degrees were widely available, but the specifics of the newer "higher degrees" remained a mystery. Attracting many of the most active and enthusiastic postrevolutionary brothers, these complex ceremonies seemed to many of them clear signs of the fraternity's high significance. Some even speculated that they showed evidence of its divine origin.

So when, in 1826, an upstate New Yorker, William Morgan, announced plans to publish a book revealing the full range of the new rituals, many area Masons were horrified. While they never sought official fraternal action, a number of brothers became determined to stop the publication and abducted Morgan. After being hidden for days in a deserted fort, he was never heard from again. Public outrage at the disappearance grew as Masons tried to cover up the crime, even going so far as to pack grand juries investigating the case with men sympathetic to the fraternity.

Avery Allyn, who had nearly refused to complete the Knights Templar degree, learned from a fellow Mason the identity of the culprit. Despite his vows of secrecy, Allyn found the knowledge so troubling that he finally decided his civic duty required him to reveal the truth. He soon went even further and turned against the Order itself. He took up the task of completing the work that Morgan never finished, publishing a "Ritual of Freemasonry" that remains the fullest source of information about postrevolutionary Masonic practice. Allyn also became a leading expert on Masonry, delivering lectures that included public demonstrations of rituals.

Anti-Masonic attacks on the fraternity did not create a national crisis. But the rise of organized opposition to Masonry did bring significant change. So many Masons left the order that it was crippled throughout the northern United States. Some states simply ceased all Masonic activities. An anti-Masonic political party ran a national presidential candidate and created the national nominating convention. The prodigious work of the anti-Masons helped train a generation of activists who led the way in many of the period's most significant social reform movements, including abolitionism. John Quincy Adams, whose extraordinary postpresidential career included years in Congress fighting slavery, ran for both the House of Representatives and the Massachusetts governorship as an anti-Masonic candidate. Adams wrote that he was particularly struck by a moment when Rhode Island legislators questioned a leading Mason desperately seeking to avoid confirming that he swore the Knights Templar oath and drank from a skull. Both the ex-president and the legislators had learned of the ritual from Avery Allyn.

Focusing attention on skulls and secret chambers, ritual elements that have long since been discarded and (until Brown's book) largely forgotten, is clearly problematic, perhaps even perverse. Masonry has always nurtured such everyday virtues as sociable interaction and charitable concern. But thrillers depend on their distance from everyday life. Few professors live lives as interesting as Robert Langdon's, and even fewer fifty-eight-year-old men climb down the Washington Monument's 897 steps hours after having had a hand chopped off. Avery Allyn and the other postrevolutionary men who passed through the higher degrees were similarly participating in the work of storytellers, not scientists. They were not just reading but were experiencing what might be considered the Dan Brown novels of their day. Brown's decision to use this earlier Masonic material in *The Lost Symbol* may reflect a recognition of that kinship, an instinctive understanding that Masonry offers, like his own work, a means of infusing serious moral and intellectual issues with high drama.

FINDING HIMSELF IN
THE LOST SYMBOL

by James Wasserman

For more than thirty years, James Wasserman has been thinking and writing about most of the issues that interest Robert Langdon in *The Lost Symbol*. Among the subjects of Wasserman's books are the Knights Templar, Aleister Crowley, the interactions of the Christian Templars and Islamic Assassins during the Crusades, the Mystery Traditions (or, as Dan Brown would have it, the Ancient Mysteries), the Egyptian Book of the Dead, the art and symbols of the occult, the Tarot deck, secret societies, the Illuminati, and King Solomon and his temple. A year before *The Lost Symbol* was released, Wasserman published his own guidebook on the influence of Masonic architecture and philosophy on the development of Washington, D.C.: *The Secrets of Masonic Washington: A Guidebook to Signs, Symbols, and Ceremonies at the Origin of America's Capital.* No traveler to Washington who wishes to explore the city in the footsteps of Robert Langdon should be without Wasserman's book. Having spent most of his adult life on his own spiritual path that includes many of the ideas familiar to readers of Dan Brown's books, we asked Wasserman, a contributor to both *Secrets of the Code* and *Secrets of Angels & Demons*, to tell us what he thought of *The Lost Symbol*.

In both *Angels & Demons* and *The Da Vinci Code,* Robert Langdon kept an emotional distance from his subject matter. The master symbolist was portrayed as brilliant, intuitive—a human calculator. But Langdon—and I suspect Dan Brown—seems to have achieved a vision of the transcendent reality behind the symbols with which he is so expert. In the last scene of *The Lost Symbol,* Langdon seems to achieve the integration of mind and heart (that I would describe as initiation) when the symbol set he discovers in the sacred architecture of Washington, D.C., finally begins to penetrate his soul. It's a transformation we have been primed to expect from the book's opening, when Brown quotes from Manly P. Hall's *The Secret Teachings of All Ages,* "To live in the world without becoming aware of the meaning of the world is like wandering about in a great library without touching the books." Robert Langdon has at last touched the books.

Langdon and Brown have grown spiritually before our eyes. There is an absence of that hostility to the Church and religion in *The Lost Symbol* that mars the earlier books. I was delighted to find Brown at peace with Freemasonry's spiritual system, which acts as a résumé of all religions. The universal nature of Freemasonry, its celebration of rationality and religion, science and symbolism, its balance between tolerance of others and the exclusivity of its own brotherhood, seems to have at last struck a chord with Langdon and his creator. The consummate outsider finds hope, the very key to the Mysteries.

It is fascinating that this would take place in communion with the same forces I hold in such reverence. For the spiritual path offered by the inner essence of America is a profound reality that has become increasingly elusive in modern culture.

Brown appears to have reached the same conclusions as many others concerning the spiritual nature of the establishment of America. The farsighted luminaries we know as the Founders shared a vision of liberty rooted in the concept of human beings as sacred participants in the Divine order—worthy of accessing the highest realms of the Holy Spirit, "endowed by their Creator with certain unalienable Rights." When Brown suggests that the Chamber of Reflection in the depths of the Capitol may be a sanctuary "for a powerful lawmaker to reflect before making decisions that affect his fellow man" (chapter 38), one can only hope a reasonable percentage of modern leaders retain such sincerity.

Brown recognizes Freemasons as the high priests of the national religion of America. Masonry's influence on our founding is beyond debate. George Washington, Benjamin Franklin, John Hancock, 16 percent of the signers of the Declaration of Independence, 33 percent of the signers of the Constitution, and 45 percent of the Revolutionary generals were Freemasons. Brown mentions the elaborate, ritualized, and very public cornerstone-laying ceremonies used to consecrate the White House, the Capitol, the Washington Monument, and so many other buildings in Washington, D.C.

I believe the spiritual forces so energetically summoned in the founding of our republic have indeed blessed this nation, and we must keep ourselves worthy of our birthright. As John Adams stated, the Constitution and the American system of government were designed for a moral and religious people. Only those capable of following the dictates of self-discipline may be free from the need of external tyranny.

I spend some time in my book, *The Secrets of Masonic Washington*, discussing the structure of the American government and its derivation from Masonic principles. One of the symbols I highlight is the triangle. Albert Mackey, renowned Masonic historian, described the triangle as "the Great First Cause, the creator and container of all things as one and indivisible." The political structure erected by the Constitution establishes three separate and competing centers of power—the executive, the legislative, and the judicial branches. Another triangular energy grid is created by the tensions between the national, state, and local governments. The Founders counted on the three-way tug-of-war that would exist between the government, the people, and the individual. For the Founders understood that the unity of the triangle is by no means a state of passive equilibrium. Rather, we find three sovereign centers held in check by one another— each boldly asserting its own individuality while trying to dominate the others, yet bound by mutual agreement to form the whole.

And this is the first great secret of the American republic. We are a nation of sovereign entities—individuals—willing to cede a limited amount of personal autonomy so that we may benefit from the common alliance we have chosen to form. The best prescription for modern Americans is that we remain as jealous of our individual liberty as our Founders were of theirs.

The profound Masonic principle of consent of the governed, proclaimed in the Revolution of 1776 and by the Constitutional Convention of 1787, transformed subsequent human history. However, we must understand today—perhaps more than ever—that the Founders were realists who refused to engage in pipe dreams of the perfectibility of human nature, or the longing for "what might be." Instead they faced human nature exactly as it is, with all its flaws and imperfections.

Let's look at another example of Masonic symbolism on which Dan Brown lavishes attention (just as David Shugarts predicted in 2005 in *Secrets of the Widow's Son*). The Washington Monument is an obelisk honoring Freemason and Founding Father George Washington. It is the central focus of the National Mall. Authorized by Congress in 1833, it was designed by Freemason and architect Robert Mills. Masonic lodges throughout America contributed to its cost. Finally on July 4, 1848, the cornerstone was laid in a Masonic ceremony. Brown mentions that a Bible was placed within that cornerstone. Twenty-two marked Masonic stones are included in the monument, contributed by various lodges and Grand Lodges.

The obelisk is an Egyptian symbol. Egypt had the most elevated spiritual teaching of the ancient world and has often been identified as the homeland of Freemasonry. Its architects, builders, and artists were responsible for some of the most timeless and enduring works in history. By choosing an Egyptian symbol to honor President Washington, the Masons were proclaiming that the eternal truths he represents would span millennia.

The design of the Washington Monument offers a profound statement of impersonality. It blends the most austere severity with the most elegant symmetry. While Washington was our first president, the victorious general who led Americans to a dramatic victory, his monument asserts that liberty is not for those who worship at the altar of man. It is a stark reminder that we, as conscious citizens, are to concern ourselves with principles rather than personalities.

The obelisk has been described as a frozen ray of the sun. And here we have another clue to the behavior expected of Americans. The solar ray represents the penetration of the celestial domain on earth. Thus we are taught that our behavior should reflect that magnificent realm of the spirit. Langdon's awakening takes place as he observes the obelisk at sunrise, finding himself flooded with solar radiance from within and without.

Symbolically, when discussing the sun, we are not merely speaking of a fiery astronomical phenomenon. In the language of sacred symbolism, the sun is a reminder of God Himself: omnipresent, the open eye, ever watchful over human behavior. Fructifying, light-giving, creative radiance, nourishing the crops, and lighting our way through the day. Its brilliant displays begin and end each day with the holy, psychedelic light shows of sunrise and sunset.

The sun represents a further spiritual truth. Swallowed by the dragon of night, he wanders far from our ability to see, illuminating hidden parts of the world of which we remain ignorant through the senses. Ancient peoples feared that he had perished and died. Yet the morning resurrection assured them of the continuity of existence; the survival of the soul after the death of the body; the impermanence of darkness; and the optimism of existence that penetrates the heart of Robert Langdon on top of the Rotunda.

The sun is ever a savior God. Jesus, Ra, Krishna, and Buddha are all identified with the sun. And if we look closer at the ceiling of the Capitol Rotunda, Brumidi's magnificent fresco *The Apotheosis of Washington* depicts President Washington in his celestial ascent as an embodied solar deity—an intercessor between God and America.

Brown's portrayal of Katherine Solomon is also worthy of note. Her scientific research is not only compatible with the spiritual teachings at the center of all religions, it will reveal those truths in scientific terms. She will help create a more glorious future for the human race through the wedding of science and spirit. Katherine is a high priestess of sacred science. In chapter 133, she reveals to Robert, "What my research has brought me to believe is *this*, God is very real . . ." And, "The same science that eroded our faith in the miraculous is now building a bridge back across the chasm it created." This is a far cry from the bitterness of Maximilian Kohler of CERN, the creator of antimatter in Brown's *Angels & Demons* who highlights the seemingly irreconcilable conflict between science and religion that runs throughout that earlier book. Further, unlike Sophie's revelations in *The Da Vinci Code* that would have destroyed religion, Katherine's truth hymns the sacred *through* the scientific. She walks in the footsteps of her illustrious predecessors—Pythagoras, Newton, Copernicus, and Bacon.

I was delighted by the character of Peter Solomon. For Solomon is truly the rock (Peter) on which the temple of Freemasonry is erected. The story of Solomon's Temple is a compelling ancient account of the conjoining of science and spirit, man and God, heaven and earth. It reveals a path of integration between sacred and profane—initiation—the illumination produced by the internalization of spiritual reality within consciousness, direct participation in gnosis. Peter Solomon is the visible superintendent of religious doctrine in *The Lost Symbol.* Contrast him with his counterparts as doctrinal authorities in Brown's previous two novels: the delusional, if sincere, camerlengo of *Angels & Demons* and the hapless Bishop Aringarosa of *The Da Vinci Code.* The other figure of spiritual leadership in *The Lost Symbol* is, of course, the Reverend Colin Galloway, a beneficent and wise anchorite who bears witness to both the highest reaches of true religion and the Masonic creed of making good men better.

I thought the fearsome character Mal'akh was well crafted. The most interesting part of his portrait to me was when he stood on his island—with all the wealth and sensual gratification one could wish for—and compared the state of his soul with his condition in the Turkish prison. This experience, known as the trance of sorrow, is the essential first step on the spiritual path. Although Mal'akh chose the "wrong side," the fact that the full satisfaction of his earthly desires proved inadequate to the nourishment of his psyche is indicative of his soul's quest for truth. Perhaps, in successive incarnations, he will learn to make better choices.

In *Secrets of Masonic Washington*, after discussing some of the archetypal teachings of *The Apotheosis of Washington*, I write that our nation's capital is "simultaneously a hymnal and a history book, a shrine and a university, a prayer and a symphony. It is a memorial to truth in a culture of lies, a beacon of freedom in a world of tyranny, and a ray of hope in the darkness of despair." The vision of America as a temple of liberty is perfectly reflected in those hallowed words inscribed at the highest point of Washington, D.C.: *Laus Deo*, Praise God.

OCCULT AMERICA

an interview with Mitch Horowitz

Mitch Horowitz is a writer and publisher with a lifelong interest in man's search for meaning. In his book, *Occult America: The Secret History of How Mysticism Shaped Our Nation,* he shows that mystical traditions are not just an artifact of history but have been an integral part of America's complex national narrative, a much-neglected and misunderstood force in the formation of our cultural and spiritual identity.

For example, the nineteenth-century practice of spiritualism—or talking to the dead—helped ignite the suffragette movement by placing women in roles of religious leadership, in this case as trance mediums. The "mental healing" movement of the mid-nineteenth century began the drive toward a therapeutic spirituality that eventually swept the American religious landscape. And the worldview of a surprising range of notable Americans—from Frederick Douglass and Mary Todd Lincoln to Henry A. Wallace and Marcus Garvey—took a leaf from occult and esoteric ideas.

Why do mystery traditions and occult beliefs endure in modern America? Because, Horowitz says, "part of the foundation of our liberal religious outlook and self-help spirituality are built on occult traditions. And a critical mass of people has found a piece of the truth in these ideas." Dan Brown among them, of course, whose novel relishes Freemasonry's secret symbols and

their ties to ethical development, as well as the "noetic" search
for the scientific proof of thought-induced personal and societal
change. No matter the vehicle, many of us are engaged in our own
personal search for The Word that can give us "hope" . . . the last
word, literally, in the novel.

Interviewed by Arne de Keijzer, here is Mitch Horowitz's
unique take on *The Lost Symbol*. Along the way the reader will learn
about the esoteric teachings behind Robert Langdon's thinking at
the near moment of his death, the Rosicrucians and their subtle
ties to Freemasonry, the dominant role of women in the occult
movement in America, the Masons' connections to Mormonism,
and our general expectation that religion should be therapeutic.
He also tells us about Manly P. Hall, the self-educated scholar of
esoteric religion and symbolism whose book, *The Secret Teachings of
All Ages*, clearly influenced Dan Brown, who used his words both
at the beginning and end of *The Lost Symbol*.

In The Lost Symbol, *Dan Brown suggests that Freemasonry played a key role in the
founding of the nation. As the author of* Occult America, *do you think Dan Brown
got it right?*

Yes, I think Brown has a very good understanding of Freemasonry's influence on early American society. Freemasonry helped introduce principles
of religious toleration and ecumenism into the American colonies. In certain respects, Brown sees that more completely and thoughtfully than
many historians of American religion.

To appreciate the nature of Masonry's influence, it is necessary to
have a sense of just how sparsely populated and agrarian a place colonial
America was in the seventeenth and eighteenth centuries. There were few
seminaries, universities, libraries, or schools. Even the city of Philadelphia
amounted to no more than about five hundred houses on the cusp of
the 1700s. People absorbed most of their ideas and philosophies through
church and civic affiliations. This is why the presence of the tightly knit

fraternity of Masonry—whose members ranked among the leading figures in colonial society—was so influential. American Freemasons extolled the liberal principle that people of different faiths could successfully coexist within a single organization or nation. This principle, as promoted by a relatively small number of educated, civically active men, produced an outsized impact on early American life and helped shape some of the founding documents of our country.

Today we think of "liberal principles" as rooted in "reason." That is, the science, political thought, and humanism of the Enlightenment. But you tie that principle to a group steeped in the occult traditions.

The Masons were classically liberal insofar as their approach to religion was nonsectarian. Early Masonry saw itself as a link in the chain of great civilizations and seekers throughout the ages who were engaged in a search for truth and meaning—one that was larger than any individual congregation or doctrine. British Masons of the 1600s—some of whom were influenced by Renaissance-era occultism—were enamored of ancient Egyptian symbolism, Hellenic mystery religions, and alchemy. They regarded alchemy not as the transformation of metals but as a metaphor for the refinement of the psyche.

Some of the imagery that Freemasons embraced looks very mysterious today, such as the pyramids, obelisks, zodiac signs, all-seeing eyes, and alchemical glyphs. Masons also used symbols of death and mortality— skulls, hangmen's nooses, and mausoleums. But these images had a spiritual purpose. As Brown indicates in his book, there exists an esoteric teaching based around the practice of trying to remember one's mortality and trying to consider the unknown hour of one's death. This can help us see ourselves in a different way. Masons were working with this idea. Freemasonry had an ethos not only of religious tolerance but self-refinement.

In TLS *Dan Brown also ties the Masons to the Rosicrucians, that mysterious seventeenth-century brotherhood that also preoccupied him in* The Da Vinci Code.

Rosicrucianism is an important and misunderstood topic. Beginning in 1614, elements of the European intelligentsia became enthralled with manuscripts authored by an invisible fraternity of adepts called the Rosicrucians. This clandestine brotherhood extolled mysticism, social help for the poor, and higher learning, while prophesying the dawn of a new era in education and spiritual enlightenment (themes that reemerged in America's alternative spiritual culture). There is doubt over whether the Rosicrucians actually existed. The whole episode may have been the provocation of a few people, such as devotees of British mathematician and occultist John Dee, who had suffered persecution after the death of Queen Elizabeth, his patron. Regardless, the Rosicrucian writings gave powerful expression to the principle of ecumenism—a nearly unthinkable ideal at the time and one that likely influenced the religious pluralism later espoused by Freemasonry in America.

In a subtle way, the drama of the Rosicrucians formed the backdrop for the appearance of Freemasonry. One of the earliest and clearest references to modern Masonry appears in the diary of British scholar and antiquarian Elias Ashmole, who in October 1646 recorded his initiation into a lodge as "a Freemason." And here the Rosicrucian connection suggests itself. Ashmole and his contemporaries were among the founders of the British Royal Society, a bastion of Enlightenment thought in the late-Renaissance era. The Ashmole circle professed a serious interest in the Rosicrucian manuscripts and sometimes referred to itself as an "invisible college"—a suggestive allusion to Rosicrucianism. Whether any "invisible college" of Rosicrucians had ever existed, the alchemical symbolism and radical ecumenism of the Rosicrucian manuscripts inspired Ashmole's circle and, hence, quite possibly, early Freemasonry.

Indeed, it is not difficult to conceive of a group of religiously liberal English educators, merchants, and courtiers, their identities concealed for reasons of political protection, seeking to build a fraternity of civic and commercial clout outside the reach of papal authority abroad and those forces at home that had condemned John Dee. In this sense, Freemasonry may be seen as one of the most radical thought movements to emerge from the Reformation.

But it wasn't just Freemasonry that introduced esoteric ideas into the early American scene. What were some of the other influences?

For one thing, there existed a very rich folklore in early American life. Before the Revolutionary War, the area of central New York state that was later called the "Burned-over District" (for its fiery religious passions) was home to the Iroquois nation. Just after the war, the colonial government pushed most of the Iroquois off that land. New American settlers in the area, many of them only marginally aware of the Indian lives that had been forced out, crafted folklore about the region once being home to a mysterious tribe, older than the oldest of the Indian tribes, maybe even a lost tribe of Israel. These ancient beings, so the story went, had been wiped out in a confrontation with the Native Americans. This story had a surprisingly widespread influence, and many Americans believed that the young nation possessed its own ancient religious mysteries and lost history. In 1830, the Mormon prophet Joseph Smith embraced this theme in his *Book of Mormon*, which depicted ancient lost tribes of Israel settling the American continent.

Speaking of the Mormons, Dan Brown never mentions in them in TLS. Talk about the connection between Masonry and Mormonism.

By the early 1840s, Joseph Smith, Mormonism's founder, had grown fascinated with Freemason rites, which he believed contained rituals dating back to the tabernacle of the ancient Hebrews. According to surviving records, Smith believed he could revive these rites, incorporate them into Mormonism, and connect his new religion with the practices of the ancient past. He blended some of Masonry's ceremonies, symbols, secret passwords, handshakes, initiation rites, and religious plays into the Mormon faith. That is one of several ways that Masonic rituals became woven into other American traditions, often to the point where the initial Masonic influence became forgotten.

Speaking more broadly, what were the most enduring themes in American occult thought and traditions?

Today, Americans widely believe that religion ought to be therapeutic. Many Americans expect religion to provide practical ideas for coping with the problems of daily life. That attitude was very foreign about 150 years ago; it was unheard of in Calvinist Protestantism. Many of the self-help ideas found today within American religion first entered our culture in the mid-nineteenth century. At that time the nation hosted a wide array of esoteric, mystical, or occult religious experiments.

One of the most important of these experiments was the "mental-healing" movement that emerged in the 1840s. In Maine, a clockmaker named Phineas Quimby began to experiment with how people's moods could influence their physical well-being. He attracted influential students, including Mary Baker Eddy, who went on to found the religion of Christian Science. Likewise, by the late 1840s, America saw the birth of Spiritualism, in which everyday people would gather around séance tables to contact departed loved ones. Again, the healing impulse was at work: American families were straining under the grief of child mortality, and people had no way to relieve their suffering. There was no pastoral counseling, no support groups, and no therapy. Hence, many people began seeking solace at the séance table. The letters and diaries of the era attest to educated people experiencing some of the most moving episodes of their lives in that way. People testified to having this experience of catharsis. You can see the stirrings of a therapeutic spirituality arising from both mental healing and Spiritualism.

Sounds as if the Spiritualist movement had more than its fair share of colorful characters.

One of my favorites is the Publick Universal Friend, a spirit channeler who became the nation's first female religious leader in 1776. She was a young woman named Jemima Wilkinson who grew up on a prosperous Quaker farm in Cumberland, Rhode Island. In the early 1770s, when Jemima entered her twenties, she converted to a fervent form of Baptism spread by the religious revival movement called the Great Awakening. By October 1776, when Jemima was twenty-four years old, she was struck with typhus fever and fell sick to her bed. After days of Jemima slipping in and out of a coma, her family wrote her off as dead. But one day she leaped from her bed—still skinny from her fever but her cheeks flushed with redness—and announced to her shocked household that the girl they had known as Jemima was now indeed dead, but the figure standing before them was reanimated by a spirit from the afterlife—and would answer only to the name Publick Universal Friend.

The Publick Universal Friend began preaching and delivering sermons around New England, upstate New York, and down to Philadelphia. Her topics were usually very tame, ranging from the ethics of neighborly love to the virtue of punctuality.

You have now mentioned two very public female religious leaders. Was there a unique presence of women on the occult scene in America?

Actually, Spiritualism provided an enormous outlet for women in the nineteenth century. In some ways, it was the first modern movement in which women could openly serve as religious leaders, at least of a sort. Most of the prominent trance mediums in the mid-nineteenth century were women. The mental-healing movement also had a number of significant female leaders and personalities. These movements provided an opening for women who wanted to participate in civic or religious culture. And both of these religious cultures helped seed the suffragette or voting-rights movement. In the mid-nineteenth century you could not find a suffragette activist who hadn't spent at least some time at the séance table. This is one of several ways in which esoteric religion and progressive politics grew up hand in hand in America.

TLS is all about books, the prime source for "The Word" Peter Solomon lives and what Robert Langdon searches for. One book that Dan Brown singles out as being influential on his thinking is Manly P. Hall's The Secret Teachings of All Ages. *Who was the author of this mysterious book?*

Manly P. Hall was a self-educated scholar of esoteric religion and symbolism. He came from very ordinary beginnings in rural Canada, where he was born in 1901 to a couple who quickly divorced. Hall was raised by his grandmother in the American West and had little formal education. But his grandmother cultivated his interests in religion and history through trips to museums in Chicago and New York. The really remarkable aspect of Hall's life is that this precocious young man published in 1928 a magisterial encyclopedia of occult philosophy—*The Secret Teachings of All Ages*—when he was just twenty-seven years old. Dan Brown said in a recent television interview that the book was a key resource for him while researching *The Lost Symbol* and that it shaped many of his own attitudes about esoteric religion and symbolism.

As a book, *The Secret Teachings of All Ages* is almost impossible to classify. It is written and compiled on an Alexandrian scale and its entries shine a rare light on some of the most fascinating and little-understood aspects of myth, religion, and philosophy. It covers Pythagorean mathematics, alchemical formulae, Hermetic doctrine, the workings of Kabbalah, the geometry of ancient Egyptian monuments, Native American myths, the uses of cryptograms, an analysis of the Tarot, the symbols of Rosicrucianism, the esotericism of the Shakespearean dramas—these are just a few of Hall's topics.

The source of Hall's knowledge and the extent of his virtuosity at so young an age can justly be called a mystery. In terms of his motives, Hall saw the very act of writing and self-publishing *The Secret Teachings of All Ages* as an attempt at formulating an ethical response to the materialism that he felt was rampant in America in the 1920s.

The book stands up surprisingly well in the twenty-first century. While its entries are at times speculative, it remains the only codex to esoteric ideas that treats its subject with total seriousness. Other works, such as *The Golden Bough*, regarded indigenous religious traditions as superstition or as interesting museum pieces, worthy of anthropological study but of no direct relevance to our current lives. Hall, on the other hand, felt himself on a mission to reestablish a living connection to the mystery traditions.

In Occult America *you discuss in some detail "Mystic Americans" and "The Science of Right Thinking." Is today's New Age movement a natural outgrowth of such ideas? What do they have in common? How do they differ?*

As noted earlier, the culture of therapeutic and self-help spirituality that permeates America today grew out of the mental-healing movement pioneered by American mystics in the mid-nineteenth century. Starting around the 1840s, a fascinating range of religious innovators in New

England began experimenting with a wide array of occult and esoteric ideas. In particular, they were interested in Mesmerism (or what we now call hypnotism), in the mystical ideas of philosopher Emanuel Swedenborg, and in the writings of the Transcendentalists. They combined these thought currents with their own inner experiences to create a philosophy of mental healing, or mind power. They believed that the mind was causative and could shape outer events. Some went so far as to suggest that the subconscious was the same as the creative power called God.

This philosophy branched off into several directions. In the mind of Mary Baker Eddy, it emerged as the new religion of Christian Science. In the hands of a wide range of American mystics, it became known by such names as New Thought, Science of Mind, and the Science of Right Thinking, to cite a few. By the early twentieth century, this positive-thinking philosophy had spread across the nation and formed the basis for the most influential self-help books of all time, such as *Think and Grow Rich* by Napoleon Hill and *The Power of Positive Thinking* by Norman Vincent Peale. It ignited a belief across the American spiritual scene that religion should not only be a force for salvation but also a force for healing and self-improvement. Today, Americans of all backgrounds and beliefs expect religion to provide practical help in facing the difficulties of daily life, such as addiction, relationship issues, financial problems, and the search for happiness. In a sense, this is the American religion. And it is rooted directly in the ideals of American mystics and religious experimenters of the nineteenth and early twentieth centuries.

Chapter
FIVE

MAN MEETS GOD, AND GOD MEETS MAN

WHAT'S BEEN LOST AND WHAT NEEDS TO BE FOUND IN OUR TIMES

an interview with Rabbi Irwin Kula

Irwin Kula is one of America's most deep-thinking and thought-provoking rabbis. Kula has inspired millions worldwide by using Jewish wisdom to speak to all aspects of modern life and relationships. A self-described "trader in the global marketplace of ideas," he has led a Passover seder in Bhutan; consulted with government officials in Rwanda; and met with leaders as diverse as the Dalai Lama and Queen Noor to discuss compassionate leadership. *Secrets of the Lost Symbol* coeditor Dan Burstein interviewed Rabbi Kula about the range of ideas, meanings, and interpretations of *TLS*.

You've just finished reading The Lost Symbol. *Your overall reaction?*

It's *The Da Vinci Code* but set in Washington, D.C. It's a lot of fun. It takes three days to read, and you can't put it down. In that respect, it's wonderful. On a more serious level, Dan Brown captures the Zeitgeist of what is happening in religion in the West. We're moving from what might be called *exoteric* toward more *esoteric* traditions . . . from an emphasis on external belief, dogma, creed, and tribal belonging–type religion to a more esoteric focusing on inner development, the cultivating of awareness, and the-raising-of-the-consciousness type of religion. Brown captures this movement in society's thinking perfectly in *The Lost Symbol*.

The two most important recent studies on American religious identity, the American Religious Identity Survey (ARIS), which came out in the spring of 2009 (now in its thirtieth year), and the Pew Study concur: all mainstream religions—that means nonfundamentalist Judaism and Christianity, basically all nonevangelical, nonfundamentalist forms of religious belief, including Catholicism—are weakening dramatically in America. In Europe it's already largely over for these religions. When we add the projected effects of generational change as Gen X, Y, and the Millennials come to dominate the culture, we are going to see a massive hemorrhaging of followers of these liberal forms of organized religion. What will replace it? A menu of wisdom and practices that can work across all boundaries, chosen from the religious and spiritual stew that already very much exists. I call this emerging cohort "mixers, blenders, seekers, and switchers." Curiously, someone like Karen Armstrong is making much the same case as Dan Brown in her new book, *The Case for God*.

On a visit to the National Cathedral, which itself plays an important role in the plot of The Lost Symbol, *I noticed that Karen Armstrong's* The Case for God *was selling in a big display in the bookstore right next to a big display for* The Lost Symbol.

In some surprising ways, they are really the "same" book. Armstrong's book is unbelievably erudite and Dan Brown's is quite obviously a work of pop fiction. But they are the same in that they both are making the claim that there is a deeper, more important truth than the simple surface read which claims that all that exists is material reality. They are also both implying and claiming that conventional religion is not working to get the job done that people need. Both books are inviting their readers to explore the more profound ideas and esoteric strands in religious traditions.

Let's talk about the Akedah—the story of Abraham and Isaac—and Dan Brown's use of that motif, which runs really from the very first moments of the book to the end. Tell us about the traditional biblical account, as well as your personal thoughts on how this story has been told in Jewish history.

I read the traditional Bible account as a terrifying story. At the end of a long relationship between Abraham and God that has spanned close to twenty chapters of Genesis and a lifetime of seeking, journeying, promises, disappointments, wanderings, and a complex but purposeful direction in Abraham's life, God orders Abraham to sacrifice Isaac, the very embodiment of the promise of his future. This is a horrifying thought, and yet there is complete silence in the text from Abraham. At the very last moment, with the knife in Abraham's hand as he is about to slaughter Isaac, an angel intervenes and says, "Stop, Abraham, I now know your full commitment to God. You're not afraid to give everything." And thus Isaac, and Abraham, get a reprieve.

This is, of course, the paradox of faith as a movement between sacrifice, death, and rebirth, which figures prominently in *The Lost Symbol:* you have to die to be able to be reborn. What does it mean to surrender so completely, as Abraham did, that one can feel and experience the depth of that alignment, that oneness and deep connection—the moth burning in the flame?

Now, the story has had every possible interpretation, from ancient times to today. There is a medieval Midrash—a commentary—that suggests Abraham actually did kill Isaac and that Isaac was resurrected. The great Danish philosopher Kierkegaard wrote one of his most important books on this subject—*Fear and Trembling*—in which he offered the argument that this is a great moment of faith that necessitates "the teleological suspension of the ethical." In other words, Abraham's intent to obey God's commandments and to submit himself to the eternal plan is considered sufficient justification to sacrifice Isaac, since it is "transethical." At the other end of the continuum, you have Woody Allen making a claim that Abraham was a madman, crazy to listen to the commandment from God to sacrifice his own son. This last interpretation, a particularly modern one, is repeated in the recent Harold Ramis movie, *Year One*.

In any event, on an important level this is a powerful, primal story about the relationship between fathers and sons, and the incredible complexity of that most basic relationship. When I read this story it is almost as if Abraham is our father and God saves us from our crazy father. But then who saves us from our crazy God? So the story is not just about saving a child from a father, but saving both from what I call a kind of parental narcissism. *The Lost Symbol* is picking up on that at a pretty significant level.

But isn't the focus in The Lost Symbol *on the son's narcissism—in other words, Mal'akh's extreme narcissism, not Peter's?*

Remember, this kid Mal'akh, who appears to be evil incarnate, is, of course, produced by Peter. We, the readers, experience Peter as this noble guy. And, yes, he is noble, but he is also flawed. Mal'akh is very much the product of Peter, "the narcissistic parent," the parent who decided to leave his son in jail to teach him a lesson.

What's so crazy in this book is that in some weird way, the Mal'akh character does understand the dethroning of self that is at the core of the Akedah story and at the core of a spiritual experience. He understands this at a much, much deeper level than Peter, who is a perfectly-in-control-of-everything self. Peter has his hand cut off and yet we don't ever see him out of control. He is in control of his sister and he is in control of politicians and he is in control of a massive house and the Masons and the big secret. He's in control of everything. He is the ultimate egocentric character. Now, just because you're egocentric doesn't mean you have to be a bad person. And Peter is not a bad person. But he is a control freak who has done great damage to his son. He is directly responsible for creating Mal'akh. But what Mal'akh understands is Spirituality 101—the dethroning of self so that one can be in the flow, that one can be at once in a state that doesn't even need a "with" in that sentence, just that one could be One. Mal'akh gets that in his perverse way. But Peter, the man with the secret, the moral paragon, doesn't. Peter is not an egomaniac, but he is the ultimate example of the separate self. He is generally a very moral guy. He wants to build a better world. But he's the least spiritual character in the book. Katherine is much more spiritual than Peter.

How do you read the choice Peter offers his son between "wealth and wisdom," between family money and knowledge of the secrets of the Freemasons that Peter is privy to?

I think that's a very Christian kind of allegory. If you are Jewish, the choice between wealth and wisdom is not as stark. We don't have the same sort of split between the material and the spiritual. Just look at King Solomon as an archetype. Who is the fountain of wisdom in the Bible? It's Solomon. But who is the wealthiest person in the entire biblical tradition? That's Solomon, too. And who has the most wives? Solomon. I believe that, while there is no necessary connection between wealth and wisdom, there's also no necessary, inherent conflict between the two.

Any of us who work with children from wealthy families understand this problem. The average reader is naturally going to identify more with Peter than with the mad, demonic son. But Peter has his share of responsibility for creating the conditions that led his son in this direction. If one steps back from the narrative, it's a very sinister story about the relationship between parent and child. And it's not the good parent versus the evil child, as it first appears. It's much more complicated. In some respects, this is the attempt of the child to actually redeem the father from being a narcissistic, controlling parent.

Speaking of the character Mal'akh, what about his name? It obviously connotes both Melech, the Hebrew word for king (as in King Solomon), as well as Moloch, the evil premonotheistic God of the Canaanites who requires child sacrifice.

I think that by choosing this name, Dan Brown is inviting us to understand that this relationship is more complex. Peter treats his son as a parental possession. There is this sense that his son is filling in one of the holes of his own psyche, rather than existing as a person in his own right. This produces profound damage. It imprisons a person—and, of course, in this case it winds up with his kid in jail. And Peter never really takes responsibility for this. At the very end of the book he begins to cry a little, but he still doesn't take responsibility. He writes Zachary off as his own independently troubled person, specifically not the father's responsibility anymore. Given that Peter is the master of the Mysteries and knows, better than anyone in the book, that everything is completely interdependent, and that there's nothing independent of the thick, intricate matrix of the cause-and-effect cycle, he should understand his own fundamental connection to Zachary. And yet the ultimate separation in the book, the ultimate lack of connection, is between Peter and his son.

Ironically, the son knows more about the Ancient Mysteries than the father and is more devoted and loyal to them. The son is leading the life demanded by the Ancient Mysteries. That's the paradox: the son actually knows the wisdom better than the father and is actually practicing at a higher level, although obviously grasping it in a deeply flawed way. The son is more spiritually developed but at a lower, indeed pathological moral level, while the father is at a higher moral level but at a lower spiritual level.

In addition to the paradox of Mal'akh, there are numerous references in TLS *to the dangers of the Ancient Mysteries. Over and over, Solomon or Langdon talk about the danger of too much knowledge or power, or of the ancient secrets falling into the wrong hands.*

There are three basic systems of religious, spiritual thought out there in the culture right now, and they are all off base in different ways. We've got this New Age system that says everything is really pretty and nice and if you just get your thoughts aligned, life will work perfectly. The New Age thought fails to recognize the powerful moral choices we have to make, the terror and burden and sacrifice of a genuine spiritual life. This line of reasoning says we can discount evil, either because it doesn't exist, is merely an illusion, a projection of our own thoughts, or because it's not inherently a part of our lives. So it mistakenly separates good and evil, splits them apart and asks us to focus on the good and the positive only.

Then we have this one-dimensional fundamentalism, which splits the other way. The fundamentalists are keenly aware that there is good and evil, but they believe they can cut off evil by defining it their way, opposing it, fighting it, and clinging to their vision of good. They think they can always be on the side of good, independent of the evil, despite the indications to the contrary. Finally, we have this kind of very heavy-handed overly materialist, atheistic view of the world, embodied by people like Richard Dawkins and Christopher Hitchens.

Those three views—New Age, fundamentalist, and materialist/atheist—are the three major perspectives within religious thinking in the

West right now and something is off in each of them. The New Age is too sweet and too easy and easily descends into a narcissistic sense which says that my thoughts create reality. The terror of life is not included here or blamed on our thoughts. The fundamentalist splitting is also too easy and simplistic. Good and evil are just not that clear and severable. Most of life is lived in very ambiguous areas regarding our motivations. There's so much essential nuance of life that's missing from the fundamentalist vision. The Dawkins/Hitchens view, meanwhile, is a disenchanted view of life. This vision is too flat to be acceptable to most people. It's T. S. Eliot's "The Waste Land." The chief exponents of this view don't seem to be logical role models. Dawkins seems so rough and Hitchens so acerbic. No one wants to be like that.

In TLS, as in Freemasonry more generally, there is a major emphasis on the "name of God"—different versions, different meanings, some singular, some plural, some renderable in Hebrew letters, some unpronounceable or that are forbidden to be pronounced.

What's interesting is not so much that there were all these editors and writers in different time periods, but that the final document that we know today as the Bible integrated all these varieties of experiences, yearnings, aspirations, images, partial glimpses—fragments of the totality of reality. That the product has many, many sources doesn't surprise me. That there isn't one name for God doesn't take away from God's holiness. That's actually a manifestation of the holiness, the inexhaustibility, the incomprehensibility of the totality of reality and existence that is just another name for God.

The more names the better, because each name is providing a touchable window into the experience of reality itself. In fact, a problem arises when any one name hardens. Today's atheism is in part a response to a moment in which one image of God has become concretized and is crowding out other depictions and ideas and images and intuitions. Basically what you have today is an atheism that is an attack on one specific image of God—the fundamentalist, voyeuristic, Peeping Tom God in the sky who rewards and punishes—in other words, the view of God that has dominated our culture for the last thirty years.

What about the difference between references to God as Elohim, which is plural, and also Adonai, which is singular?

The use of Elohim begins early on. It seems to me it is an early generic name for God that brought the pantheon together. Through the grammatical plural form, you're getting a tiny glimpse into what it was like before there was One God. Here's a reference point I give people to help them understand the premonotheistic mind-set: I ask: "How many interior voices do you have?" And a person responds, "What do you mean, I'm just me." And I say, "Well, I'm curious. Do you ever hear your parents' voices? Do you ever hear your colleagues' voices? Do you ever hear Glenn Beck's voice? Do you ever hear your greedy voice? Your envious voice? Your lustful voice? Your angry voice? How many selves do you have?" Now imagine that each of those voices is the voice of a different god. There are many voices with many characteristics, thus many gods. I hear all of those voices and more. But there is still some chairman of the board who I imagine speaks for me, balancing all the different voices, poles, inputs. Now project that out onto a cosmos. And you can see what ancient peoples were doing. They didn't yet have the split between the external and the internal like we do.

This split is really a recent Western one that has come at great cost. This dichotomy between interiors and exteriors; the internal and external is only a partial truth, but in some ways a very beneficial one. We can cure cancer because of this truth, go to the moon, build dams, etc. But it remains only a partial truth. That's where *The Lost Symbol* comes in. We have lost contact with the truth beyond the material, the truth beyond appearances, the truth that before the modern Enlightenment, people could more easily understand and feel their inherent connectedness to one another and to the universe. That moment when something was different, when everybody was connected at the deepest level of truth about the oneness of the world, is gone, and we consequently feel a sense of loss.

Was it really ever that way? Did the ancients "know" more than we moderns do in a spiritual sense?

The experience of something lost is a constituent of what it means to be human. I start with that as a base. At some point in our very early development, there is this experience of loss. The loss is the experience of some deeper, more profound harmony. One cannot recognize oneself as a person without separation, a split consciousness so to speak. Now, whether that happens at six months when the separation from the breast occurs, or at thirteen when teenagers reject their parents and teachers, or at some other age or stage, the fact is, there can be no identity without separation. But it turns out that the second you experience yourself as separate, a sense of loss, longing, and yearning also develop.

The tremendous advances of the last three hundred years from the point of view of material wealth and well-being, health, life span, knowledge, communication, and medicine make the last few hundred years leading up to the present moment the best time in the history of the human being. But at the same time that our society has reaped these unbelievable gains, something has been crowded out. To me, what has been crowded out are the other dimensions of the human experience of reality that are necessary for us to feel happy, creative, loving, compassionate, generous. We are seeing now that we are incomplete without those experiences. This is what it means to be at the end of the modern era and be moving to the postmodern era. We're beginning to know that we have to recover some lost wisdom—perennial wisdom, if you will—from previous eras.

DAN BROWN'S RELIGION

Is It Me or We?

an interview with Deirdre Good

As we have seen in the previous interview with Rabbi Kula, *The Lost Symbol* provokes discussions on some of the most important themes in religion. We asked Deirdre Good, a professor of the New Testament at the General Theological Seminary in New York City, to assess Dan Brown's overall belief system. Can it be characterized as amounting to a theology? Are the biblical verses and the context in which Brown uses them a reliable interpretation of the book he honors as "the Word"? Is his interpretation of the phrase "Ye are gods" from Psalm 82 accurate? Why is the dean of the National Cathedral blind?

Good's answers to these and other questions are thoughtful, and often surprising. Dan Brown is conveniently selective at times, she says, using snippets from the more complete verses virtually as sound bites. And, she asks rhetorically, what happened to Dan Brown's worship of the sacred feminine, so extensively seen in *The Da Vinci Code*?

Deirdre Good is a widely respected scholar of religion whose work centers on the Gospels, noncanonical writings, and the origins of Christianity. She has been a contributor to three prior books in the *Secrets* series, *Secrets of Mary Magdalene, Secrets of the Code,* and *Secrets of Angels & Demons.* **Her latest book is** *Starting New Testament Study: Learning and Doing.*

What did The Lost Symbol *tell you about Dan Brown's point of view on religion?*

In this book Dan Brown conveys a very individualized notion of religion. It's all about individual growth, individual purification, and individual sacrifice. In that regard, I suppose his ideas are a reflection of our times, including my world of Christian seminaries as well as the wider world of spiritual quests. It's a kind of religious perspective that says, "My own quest is the thing that I'm engaged in, and as long as I don't harm anyone else through it, then it's perfectly okay for me to keep pursuing it."

What is wrong with that?

I strongly believe that at its core, religion calls us to collective action instead of simply a process of individual self-realization. For example, many more spiritual insights can be gained from communal prayer, singing, chanting, or interpretation of Scripture than when you do that same activity alone.

Still, The Lost Symbol *talks about the "collective truth" and the "collective unconscious."*

True, but Brown limits his support of this collectivism to the "science" side of his story. In chapter 133, the last chapter of the book, Katherine tells Langdon, "We've scientifically proven that the power of human thought grows *exponentially* with the number of minds that share that thought." That's a great idea precisely because it moves us away from individualism. It is saying, "You can't just have a single person and hope that the power of that one person's mind is going to affect anything." Perhaps a person acting alone can have an impact on something, but surely it is the collective action that ensures change. As the Bible says, "For where two or three are gathered together in my name there am I in the midst of them" (Matthew 18:20).

The problem arises when Katherine, in that same paragraph, says that the new spiritual awareness can be conveyed through the power of the new technologies—Twitter, Google, and Wikipedia. That these in themselves allow us to link together "to transform the world." The irony is that those resources often complicate our relationship to religion; I don't believe the links we forge that way can create the same spiritual fulfillment as those we make in person, and I do not believe that is where we'll discover the exponential power of collective minds. I think in the end it just isolates us further. People hold online prayer groups all the time, but aren't they a substitute? If you can, why not pray in the flesh, in real time, with other human beings?

What do you think of Dan Brown's use of the phrase "Ye are gods"?

First, he is being very selective, as is his wont. "Ye *are* gods" is only one part of Psalm 82, verse 6. Brown uses it to demonstrate human potential, but if you look at the whole verse, the psalmist is saying in the voice of God, "I have said 'ye *are* gods. . . .' And all of you are children of the most High." Then the next verse says, "But you shall die like human beings," which Dan Brown has chosen to leave out. In other words, while God recognizes human aspirations, it is impossible to create "one-ness" with God.

What the psalm is perhaps expressing is that while you can be elevated by your connection to the divine, your life will end just like everybody else's. You will indeed die. Only God is infinite. What Brown gives us is tantalizing, but it's just one of those little snippets he carries around like instant mantras.

What about Brown's use of the phrase "The kingdom of God is within you" (Luke 17:20)?

The verse can be interpreted two ways, and both are presented in any Bible that has footnotes. It's not only that the verse could be about individual potential, but that it also discusses another possibility: the kingdom of heaven is in our midst. In other words, it uses the plural "you." The kingdom of heaven is among us collectively, not in the middle of your psychological development. That's a very different reading from Brown's interpretation of individuated divine potential.

Resurrection is another major theme in The Lost Symbol.

Definitely. Robert Langdon "comes back to life" after having ostensibly died. The method of Langdon's "drowning," made possible by technology, provides a way for regular people to appear to have been resurrected. Human beings are thus accruing to themselves the power of life over death. And if human beings have the ability to control death, then the meaning of life is going to radically change.

Coming to terms with one's own death is the last great challenge of life. All of us face it. So it's interesting to note that Robert Langdon doesn't seem to want to come back to life after they drag him out of the tank. He wants to stay in that womb. "His body returned to him, although he wished it had not," says the narrator of *TLS* at the start of chapter 113. "This world felt hard and cruel." Brown seems to suggest that perhaps death is not the frightening thing that we so often make it out to be. But is this an adequate response to death?

What do you think is the significance of Dan Brown's use of the Akedah story—the binding of Isaac—in this novel?

When you think of Bible stories that could be central to a book that wanted to talk about religious values, assuming this one does, why choose the sacrifice of Isaac? Yes, it is an important story and it serves the novel's ideas about sacrifice—Peter losing his hand, Katherine her lab, Mal'akh probably his life—but it is not an obvious selection, and it seems to me like a deliberate choice against the collective.

Brown could have used, for example, the story of the deliverance of the Israelites at the Red Sea—a fantastic tale of liberation that is absolutely central to Judaism's notion of its people's relationship to God. In both Christian and Jewish tradition, it's a story about many things— redemption, salvation, and the creation of community. But as the Akedah story is usually interpreted, it's all about an individual and his relationship to his father—or in the case of *The Lost Symbol*, it's about Peter Solomon's remorse and grief around the loss of his relationship with his son.

The question that doesn't get asked is: where is Isaac's mother? This is one of the great issues in the interpretation of Genesis 22: God does not to reach out to Sarah. I contend that by choosing this story Brown has chosen also, in the end, to marginalize women and to reduce religion to issues of relationships between fathers and sons.

Are you saying that the same novelist who celebrated the sacred feminine in his previous books now chooses to push women aside, both as characters and as spiritual figures?

Well, how many women are practitioners of Masonic traditions? None. It seems strange for Dan Brown, who was so focused on the role of the sacred feminine in *The Da Vinci Code*, to retreat from that idea now. But in *The Lost Symbol*, he chose Masonic traditions and the Akedah to express the book's values, and both exclude women. I think no matter how much Brown as author and we as readers may maximize Katherine's role, she is the exception that proves the rule.

Are there other things that you found odd in your reading of The Lost Symbol?

Yes. Take Brown's interpretation of the Book of Revelation. It's peculiar. I wonder if he may be using it as a counterpoint to the *Left Behind* series, which takes a very militaristic approach to Revelation. In this approach, the world is going to end in a giant conflagration and the few that are saved will survive. But there is nothing to do with war in the way Dan Brown reads Revelation. He never mentions war. He treats the text like the symbologist he is; Revelation is just a symbol system. The book isn't in and of itself of interest; it's an invitation for Langdon to decode its symbol system until he uncovers what has been obscure. It is an odd way to read Revelation.

I also found his portrait of the Reverend Colin Galloway, the dean of the National Cathedral, rather odd. You would think that having grown up an Episcopalian (Brown's mother played organ at Christ Church in Exeter, New Hampshire) that Dan Brown would know that deans of cathedrals usually say much more mundane things about church business. A dean is also the officiant in all services at a cathedral, but Galloway is blind. I can only speculate on why Dan Brown describes him thus. Is he blind because he sees in a "different" way? It is hard to get into the mind of Dan Brown on this one.

Finally, I don't think Brown does justice to the effort and discipline required for transformation through mental power to occur. I completely believe that the power of the human mind is limitless, but it's not a question of hooking yourself up to instruments in a lab. If, for example, you were to look to Buddhist meditation and chanting as a means of transformation, it's not a question of going off for three weeks to Tibet and suddenly something changes. No, this is a lifetime of discipline. We know from people who do this that it requires an immense commitment and long training. It's the kind of activity that we need to start with on page one if we're really serious about what it implies. Yet from a base of ignorance, Robert Langdon seems to accomplish it literally overnight. This is the promise of the human potential movement; it is not a practicing faith.

In The Lost Symbol, *Brown asserts that all religious traditions share a fundamental core that, if we were only able to access and understand it, offers the promise of a kind of world harmony. Do you agree, or do you think different religious traditions have their own truths that are largely irreconcilable with those of others?*

I think we have to bring our best selves, including our minds and our souls and our spirits, to bear on issues of crucial importance to human beings. By this I mean, of course, the healing of the human body, but also the survival of the planet, and the transformation of the world away from destruction toward sustainability. Whether that involves reaching across all of these traditions we will have to wait and see. But I do think religions are playing a crucial role in a common realignment of values. Compassion, for example, is certainly a universal religious statement. What great things might be achieved if we focus together on a value like that?

SCIENCE AND RELIGION
FACE THE BEYOND

by Marcelo Gleiser

Were Robert Langdon an actual person, he would certainly know Marcelo Gleiser, a professor of physics and astronomy at Dartmouth College and a likely soul mate. Gleiser, too, has an appreciation of the Ancient Mysteries and, as is clear from his essay that follows, seeks to give new life to a time before the matter-spirit duality was broken in the wake of the rise of modern science.

Gleiser is concerned primarily with the interface between the universe as a whole and particle physics as well as the origins of life on earth and the possibility of life elsewhere in the universe. In his first book, the award-winning *The Dancing Universe: From Creation Myths to the Big Bang,* Gleiser addressed two fundamental questions: Where does the universe and everything in it come from? And how do religion and science explain the riddle of creation? His current book is *A Tear at the Edge of the Universe: Searching for the Meaning of Life in an Imperfect Cosmos.*

Gleiser, who is active in the science-religion debate, enthusiastically took up our request to comment on *The Lost Symbol.* He starts with a thought-provocation: *TLS,* he says, was for him a sad book, in the sense that page after page of it was all about loss. It is a loss, he then explains, that came with the Enlightenment's drive "toward the complete rationalization of knowledge, the eradication of anything mystic." Gleiser also discusses the novel's hoped-for reawakening of humankind's inner divinity, and the proposition that scientists could become "the prophets of a new age of enlightenment."

> If there is nothing in here but atoms, does that make
> us less or does that make matter more?
> —*Carl Sagan*

We spend our lives torn between light and darkness, between the bliss of love and the pain of loss. Herein lies the great drama of being human, to have an awareness of the passage of time, to know that our existence is bracketed between a beginning and an end. We know that we will die; we know that our loved ones will die. The pain of seeing someone you hold dearly in your heart depart from this world never heals. I lost my mother when I was six, and I can honestly say that the loss doesn't go away. It transforms, it takes on different meanings as time passes. But the void remains, in one way or another. And it must be filled somehow. Much of human creativity, of our art, our faith, our science, is an attempt to deal with our bracketed existence.

"We are builders," Dan Brown's protaganist Robert Langdon thinks in *The Lost Symbol*. "We are creators." And so, as Langdon suggests, if we can't live forever, maybe our deeds can. Or, perhaps, we *do* live forever, just not with our mortal material shells.

As I read *The Lost Symbol*, the same thought kept coming back to me, page after page: this is a book about loss, about the often-desperate human struggle to cope with it. There is heart-wrenching human drama brought about by the loss of loved ones and by the harsh antagonisms of family life. There is the loss of religious faith brought about by modern science, and the resulting spiritual void that haunts so many. There is the loss of trust in our institutions and fellow human beings, resulting in the widespread belief in all sorts of secret conspiracies. At the core of Brown's narrative lies the split between science and religion and his hope that a possible compromise can be forged through a new kind of mystical science called "noetic science": scientists turned into the prophets of a new age of enlightenment.

Before the advent of modern science, things were simpler. Most people in the world believed in life after death. For Christians and Muslims, there was the day of judgment and the promise of resurrection and eternal life; for Jews, the eternity of the soul; for Hindus, there were the cycles of reincarnation, or "atma," that continue on until the soul matures and tires of material pleasures, finally joining spiritual eternity with "Brahman," the One. Different creeds would state it differently, but most would uphold the theory that our few decades of mortal life, anchored to a frail shell of flesh and bone, are not the whole story. Most would also claim that the soul, being a part of God, is eternal. So, if we are carriers of a part of God, we are all gods, at least potentially. "It's not our *physical* bodies that resemble God, it's our *minds*," says Peter Solomon, the man of wisdom in *TLS*. When our bodies die, our drop of divinity remains. Until the end of the Renaissance, immortality was a simple matter of faith: for the believer, existence was not bracketed between a beginning and an end. Religion freed man from the chains of time. For many, it still does.

During the mid-seventeenth century, the French philosopher René Descartes brought this mind-body dualism to the heart of philosophy. He saw the body as having extension (that is, occupying a volume in space) and being material, and the mind as having no extension and being immaterial. This split, although pleasing from a theological perspective (the mind could then easily be equated with a divine-like soul), caused a problem: how would something immaterial (the mind) interact with something material (the brain)?

Remarkably, the same mystery would reappear at the foundation of one of the greatest physical theories of all time, Isaac Newton's universal theory of gravity, proposed in 1687. The theory describes quantitatively how gravity works as an attractive force between any two chunks of matter, which weakens with the square of the distance between them.

Newton, whom the influential British economist John Maynard Keynes called "not the first of the age of reason [but] the last of the magicians, the last of the Babylonians and Sumerians," puzzled over the nature of this force. How could the influence of one mass upon another—the sun upon the earth, for example—be felt across the vastness of space? When asked about the nature of gravity by Oxford theologian Richard Bentley, Newton replied:

> It is inconceivable that inanimate brute matter should, without the mediation of something else which is not material, operate upon and affect other matter without mutual contact. . . . That gravity should be innate, inherent, and essential to matter . . . without the mediation of anything else . . . is to me so great an absurdity that I believe no man who has in philosophical matters a competent faculty of thinking can ever fall into it.

And so, according to Newton, gravity, the engine that propels the cosmos forward in time, also carries within it the mystery of the matter-spirit duality. Science could go only so far in explaining nature through the actions of matter upon matter. John Maynard Keynes was indeed correct in calling Newton the "last of the magicians," and Brown explores this notion brilliantly in his exciting book. Newton did believe in the wisdom of the ages, in the existence of secrets too precious to be revealed to the common man. "The event of things predicted many ages before will then be a convincing argument that the world is governed by Providence," he wrote.

The science-religion split that characterizes the modern world happened after Newton, the unintended consequence of the success of his physical theories. During the eighteenth century the rational approach to the study of Nature became the *only* accepted game in town. "Enlightenment" was seen as the complete rationalization of knowledge, the eradication of anything mystic. A "man of science" became synonymous with someone who would consider only material explanations for natural phenomena. The joining of natural and supernatural causes, that to men

like Descartes and Newton was a given, became anathema to the enlightened man. The "wisdom of the ancients" became a historical curiosity,
ridiculed by the new scientific way of thinking. As a result, people of faith
became disoriented and felt threatened. Some joined secret societies where
the ancient mystical practices were still celebrated. Others retreated into
blind orthodoxy, negating scientific advances. Science was "stealing God
from them," as someone, to my horror, once accused me of doing during
a live interview in Brazil. This angry attitude toward science is easy to
understand: if God is gone, so is the promise of immortality. What can
science offer in return?

Not immortality. Of course, there is medicine and the ever-increasing
life expectancy. There are the comforts and gadgets of modern technology. There are wondrous revelations of worlds too small and too far to
be seen with the naked eye, atoms and subatomic particles, black holes,
the Big Bang, realities that no one could have dreamed of. But the natural
course of science is to drive an ever-deepening wedge between the natural
and the supernatural, leaving modern man in a state of deep confusion.
Where does love fit in all this? Where does loss fit? Are we all going to
end as we began, as stardust dispersed through the cold, interstellar void?
If that's the case, science doesn't offer a very redeeming view of the end
of life. . . .

Brown offers a solution: mind, the last frontier. We know so little
of how the brain works, of how a (huge) collection of neurons is able to
create and sustain our awareness, our notion of self. So many mystical traditions have tapped into the human mind and found tremendous powers.
Could Descartes' and Newton's ideas of an immaterial substance be right?
There are so many accounts of visions, of miracles, of reaching nirvana,
of mind-expanding drugs, of near-death experiences, all pointing toward
new realms of existence not yet known to science. Wouldn't it be wonderful if, indeed, we were all, much more than we are, capable of tremendous
feats? Wouldn't it be wonderful if we were all gods?

This urge for divinity is found in every culture throughout history
and even at an individual level. As an example, I tell a tale from my own
youth, a striking illustration of how life imitates fiction. When I was

an undergraduate in physics, I wanted to prove—scientifically—that we have an immortal soul. To this end, I devised an experiment to measure its weight; the experiment was simple, a system of scales to measure weight loss and devices to measure electromagnetic activity. To my amazement, Katherine Solomon, the scientist heroine in Brown's book, does the same. With the aid of fiction, she succeeds. I, of course, did not.

The main message of *The Lost Symbol* is that we humans are godlike; we have untapped powers, hidden in our minds. Brown creates a hopeful vision of the future, where God is only "a symbol of our limitless human potential," and that this symbol, lost over time, is about to be rediscovered: the wisdom of the ages. To realize this potential requires the ultimate meeting of the minds. As Katherine argues, each mind has the ability to interact with matter. However, the power within each individual is small and is revealed only after much training. (Readers who practice yoga or play an instrument know how hard it is to achieve mastery.) But when it is, and more and more minds come together, "the many will become one," and positive change could happen in the world.

Brown's book is itself a symbol, a symbol of his (very noble) belief in our ability to change the course of history, to change the world. Hopefully, the book will inspire millions to do their best. I am sure that was Brown's intention in writing it, although he points out, through Robert Langdon's concerned voice, that any new scientific discovery can be used for either good or evil. As explained in *TLS*, during the Cold War, both the CIA and the Soviet KGB had a keen interest in exploring the possibility that the human mind could interact with matter. For my part, I hope that the book will not rekindle a revival of crooks claiming to have telekinetic powers, as Uri Geller and countless others have done in the past. I should make it quite clear that there isn't an inkling of hard evidence in support of any such claims. If the human mind can physically affect matter, it is through our thoughtful actions to improve (and, sadly, sometimes destroy) our lives and those of others.

There is another, more realistic way to see how modern science can inspire us to do our best. Although it falls within the same symbolic category as Brown's "all minds as one," it is based on a more concrete proposal that I detail in *A Tear at the Edge of Creation: Searching for the Meaning of Life in an Imperfect Cosmos*. During the past decades, we have learned a tremendous amount about the origin of life on earth and the possibility of life elsewhere in the cosmos. Eager to find companionship, we have traveled to our neighboring worlds in the solar system, only to find them to be barren, hostile lands. If there is life in the Martian underground, or in the subterranean oceans of Jupiter's moon Europa, it will certainly be very primitive. The more we explore the cosmos, the more we understand that simple life-forms may possibly exist in distant worlds out there. However, we also learn that the complexity of life found on earth makes it a rare jewel, an oasis floating precariously in the emptiness of space.

The study of earth's past history points to a startling fact: we are the products of a sequence of environmental accidents that greatly affected the evolution of life. If this sequence had been different, we wouldn't be here. As a consequence, to have evolved from simple unicellular organisms to complex multicellular ones and, ultimately, to thinking beings, was a real fluke. Furthermore, even if there are other thinking beings in the cosmos, they are so very far away from us as to be nonexistent in any practical sense. Contrary to UFO reports, aliens haven't been here and were certainly not the originators of the wisdom of the ages; we built the pyramids ourselves, through our wonderful inventiveness. We are precious because we are rare: in this way, as the lone creatures capable of self-awareness and of amazing technological feats, we are indeed godlike.

Our cosmic loneliness dictates a new directive for humankind: to preserve life and protect the world we have. Our awareness of life and death, of love and loss, is our strongest weapon against collective oblivion. Modern science has confirmed that we have a chance only if we fight as one to save our planetary home. Only then will the many become one, and we will realize our true human potential: to rejoice in our knowledge of the world and, through it, become one with the cosmos.

And Never the Twain
Shall Meet?[*]

commentary by Karen Armstrong and Richard Dawkins

At the core of Dan Brown's narrative lies the effort to reunite the earthly with the divine through the embracing of a new science. The novelist puts forth a worldview in which science (pseudoscience, if you prefer), mysticism, and mythology unite to link past to present and to advance human understanding. But can such a bridge be built? Reading Karen Armstrong, whose latest book is *The Case for God*, and then Richard Dawkins, author of *The God Delusion* and, most recently, *The Greatest Show on Earth*, sows the kind of doubt even the noetically informed Katherine Solomon, the scientist in the novel, might find daunting.

Karen Armstrong argues here that our historic objectification of God exposes Him to potential demise at the hands of evolutionary theory. Instead, in a thesis Robert Langdon would no doubt accept, she encourages us to move toward a God who is beyond reason—a symbol or a metaphor for something greater than man can put into words, something that can be reached only through myths and rituals: As Rabbi Irwin Kula tells us in this chapter, Karen Armstrong's *The Case for God* and Dan Brown's *The*

Lost Symbol, despite the obvious differences between a scholarly nonfiction book and a pop-culture potboiler, are, essentially, the same book in terms of their efforts to redress modern society's lost sense of wonder and to stimulate the search inward to find divinity.

To which Richard Dawkins might respond, "Why even try to cross a bridge when there is nothing on the other side with which to connect?" He scoffs at a divine presence of any sort, arguing here and elsewhere that science, through evolution, has eliminated the possibility of a supernatural creator. Some might argue that this kind of zealousness for the material world—and nothing but the material world—robs us of our sense of wonder and connectedness to the universe. Yet Dawkins told us as far back as 2005, when he was interviewed for our *Secrets of Angels & Demons* book, "The suggestion that science robs us of wonder is utterly preposterous." He added that he hoped that someone in a Dan Brown novel would make that point. After *TLS,* he is probably still waiting. . . .

WE NEED GOD TO GRASP THE WONDER OF OUR EXISTENCE

by Karen Armstrong

Despite our scientific and technological brilliance, our understanding of God is often remarkably undeveloped—even primitive. In the past, many of the most influential Jewish, Christian, and Muslim thinkers understood that what we call "God" is merely a symbol that points beyond itself to an indescribable transcendence, whose existence cannot be proved but is only intuited by means of spiritual exercises and a compassionate lifestyle that enables us to cultivate new capacities of mind and heart.

But by the end of the seventeenth century, instead of looking through the symbol to "the God beyond God," Christians were transforming it into hard fact. Sir Isaac Newton had claimed that his cosmic system proved beyond a doubt the existence of an intelligent, omniscient, and omnipotent creator who was obviously "very well skilled in Mechanicks and Geometry." Enthralled by the prospect of such cast-iron certainty, churchmen started to develop a scientifically based theology that eventually made Newton's Mechanick and, later, William Paley's Intelligent Designer, essential to Western Christianity.

But the Great Mechanick was little more than an idol, the kind of human projection that theology, at its best, was supposed to avoid. God had been essential to Newtonian physics but it was not long before other scientists were able to dispense with the God hypothesis and, finally, Darwin showed that there could be no proof of God's existence. This would not have been a disaster had not Christians become so dependent upon their scientific religion that they had lost the older habits of thought and were left without other resources. . . .

Throughout history, most cultures believed that there were two recognized ways of arriving at truth. The Greeks called them *mythos* and *Logos*. Both were essential and neither was superior to the other; they were not in conflict but were complementary, each with its own sphere of competence. Logos ("reason") was the pragmatic mode of thought that enabled us to function effectively in the world and had, therefore, to correspond accurately to external reality. But it could not assuage human grief or find ultimate meaning in life's struggle. For that people turned to mythos, stories that had no pretensions to historical accuracy but should rather be seen as an early form of psychology; if translated into ritual or ethical action, a good myth showed you how to cope with mortality, discover an inner source of strength, and endure pain and sorrow with serenity. . . .

Religion was not supposed to provide explanations that lay within the competence of reason but was to help us live creatively with realities for which there are no easy solutions and to find an interior haven of peace; today, however, many have opted for unsustainable certainty instead. But can we respond religiously to evolutionary theory? Can we use it to recover a more authentic notion of God?

Darwin made it clear once again that—as Maimonides, Avicenna, Aquinas, and Eckhart had already pointed out—we cannot regard God simply as a divine personality who single-handedly created the world. This could direct our attention away from the idols of certainty and back to the "God beyond God." The best theology is a spiritual exercise akin to poetry. Religion is not an exact science but a kind of art form that, like music or painting, introduces us to a mode of knowledge that is different from the purely rational and that cannot easily be put into words. At its best, it holds us in an attitude of wonder, which is, perhaps, not unlike the awe that Richard Dawkins experiences—and has helped me to appreciate—when he contemplates the marvels of natural selection. . . .

GOD IS NOT DEAD. HE WAS NEVER ALIVE IN THE FIRST PLACE.

by Richard Dawkins

Before 1859 it would have seemed natural to agree with the Reverend William Paley, in "Natural Theology," that the creation of life was God's greatest work. Especially (vanity might add) human life. Today we'd amend the statement: evolution is the universe's greatest work. Evolution is the creator of life, and life is arguably the most surprising and most beautiful production that the laws of physics have ever generated. Evolution, to quote a T-shirt sent to me by an anonymous well-wisher, is the greatest show on earth, the only game in town. . . .

But what if the greatest show on earth is not the greatest show in the universe? What if there are life-forms on other planets that have evolved so far beyond our level of intelligence and creativity that we should regard them as gods, were we ever so fortunate (or unfortunate?) as to meet them? Would they indeed be gods? Wouldn't we be tempted to fall on our knees and worship them, as a medieval peasant might if suddenly confronted with such miracles as a Boeing 747, a mobile telephone, or Google Earth? But, however godlike the aliens might seem, they would not be gods, and for one very important reason. They did not create the universe; it created them, just as it created us. Making the universe is the one thing no intelligence, however superhuman, could do, because an intelligence is complex—statistically improbable—and therefore had to emerge, by gradual degrees, from simpler beginnings: from a lifeless universe—the miracle-free zone that is physics. . . .

Darwinian evolution is the only process we know of that is ultimately capable of generating anything as complicated as creative intelligences. Once it has done so, of course, those intelligences can create other complex things: works of art and music, advanced technology, computers, the Internet, and who knows what in the future? Darwinian evolution may not be the only such generative process in the universe. There may be other "cranes" (Daniel Dennett's term, which he opposes to "skyhooks") that we have not yet discovered or imagined. But, however wonderful and however different from Darwinian evolution those putative cranes may be, they cannot be magic. They will share with Darwinian evolution the facility to raise up complexity, as an emergent property, out of simplicity, while never violating natural law.

Where does that leave God? The kindest thing to say is that it leaves him with nothing to do, and no achievements that might attract our praise, our worship, or our fear. Evolution is God's redundancy notice, his pink slip. But we have to go further. A complex creative intelligence with nothing to do is not just redundant. A divine designer is all but ruled out by the consideration that he must be at least as complex as the entities he was wheeled out to explain. God is not dead. He was never alive in the first place.

Now, there is a certain class of sophisticated modern theologian who will say something like this: "Good heavens, of course we are not so naive or simplistic as to care whether God exists. Existence is such a nineteenth-century preoccupation! It doesn't matter whether God exists in a scientific sense. What matters is whether he exists for you or for me. If God is real for you, who cares whether science has made him redundant? Such arrogance! Such elitism."

Well, if that's what floats your canoe, you'll be paddling it up a very lonely creek. The mainstream belief of the world's peoples is very clear. They believe in God, and that means they believe he exists in objective reality, just as surely as the Rock of Gibraltar exists. If sophisticated theologians or postmodern relativists think they are rescuing God from the redundancy scrap heap by downplaying the importance of existence, they should think again. Tell the congregation of a church or a mosque that existence is too vulgar an attribute to fasten onto their God and they will brand you an atheist. They'll be right.

SCIENCE REQUIRES THAT YOU STEP OUTSIDE THE MENTAL COCOON

an interview with George Johnson

Dan Brown opens *The Lost Symbol* with a note stating that "All rituals, science, artwork, and monuments in this novel are real." Yet how real is the science? Can readers take what Brown presents in this novel as "fact"?

To address this issue, we turned to George Johnson, the well-known science writer for the *New York Times* and a cohost of *Science Saturday* on www.bloggingheads.tv. His book credits include *The Ten Most Beautiful Experiments*, about the people behind great scientific moments; *Fire in the Mind: Science, Faith, and the Search for Order*; and *Architects of Fear: Conspiracy Theories and Paranoia in American Politics*. Johnson's depth of knowledge about science, the connection between science and faith, and the foundation of conspiracy theory puts him in a rare position to comment on how true Dan Brown has been to these themes in *The Lost Symbol*.

The Lost Symbol *regularly associates the Freemasons with "esoteric traditions" and the use of symbols that go back to the Rosicrucians, but avoids the links "the brethren" may or may not have had to various conspiracies—the Illuminati, for example—that have run parallel to their history. Does this seem strange to you?*

Freemasons have long entertained the legend that their organization is descended from ancient guilds of stonecutters—who built everything from the Egyptian pyramids to the castles of medieval Europe—and that these brotherhoods were in possession of some kind of esoteric knowledge. Maybe the original masons were just protecting trade secrets, like how to hold a chisel, but the nature of their wisdom has been subject to all kinds of wild speculation. The Freemasons themselves invite this with rituals that suggest an appreciation for other ancient societies like the Rosicrucians and the Knights Templar. But the pageantry alone doesn't mean that the connections are real.

In the eighteenth century, the secrets protected in the Freemasonic lodges resembled what came to be called secular humanism—the notion that truths are discovered by the free human mind, not imposed top down by some ecclesiastical authority. Freemasons and similar underground societies like the Bavarian Illuminati believed that skepticism is noble, not heretical. That things happen for a reason, not by supernatural fiat. These are the ideals of the Enlightenment. No wonder Jefferson and Franklin were attracted to the cause.

For the established order, secularism was as threatening as the challenges posed earlier in history by heretics like the Gnostics and the Cathars. Through a weird kind of symbiosis, the maverick, freethinking spirit of the Freemasons interacted with the paranoid fears of the established order to give rise to a fantasy of an ancient, enduring struggle between light and darkness. It's a theme that runs deep in the human psyche. It resonates with our brains. And it helps sell novels.

The presumed connection between the Freemasons and the Rosicrucians seems to be especially rich source material for conspiracy theorists.

The legend began in the seventeenth century when manifestos appeared in Europe claiming to be written by a secret society of mystics and philosophers called the Order of the Rose Cross. These Rosicrucian documents may have been a hoax, but some historians think they were an inspiration for the founding of the Invisible College, a precursor to the Royal Society of London—which became Europe's preeminent organization devoted to scientific research. The Freemasons also incorporated the Rosicrucians into their legends and rituals—there is a Masonic degree called "Knight of the Rose Croix." But again, that doesn't mean there was an actual link between the two groups—other than in the minds of the Masons and the conspiracy theorists.

You have written about the "safe houses" that gave shelter "to gentlemen [Freemasons] interested in new ideas." These ideas represented "the thin line then between hard-core science and what we now dismiss as the occult." It seems that Dan Brown wants to blur that line or even make it disappear. What do you make of this?

That is the most fascinating thing about this whole subject. In the eighteenth and even the nineteenth centuries, the line between what is and is not accepted as science was not so cleanly drawn. Scientists like Michael Faraday were showing that a current flowing through a wire could make a compass needle move. Wrap an iron nail with wire and connect one end to a piece of copper and the other to a piece of zinc, submerge both metals in a mildly acidic solution, and the nail becomes a magnet. Hold two of these coils near each other but not touching and one will influence the other through invisible waves. What could seem more magical? Later William Crookes used electricity to generate mysterious rays in a vacuum tube. He thought he was seeing ectoplasm. He and other physicists of the time dabbled in séances and spiritualism. But the scientific method slowly weeded out sense from nonsense. However, the nonsense never goes away, as evidenced by *The Lost Symbol*.

Nor does the sense of suspicion surrounding the Freemasons, even in a novel that treats them so reverently. Toward the end of the book, Brown suggests that the release of a video showing prominent lawmakers in a Masonic ritual would have cataclysmic effects on democracy. Do you think this would truly be the case?

It's really pretty funny that the director of the CIA's Office of Security is illegally detaining innocent people and threatening them with guns just to prevent a video from leaking out showing some senators and other high-level government officials playacting at the local Masonic lodge. In real life, Sarah Palin would probably take the revelations as evidence of devil worship, and right-wing radio talk-show hosts would go nuts. But a threat to democracy? Probably not.

The other major notion is that the secrets Katherine Solomon is nearly ready to reveal via her "noetic science" experiments will change the world. What is your perspective on "noetic science"?

Early in the book (chapter 18), Katherine makes what is intended as a dramatic pronouncement: "What if I told you that a thought is an actual *thing*, a measurable entity, with a measurable mass?" Well, what if she did? Thoughts are patterns of electrochemical pulses in the brain. They are made from matter: ions and molecules. Of course they have mass. And of course a thought can change the world. You can invent the atomic bomb, declare war on Iraq, or just decide on a whim to pick up a rock and throw it through a window.

Noetics, at least as described in the novel, is making a more radical claim: that the mind is somehow separate from the brain—philosophers call this "substance dualism"—and has powers that transcend the forces known to physics. If you concentrate really hard, your thoughts alone can move matter. That made for a great plot in Stephen King's *Carrie*. But the phenomenon—telekinesis—isn't real and doesn't hold up to scientific scrutiny. We never learn much in the novel about Katherine's experiments. But they can't have gotten very far or she could have wished her way out of the clutches of the scary illustrated man.

The Lost Symbol is fiction, so the author can make up anything he wants. But at the beginning of the book he writes, "All rituals, science, artwork, and monuments in this novel are real." When it comes to the science, he breaks that pact with the reader again and again. We're told that it has been "categorically proven that human thought, if properly focused, [has] the ability to affect and change *physical* mass" (chapter 15). Brown is actually claiming that psychokinesis is established science. In a typical experiment, human subjects are asked to concentrate very hard and try to influence the output of some sequence of random events—like trying to make a coin come up heads more often than tails. *Order from chaos!* But in one experiment after another, any deviations from the norm have been so slight that only people already predisposed to believe in psychic powers are impressed. Even if the deviations from randomness are more than just experimental noise, it is impossible to rule out other, more mundane explanations. Pure randomness is very hard to generate. The coin or the dice might be uneven. An electronic random-number machine may be biased in subtle ways.

Brown also exaggerates the progress superstring theory has made toward becoming established science. He says the idea that the universe has ten dimensions is "based on the most recent scientific observations" (chapter 15). But it's not. It is a fascinating theory and an impressive feat of mathematics, but it is purely speculative and in something of a crisis because it cannot be experimentally tested. Elsewhere in the book, we're credulously informed that a New Age superstition called Harmonic Convergence is a subject of serious consideration by cosmologists (chapter 111), and that a phenomenon in physics called quantum entanglement was presaged in shamanic texts and has something to do with remote healing.

In a typical conspiracy theory, scraps of historical truth—there *was* an organization in Bavaria called the Illuminati and they did interact to some extent with French Freemasons—are ripped from their context and woven into fantasies. This is how Brown treats science. It is true, as he writes (chapter 78), that the CIA funded experiments in "remote viewing." What he doesn't say is that the experiments were failures. It's true that neuroscientists have scanned the brains of yogis to see what parts of the cortex light up. But they did not find that meditating brains "create a waxlike substance from the pineal gland [that] has an incredible healing effect" (chapter 133). "This is real *science*, Robert," Katherine says. In truth, it's not even good science fiction.

Again this is just a novel. But a lot of readers are going to come away from it with their scientific literacy knocked down another notch.

Brown even suggests that the connection between science and spirituality had an impact on the Founding Fathers, using Benjamin Franklin as an example. Did the belief in this connection really influence the political thought of the time?

In a word: no. Franklin wasn't particularly religious or spiritual. He was a rationalist and was inspired like other leaders of the American cause by Enlightenment philosophers—Locke, Rousseau, Montesquieu. They weren't talking about finding links between science and mysticism, but about the ideals of democracy and the rights of man, about how to balance power and construct sturdy governments.

The subtitle for your book, Fire in the Mind, *is* Science, Faith, and the Search for Order. *This seems to speak directly to the themes Dan Brown is playing with in* The Lost Symbol. *Can you expand on this a bit as it might apply to the novel?*

Science, theology, and even conspiracy theories are driven by the same phenomenon: the brain's compulsion to find order—or to impose it when it is not actually there. A major theme of *Fire in the Mind* is the human dilemma posed by never knowing for sure whether the orders we see are real or invented. Science is far better than religion at making the distinction. A theology or a conspiracy theory is taken as "correct" as long as it is internally consistent. Science requires that you step outside the mental cocoon and subject each idea to a reality test—a scientific experiment.

A very good point. However, while one could easily argue that "noetic science" has failed to prove anything with the "evidence" it offers, one of the things TLS *suggests is that scientific proof of the existence of the soul and the power of mind over matter would dramatically alter life as we know it. How true do you think this is?*

If, after all the failures and embarrassments of parapsychology research, psychic powers are ever demonstrated to exist, that would certainly shake the foundations of science. Mind might turn out to be something more than patterned energy and matter. The "ghost in the machine" would be real. Once they had absorbed the shock, scientists would be more excited than anyone else. They would have new territories to explore.

—*Interviewed by Lou Aronica*

Chapter
SIX

YE ARE
NEW AGE
GODS

THE ENERGY THAT CONNECTS THE UNIVERSE

an interview with Lynne McTaggart

Katherine Solomon turns out to be more than a fictional character. In fact, she's an amalgam of several very real people. To create Katherine, Dan Brown drew perhaps most strongly on the accomplishments of author Lynne McTaggart. Her book *The Field* chronicled the efforts of a number of frontier scientists to prove the existence of an energy field that connects everything in the universe. In 2007 she published *The Intention Experiment*, which tells of her work with scientists to explore the power of thought. This research bears a strong similarity to the work Katherine Solomon is doing. "What if group thought could heal a remote target?" Lynne wrote in a recent blog on *The Huffington Post*. "It is a little like asking, what if a thought could heal the world? It is an outlandish question, but the most important part of scientific investigation is just the simple willingness to ask the question."

We spoke with Lynne McTaggart to ask her what it's like to become a fictional character, what she thinks of the attention Dan Brown has brought to the field of noetics, how much of what she writes about is accurate, and how she responds to a less-than-receptive scientific establishment.

Did you have any communication with Dan Brown before the publication of the book?

No, absolutely none. The book was a complete shock and surprise. When I first heard about it, I had my head down writing my new book. My editor e-mailed me, saying something to the effect of, "You're featured in *The Lost Symbol*." I didn't know what *The Lost Symbol* was. I thought someone had written a book annotating *The Intention Experiment*. I had to Google *The Lost Symbol* to find out what it was. Then I found out it was Dan Brown's new novel, and after I picked my jaw up from the floor, I ran to the phone and called my husband to tell him to get a copy. It was surreal. You expect your work to generate a certain amount of publicity, but you don't expect this publicity to come from a blockbuster novel. I was a little bit out of my body for a week or so.

How good was he with the facts?

It was fun to see how careful he was in creating a crazy quilt of sorts to describe Katherine Solomon and the field in which she works. He was very faithful to the details. He based all of the equipment Katherine uses on equipment that's out there. She uses random event generator machines, which a physicist named Helmut Schmidt invented to test the power of thought on electronic equipment, and which were used most famously by Princeton University's former dean of engineering Robert Jahn for his PEAR (Princeton Engineering Anomalies Research) program. She uses CCD cameras to record the light coming from the hands of healers. University of Arizona psychologist Gary Schwartz, one of my partners in the Intention Experiment, has done that. We just finished carrying out a clean water Intention Experiment using similar equipment. Katherine does experiments in making seeds grow. We've made food grow faster and seeds sprout higher with thought. I've run that particular experiment with Dr. Schwartz and replicated it six times. Katherine's experiments on the magnification effect of group intention also owes a great deal to our work. Even the Cube that Katherine uses as her lab is similar to the special experimental unit used by Marilyn Schlitz, the president of the Institute of Noetic Sciences, and its senior scientist, Dean Radin.

Just a few small details about noetic science in *The Lost Symbol* could be said to stretch the limits of what is now possible. For instance, Katherine's Cube lab is supposed to be able to block out thoughts. Thoughts appear to be impervious to most barriers or distance. And the electrically shielded room in the IONS lab doesn't block out the effects of intention. Nevertheless, experiments with special magnetically shielded rooms do affect the ability of healers to send healing thoughts to others.

What kind of impact does this massive bestseller have on the attention given to noetics?

It's huge. Just judging by my own experience, my book sales in the United States increased by up to three hundred percent and our Web traffic at the Intention Experiment Web site (www.theintentionexperiment.com) has quadrupled. At this writing, *The Lost Symbol* hasn't been released outside the English-speaking world yet. When it does, I assume it will also increase sales of my books in foreign languages. The only person on our team who isn't enamored of Dan Brown is our Webmaster, because we suddenly may need a far bigger server to run intention experiments.

Has being such a major theme in The Lost Symbol *legitimized noetics?*

Featuring this kind of frontier science in a bestselling blockbuster has certainly brought these ideas to a massive mainstream audience. If their interest is sparked, they can discover through my books and the work of many scientists just how much evidence there is to support what appear at first glance to be fantastical ideas. It's also given a good deal of attention to the term *noetic science,* a phrase I believe was coined by the former astronaut Edgar Mitchell, who founded the Institute of Noetic Sciences. Among most scientists involved with studying the power of thought, this science is generally considered consciousness research. Their work suggests that the mind can receive information through extrasensory means and that it can have an effect on the physical world. This includes "mind over matter": the power of thought—or intention—to affect and change the world.

This novel seems to have a very hopeful sensibility to it. Does it seem that way to you as well?

I think that it is very hopeful. Dan Brown is signaling a new age that returns power back to the individual. For a very long time, we have accepted the notion that the universe is composed of a lot of separate entities jostling around in space, and that human beings are essentially lonely people on a lonely planet in a lonely universe. Dan Brown is very much advocating the idea that we create our world and that we can affect it for the good. That's what Katherine Solomon is doing. She's very much an idealist—a woman after my own heart—talking about a second age of enlightenment, where we finally recognize that we are masters of our fate, and that we create our reality. Katherine believes that the power of thought has the capacity to change matter. The idea that we are cocreators of our world is ultimately an extremely optimistic message.

In the book, Katherine claims to be on the verge of substantial scientific breakthroughs. How close do you think we are to those breakthroughs?

Well, I think she's a little further along than we are on the Intention Experiment, that's for sure. We're just taking baby steps right now, trying to prove the effect of mass thought. I've run nineteen intention experiments with our scientists and sixteen have shown very significant positive results, from making food grow faster to altering essential properties of water, to even lowering violence. It's been gratifying to see that the experiments have captured the public imagination, attracting thousands of participants from ninety countries, in every continent except Antarctica, who come on the Intention Experiment Web site and follow our instructions to send the same thought at exactly the same moment to a target sitting in a laboratory thousands of miles away.

I created the Intention Experiment out of frustration. When I was researching the power of intention for my book, I was especially interested in the power of group thought and whether it magnifies the effect of intention generated singly. I found a lot of tantalizing evidence about this, but nothing conclusive. One night, my husband said to me, "Why don't you run these experiments yourself?" That sounded ridiculous to me because I'm not a scientist and I hadn't done an experiment since tenth-grade biology class. But I realized I was in a unique position because I had lots of readers around the world—my books are in twenty languages—and these readers could provide an enormous potential experimental body that most scientists don't have. My primary role in the Intention Experiment is to enlist scientists who will work with me to design experiments testing the power of group thought to heal aspects of world problems. As a writer, I try to bring attention to this important work and communicate complicated ideas about this cutting-edge science and these experiments in a comprehensible way for laypeople.

When we started, I immediately wanted to test whether we could do something to alleviate the catalog of suffering on the planet. Let's save cancer victims, let's save people from starving, I thought. When Dr. Schwartz generously agreed to run experiments with me, he said, "Let's start with a leaf." I was really let down. I said, "A leaf? That's hardly going to set the global mind on fire." He said, "We're trying to do something that's never been done before. We have to start with something simple." So we began there and the results have been astounding. They've surprised everyone working on this project. If you do something once in a scientific experiment, it's a demonstration. If you replicate it six times, you're moving toward something more conclusive. The results of our various experiments are available on the Intention Experiment Web site, as is information about how people can participate in our global experiments.

One of the points The Lost Symbol *makes is that everything we need to know is already out there, that the ancients had uncovered all of these secrets long ago, but that history and other agendas have buried this knowledge. Do you agree with that sensibility?*

I think science is now proving what the ancients have espoused. Belief about the power of thought is nothing new; what's new is the scientific explanation for it. Other new ideas in frontier science aren't revolutionary in many cultures. Only Western minds believe that we are all separate entities that end with the hair on our skin. Many other cultures past and present don't see the world this way.

If a scientist—a real-life Katherine Solomon—were able to offer unassailable proof of these discoveries, what kind of impact would that have on the world?

Scientists *are* offering unassailable proof. There have been many, many studies showing that thought can have an effect on everything from machinery and equipment to cells to full-fledged organisms like human beings. The problem is that science is ruled right now by scientific fundamentalists who consider anything outside the accepted paradigm "junk" science. Frontier science is always about asking the impossible questions. Can I make a big, heavy object fly? Will I fall off when I get to the end of the earth? Those questions move science forward; if we didn't have impossible questions, we'd never have any kind of progress.

But right now, a lot of scientists—the neo-Darwinians, for instance—believe that the scientific discoveries from several centuries ago have already given us all of the answers. They aren't willing to acknowledge that science is a story. Somebody will write a chapter and it will be valid for a while. Then someone will rewrite these chapters and add new ones. We have to understand that it's an ongoing process. The discoveries made by the real-life Katherine Solomons are creating a new paradigm. They *will* be accepted, but probably not for another generation or so because that's what happens with frontier science. Most of the discoveries I wrote about in *The Field* were made thirty years ago, and it's going to take another twenty years for them to be accepted.

So this resistance we're seeing now is not anything new?

Frontier scientists and true explorers of every variety have always been treated as heretics. I think what conventional scientists find most threatening about these new ideas is that they overturn our accepted paradigm of the way things work. Our central idea, that consciousness affects matter, lies at the very heart of an irreconcilable difference between the worldview offered by classical physics, the science of the big, visible world, and that of quantum physics, the science of the world's most diminutive components. The discoveries made in consciousness research offer convincing evidence that all matter in the universe exists in a web of connection and constant influence. This overrides many of what conventional science now considers the laws of the universe. The world is a good deal more complicated than we once thought, and it is fundamentally different from the well-behaved universe of traditional Newtonian science.

Because of The Lost Symbol, *the blogosphere is burning up with a wide range of discussions about noetics. Some of it is very dismissive. How do you answer critics who say that the methods used by you and others in this field are not scientifically based?*

I'd say they haven't looked at the vast body of research in this area. Many critics have a vested interest in debunking consciousness research because they are committed to a very comfortable paradigm that they don't want shaken. Some have invested entire careers in their worldview.

Our Intention Experiments, for instance, don't just have controls. We have controls of the controls. The scientists involved in consciousness research are not fringe scientists. They are prestigious academics at Princeton, Stanford, the University of California, the University of Arizona, the University of Edinburgh, and so on. These are top physicists, biologists, engineers, and psychologists. The only difference between them and conventional scientists is that they're open-minded.

Consciousness research is not only the stuff of fiction. With every unorthodox question asked, with every unlikely answer, frontier scientists such as those featured in my books—and now Dan Brown's—remake our world.

—*Interviewed by Lou Aronica*

NOETICS

The Link Between Modern Science and Ancient Mysticism?

by Lou Aronica

In his first Robert Langdon book, *Angels & Demons*, Dan Brown explored the tension between science and religion, set off in history through the conflict between Galileo and the Vatican. He suggested there were two nonoverlapping magisteria, to use Stephen Jay Gould's phrase, one the Cathedral of Science (the advanced physics lab at CERN), the other the Cathedral of Religion (St. Peter's Basilica). Still, there were hints that Dan Brown was thinking about a grand reconciliation. Among the clues was a copy of Fritjof Capra's *The Tao of Physics*, a real-life book that was on the bookshelf of the fictional physicist Leonardo Vetra, and one among four dealing with the full spectrum of the science/religion debate. Capra's argument is that humanity needs both physics and Eastern mysticism.

Seven years later, it is clear that Dan Brown has fully adopted this argument in *The Lost Symbol*, using noetic science as his vessel. (Brown here also continues his tradition of mentioning real books and real persons. In *TLS* the mind-altering possibilities of science are reflected in the reference to *The Dancing Wu Li Masters*, and the real-life tribute is to two of the most visible proponents of noetics, Lynne McTaggart and Marilyn Mandala Schlitz, both of whom are featured in this chapter.)

Noetic science has its champions, but it also has more than its share of critics, "hard" scientists chief among them. The doubters point to the fact that there have been no independent, double-blind experiments that support the thesis that mind moves matter, mind heals bodies, or that the soul literally resides in the body. Neil deGrasse Tyson, the noted astrophysicist, once wrote a column in which he cleverly reflected the prevailing view of all such "mental" science: ". . . the persistent failures of controlled, double-blind experiments to support the claims of parapsychology suggest that what's going on is non-sense rather than sixth sense."

To sort this out for us, we asked Lou Aronica to take a more detailed look at Dan Brown's new favorite science. Aronica has been a highly successful writer and publisher. Among dozens of other titles, he published Lynne McTaggart's *What Doctors Don't Tell You*. As a writer he has authored numerous books, among them *Miraculous Health: How to Heal Your Body by Unleashing the Power of Your Mind* (with Rick Levy). His latest book is *The Element* (written with Sir Ken Robinson), which is a *New York Times* bestseller. He starts us off with an apt quote.

Any sufficiently advanced technology is indistinguishable from magic.
—*Arthur C. Clarke*

The late, great Arthur C. Clarke was a "hard scientist." He is credited with developing the concept of the geosynchronous satellite and he is the author of numerous bestselling works of science fiction and nonfiction, most notably *2001: A Space Odyssey*. Yet Dr. Clarke was also fully aware, as the quotation above indicates, that much that we now regard as science once seemed purely fanciful. If you asked an eighteenth-century scientist about space travel, beaming sound across the globe, or a box with vast computational capacity he would have scoffed. Such notions would have seemed back then like nothing more than so much hocus-pocus (or, as Dan Brown might render it, *Avra KaDabra*, the child magicians' "abracadabra," "I create as I speak" in ancient Aramaic). What, then, feels like magic to us now that we will regard as hard science in the future? In some ways, this is the question posed by those who work in the field of noetic science.

The potential discoveries made by noetic science underlie one of the most pervasive and compelling themes in *The Lost Symbol*, one that drives it from beginning to, literally, the final word. Katherine Solomon has dedicated her life to this study and her brother, Peter, has built a lab for her at the Smithsonian Museum Support Center where she can confirm discoveries that she believes will change the way every person on the planet thinks. In chapter 11, according to the omniscient narrator of *TLS*:

> Katherine's experiments had produced astonishing results, particularly in the last six months, breakthroughs that would alter entire paradigms of thinking. Katherine and her brother had agreed to keep her results absolutely secret until the implications were more fully understood. One day soon, however, Katherine knew she would publish some of the most transformative scientific revelations in human history.

In later chapters, Katherine notes that "We have barely scratched the surface of our mental and spiritual capabilities," and that "Experiments at facilities like the Institute of Noetic Sciences (IONS) in California and the Princeton Engineering Anomalies Research Lab (PEAR) had categorically proven that human thought, if properly focused, had the ability to affect and change *physical* mass." She mentions how random event generators became less random after the terrorist attacks on 9/11 caused much of the world to come together in response to a shared tragedy, and how she finds Lynne McTaggart's book *Intention Experiment* fascinating. In chapter 15, we hear further that:

The most astonishing aspect of Katherine's work, however, had been the realization that the mind's ability to affect the physical world could be *augmented* through practice. Intention was a *learned* skill. Like meditation, harnessing the true power of "thought" required practice. More important . . . some people were born more skilled at it than others. And throughout history, there had been those few who had become true masters.

This is the missing link between modern science and ancient mysticism.

The search for the place where science and religion meet has deep roots. Pierre Teilhard de Chardin, a young French Jesuit, found inspiration in exploring the connection between theology and evolution in the early part of the twentieth century. He promoted a concept he called le Tout (the All) that explored the interrelatedness of everything in the universe and the constant change that took place within this universe. He once wrote, "The life of Christ mingles with the life-blood of evolution." He believed that the allegories in the Bible and the evidence provided by science of the earth's history were compatible, observing that, while evolution was in his opinion irrefutable, life evolved in a fashion too orderly to be simply a matter of natural selection. Perhaps Teilhard's most enduring contribution to this conversation is his conception of the "noosphere," a collective consciousness, essentially a thinking planet that rose from mankind's evolution and the evolution of the world around him. He also envisaged the "Omega Point," a theory of evolution as arriving at some eventual, godlike place.

Around the same time Teilhard was making his breakthroughs, Duncan MacDougall, an American doctor, was attempting some breakthroughs of his own. MacDougall believed he could use science to prove the existence of the soul. He posited that the soul had physical mass, and therefore could be measured by noting the weight loss that took place the instant a person died (the moment when the soul presumably left the body). In 1907, he built a special bed in his office, set it on a finely calibrated scale, and then placed dying volunteers on it, waiting for the moment they expired. MacDougall had made accommodations in advance for normal fluctuations in body weight, so he was convinced that any drop that came in the moment of death would be the weight of the soul. He conducted the experiment six times, concluding that the soul weighed approximately twenty-one grams. He then ran a similar experiment on fifteen dogs (the assumption being that animals didn't have souls) and determined that none of these dogs experienced any measurable weight loss.

MacDougall published his work quickly, though his sample size was extremely small. The scientific establishment assailed him equally quickly. They pointed to the inconsistency of his findings: in fact, only one body measured by MacDougall lost twenty-one grams. Another lost fourteen, yet another forty-five, and a third actually gained weight initially. MacDougall threw out one trial because he'd failed to adjust the scales properly and another because the subject died on the bed before MacDougall and his associates had completed all the necessary adjustments. In spite of these inconsistencies, MacDougall maintained his position that the soul weighed twenty-one grams. And, somehow, this turn-of-the-century urban legend persists to this day, even finding a foundational place in Alejandro González Iñárritu's feature film *21 Grams* (starring Naomi Watts, Sean Penn, and Benicio del Toro), as well as a recent song by Aerosmith guitarist Joe Perry titled "Oh Lord (21 grams)."

In *The Lost Symbol*, Katherine Solomon conducts a high-tech version of this experiment, utilizing a high-precision microbalance and an airtight plastic pod in which to rest the dying body. Dan Brown is clearly paying homage to MacDougall with this, though he never mentions the doctor by name, nor does he mention twenty-one grams (chapter 107):

> Moments after the man's death, the numbers on the scale had decreased suddenly. The man had become *lighter* immediately after his death. The weight change was minuscule, but it was measurable . . . and the implications were utterly mind-boggling.
>
> Katherine recalled writing in her lab notes with a trembling hand: "There seems to exist an invisible 'material' that exits the human body

at the moment of death. It has quantifiable mass which is unimpeded by physical barriers. I must assume it moves in a dimension I cannot yet perceive."

From the expression of shock on her brother's face, Katherine knew he understood the implications. "Katherine . . ." he stammered, blinking his gray eyes as if to make sure he was not dreaming. "I think you just weighed the human soul."

Noetic science gained tremendous momentum—and its name—in the early seventies, literally from a cosmic source. Astronaut Edgar Mitchell was a member of the crew of *Apollo 14* that embarked on a nine-day mission including two days on the surface of the moon. As dazzled as Mitchell was by his extraterrestrial jaunt, the return trip turned out to be truly life-changing. A view of the earth from space struck him with a sense that everything was connected in ways he'd never understood before. "The presence of divinity became almost palpable," Mitchell was quoted as saying, "and I knew that life in the universe was not just an accident based on random processes. . . . The knowledge came to me directly."

From that moment, Mitchell became committed to seeking deeper truths than his scientific training had afforded him up to that point. He believed that he needed to explore the inner space of consciousness with as much passion as he had explored outer space, and that accessing a new combination of empirical and conjectural (at least from a hard-science perspective) would lead to a new understanding of our universe. He sought to create a laboratory for exploring the "inner world of human experience" with the same attention to detail with which others explored the sciences that propelled him to the moon.

In 1973, Mitchell helped found the Institute of Noetic Sciences (IONS), the real-life institute referred to by name in *TLS*. The term *noetic* derives from the Greek word *noesis* and was defined by philosopher William James more than a century ago as "states of insight into depths of truth unplumbed by the discursive intellect. They are illuminations, revelations, full of significance and importance, all inarticulate though they remain; and as a rule they carry with them a curious sense of authority."

IONS, located in Petaluma, California, has sponsored hundreds of projects (its Web site lists "a comprehensive bibliography on the physical and psychological effects of meditation, an extensive spontaneous remission bibliography, and studies on the efficacy of compassionate intention on healing in AIDS patients" among these), has nearly thirty thousand members, and has three hundred associated community groups around the world. Said former president of IONS Willis Harman,

> For the first time there is hope that this knowledge can become not a secret repeatedly lost in dogmatization and institutionalization, or degenerating into manifold varieties of cultism and occultism, but rather the living heritage of all humankind. In part, at least, we are dealing here with the rediscovery of truths that in some sense have been discovered over and over again, and have left their track in the culture more rapidly than in the scientific community.

This, of course, is in synch with the fictional work Katherine Solomon is doing in Pod 5 at the Smithsonian Museum Support Center. As encouraged by her brother, Katherine has become a scholar of both cutting-edge science (entanglement theory, superstring theory, etc.) and ancient wisdom (the Zohar, the Kybalion, and translations of Sumerian tablets from the British Museum, among others). She thinks very much like a member of IONS, and she name-checks the organization in several places.

As she does Lynne McTaggart. By all indications, Dan Brown did not know McTaggart personally when he was writing *The Lost Symbol*, yet he's made Katherine Solomon—at least partially—in her image. McTaggart (interviewed in this chapter) is approximately the same age as Solomon, has the same color hair, and has published two bestsellers on noetic science. Solomon has conducted several of the experiments that McTaggart chronicles in her books *The Field* and *The Intention Experiment*, and is very actively involved in the intention work that forms the foundation of

McTaggart's current pursuits. In the kind of thing that can happen only in a certain type of fiction (thriller writers and graphic novelists seem to have cornered the market on this), Katherine Solomon seems at once to *be* Lynne McTaggart and to be McTaggart's *successor*. She references McTaggart while at the same time claiming to do things that McTaggart has done, but also claims to have taken her work to entirely new levels.

Lynne McTaggart had already established herself as an award-winning investigative journalist with her books *The Baby Brokers* and *What Doctors Don't Tell You,* the latter of which I had the pleasure of publishing when I was publisher of Avon Books. In the late nineties, she started examining the work of the scientists researching the existence of the Zero Point Field (a theoretical energy field that connects everything in the universe). This led her to write *The Field,* whose opening paragraph will sound very familiar to anyone who has read *The Lost Symbol:*

> We are poised on the brink of a revolution—a revolution as daring and profound as Einstein's discovery of relativity. At the very frontier of science new ideas are emerging that challenge everything we believe about how our world works and how we define ourselves. Discoveries are being made that prove what religion has always espoused: that human beings are far more extraordinary than an assemblage of flesh and bones. At its most fundamental, this new science answers questions that have perplexed scientists for hundreds of years. At its most profound, this is a science of the miraculous.

McTaggart followed *The Field* with a book even more ambitious and more distinctive in its conceit. *The Intention Experiment* sought to prove, through the exploration of the work of scientists at leading institutions, that thoughts could have a real effect on the world. In the book, she invites readers to come to her Web site (her Web traffic has grown exponentially since the release of *The Lost Symbol*) to become part of the ongoing research in this area. Using the Web site, McTaggart brings together large groups of people from all over the world to focus their thoughts on a variety of benevolent pursuits. She has weekly "intentions" directed at individuals in need of help, and less frequent wide-scale intentions directed at huge problems like combatting pollution, Alzheimer's, and ADD. She believes that her Peace Intention Experiment might have had a direct impact on bringing peace to regions of Sri Lanka. She holds these experiments under lab-controlled conditions, and engages physicists and psychologists from the University of Arizona, Princeton University, the International Institute of Biophysics, Cambridge University, and others.

Lynne McTaggart is not the only person who sees herself in Katherine Solomon. Marilyn Schlitz, the current president of IONS, noted in a recent blog post, "short of olive-colored skin, long hair, a wealthy family, and a crazy sociopath pursuing her, there are some exceptional similarities in our mutual bios." Schlitz, who also makes a contribution in this book, notes that a paper she published on remote viewing drew the attention of the CIA (referenced in the novel), and that she, too, has conducted intention experiments, that she has run experiments regarding the impact of intention on random number generators and on water, and that she has done extensive research on entanglement theory, string theory, complexity, and other areas that Katherine Solomon also pursues. Her lab at IONS is an electromagnetically shielded room very similar to Katherine's Cube, and two wealthy patrons donated the room and the equipment in it. "I've even presented this work at the Smithsonian Institution, including a discussion of ancient lore about biofields and subtle energies," Schlitz notes. "Like Katherine, my work is dedicated to bridging science and ancient wisdom. It is at the interface of these two ways of knowing reality where we believe great breakthroughs lie."

Another noetic scientist who plays a prominent role in this subplot but doesn't receive any mention by name is Masaru Emoto. In several places in *The Lost Symbol*, reference is made to experiments which show that concentrated thought has an impact on water molecules. The most famous of such experiments in the world outside Dan Brown's fiction are those conducted by Emoto and chronicled in his wildly popular books, *Messages from Water* and *The Hidden Messages in Water*, among others. Emoto photographed newly formed water crystals that had been exposed by concentrated thought to loving words (for example, *love, gratitude, thank you*), angry thoughts (*Adolf Hitler, demon*), and beautiful music (Beethoven's *Pastorale*, "Amazing Grace"). The water exposed to positive messages formed jewel-like, proportional crystals, while the water exposed to negative messages formed jagged, scarred crystals. Emoto, a bestselling author who lectures around the world, believes this offers proof that our thoughts have a dramatic impact on the physical world around us.

Another figure referenced yet unnamed in *The Lost Symbol* is Dr. Gary Schwartz, a psychologist at the University of Arizona. In the novel, Katherine mentions that she has used CCD (charge-coupled device) cameras to show the energy coming from a healer's hands. CCD cameras are cooled to minus 100 degrees centigrade to take images of biophoton emissions. In his 2006 paper, "Research Findings at the University of Arizona Center for Frontier Medicine in Biofield Science: A Summary Report," Dr. Schwartz, director of that center, offers CCD photographs of precisely this.

Many people encountered the concepts of noetics for the first time in the 2004 film *What the #$*! Do We (K)now!?* (*What the Bleep Do We Know!?*), which was rereleased in an expanded version in 2006 called *What the Bleep!?: Down the Rabbit Hole*. The film, which featured both Emoto and, in the expanded version, McTaggart, was a lavishly produced part story/part documentary that followed a woman named Amanda (played by Marlee Matlin) on an unanticipated quest for enlightenment. Her quest exposes her to great secrets and changes her life forever. To underscore Amanda's discoveries, fourteen experts on everything from quantum mechanics to string theory to psychic phenomena act as what the filmmakers call a "Greek chorus" to drive home the message that science and religion are pointing in the same direction and that the universe has many more possibilities than most of us have acknowledged.

What the Bleep was a surprise hit by documentary standards (though it was also a surprise *documentary* by documentary standards, since it includes quite a bit of narrative). It did well at the box office and phenomenally in ongoing DVD sales and rentals. (An interview with the producer, script writer, and director of the film, William Arntz, is also in this chapter.)

What the Bleep moved the conversation about noetics away from the

New Age fringes and toward the mainstream. *What the Bleep* viewing parties popped up all around the country, and the film gained the kind of cocktail-party-chatter status that other works on this subject had never generated before. It was in wide circulation in the same 2004 to 2005 period that Dan Brown's *Da Vinci Code* continued to dominate the bestseller lists and the audience for *The Da Vinci Code* and *What the Bleep* had a high degree of overlap. The scientific community has been largely dismissive of noetics; so dismissive, in fact, that it is difficult to find scientists who consider themselves pure scientists who will even acknowledge that noetics is a legitimate field of study. The overwhelming criticism of noetic experiments is that they fail to hold up to the rigors of the scientific method. Because this is the case, most noetic researchers base their conclusions on observation, and they conclude their findings on the selection of a particular event in a study rather than the consistent appearance of that event. Masaru Emoto, for instance, has been repeatedly unwilling to share details of his methods with the scientific community. He is known to select particular photographs because they confirm his hypothesis and has resisted exhortations to subject his experiments to double-blind testing. Institutes such as the U.S. National Academy of Sciences have also commented on the lack of scientific evidence in the claims of parapsychology (a field analogous to noetics).

Perhaps the most significant blow to the legitimacy of noetic science was the closing of the Princeton Engineering Anomalies Research program (PEAR). In *TLS*, we are told by Dan Brown that experiments at PEAR "had categorically proven" that human thought, if properly focused, could affect and change physical mass, a claim most skeptical scientists would find preposterous. PEAR's work is treated with reverence in *TLS*, with Brown, Langdon, and the Solomons apparently unaware that PEAR was terminated as a Princeton project in 2007. According to a press release from the university, PEAR conducted an "experimental agenda of studying the interaction of human consciousness with sensitive physical devices, systems, and processes, and developing complementary theoretical models to enable better understanding of the role of consciousness in the establishment of physical reality." But it fell under regular criticism from academics. Most damning, though, was the limited impact of the results it claimed. After conducting millions of trials on intention, they concluded that intention could have an impact on two or three events out of *ten thousand*. Robert L. Park, a former executive director of the American Physical Society, said of PEAR, "It's been an embarrassment to science, and I think an embarrassment for Princeton. Science has a substantial amount of credibility, but this is the kind of thing that squanders it."

Ultimately, though, it comes back around to Arthur Clarke's observation. If noetics is in fact a "sufficiently advanced technology," then perhaps the naysayers are wrong in dismissing it. Centuries from now, maybe people will look back on the scientific community's unwillingness to accept the findings of noetic science as an egregious case of small-mindedness.

On Becoming a Fictional Character in a Dan Brown Novel

by Marilyn Mandala Schlitz

Dan Brown loves to base his characters on real people. Though he name-checks Lynne McTaggart in the field of noetics, Katherine Solomon's closest living equivalent may equally be Marilyn Mandala Schlitz, the daughter of a Freemason, a scientist by training, and president of the nonfictional Institute of Noetic Sciences (IONS). Schlitz says that she was not in touch with Dan Brown during the research stage of the book.

IONS, based in Petaluma, California, was cofounded in 1973 by former *Apollo 14* astronaut Edgar Mitchell and other like-minded people who "felt the need for an expanded, more inclusive view of reality" than contemporary science was willing to explore. Its mission, "to expand our understanding of human possibility by investigating aspects of reality—mind, consciousness, and spirit—that include but go beyond physical phenomena," is echoed in Katherine's research in the novel.

Schlitz has worked on many of the same studies and experiments as the fictional Katherine. She has even conducted tests from an electromagnetically shielded room, which she now refers to as "the Cube." Here, the Institute of Noetic Sciences president gives her version of what she (and Katherine) are trying to achieve.

Out of the blue my colleagues and I have become part of the plotline in *The Lost Symbol*. The lead, Katherine Solomon, is a noetic scientist with whom I can relate. Indeed, short of olive-colored skin, long hair, a wealthy family, and a crazy sociopath pursuing her, there are some exceptional similarities in our mutual bios.

I begin with a theme that pervades *The Lost Symbol:* the Masons. Both my father and brother were 32° Masons and members of the Scottish Rite. They both learned mysterious symbols that could not be shared with me, despite my many probing questions. My father wore the iconic Masonic ring, which was passed down to my brother after his death, just as it was in the character Katherine's family.

As noetic scientists, Katherine and I share a mutual fascination with the powers and potential of consciousness, and we have both pursued careers well outside the mainstream.

As president/CEO of the Institute of Noetic Sciences, I know the value and the urgency of our studies, as well as the complexity of explaining our work to the world. For both of us, noetic science is a multidisciplinary approach that seeks to understand the role that consciousness plays in the physical world, and how understanding consciousness can lead to creative new solutions to age-old problems. We have been inspired by breakthroughs that were sourced through intuition and inner knowing and expressed through reason and logic. We believe that consciousness matters.

Like Katherine, my career began at nineteen. And early on, my mentor was a neurophysiologist who introduced me to ancient Egyptian texts and modern scientific views of consciousness. As an undergraduate at Montieth College, Wayne State University, I read Newton, Ptolemy, Pythagoras, and Copernicus, as well as on spiritualism, theosophy, parapsychology, and comparative religion. Like Katherine, I was looking for ways to broker a paradigm shift for our modern age.

I began as an experimental parapsychologist, studying the interface of mind and matter. I published my first paper on remote viewing in 1979; this attracted members of the CIA/DIA (Defense Intelligence Agency) team doing classified work on psychic phenomena. Years later

I gained security clearance through my work in the Cognitive Sciences Laboratory at SAIC (Science Applications International Corporation), a large government-sponsored research site where I conducted research on mind over matter. Throughout the past three decades, I have conducted laboratory-based and clinical studies involving distant intention, prayer, altered states of consciousness, contemplative practice, subtle energies, and healing. Like the Noetic Sciences program in *The Lost Symbol*, my experimental research has included studies of distant intention on living systems, including microorganisms, mice, and human physiology. My research on distant mental influences on living systems (DMILS) has been replicated in laboratories around the world, moving it beyond fiction and into peer-reviewed journals.

I conducted RNG-PK (random generator) experiments in the mid-1980s with Helmut Schmidt, the physicist who developed this research area. In our published report, we found that intention and attention appeared to have an impact on the outcome of random event generators, or what can be thought of as electronic coin flippers. In particular, we found that meditation practitioners did better than the average population on shifting randomness. I'm pleased to note that Katherine confirmed our findings.

Several years ago, I convened the first international meeting of the global consciousness project at the Institute of Noetic Sciences. We were able to establish a network of random generators around the world that allowed us to extend our laboratory research into the field and track the role of collective attention on the creation of order from randomness.

As we have sought to gain a theoretical understanding of our noetic science data, my colleagues and I consulted experts in the area of quantum theory. I learned from the best, including Brian Josephson; Richard Feynman; Hans Peter Duerr; Roger Penrose; Henry Stapp; and IONS founder Edgar Mitchell, among others. In addition to research on entanglement and nonlocality, I continue to track complexity, emergence, and string theory, research areas that have also been central to Katherine's studies.

Our laboratory at the Institute of Noetic Sciences includes a two-thousand-pound electromagnetically shielded room, which we now affectionately refer to as "the Cube." Two wealthy patrons donated funds to build our lab, believing we are on the verge of a breakthrough. In it, my colleague Dean Radin and I have conducted studies of intuition, gut reactions to distant emotional stimuli, order in randomness, the role of intention on water crystals, and the potential nonlocal nature of nondual consciousness, all topics that have been considered in *The Lost Symbol*. I've published the results in my two main books, *Consciousness and Healing* and *Living Deeply*, and in many journal articles (just as Katherine has done). I've even presented this work at the Smithsonian Institution, including a discussion of ancient lore about biofields and subtle energies.

Like Katherine, my work is dedicated to bridging science and ancient wisdom. It is at the interface of these two ways of knowing reality where we believe great breakthroughs lie. In our detailed study of consciousness transformation, we studied practitioners from sixty different transformative traditions, some ancient and some modern. Bringing the lens of science to these diverse practices, we identified the factors that stimulate, support, and sustain positive changes.

IONS has also sponsored research and conferences on the potential survival of consciousness after bodily death. We have studied cross-cultural cosmologies of the afterlife and collaborated with Ian Stevenson and others on reincarnation and mediumship. As I have written in several publications, the fact of our mortality and what happens when we die are critical issues as we seek a path to peace within ourselves and across cultures.

Katherine and I share a deep commitment to the positive unfolding of life on our planet. Like the final message in *The Lost Symbol*, I believe that human beings are poised on the threshold of a new age; noetic science may help lead the way.

Bending Minds, Not Spoons

an interview with William Arntz

The power of thought to transform water molecules. The mind's ability to alter the material world. The promise of an alternate spirituality that unites all mankind. Yes, it's *The Lost Symbol*, but they're also the main ideas behind the sleeper-hit documentary film *What the Bleep Do We Know!?* Released at about the same time as Dan Brown's earlier bestseller, *The Da Vinci Code*, it almost certainly was a source of inspiration for this latest novel.

What the Bleep Do We Know!? was conceived, funded, and codirected by William Arntz, a research physicist-turned-Buddhist-turned-software-developer-turned-filmmaker. Released in February 2004, the film has been shown in more than thirty-five countries and has grossed more than $10 million.

What the Bleep explores the intersecting worlds of quantum physics and spirituality. It features documentary-style interviews with specialists in fields such as physics, neuroscience, molecular biology, anesthesiology, and psychiatry. It explores a range of hypotheses, including multiple universes, an alternate definition of consciousness, and the power of human thought. Here, Arntz talks about the parallels between his film and the ideas of *The Lost Symbol*.

What did you make of The Lost Symbol*?*

The message he is conveying is great. And I am familiar with many of the ideas he explores because they are very similar to what I was doing in *What the Bleep*.

You and Dan Brown both seem to have an interest in the merging of science and religion.

I have a degree in physics and my first job was as a laser physicist. Then I did a lot of spiritual study. Science has pushed far enough now to start verifying a lot of these ideas.

And you and Dan Brown are both fascinated with noetics.

Yes. I, too, believe there are serious scientists looking at the most interesting and pressing questions of today, both from a scientific point of view and also from a metaphysical or spiritual point of view. What would happen if people really knew that the concentrated attention of our minds can move matter? What if praying for someone does help cure them? Such abilities could have immense ramifications around the world.

And yet many people, including the character Robert Langdon, remain skeptical.

We got a lot of grief from journalists for *What the Bleep*. But by far the largest group of critics was scientists. They hated it. They were outraged: "How dare you do this? You know you're not properly credentialed!" It was like priests saying in the Middle Ages, "How can you talk about this? You're not ordained as a priest, you can't speak Latin, so you can't talk about it!"

But if you look at the history of science, this always happens. When you read about Einstein first publishing his theories, a lot of his critics didn't attack his work scientifically, they just said, "Who would believe a patent clerk from Switzerland?" And basically that's what they did with *What the Bleep*.

What about the criticism that noetics and other related fields do not stand up to the same rigorous tests as, for want of a better phrase, "real science"?

In the early days, I think a lot of claims were made that just seemed kind of crazy. But today it's much better. I've read reports and seen studies and it's very, very rigorous. For example, Bill Tiller, a professor emeritus at Stanford, has done experiments in which four mediators, people with very focused minds, change the pH of water by using the power of thought. That's unheard of. He has also changed the reproduction rate of fruit fly larvae. Tiller backs this up with a whole bunch of mathematics to explain what's going on. It's really fascinating stuff.

Then why does so much skepticism remain?

One of the weird things about noetics is that the person running the experiment has an effect on the experiment. I think they call it the "garage effect." In other words, you have a scientist working in his or her garage, and he's able to have this amazing thing happen. But when someone else comes in to replicate the experiment, it doesn't work. And then the original scientist comes back and runs the experiment, and it does work.

In the materialistic scientific model, the person running the experiment is immaterial, because the assumption is that there's nothing an observer can do that is going to affect the experiment. But as soon as you cross over to noetics, the person running the experiment can have a profound effect, even though there's no "physical interaction." So this causes a lot of trouble when people try to replicate these experiments, especially if the skeptics get there and the experiment doesn't work for them.

One of the most memorable experiments Brown mentions in The Lost Symbol *is the one in which water molecules are changed by using the power of thought.*

Distilling water is like erasing the memory on a hard drive; distilled water has no form or shape. Masaru Emoto, who is featured in *What the Bleep*, takes distilled water samples and has people focus intention on them. Then he takes the water and freezes it in a certain way. He looks at it through a microscope, in a lab that's something like ten degrees below zero, and watches the crystals form in different patterns based upon the mental input.

Are there any other noetic studies not in the novel that you would have liked to have seen in The Lost Symbol?

I probably would have mentioned that IONS (Institute of Noetic Sciences) has been running "sending and receiving" experiments. I have taken part in one of these. They locked me in a room that's about a five- or ten-ton cube, about ten feet tall, resting on shock absorbers. It's like a huge Faraday cage, completely isolated from everything. And then they mark someone one hundred yards away and we're both wired up to EEGs. Then someone has a thought and the other person responds. We actually filmed this experiment and included it in an extended, five-hour version of our film, called *What the Bleep!?: Down the Rabbit Hole.*

Describing some of these experiments in just a little more detail would have let people know that this isn't just a bunch of people trying to bend spoons. It's really serious scientists going to great lengths to make sure their procedures are impeccable.

One area in which you push the envelope further than Dan Brown did is the concept of parallel universes.

I can see why he wouldn't touch that one, because it's a theory that is still quite experimental. There's also a multiuniverse theory, where for every decision that's made, both sides of the decision happen and the universe splits in half. Then there's past-life regression. Some of the past-life regression studies are amazing. For example, a four-year-old will start speaking in a dialect from a place in Asia, where it hasn't been used since the nineteenth century. He or she describes life in the village, and all this kind of stuff. But there are forces out there that really don't want you to talk about past lives.

In *What the Bleep* we included interviews with Ramtha, who claims to be someone from thirty-five thousand years ago who is channeled through this woman J. Z. Knight. By including him in the film we are saying, "Look, there is more to reality than just the physical." If you have a being that can communicate through someone else's body, that means we're not our bodies. And as soon as you say that we're not our bodies, that completely blows open the whole perspective about scientific materialism that says reality is only what we perceive with our senses.

It reminds me of the passages in *The Lost Symbol* where you think that Langdon has died, where I suppose you could argue he has an out-of-body experience. If you take that in tandem with the idea of Katherine discovering the weight of a human soul, then you get a similar kind of message, albeit in a different way.

Have you met people who have had an out-of-body experience?

Yes, and let me tell you, they're not normal for a while. Their minds have literally been blown, especially if they are skeptics, because their whole worldview has just crumbled. I would have guessed that Langdon, after having all of that happen, would have been a little more melted down, like a newborn baby.

Both What the Bleep *and* The Da Vinci Code *were popular around the same time. Did you notice any parallels between your movie and Dan Brown's novel?*

Definitely. Dan Brown was drawing on information that was already out there. And so were we. It is similar to what Dan talks about in *The Lost Symbol*—this whole idea that what was hidden is now coming to light.

My favorite parallel is the one based on old Celtic culture. The bard was considered a sacred position because he would take wisdom from the priests and communicate it in an artful form to the population. When the bard came to town, all work stopped. Everyone got around the fire and didn't leave until the bard put the harp down. Dan is like a classic bard. He's taking the more esoteric knowledge that's hidden in plain view for everyone and communicating it in such a way that people understand it.

—*Interviewed by Paul Berger*

"Ye Are Gods"

by the Editors

Robert Langdon, in conversation with Reverend Colin Galloway, dean of the Washington National Cathedral, remembers an ancient Hermetic precept this way: "Know ye not that ye are gods?" (chapter 82). Langdon refers to this as "one of the pillars of the Ancient Mysteries" and a "persistent message of man's own divinity" in many ancient texts, including the Bible. The insinuation is that man is God or at least can become God—and that this is what the ancient philosophers, the editors of the Old Testament, and the Freemasons all believe.

This theme is also echoed by Warren Bellamy, Architect of the Capitol and a Mason, when he tells Langdon: "[T]he Ancient Mysteries and Masonic philosophy celebrate the potentiality of God within each of us. Symbolically speaking, one could claim that anything within reach of an enlightened man . . . is within reach of God" (chapter 49). The universality of the assertion of man's inherent divinity is reinforced further in chapter 131, when Peter Solomon gives Langdon a quick rundown of instances in Christianity, Hinduism, Islam, and Buddhism where similar assertions have been made.

Langdon, who elsewhere says he is not much of a Bible scholar (a bit strange for a Harvard professor with an eidetic memory who is so steeped in symbols and their meanings), remembers the phrase from Psalm 82, A Psalm of Asaph:

1 God standeth in the congregation of the mighty; he judgeth among the gods.

2 How long will ye judge unjustly, and accept the persons of the wicked? Selah.

3 Defend the poor and fatherless: do justice to the afflicted and needy.

4 Deliver the poor and needy: rid *them* out of the hand of the wicked.

5 They know not, neither will they understand; they walk on in darkness: all the foundations of the earth are out of course.

6 I have said, <u>Ye *are* gods</u>; and all of you *are* children of the most High.

7 But ye shall die like men, and fall like one of the princes.

8 Arise, O God, judge the earth: for thou shalt inherit all nations.

There are several arguments against commingling the Hermetic injunction, "Know ye not that ye are gods," with the reference "Ye *are* gods," in Psalm 82.

First, most biblical scholars tend to believe that the Psalm's reference is really critiquing those mortal men who have come to see themselves as gods—noting that they will die, just like men. (See Deirdre Good's essay in chapter 5.) Rather than man's inherent divinity, this reference seems to most readers to point to man's hubristic assumption of a god-like role.

Second, this specific passage of Psalms uses "gods"—*elohim* (סיהלא) in Hebrew. While Elohim is one of the many names for God, the fact that it is a plural form has been interpreted to mean "kings," "angels," or, commonly, "judges."

Charles H. Spurgeon, a nineteenth-century Baptist preacher and author of the *Treasury of David*, explained: "To the people of Israel this kind of appellation would not seem over bold: for it was applied to judges in well-known texts of the Law of Moses." The British Methodist theologian Adam Clarke argued that *elohim* refers to man as God's representative on earth imbued with his "power and authority to dispense judgment and justice."

In other words, according to religious scholars, Psalm 82 may refer to man's responsibility on earth to act as a judge, not the Hermetic meaning that divinity lies within man.

Finally, at least some Freemasons have taken issue with Brown's assertion that the inherent divinity of man is a Masonic belief. According to a report on Beliefnet, Most Worshipful Brother Reverend Terry Tilton, a retired Masonic leader from Minnesota, points out, "There can be no real substitute for perfection, the infinite and divine truth. And that is why just because God is God and we are not, human beings can never fully bridge the gulf of understanding and perfection in this world."

As readers of *The Da Vinci Code* know, Dan Brown has a great interest in alternative histories and alternative interpretations. He emphasizes the importance of the Gnostic Gospels over the traditional Gospels. In particular, he has previously called readers' attention to the Gnostic principle that God is interior to us, not exterior, and that through various mystical means, journeys, and truth-seeking, men and women can realize their inner divinity.

While this is, indeed, a view found in some of the Gnostic Gospels such as the Gospel of Thomas (see the outstanding book by Elaine Pagels, *Beyond Belief*), it is not the traditionally expressed view of either the Old Testament or the New Testament. But a Gnostic reading of "Ye are gods" does converge snugly with Dan Brown's plotlines in *The Lost Symbol*. From a Gnostic perspective we are all divine and human at the same time; we are all gods.

Chapter
SEVEN

MYSTERY
CITY ON
THE HILL

A MASONIC PILGRIMAGE
AROUND WASHINGTON, D.C.

by David A. Shugarts

Like *The Da Vinci Code*, which could be read as a tour of Paris, and *Angels & Demons*, which could be read as a tour of Rome, *The Lost Symbol* is, among many other things, a tour of Washington, D.C. The locations visited by the book's characters—the Capitol Rotunda, the Library of Congress, the House of the Temple, the National Cathedral, the Washington Monument—are all noticing an upswing in visitors making their own *Lost Symbol* pilgrimages. David Shugarts, who correctly predicted Dan Brown's use of every single one of these locations in his 2005 book *Secrets of the Widow's Son*, explains what Brown does and does not tell us about these places, all rich with their own mysteries, symbols, and Masonic connections.

Quick, look at the architecture of Washington!

In *The Lost Symbol*, Dan Brown takes us on an extremely abbreviated tour of Washington. The plot-driven novel affords hero Robert Langdon only a few seconds to pause and absorb the significance of any given painting, sculpture, or massive building. Luckily, Langdon always recognizes the meaning and history of everything he sees. Or does he?

In a city full of art and architectural treasures, it's a very short list of stops. Disregarding the Smithsonian Museum Support Center in Maryland, which isn't open for public tours, the action of *The Lost Symbol* is confined to just a handful of cinematic settings in public buildings in the District: the Capitol, the Washington Monument, the Library of Congress, the U.S. Botanical Garden, the National Cathedral. And there's one building owned by the Freemasons: the House of the Temple.

The Lincoln Memorial, Jefferson Memorial, the "Castle" that is the original home of the Smithsonian Institution, are merely covered in quick descriptions from afar. Langdon and the book's female lead, Katherine Solomon, never actually visit any of these places. And there are innumerable fascinating places that Dan Brown might have utilized but didn't— the Albert Pike statue in Judiciary Square, honoring the prime mover of Freemasonry in the nineteenth century, being a notable example.

A Masonic connection ties together most of the buildings they do visit. In 1793, George Washington led a parade up to the site of the new Capitol Building and laid its cornerstone. Washington presided in the ceremony in his Freemason's apron; offered the Masonic libations of corn, wine, and oil; and used a special trowel to spread the mortar. The silver trowel, with an ivory handle, had been specially made for the occasion by Masons.

The same silver trowel would be used on many, many similar occasions for the next two centuries. It was used to lay the cornerstones of the Washington Monument, the National Cathedral, the Library of Congress, and the House of the Temple. The trowel was also used at the George Washington National Masonic Memorial, in Alexandria, Virginia, a spot that Robert Langdon uses as a diversion but didn't visit in the story. That's in fact where the trowel resides today, kept by Washington's old lodge, Alexandria Lodge 22. (A tour guide at this location acknowledges that the museum staff wish they had received an actual visit from Langdon in the story, instead of being used as a mere diversion, although they were initially worried that their 333-foot-tall tower might have been used as a backdrop for a murder.)

Washington's trowel was also used at the Jefferson Memorial, the U.S.

Supreme Court, the Department of Commerce, the National Education Building, the U.S Post Office Building, and the State Department Building, just to name the highlights. (There was also a Masonic ceremony in 1790 for the cornerstone of the White House, called the President's House at the time, but Washington was not present and the trowel hadn't been created yet.) Thus, it seems as though the Masons did have an ever-present hand in building the nation's capital, even if it was only a ceremonial hand.

But the real question is, what is Masonic about the architecture? Since there are so many Masonic forms and symbols that come from other traditions, it's hard to say which are exclusively Masonic. There are a lot of great architects who turn out to be Masons, and the role of geometric principles, the use of light, and allusions to classic Greek, Roman, and Egyptian civilizations in Masonry certainly play a role in their thinking.

Masons often use motifs of squares and circles, for instance, and a checkerboard floor is one of the most common features of a Masonic lodge. There are lots of squares, circles, and checkerboards in the floors of Washington's great buildings. Masons love shapes like triangles (right triangles or equilateral) and stars. They love stars with five points or six (or seven or eight or nine). They like spheres and cubes, or almost any geometric shape, including pyramids, which do show up in a lot of Masonic buildings. But they also admire the classical orders of columns, such as the Doric, Ionic, and Corinthian, which are found throughout Washington. Symbols of light, of illuminating knowledge, and of enlightenment, are greatly cherished by Masons, but also good use of light is a technique employed by most architects.

There are lots of symbols and symbolic references in the architecture of Washington. But these symbols are very old, and, in most cases, the Masons did not create them but merely adopted or chose to emphasize them. The signs of the Zodiac, as well as depictions of Greek and Roman gods, can be found all over Washington's architecture and art, but these are not the exclusive work of Masonic architects and artists.

One of the archetypal classical structures to keep in mind is the Pantheon of Rome, built as a temple where the people could worship multiple gods, rather than just one. A feature of the Pantheon is a round hole in the dome called an oculus that lets in light from above. It literally represents the all-seeing eye of heaven. In *Angels & Demons*, the Pantheon in Rome figured as a stop on that plot's tour. And in *TLS*, Dan Brown refers (often in a factually muddled way) to oculi eleven times and pantheons ten times.

One of the themes held in common by Freemasonry and by the architecture of Washington is an attempt to go beyond differences between religions by tolerating all religions. Freemasons accept any man who believes in a supreme being but they avoid debate about specific deities. By avoiding overtly religious symbols (e.g., a crucifix), but accepting classical Greek and Roman gods, the architectural tradition of Washington aims to achieve the same thing. Separation of church and state is an American inheritance from the deists who were the Founding Fathers in the Age of Enlightenment. Not all deists are Masons and not all Masons are deists, but there is a strong connection and frequent overlap.

Amid his scurrying to different stops in *TLS*, Langdon slowly peels the layers of this onion.

In *TLS*, Langdon is told first to report to the Capitol. His entry comes through the new Capitol Visitor Center, still under construction, which takes him underground and thus he cannot take any note of dozens of sculptures and reliefs on the east face of the building. He does get a glimpse of the dome towering above, and remarks on the Statue of Freedom that adorns the dome. There is a vast wealth of art in the Capitol, but Langdon is in a rush to report to the National Statuary Hall, and doesn't stop to gaze. "Normally, Langdon would have taken a full hour in here to admire the architecture," writes Dan Brown in *TLS*.

Langdon recollects correctly that the National Statuary Hall was once the Hall of the House of Representatives, but doesn't remark on the specifics of the many statues there. The statues are a collection that was assembled over the years from 1864 onward, when each state was invited to send two statues of their favorite sons. Statues of William Jennings Bryant, or Sam Houston, or even Will Rogers were sent. But the hall was not large enough to hold so many statues, so in 1933, when it was already overcrowded with sixty-five of them and their weight was endangering the structure, they were distributed to various other rooms and corridors. Today, only about thirty-five statues, out of a full collection of one hundred, remain in the hall itself. Interestingly, states are allowed to make substitutions, so in 2003 Kansas put in President Dwight Eisenhower instead of George Washington Glick, and in 2009, California swapped President Ronald Reagan for Thomas Starr King. A few favorite daughters have begun to show up as well.

But Langdon can't tarry in the Statuary Hall; he must hurry to the next scene, in the Capitol Rotunda.

Dan Brown abbreviates the Rotunda to emphasize its high and low points. He basically directs the reader's attention to the floor and to the ceiling, missing out on the rest of the art-filled room. He reveals that there was once a hole in the floor, and he focuses on the fresco overhead, Constantino Brumidi's *Apotheosis of Washington*, with its collection of Roman goddesses in odd contexts, accompanying George Washington as he ascends to become a deity.

"There are symbols all over this room that reflect a belief in the Ancient Mysteries," Langdon instructs Sato and Anderson early in the book. And Sato, on cue, replies that what Langdon is highlighting "hardly fits with the Christian underpinnings of this country" (for more detail on the *Apotheosis of Washington*, see "The Clues Hidden in Circles and Squares" in chapter 8).

But Brown is being highly selective in what he chooses to reveal to readers about the Rotunda. What is being overlooked? Well, the walls are lined with eight giant paintings, including the *Declaration of Independence* by John Trumbull, and others depicting scenes from American history. Each painting is eighteen feet wide and twelve feet tall. There are many statues of Washington, Lincoln, and Jefferson, not to mention James Garfield and Ulysses S. Grant; there is a bust of Dr. Martin Luther King Jr. The visitor eager to get the broader Masonic tour of the Capitol will want to know that Vinnie Ream is the sculptor of the Lincoln statue—Ream was a friend and disciple of Albert Pike and was the first woman to receive a commission for a sculpture from the U.S. Congress.

Above the paintings and entrances are stone sculpture reliefs, representing early explorers and historic American events. In a band that is fifty-eight feet above the floor, an eight-foot-high frieze circles beneath the dome's windows. The frieze is almost three hundred feet in circumference and includes nineteen scenes, such as "The Landing of Columbus," "William Penn and the Indians," and "The Birth of Aviation."

Thus, even though Dan Brown only uses the Rotunda to underline certain pagan allusions, such as goddesses on the ceiling and the notion of apotheosis—man becoming god—the real sense and purpose of the room is to depict the march of American history.

Brown is also inventive about the room's own history. He says the Rotunda was designed as a tribute to the Temple of Vesta in Rome. (Vesta, goddess of the hearth, had an eternal hearth fire burning in her temple.) Brown says there was a hole in the center of the Rotunda floor in order for visitors to see an eternal flame in the crypt below, which he implies was kept burning for fifty years.

However, most authorities say the Rotunda was actually modeled after the Pantheon of Rome, not the Temple of Vesta. The spurious reference to Vesta, however, allows Brown to work in an allusion to the vestal virgins, important priestesses in ancient Rome, and a throwback to Brown's emphasis on the role of the sacred feminine in *The Da Vinci Code*. Also, the details of the Rotunda's construction phases do not bear out the notion that it had the hole and the flame for fifty years. In the early stages of the Capitol construction, it was planned that George Washington's remains would rest in the crypt. A hole was constructed when the Rotunda was first completed in 1827, so that visitors could (someday) gaze upon his tomb. But the Washington family would not consent to move his remains there, and the plan was abandoned.

By 1832, the hole was filled in, because of a new plan to place a statue of Washington in the center of the Rotunda. This statue, the rather amazing Horatio Greenough sculpture of Washington as Zeus, was eventually installed in 1841. But it was unpopular and its weight of twelve tons began to crack the floor, so it was moved out onto the Capitol's lawn and then became a white elephant. Eventually, it ended up in its current home, the National Museum of American History.

Langdon pauses to relate the tale of the Washington/Zeus statue. Then Langdon is descending into the labyrinthine Capitol basement via the crypt, with the book noting in passing the statues there, as well as the compass set into the floor that marks the center of the numbered street system for the District of Columbia.

In short order, Langdon is rushing through underground corridors and tunnels to the Library of Congress.

The Library of Congress (LOC) originally occupied a portion of the Capitol building and was funded in 1800 by an appropriation of $5,000 for the purchase of books for Congress to use. In the War of 1812, the British burned the Capitol, along with the library, and it was retired President Thomas Jefferson who saved the day, offering his own very large library of 6,487 books to restart the Library of Congress. Even though the LOC by the 1870s was clearly outgrowing the space available in the Capitol, it was not until 1897 that the grand new LOC building was opened to the public. This is now called the Thomas Jefferson Building and two others have been added to the LOC campus, the John Adams Building a block east, and the James Madison Building a block south.

Dan Brown gives a pretty good account of the Great Hall and the Main Reading Room of the LOC. It is incredibly ornate, a rich tapestry of sculpture, paintings, and architectural details. Brown pokes a bit of fun at the odd sculpted cherubs, or *putti*, in the banisters of the staircases of the Great Hall. One is an electrician holding a telephone and another is an entomologist capturing butterflies. Fanciful cherubs were the specialty of the sculptor, Philip Martiny, and his cherubs were part of a theme representing "the various occupations." But Martiny was only a minor artist among some forty or fifty who were commissioned to fill the LOC with hundreds of pieces of art.

Above the Main Reading Room, along the balustrade of the galleries, are sixteen bronze statues, paired to represent eight categories of knowledge. They include everything from Plato and Francis Bacon ("Philosophy") to Beethoven and Michelangelo ("Art"). In a rush, of course, Langdon can only muster a flick of the eyes toward these statues, not even remarking on what they represent. (For more detail on the Library of Congress, see "Hiding Out in Jefferson's Palace of the Book," later in this chapter.)

Getting a very quick passing mention in *TLS* is the Folger Shakespeare Library, just north of the Adams Building. Langdon recognizes that it has a copy of Francis Bacon's *New Atlantis*. The Folger Library has more than 250,000 books, many copies of Shakespeare's plays, manuscripts dating back to Elizabethan times, and even an Elizabethan Theatre. As Dan Brown knows, the library is administered under a trust arrangement by Amherst College, Dan Brown's alma mater. It was a bequest from Henry Clay Folger, a Standard Oil chairman and Amherst graduate.

There's a diversionary reference to the George Washington Masonic National Memorial, across the river in Alexandria, Virginia. The Memorial was created by Freemasons in the twentieth century to honor George Washington's role as the foremost Freemason in American history. Dan Brown gives an extensive description of this structure, even though it does not figure into the plot. Rising 333 feet and crowned by a pyramid with a flamelike finial, it is partially based on the legendary lighthouse in Alexandria, Egypt. The columns of the three major sections of the tower denote the Doric, Ionic, and Corinthian orders admired by the Freemasons. There are actually ten stories within the Memorial, containing many specialized rooms with allegorical scenes dear to Freemasons, including the Temple of Solomon and the Ark of the Covenant. The main floor's Memorial Hall contains a seventeen-foot-tall bronze statue of Washington in Masonic regalia.

But Langdon and Katherine Solomon don't actually arrive at the Memorial, since they are sneaking off to the Washington National Cathedral, in the northwest of the city.

The National Cathedral gets largely condensed in *TLS* into just three special items that figure into a riddle for Langdon to solve as he looks for a place that contains "ten stones from Mount Sinai," one from "heaven itself," and one with the "visage of Luke's dark father." Child's play for

The George Washington National Masonic Memorial (completed in 1932).
(*Photograph by Julie O'Connor*)

Langdon. He solves this riddle instantaneously, since he immediately recalls that in the floor of the National Cathedral near the altar are ten
stones from Mount Sinai; that there is a grotesque of Darth Vader on the
northwest tower; and there is a small piece of an actual moon rock embedded in a stained-glass window, which is known as the "Space Window"
commemorating the astronauts.

These are just tokens, since there are more than two hundred stained-
glass windows, dozens of grotesques and gargoyles, and many special
stones in the vast neogothic cathedral, the sixth largest in the world. For
instance, the altar's stones include some that were brought from Solomon's Quarry, near Jerusalem, where the stones of Solomon's Temple were
said to have been quarried, and the pulpit was carved from stones brought
from England's Canterbury Cathedral. In addition to many religious
scenes, some of the stained-glass windows also depict the Lewis and Clark
expedition, or the raising of the American flag at Iwo Jima.

The cathedral occupies a carefully nurtured place in American life as
"the national house of prayer." It is an Episcopal cathedral but has been
open to congregations of many kinds. Many funerals of state or memorial ceremonies have been held there, including the funerals of President
Ronald Reagan in 2004 and President Gerald Ford in 2007. Although
it seems like an official cathedral, none of its funds, for construction or
operation, come from the government. And although its focus is undeni-
ably Christian, it is also emblematic of the cathedral's attempt to fulfill
a national, ecumenical role. There are statues of Washington and Lincoln, and seals and flags of the fifty states, and many pieces of art that
relate to secular historical events. On sale in the bookshop are a variety
of titles that would please the one-world spiritual vision of Galloway and
the Solomons. These range from the Dalai Lama to the Koran, from the
Gnostics to the noeticists. In the fall of 2009, there was a large display of
The Lost Symbol on sale here.

Langdon eventually finds himself racing to the House of the Temple,
headquarters of the Supreme Council 33°, of the Ancient and Accepted

Scottish Rite of Freemasons, Southern Jurisdiction. Patterned after the Mausoleum of Halicarnassus, this structure is a veritable treasure house of Masonic symbolism and architecture. It is the Scottish Rite that confers Freemasonry's thirty-third degree, so it's no coincidence that the House of the Temple has thirty-three columns, each thirty-three feet tall. It has a pair of massive sphinxes guarding the front stairs, which are built in sets of three, five, seven, and nine steps—numbers significant to Masons—leading to two massive bronze doors weighing twenty-four hundred pounds each. (Although the bronze doors may appear intimidating, the Scottish Rite Freemasons actually accept visitors and conduct regular tours.)

Inside the doors there is a large atrium lined with black marble columns and a staircase leading up to the Temple Room, where much of the action of *TLS* takes place. The roof of the House of the Temple is built as a thirteen-layer pyramid, topped by a square skylight. Dan Brown depicts this skylight as an oculus for dramatic purposes, as a conduit to the heavens. Beneath it is the Temple Room, the centerpiece being an altar. In *TLS*, this is staged as a sacrificial altar, but for the Masons it holds the sacred books of the major religions, such as the Bible, the Old Testament, and the Koran.

The House of the Temple also contains a large library, with many rare books, as well as a special alcove where the remains of Albert Pike are interred. Pike was a lawyer, Civil War general, poet, and scholar who led the Scottish Rite in the late 1800s. There are special rooms dedicated to famous Masons, such as the Founding Fathers, Burl Ives, J. Edgar Hoover, and several U.S. astronauts who were Masons.

———————

In *TLS*, Peter Solomon ends his evening by showing Robert Langdon the views from the top of the Washington Monument. This is staged so that he can reveal the full meaning of the "Masonic Pyramid" and the gold capstone talisman that Langdon has been lugging around all night.

By a very loose interpretation of the structural forms of the Washington Monument, Solomon and Langdon are at the end of their allegorical journey, finding themselves, as called for by all the puzzles and riddles and codes, beneath a pyramidal stone, under which is a "spiral staircase

Detail of the Sphinx statue from the House of the Temple of the Scottish Rite of Freemasonry (completed in 1915). (*Photograph by Julie O'Connor*)

winding down hundreds of feet into the earth, where the lost symbol is buried."

It's true that the top of the monument forms a thirteen-layer pyramid, or pyramidion, the topmost stone being also pyramidal in shape and weighing thirty-three hundred pounds. Capping that is an inscribed one-hundred-ounce pyramid of aluminum, with Brown's oft-mentioned "Laus Deo" inscription on its east face. And it's true there is a staircase, although it doesn't descend "into the earth," but merely to ground level, via 897 steps. Somewhere in the base of the monument is the original cornerstone, its exact location now unknown. In a recess of the cornerstone, we are told by *TLS*, lies the "Lost Word."

Thus Dan Brown works hard to make the pyramidal form carry the symbolic potency. One has to ascend to the top of a 555-foot obelisk to experience its mystical emanations, which somehow are supposed to transmit to the base of the monument, following a variation on the hermetic world view, "As above, so below."

In stretching to make the Washington Monument obelisk into a conceptual pyramid, Dan Brown fails to mention that a pyramid is exactly what was first seriously intended for George Washington's tomb.

While Washington was still alive in the 1790s, it was assumed that a great equestrian statue would be erected to honor him, at approximately the same location where the monument now stands. However, this plan was set aside after his passing in late 1799.

In 1800 Congress resolved to build a mausoleum for him "of American granite and marble in pyramidal form." Thus, if Congress had had its way, George Washington would have been entombed like an Egyptian god-king.

Since Congress never got that plan to work (partly because of lack of funds and partly because the Washington family would not allow Washington's remains to leave Mount Vernon), the stage was set for a long and fitful birth of what would become the mighty obelisk we have today.

Along the way, many designs were proposed and dismissed, including a truly massive pyramid offered by Peter Force in 1837. The pyramid imagined by Congress would have been one hundred feet on a side, but

Washington Monument (completed in 1884). (*Photograph by Julie O'Connor*)

Force's pyramid would have been on the scale of the pyramids of Giza, several hundred feet on a side.

But a pyramid was not to be. In the 1830s when a serious effort was made to get started on the long-discussed monument, the winning design was a combination of a six-hundred-foot obelisk with a nearly flat top, surrounded by a circular colonnade that was intended to house statues of the Founding Fathers. The designer, Robert Mills, called it a "National Pantheon." However, the design was modified over the years and the colonnade was omitted in favor of a very Egyptian obelisk with its pyramidal top.

The cornerstone was laid on July 4, 1848, in a full Masonic ceremony. Construction began, but it was halted in 1856 when only the first 150 feet had been built. The monument then sat as an eyesore for almost three decades until it was finally completed in 1884. At the time, it was the tallest structure in the world, and even today it is the tallest free-standing stone structure.

The monument was funded by donations, and an invitation was made for citizens from all over the country, and many civic organizations, to donate decorative stones that would line the interior walls. Altogether, some 193 stones were eventually installed, to be seen at landings along the stairs. Many of the stones were donated by Freemason groups, but there were plenty of other organizations, such as the Sons of Temperance, the Odd Fellows, and the Order of Red Men. Today, most visitors do not get to see all these stones because the stairs are only open for occasional walk-down trips, but visitors can glimpse some stones through a window in the elevator car.

One stone, known as the "Pope's Stone" because it was sent by the Vatican under Pope Pius IX, was mysteriously stolen in 1854 when it sparked the enmity of the American Party, also called the "Know-Nothings." The Know-Nothings, who were opposed to immigrants and Catholics, viewed the stone as a beachhead for an eventual invasion by the Vatican, and they vowed that it would never become a part of the monument. The stolen stone was never recovered and it may have been smashed to bits or dumped into the Potomac. But in 1982, a replacement stone from the

Vatican was quietly installed at the 440-foot level. Brown references none of this fascinating history, although it is lurking in the shadows of his historic themes.

A big mystery is the location of the Washington Monument's cornerstone. Although it had been laid in a very public ceremony, it became lost from view as the different stages of construction progressed. Thus, no one knows exactly where it is today.

In *TLS*, Dan Brown makes it seem as though a Bible was secretly put into the cornerstone by the Masons as the hidden "Lost Word."

Actually, there were at least fifteen thousand witnesses to the laying of the cornerstone, including then-president James Polk (a Freemason) and many dignitaries. In a zinc case recessed into the 24,500-pound stone was placed a very eclectic collection of many dozens of items that had been contributed by many different groups. There was indeed a Bible, but it was given by the Bible Society (not the Freemasons).

But also, there were nearly two hundred other items, including copies of the Constitution and the Declaration of Independence, a portrait of Washington, all U.S. coins then in use from the ten-dollar gold eagle to the half-dime, an American flag, a copy of the U.S. census from 1790 through 1848, a description of the telegraph machine, a one-cent coin minted in 1783, some almanacs and various nautical maps and charts, not to mention seventy different newspapers from fourteen states. There were many dozens of other odd items, contributed by all kinds of groups and individuals. The entire list of items was not secret at all, but was published during the dedication of the monument. Thus, if the Bible is to be considered the "Lost Word"—lost in the mystery of the missing Washington Monument cornerstone—must we also assume that the "Annual Report of the Comptroller of the State of New York on Tolls, Trade, and Tonnage on the New York Canal System"—just one of the two hundred documents buried in this time capsule—is also a repository of mystical knowledge?

Finally, there's the big picture: Langdon eventually takes a little time to ponder the overall layout of Washington. In one passage Langdon dismisses the theories that the street layout forms satanic pentagrams and other Masonic or arcane symbols. This by itself must be a major disappointment to conspiracy theorists who have long bubbled their wares just below the surface of public consciousness, waiting for Dan Brown to legitimize these themes.

But Langdon, near the end of *TLS*, does perceive meaning in the layout of the city. He carefully contemplates the cross-shaped formation of the major vistas, the Capitol to the Lincoln Memorial on the east-west axis and the White House to the Jefferson Memorial on the north-south axis, with the giant obelisk at the crossing. Langdon perceives this as "the crossroads of America" and also likens it to a Rosicrucian cross.

This doesn't exactly fit the origins of the city design, which didn't have space for such a cross. It was first laid down by Pierre Charles L'Enfant (who either was a Mason or was well-versed in Masonic thinking) around 1791, when the Potomac lapped its bank just west of the current site of the Washington Monument. For about one hundred years after the plan was laid, the areas where the Jefferson and Lincoln memorials now stand were underwater. Rather than a cross, the major vistas of Washington would have formed a large "L" or a large right triangle, perhaps of mystical interest to the Pythagoreans among us. Whatever monument was erected for George Washington—and many ideas were considered—would have stood on the banks of the Potomac.

Of course, the city plan evolved, and in the 1880s and 1890s, the Potomac was filled in and the land was built on, yielding the magnificent cruciform layout we have today. Whether this was governed by a larger, Masonic plan or was merely the result of great designers falling into step with a broad classical concept over the years, is open to endless debate. Certainly, there were plenty of Masons involved in the building of the city throughout its many phases, but there were plenty of non-Masons, too.

Langdon's notion of the "crossroads of America" is apt in several ways. First of all, no visitor to this location can fail to miss the power, majesty, and interconnectedness of the Founding Fathers to modern America, and of the seat of Congress to the White House, and other themes crucial to our democracy. But there is another way in which the "crossroads" allusion is appropriate, if off by a few hundred feet in a technical sense.

In *The Da Vinci Code*, Dan Brown focused on various competing attempts in the late eighteenth and early nineteenth century to define the world's prime meridian, or zero point of longitude, including a "Rose Line" that went through the heart of Paris. As the new American nation unfolded, Thomas Jefferson in 1804 launched an effort to create a prime meridian centered where the Washington Monument was intended to be built.

But because of the soft soil, the monument's center was moved several hundred feet south and east. The marker that remains in the true center of the cross is a knee-high stone known as the Jefferson Pier Stone. It was the zero longitude of American maps for a long time, but was eventually superseded after an international agreement in 1884 selected Greenwich, England, as the world's prime meridian.

While the Washington Monument's present location may not be the technical crossroads of anything, there are few visitors to its top who are not moved at least in some small way by seeing the vision of the founders of American democracy spelled out before their very eyes. And therein lies the beauty of fiction. Dan Brown may have many of his facts wrong, but in the closing chapters of *TLS* he has painted a good picture of the overall spiritual quality of at least one important strand running through the American tapestry of experiences.

THE LOST SMITHSONIAN

an interview with Heather Ewing

Dan Brown conjures up a Smithsonian Institution that few people have ever seen. From the incredible, hidden collections of its Museum Support Center—meteorites, poisoned darts, and fantastic sea creatures—to the enormous, hangar-size pods where, Brown hints, cutting-edge, secret experiments could be carried out without the world's knowledge, the Smithsonian seems like a wonderful yet weird place. However, the real-life Smithsonian story is only half-told in *The Lost Symbol*.

As surprising as it might seem, Brown neglected to mention the mysterious backstory to the founding of the institution. It is a tale hinted at, but not told, by Peter Solomon during a lecture at Philips Exeter Academy when he says the Smithsonian was established thanks to the bequest of an English scientist, James Smithson, who "envisioned our country to be a land of enlightenment." But what Solomon fails to mention is that Smithson had never visited America. Even today, questions remain about who he was and why he chose the United States as the beneficiary of his fortune.

Heather Ewing is an architectural historian who worked at the Smithsonian during the 1990s and who recently published a biography of James Smithson and an architectural history of the Smithsonian's buildings. Here, she discusses the institution's fascinating history and examines what Dan Brown got right—and wrong—about the Smithsonian today.

Peter Solomon portrays James Smithson as a man who left his fortune to the United States because he viewed it as a "land of enlightenment." Do you agree?

I do believe that Smithson saw the U.S. as a land of enlightenment and possibility. But there's an awful lot of mystery to his bequest. It's certainly not as absolute as Brown makes it seem.

For a start, Smithson actually left his fortune to his nephew but because the nephew died at a young age, the fortune passed on to Smithson's second choice: the United States. Also, Brown omits Smithson's personal story, which is that he was the illegitimate son of a British aristocrat. That weighed heavily on him his whole life. He was probably attracted to America as a place where inherited privilege was being rejected and where a country based on laws and reason was being established. He was also probably snubbing England, a place that had rejected him.

There are many questions surrounding Smithson's life; what do we know about him?

He was born around 1765. We don't know the exact date because he was born in secret in Paris, where his mother had gone to have the child away from English society. His father was the first Duke of Northumberland and his mother was a wealthy widow, a cousin of the Duchess of Northumberland.

Smithson grew up in a society in which name and background meant everything. He had a very strong mother who instilled in him the idea that he was descended from kings and destined for great things. Yet, as an illegitimate child, he felt outside accepted society.

But in the scientific world he was very highly regarded.

Yes, the late eighteenth century was a very exciting time for chemistry and Smithson was at the heart of this new field.

He lived a very peripatetic life. He knew virtually all the great minds of his generation and spent time in all the major scientific circles in Europe.

He believed that advances would come only by working collaboratively. And he felt very strongly that there was a community of scientists who were above the idea of nations.

He became the youngest Fellow of the Royal Society, at the age of twenty-two, and part of an inner circle of chemists playing a very active role in the organization. He traveled all over Europe, including France, Italy, and Germany, searching for minerals and conducting experiments. He wrote papers on all sorts of topics, from an analysis of a substance called tabasheer, sometimes found inside bamboo, to "an improved method of making coffee." He also identified a zinc carbonate, smithsonite, which was named after him. He thought everything was worthy of study, from a lady's tear to what makes a blackberry the color that it is.

The Royal Society also rescued him when he was taken prisoner during the Napoleonic Wars. The president of the Royal Society, Joseph Banks, helped imprisoned scientists from both sides by arguing that scientists were not at war—that the work of scientists benefited all nations—and he arranged for Smithson's release.

So there is a picture here of a man who sees no national borders in the world of science?

Absolutely. His Smithsonian bequest, which has always seemed so enigmatic and bizarre, when viewed in that light actually starts to make some sense.

Smithson dedicated his whole life to science. He never married and had no children. And at the end of his life, he wrote a will in which, in the event that he had no heirs, his fortune would go to the United States of America "to found at Washington, under the name of the Smithsonian Institution"—he specifies that much—"an Establishment for the increase and diffusion of knowledge among men."

How much was the bequest worth?

Through investing, Smithson had increased his inheritance from his mother tenfold. His bequest was worth about half a million mid-nineteenth-century dollars—vastly more today. I think it's more effective to imagine it as 1/66th of the entire federal budget in 1838.

What was the response to the Smithsonian bequest in America? Is it fair to say the debate mirrored some of today's debates over the role of the federal government?

It was extremely contentious. It came at a time when the first seeds of the Civil War were brewing. President Jackson didn't know whether he had the authority to accept such a gift, so he turned it over to Congress. The idea of a national institution in the nation's capital was very problematic for some Southern senators who were fighting for states' rights.

There was also a debate about what exactly this "institution for increase and diffusion" would be—a university, a library, a teacher-training college? John Quincy Adams wanted it to be an astrophysical observatory. Everyone had a different idea. In the end, it was something of a classic congressional compromise; they threw everything into the bill: laboratories, a library, an art gallery, meteorological research, and so on. And that's how we got the Smithsonian we have today, which has a little bit of everything.

So the building of the Smithsonian became a major event?

Yes. Its governing body included the vice president of the United States and the chief justice of the Supreme Court. Three congressmen and three senators sat on its board of regents, as well as seven citizen regents, from around the country. This is still true today.

I was surprised to see that Dan Brown made a big deal of the Masonic cornerstone-laying ceremonies for major D.C. buildings like the U.S. Capitol, but he didn't mention that the Smithsonian building also had a Masonic cornerstone-laying ceremony. President Polk used the same gavel that George Washington had used when he laid the cornerstone for the Capitol and he used Washington's Masonic apron as well. There was a huge parade from the White House down to the Mall. The Smithsonian also has a number of Masonic items in its collections.

Was Smithson a Mason?

The Masons do like to claim him. But I looked into that quite extensively and there's no way to prove it.

But the Masons were involved in the cornerstone ceremony?

Freemasons came from all over the East Coast. The grand chaplain of the Grand Lodge of Maryland, who led the ceremony, said that he hoped the Smithsonian building would be a "central sun of science about which systems may revolve and from which light and knowledge may be reflected throughout every clime and kingdom of the globe." That sort of idea has a lot of resonance with Smithson's bequest.

In what way?

I like to think Smithson chose the States as his beneficiary not because he was giving something just to the U.S., but because he felt that we were the best trustees of this gift for the whole world; and that we, as this new, enlightened nation, based on laws and science, would be best able to execute his ideals.

The Castle is the original Smithsonian building. Is Dan Brown correct in his description of it as a "quintessential Norman castle"?

Yes, and no. It is inspired by Norman Romanesque architecture. But it is very much a nineteenth-century building. There's a sort of pastiche quality to a lot of nineteenth-century architecture, and whimsy, too, and it's all there.

It is a very important building in American architecture. If you imagine Washington in the 1830s, it's a city of great big neoclassical white buildings, either marble or Aquia sandstone. They're Greek- and Roman-inspired monuments. You have the White House, the U.S. Capitol, the Treasury Building, and the U.S. Patent Office. The Smithsonian building was really one of the first public buildings in a medieval style in the United States.

So what was inside?

It originally housed a library, a natural history museum, a little art gallery, scientific laboratories, offices, meteorological research, and a publications exchange. There was a lot of mailing out of publications in the early days;

that was the early interpretation of what "the diffusion of knowledge" would be.

The building also housed the head of the Smithsonian, who lived there with his family. Many of the young naturalists lived in the towers while they were cataloging the collections coming in from government expeditions exploring what would become the western United States.

And it was all funded by this one bequest?

Actually, the Smithson money was almost lost early on. Congress deposited the bequest in some state bonds, Arkansas and others, which some of them subsequently defaulted on. The government had to make up the money. John Quincy Adams rails in his diary about getting the Smithson funds out of "the fangs" of Arkansas.

The Smithsonian's first secretary, Joseph Henry, became concerned that Smithson's bequest for scientific research was going to be swallowed up by the responsibilities of taking care of the government collections. So, he arranged for an annual appropriation from Congress. Today, the Smithsonian receives about 70 percent of its budget from Congress.

Is it true that Smithson's papers were destroyed in a fire?

Yes, Smithson's papers were all lost in a fire at the Castle in 1865. It was a very cold day in January. Some workmen had brought in a stove while they were moving paintings around on the second floor. The building caught fire, taking the whole second floor. Smithson's books, which were on the ground floor, were the only part of his legacy that survived. All his belongings—his mineral collection and his papers—were gone.

Moving to the modern Smithsonian, is Dan Brown correct in saying that the Smithsonian Museum Support Center (SMSC) is "the world's largest and most technologically advanced museum" and that it holds more objects than the Hermitage, the Vatican, and the Metropolitan Museum of Art put together?

That is true. There are some fifty-four million items at the SMSC, while the Hermitage contains more than three million and the Metropolitan Museum of Art more than two million. But when you're dealing with huge study collections of fossils, insects, pressed plants, etc., you can imagine how quickly your collections would grow.

What about Brown's characterization of the SMSC building?

It's very well done, though the place is not quite as secretive as Brown makes out. It's very bright and modern and high-tech. There were four pods in the original construction. They are all larger than football fields and several stories high. The zigzag structure was chosen to allow for additional growth.

The Wet Pod used to be in Pod 3—but not anymore. The Natural History Museum stored a lot of its collections in ethanol, formalin, and other alcoholic spirits, which are highly toxic and flammable, in its basement on the National Mall. But you don't want these things where they pose a danger to your museum and visitors. So Pod 5 was opened in 2007 to put all the wet collections together.

Brown seems to have situated the book in that moment in time when Pod 5 is under construction and some of the wet collections are in Pod 3.

And is that where you can now find architeuthis and coelacanth?

Actually, anybody can see them now. The Smithsonian opened a new Ocean Hall in 2008 that has a coelacanth and two giant squid (*architeuthis*), a male and a female. The female was flown in from Spain. Because she was submerged in formalin and you're only allowed to transport a certain amount of alcohol into the country, the U.S. military was involved in bringing her to Washington. They called it Operation Calamari.

How did Smithson himself end up in the museum's collections?

Smithson died in Italy, in 1829. Around 1900, the city of Genoa was quarrying the cliff where the cemetery was located. They contacted the Smithsonian to say that they were going to move all of the remains. The board of regents said that it was fine to move Smithson to another burial place in Genoa. But Alexander Graham Bell, who was on the board—and also, coincidentally, a Mason—felt that Smithson should be honored in the United States for his exceptional bequest. Bell's son-in-law, Gilbert Grosvenor, the head of the National Geographic Society, launched a media campaign to bring Smithson to the U.S. Bell and his wife went off to Italy, and Mrs. Bell photographed the whole thing, so there are these wonderful photographs of the exhumation.

They brought Smithson back to a huge reception. There was a big procession from the Navy Yard to the Smithsonian, with the president and Supreme Court justices and other dignitaries leading the way. Smithson lay in state in the Castle building. Then they put him in a crypt in the Castle, which is where he is today.

He finally made it to America.

DANGER IN THE WET POD

Fact and Fiction About the Smithsonian

by the Editors

Chances are good that you've been to one of the museums that comprise the Smithsonian Institution. It is, after all, the world's largest museum and research complex, and more than twenty-five million people will visit in any given year. In addition to the well-known Air and Space, Natural History, and National Portrait museums in D.C., and the Cooper-Hewitt National Design Museum and the Heye Center of the National Museum of the American Indian in New York, there are 156 Smithsonian affiliates around the country. Still, even if you are a regular patron, there's an excellent possibility that the first time you heard of the Smithsonian Museum Support Center (SMSC) was in the pages of *The Lost Symbol*.

The SMSC is the setting for some of the most chilling scenes in the novel, including the one where Trish Dunne meets her unfortunate fate as roommate-for-eternity (or at least until they fish out her ethanol-soaked corpse) with a giant squid, and Katherine Solomon's nail-biter of a confrontation in the absolute darkness with Mal'akh, someone she'd probably bounced on her knee at some point much earlier in their lives, not knowing then of his predilection for ink and grudges.

Dan Brown presents the SMSC as a gargantuan warehouse storing the wide array of treasures not on museum display—calling it a "secret museum" and "the world's largest and most technologically advanced museum." He describes Pod 5, the home of Katherine's lab, as a massive football field–size space not yet wired for electricity. This requires Katherine to make a blind daily trek to her work space with nothing but a thin strip of carpeting to guide her. Katherine has nicknamed her lab "the Cube." It runs on the power of hydrogen fuel cells, and is fully sealed off from the world by a lead-lined door. Within the Cube she delves deep into the secrets of noetic science, backing up her apparently vast experimental data on two redundant holographic memory storage units.

While the SMSC of *The Lost Symbol* is a strange and mysterious place, the real SMSC is nearly as fascinating—even if the reality is different from the fantasy version described by Dan Brown. Though most of the public isn't even aware of its existence, it is far from a secret museum. One doesn't simply walk through the front doors as one might the National Air and Space Museum or the National Portrait Gallery, but there are tours every Wednesday and appointments available to those who contact one of the Smithsonian museums with a request to see a particular collection not currently on display. The Smithsonian is quick to acknowledge that the treasures stored in the SMSC are the property of the taxpayers of the U.S. and that they therefore have a right to view this property. The only thing secretive about the Museum Support Center is that, in an attempt to save the items in their collection for generations to come, they don't make these things as easily visible to the public as those on the National Mall.

The SMSC is located on a four-and-a-half-acre lot in Suitland, Maryland, about seven miles from the heart of Washington, D.C. The long, low building has a distinctive zigzag design and it opened in 1983 to serve as a storage and research facility for the overwhelming majority of items owned by the Smithsonian (only 2 percent of the collection is actually on display in the museums at any one time). There's a little bit of everything here: giant Venezuelan rats, for example, along with Edward Curtis frontier photographs, meteorites, and the skulls of the elephants Theodore

Roosevelt brought back from safari (as it turns out, the elephants you can see in the Museum of Natural History don't have these heads any longer). There's even the brain of Western explorer John Wesley Powell, which arrived at the Smithsonian via a bet. All told, there are somewhere around 54 million artifacts, and the Smithsonian can actually tell you what everything is and where everything is located thanks to a propri-etary coding and cataloguing system. Rather humbling for those of us who often forget where we put our car keys.

The zigzag nature of the structure lets the storage pods remain sepa-rate from the offices and labs on the SMSC site and allows for expansion without breaking from the original design. Between the pods (which are fully sealed for the sake of preservation and security) and the offices is a huge corridor that SMSC staffers refer to as "The Street." One can only access the pods through this corridor, which has just two entry points, one for visitors and one for items in the collection. Security is very high, with a combination of checkpoints, security officers, and electronic moni-toring devices in use.

The temperature of the facility is set for 70 degrees (with a variance of 4 degrees in either direction) and relative humidity is 45 percent (with a variance of 8 percent up or down). Of course, for the sake of main-tenance, some sections of the SMSC are considerably colder: there are samples here stored at 200 degrees below zero. Enormous industrial fil-ters work overtime to keep the air within the entire complex scrubbed clean. The upside for employees is that allergens are virtually nonexistent. The downside is that you can't open your window on a spring day or even have a sandwich at your desk because doing so will contaminate the near-perfect atmosphere.

As with Katherine Solomon, there's a great deal of scientific research going on at the SMSC. Because the collection is so comprehensive and so well archived, scientists and scholars travel from all over the world to examine the holdings. It isn't unusual for foreigners to come to the SMSC to discover critical details about their own native flora and fauna because the Smithsonian collection is more extensive than any they have in their homelands.

It is curious that Brown decided to describe Pod 5 as a dark, empty space, since the pod has been up and running—utilizing the latest in museum storage technology, including electricity—since 2007. There are accounts of his visiting the SMSC in 2008, so he must have known all about this. However, he might have deemed it too late to change an essential part of his novel. One can appreciate his decision to stray from the facts for the sake of his story. Depicting Pod 5 as it is today would have stripped much of the drama and mystery from the scenes set there. However, one does have to wonder why Katherine and friends continuously made that long walk to the entrance of the Cube without *portable* illumination. A flashlight would have done the job very well. A Zippo would have been an improvement over following the floor runner. For that matter, if you're going to the effort of outfitting the Cube with a hydrogen fuel cell, couldn't you run an extension cord or something to allow for a lamp? That chase scene with Katherine and Mal'akh truly was terrific, but it requires massive suspension of disbelief to get there.

While the Cube itself doesn't exist (at least no one will admit that it exists), much of its technology does. Hydrogen fuel cells are around and they pack considerably more juice and maintain their power for much longer than traditional batteries. They would easily service the energy needs of the Cube were Pod 5 actually devoid of electricity.

Holographic memory is already in limited use, though it is currently far too costly for most applications and is generally seen as unnecessary, even for massive data needs. Of course, given Peter Solomon's fortune, money would not be an impediment. Even the safeguards against contamination are plausible, though only noetic scientists seem to believe at this point that anything can filter out the "thought emissions" that others working around the real Pod 5 would generate.

The real Pod 5 is the new "Wet Pod," a 125,000-square-foot space that serves as the home of vertebrate, invertebrate, and botanical collections stored in alcohol, ethanol, and other preservation fluids. There is indeed a forty-foot squid there, just as is depicted in the scene in *TLS* when Trish shows Mal'akh, posing as Dr. Abaddon, around what is said to be Pod 3 (which Brown refers to as the Wet Pod). In addition, there are

25 million other specimens that comprise the National Museum of Natural History's biological collections, including some gathered by Charles Darwin himself. At the moment, Pod 5 is the most technologically current of the five pods, though Pod 3, the former Wet Pod, is getting a face-lift scheduled for completion in early 2010.

In a blog post, Megan Gambino, an editorial assistant at *Smithsonian* magazine, said of Dan Brown, "The bestselling writer is notorious for blurring the boundary between fact and fiction, and his latest book is no exception. The Smithsonian plays a dominant role in the plot. A major character works at the Smithsonian's Museum Support Center. . . . The true-life address of that facility is even revealed." Of the pods, she noted that Brown correctly captured the numbering system and some of the description, but "took some liberties with their uses. . . ."

While the SMSC is a central setting in *The Lost Symbol*, the Smithsonian as a whole plays an important role both directly and metaphorically in the novel. Peter Solomon is said to be the secretary of the Smithsonian, a position that tops the institution's organizational chart. In real life, G. Wayne Clough holds that position. Where Peter Solomon is a 33° Mason with nearly unimaginable wealth, Clough grew up modestly in Georgia and there is no indication that he has any affiliation with the Masons. However, Masons did build many of the Smithsonian's structures, including the building known as the Castle that houses the institution's administrative offices as well as the crypt of James Smithson. Smithson, the great endower of the Smithsonian, is said by a number of sources to have been a Freemason.

The Smithsonian plays one other considerable role in *The Lost Symbol*, though it is quite indirect. Toward the end of the novel, Mal'akh attempts to release a video of a "gathering of the most decorated and accomplished Masons in the most powerful city on earth." People captured on the video included, among others, two Supreme Court justices, the Speaker of the House, and three prominent senators. Brown's implication is that the release of this video, pinning major lawmakers to a ceremony that involved drinking from a human skull, would shake the government to the core, perhaps toppling American democracy and the Masonic tradition in an instant. Whether such video revelations would have had such cataclysmic consequences is open to debate. However, Dan Brown may have found inspiration for his selection of high-ranking Masons from the board of regents of the Smithsonian Institution. That board includes, on an ex-officio basis, the chief justice of the Supreme Court and the vice president of the United States, as well as three senators, three congressional representatives, and a group of prominent private citizens, which today includes at least three real-life billionaires.

James Smithson himself is a man veiled in mystery. When the British scientist drew up his will, he stipulated that his considerable fortune be bequeathed to his nephew. However, if his nephew died without heirs (which happened in 1835, six years after Smithson's death), the remaining money would go "to the United States of America, to found at Washington, under the name of the Smithsonian Institution, an establishment for the increase and diffusion of knowledge among men." Nearly nothing is known about why Smithson decided to make such a generous contribution to establish this kind of institution in a land he never visited. Much of what we might have learned about James Smithson turned to ash on a frozen January day in 1865 when the Castle caught fire and destroyed all of Smithson's personal effects that had been shipped to America.

It's unfortunate that the SMSC didn't exist in that earlier era. If it had, Smithson's effects would likely be in pristine condition today, and we might all have a better picture of the man who made possible the institution that bears his name.

HIDING OUT IN JEFFERSON'S PALACE OF THE BOOK

Why Robert Langdon's Adventure Takes Him Inside the Library of Congress

by the Editors

The Lost Symbol is many things: a thriller, an intricate puzzle, an elaborate tour of the "secret" Washington, D.C., and more. But perhaps beyond all of this, it is a love song to books, the written word, and the accumulation of knowledge and wisdom. A book lies at the heart of its mystery, the "Lost Word" is its deepest secret, and its prevalent message is an exhortation to open the mind. Dozens of specific books and authors are mentioned by name in *TLS*, and numerous proverbs and aphorisms related to books are cited, such as, "Time is a river . . . and books are boats. . . ." In fact, one could read the entire work as an argument for the extraordinary power of words and books.

If one were going to pay tribute to books and words in a novel set in America—and certainly in a novel set in D.C.—one would naturally find one's characters gravitating toward the Library of Congress, the most elaborate and inclusive home for books in the country. "It's my favorite

Library of Congress Main Reading Room. (*Courtesy of the Library of Congress*)

room in all of D.C.," Dan Brown has said of its main reading room. Brown sends his characters there in a particularly clever way that underscores the central place books have in his novel: he literally makes those characters part of the library's distribution system.

In chapter 59, Robert Langdon, Katherine Solomon, and Warren Bellamy travel deep into the library's stacks to elude pursuit. Upon the realization that he's within the labyrinthine stacks, Langdon notes that "he was looking at something few people ever saw," and he steps away from the tension of the moment to express the proper level of awe and reverence at being in the presence of such an overwhelming collection of books. Bellamy convinces Langdon that the only escape route is via one of the conveyor belts used to get a volume from its place in the stacks to one of the three buildings that comprise the library. Langdon observes that the belt "extended a short distance then disappeared into a large hole in the wall," immediately seizing his mind with claustrophobic visions and causing him to seek other options. He soon discovers, though, that if he's going to get away from the CIA agents trying to chase him down, he is going to have to go hardbound. By chapter 62, Langdon has gotten over his phobias (or rather Bellamy convinces him that he has no other choice but to do so) and he rides the conveyor toward his delivery in the library's Adams Building and temporary freedom. Brown makes the Library of Congress seem at once awe-inspiring and mildly sinister, and he uses its unique properties to grand effect.

The Library of Congress serves many functions, though helping symbologists stay free from misguided government functionaries is not supposed to be one of them. It is the primary research facility for the U.S. Congress. It is the location of the U.S. Copyright Office. It is the home of America's poet laureate. But it is first and foremost a library, much like the one you would find in your community . . . assuming your local library housed 130 million items . . . and that it included 650 million miles of bookshelves . . . and that it had a staff of nearly 4,000.

Established by act of Congress in 1800, it was originally housed in the Capitol building and was intended then for use exclusively by members of the legislative branch. The British, perhaps sensing that someday their own British Library would be in competition with the Library of Congress for the largest in the world, burned its contents—then about three thousand volumes—to the ground in an 1814 invasion during the War of 1812. Thomas Jefferson, in need of an infusion of cash (and, according to some reports, unwilling to part with his extensive wine holdings), agreed to sell his entire collection of 6,487 books—the largest collection in America at the time—to the Library of Congress for $23,950.

The famously well-read and intellectually curious Jefferson's library included a wide variety of volumes, many of which were on subjects the original library had not included. Some within the legislature expressed concern at the breadth of the material, believing that a few of the topics fell outside the scope of the library's original charter. Jefferson called his fellow politicians to task over such a suggestion, saying, "I do not know that it contains any branch of science which Congress would wish to exclude from their collection; there is, in fact, no subject to which a Member of Congress may not have occasion to refer." In other words, he was pushing the lawmakers of our nation to expand their minds, much as Peter Solomon suggests we all need to do at the end of *The Lost Symbol*.

Although Thomas Jefferson himself was not a Freemason, many of his contemporaries were Masons and their reverence for books was cut of the same intellectual and moral cloth as their emphasis on science, progress, tolerance, open-mindedness, and self-improvement. James Billington, today's Librarian of Congress, and a well-known historian, has pointed out that it is no surprise that the Freemasons were integral to the American Revolution. Freemasonry, he once said, was "a moral meritocracy—implicitly subversive within any static society based on a traditionalist hierarchy." Much of the impetus to find and believe in the moral compass of eighteenth-century Masons, deists, and Founding Fathers came from the deep rationality, richness, and importance of books in the early American experience.

Jefferson's influence on the Library of Congress was profound and extended far beyond the volumes he sold to revive it. He claimed that he could not live without books and the Library of Congress became the ultimate manifestation of a book lover's dream. While it does not contain every book ever printed in the United States (a commonly held myth), its collection is the most comprehensive compilation of American writing ever amassed. Jefferson believed there was a direct connection between the values of democracy and the quest for knowledge, and in that spirit the library seeks to be as inclusive as possible and as accessible as possible, its librarians having long ago cast aside the notion that it should exist solely for our nation's lawmakers.

The library collection grew dramatically and quickly from Jefferson's collection. Its home remained the Capitol building until the end of the nineteenth century when a shortage of shelf space clarified the need to give the Library of Congress a place of its own. And quite a place it was. Designed by architects John L. Smithmeyer and Paul J. Pelz, it was created in the style of Florentine Renaissance buildings. This itself makes it distinctive in a city where major buildings tended to source their inspiration from the Romans and the Greeks. From the start, the goal was to create a library that surpassed all others in the world for splendor. The intention was to create nothing less than a palace for books. The original building (known now as the Jefferson Building) is a vast study in marble, its columned entrance giving way to sweeping staircases, ornately carved pillars, huge vaults of space, and, most dramatically, a massive 23-carat gold-plated dome that rises 195 feet above the main reading room. Tablets featuring the names of ten great creators of the written word encircle the dome—Dante, Homer, Milton, Bacon, Aristotle, Goethe, Shakespeare, Moliere, Moses, and Herodotus. Cervantes, Hugo, Scott, Cooper, Longfellow, Tennyson, Gibbon, and Bancroft get tablets elsewhere. Standing under the dome, one gets the impression that one has entered a cathedral. And indeed, in many ways, one has.

Two additional buildings now complete the huge sprawl of the Library of Congress. The Adams Building opened in 1938, its architecture and lines less elaborate. The Madison Building, also a much simpler structure, was completed in 1981 and serves as home to the librarian's office, the copyright office, the Congressional Research Service, and the law library as well as the country's official memorial to James Madison.

While the Library of Congress itself is a work of art, it is also home to many great works of sculpture and painting. More than forty artists have been commissioned to create major pieces for the library. The exterior includes the massive *Neptune* fountain created by sculptor Roland Hinton Perry and boasting sea nymphs, sea monsters, the sea god Triton (pictured before he bulked up for his powerful supporting role in Disney's *The Little Mermaid*), and a majestic twelve-foot rendition of Triton's father, Neptune. Circling the building as ornaments to the first-floor windows are the ethnological heads, studies in granite by William Boyd and Henry Jackson Ellicott of thirty-three ethnicities from around the globe. Three massive bronze doors greet visitors at the entrance. Commemorating writing, printing, and tradition as interpreted by three different sculptors, they are fourteen feet high and a combined three and a half tons in weight.

Among the artistic highlights inside the library are the eight statues in the main reading room representing philosophy, art, history, commerce, religion, science, law, and poetry. There are bronze statues at the staircases, mosaics depicting thirteen disciplines of knowledge, and Edwin Howland Blashfield's mural *Human Understanding*, set inside the lantern of the dome. There's Henry Oliver Walker's mural *Lyric Poetry* celebrating the work of American and European poets in the South Corridor, Walter McEwen's paintings of Greek heroes down the Southwest Corridor, and a marble mosaic of Minerva by Elihu Vedder along the staircase that leads to the Visitor's Gallery. In the Adams Building, one can find the history of the written word as sculpted in bronze by Lee Lawrie, and Frank Eliscu's four-story bronze relief *Falling Books* presides over the main entrance of the Madison Building. As Langdon waits for Bellamy to explain what's going on with Peter and the Masonic Pyramid, they stride by the Gutenberg Bible. Overhead is John White Alexander's six-panel painting entitled *The Evolution of the Book*, which traces the history of the word from cave paintings to hieroglyphics to illuminated manuscripts to the printing press.

Nearly all of the 29 million volumes the library holds are housed in sixteen-story stacks inaccessible to the general public, hence Langdon's observation that he'd been where few others had. One doesn't browse stacks of the Library of Congress to do research, to read the works of one of the writers immortalized on the library's tablets, or to take something home to read to the kids. To get a book from the library, you must place a request and wait perhaps an hour or more to receive the book you desire. This delay comes from the fact that your book might indeed have a very long way to travel from the bowels of the stacks, perhaps riding the very same conveyor belt that took Robert Langdon on his claustrophobic ride to freedom. (While a conveyor system actually does exist and is currently being upgraded, Langdon's ride itself would be much more of a challenge than Dan Brown suggests. According to a spokesperson for the library, "Since it is designed for boxes carrying books and has a significant number of horizontal and vertical switching points [e.g., going from the Jefferson basement level to the Jefferson cellar level], it would not be possible for a person to fit on it and ride from the stacks in the Jefferson Building to the Adams Building.")

It is interesting to note that this ornate "temple of books" might seem out of proportion to the general perception of the place of books in the life of the average contemporary American. Charles McGrath, former editor of the *New York Times Book Review,* said about the Library of Congress in a 2009 *Times* article, "It's gratifying that someone once thought books deserved such an impressive home." His suggestion, of course, is that most of us no longer read books regularly or value books and libraries, that no one has time to read entire books anymore, and that the Internet is supplanting the book as an information resource. Film and television draw much larger audiences. Far more people will download the latest Jay-Z album on their iPods (especially if one includes illegal downloads) than will buy the typical number one *New York Times* bestseller. Even the book's newest incarnation, the electronic book, is a kind of repudiation of the book as a physical work worthy of a grand physical home.

In *TLS*, there are numerous references to lost words, lost books, and the lost wisdom of the ancients. We all know the cautionary tale of the fire at the Library of Alexandria where the world lost much of its physical storehouse of knowledge, not to be recovered until the Renaissance. (Much of Thomas Jefferson's original collection in the Library of Congress was lost in a fire; ditto for James Smithson's papers in the early years of the Smithsonian.) *TLS* is filled with the sense of loss and regret for a more golden, wiser epoch—and also filled with the encouragement to revive those long-gone traditions.

But now consider this: three of the biggest and most enduring cultural phenomena of the past decade have come from the book world via Dan Brown, J. K. Rowling, and Stephenie Meyer. Has anything from the film world come close to matching the impact of these three authors in the last ten years? In fact, five of the top-grossing films of all time as well as five of the annual top-grossing films in the last ten years were based on books. Nothing in the music world has come close. Amazingly, in the aftermath of the death of singer Michael Jackson, the King of Pop's *Thriller* CD was often cited for its phenomenal sixty million copies sold worldwide. But Dan Brown's *Da Vinci Code* actually outsold *Thriller* by more than twenty million copies.

Sure, television shows regularly draw bigger audiences than those that buy books by these authors. Stephenie Meyer's novel *Twilight* has had somewhere around the same number of readers (though that number is still growing dramatically) as a show like *America's Got Talent* has viewers. For that matter, more people saw *G.I. Joe: The Rise of Cobra* than bought the latest Harry Potter book. But how many were still talking about those other entertainments a week later (or an hour later, for that matter)? We know that readers can't stop talking about Edward and Bella or Harry and Voldemort—or Robert Langdon and whichever brainy female partner is along for the adventure. One could therefore argue that books have had a more dramatic influence on pop culture in the last decade than any other creative art form.

So the future of books may not be as bleak as some fear. It is a challenged future, no doubt. And for that reason, it's probably a good thing that among all the other ideas in *TLS*, Dan Brown rightly celebrates the written word. And part of that celebration is an evocation of the book's most deservedly sumptuous shrine, the Library of Congress.

WHAT DOES *THE LOST SYMBOL* GET WRONG ABOUT THE NATION'S CAPITAL? EVERYTHING.

by David Plotz

As a fan of Washington conspiracies and a native of D.C., *Slate*'s editor David Plotz was eager to see what Dan Brown would conjure up from his city. A former political reporter and almost lifelong resident, Plotz knows the Washington people and places mentioned in *The Lost Symbol* better than most. He went to school on the grounds of the National Cathedral, his office overlooks Dupont Circle (where Langdon lands in a helicopter), and he is a friend of the current chair of the Smithsonian Institution. Moreover, as author of *Good Book: The Bizarre, Hilarious, Disturbing, Marvelous, and Inspiring Things I Learned When I Read Every Single Word of the Bible*, Plotz is more than familiar with the text within which, according to Brown, the "Lost Word" is concealed.

Here, Plotz explains why *The Lost Symbol*, devoid of sex and money, and fixated upon a spiritual quest for power, may be "the strangest novel ever written about Washington."

In the mid-1990s, just before Dan Brown discovered angels and demons, Washington, D.C.'s, alternative weekly, the *City Paper*, published a popular column in which it tried to solve local mysteries sent in by readers— uncovering the truth about the capital's baffling buildings, locations, and phenomena. The column was called "Washington's Mundane Mysteries" because, it turned out, that's what all of them were. Those sinister brown metal boxes on certain downtown street corners? Merely storage bins for extra copies of the *Washington Post*. That massive vault looming over Rock Creek Parkway? Just a Department of Public Works pump house.

But this is not the Washington you will meet in Dan Brown's new novel, *The Lost Symbol*. In Brown's world, there are no mundane mysteries in the nation's capital, no mysteries that can be solved with a quick Google search or a phone call or two. There are only two grand mysteries— mysteries so elaborate they make the Watergate conspiracy look like a nursery school picnic.

When I heard that Brown was setting his newest book in the city where I've spent my entire life, I was secretly excited and curious. I'm an addict of D.C. books, a sucker for conspiracies in the halls of power. Having slogged through *The Da Vinci Code*, I knew that Brown's Washington wouldn't exactly be the city as seen on C-SPAN. I certainly expected a heavy dose of Freemasons—though I underestimated just how heavy that dose would be—but also hoped he could offer his cunning take on theologically suspect Supreme Court justices, ominous senatorial rituals, and the secrets of the White House. ("Robert Langdon slid the West Wing blueprints on top of the 3,900-year-old Codex Hammurabi, until the matching crescent symbols intersected. He stared at it, dumbstruck: so that was why it had to be an Oval Office!")

But I am sorry to report that *The Lost Symbol* turns out to be perhaps the strangest novel ever written about Washington. It is awesomely wrong about what makes the city compelling.

TLS recounts—and recounts, and recounts—Harvard symbology professor Robert Langdon's race to discover the secret of the "Ancient Mysteries," a long-concealed method of unlocking the power of the human mind, guarded for centuries by the Freemasons and hidden right here in the nation's capital. All the while he is pursued by a biblically inspired, steroid-enhanced, excessively tattooed eunuch/psychiatrist—don't even ask!—and the CIA through the crypts of the Capitol, the Reading Room of the Library of Congress, and the ceremonial hall of the Scottish Rite Temple. Among these and yet more postcard stops, Langdon uncovers a conspiracy involving ancient Egyptian adepts; the Rosicrucians; mathematical puzzles secretly encoded in the prints of Albrecht Dürer; "The Order"; the machinations of the Invisible College; an encrypted Masonic pyramid; the Institute of Noetic Sciences; Isaac Newton; the House of the Temple; the "Lost Word"; the circumpunct; the arcane symbol that will unlock . . .

Oh, never mind. It's beyond parody. Or maybe it's not. At *Slate*, the magazine where I work, we built a Dan Brown Sequel Generator. You plug in a favorite city and organization, and our computer did the rest. Mormons in New York City? Robert Langdon is summoned to the New York City Public Library, where he discovers a hideously mangled corpse, and evidence of the resurgence of the Trumifori, a secret branch of the Mormon Church with a legendary vendetta against its ancient enemy, the Vatican. . . .

The Teamsters in Jerusalem? Robert Langdon is summoned to the Church of the Holy Sepulchre where he discovers a secret rune, and gruesome evidence of the resurgence of the Inquinati, a secret branch of the Teamsters Union. . . .

Brown's Washington does overlap with the Washington I know in some unexpectedly gratifying ways. The eunuch, for example, kidnaps the head of the Smithsonian, chops off his hand, and carries out grisly demonic rituals on him. In real life, the chairwoman of the Smithsonian is a friend of mine, with both her hands. Brown sets critical scenes at the National Cathedral, where I went to high school, conducts "harsh interrogations" at the U.S. Botanical Garden where I take my kids, lands a helicopter in the traffic circle outside my office window, and gives his psychopathic eunuch a sinister hideout a few blocks from my house.

But don't get me started about Brown's supposed mania for accuracy! Langdon drives north to get from the cathedral to Kalorama Heights?

The eunuch crosses the Anacostia River into Maryland on Independence Avenue? The tip of the Washington Monument is the highest point in the city? If I can't trust Brown to get the location of the Tenleytown Metro station right, how can I trust him to reveal the truth about the Kether, the highest Sephiroth, the Monad, the Prisca Sapientia, the "at-one-ment of the mind and soul"? Also, he has the Washington Redskins making the playoffs. Please.

But I digress. Despite Brown's Google Maps checkoff of Washington landmarks, he managed to miss the city itself. *The Lost Symbol* is a novel about a Washington conspiracy, but it's not the kind of Washington conspiracy you've ever heard about. There are no murdered Supreme Court justices, no slutty press secretaries or dissipated journalists. In fact, there are hardly any people at all. By cramming the events of the novel into a single Sunday night, Brown conveniently ensures that none of the people who actually make Washington Washington will intrude on his nutter antics. The closest he gets to a Washington notable is Warren Bellamy, his heroic Architect of the Capitol. In real life, the architect of the Capitol is a bureaucratic functionary who might barely be able to count the beans in the Senate bean soup.

The fundamental premise of *The Lost Symbol* is that Washington is a "mystical city," and it is this error that makes the book so maddening. In Brown's Washington, the marble, the wide streets, and the monuments all signify some kind of connection with the divine. The city encodes transcendental secrets about God and the potential of the human mind. But anyone who has spent more than a tourmobile ride in D.C. knows that what makes Washington interesting is its very smallness, the contrast between its grand architecture and the human machinations that take place within it. From high to low, from *Democracy* to *The Pelican Brief,* Washington novels have exploited and reveled in the human spectacle this presents, the way in which ambitious, idealistic, flawed Americans wrestle each other for power and wealth.

Yes, there are conspiracies in Washington, but not the sort Brown imagines. They are conspiracies about money, sex, elections, and public policy. These are absent from Brown's Washington. Every few years, for example, Washington is diverted by the spectacle of a powerful figure done in by sexual weakness. But Brown's characters are sexless. There's that eunuch, of course, and the others might as well be. They float in a world of pure thought—nonsensical thought, but pure.

Money, too, has no place in Brown's world. Everyone has way more than enough of it, making the private jet rides, booby-trapped mansions, and lavish secret laboratories easy to come by. But no one in *The Lost Symbol* is motivated by anything so pedestrian as greed, or ever has even a momentary thought about using their knowledge to make a profit for themselves, or their friends. Again, this makes them unlike practically every person who has ever lived in Washington, whose prominent citizens are all too aware of the power of the purse.

Most of all, Washington conspiracies concern power: which branch of government did what to whom? The Supreme Court case that will upend the environment; the congressional bill that will wreck trade policy. But neither power nor the business of the nation interests Brown. In his view, the epic events that occur in the nation's capital are dust in the wind next to the coming grand revelation of the ancient wisdom. In real Washington, ideas are practical tools, ways to change the country to advance some interest, to win billions of dollars, to improve the lot of citizens, to tilt the global balance of power. But Brown treats this all as beneath notice. His ideas, you see, concern transcendence, the portal that will turn Washington's all-too-mortal men into divine, philosophical supermen.

Brown posits a Washington oozing with spiritual energy and secrets of the known universe. But in the real Washington, if you held a panel about the Ancient Mysteries, the unification of religion and science, and all that other Brownian hoo-ha, you couldn't fill a small conference room at the Brookings Institution—even if you served a free lunch and invited all the interns. Washington may strike the visitor as majestic, but at its heart it is the least spiritual, and least mystical, place imaginable: no one has thought about their immortal soul here since *Damn Yankees*.

The Lost Symbol bizarrely resembles those other well-known mega bestsellers about ancient prophecies, the *Left Behind* books. That series chronicles the end of days, as recounted in the Book of Revelation, from the Rapture to the Antichrist to the Second Coming. Like *The Lost Symbol,* the *Left Behind* books mock the reality of actual life as mere trivia, when we all should really be concentrating on our immortal souls. And though the Brown books reach radically different conclusions than the *Left Behind* series—one follows Christian fundamentalism, the other New Age pantheism—they also share a similar apocalyptic mania about the Bible.

Having recently published a book about reading the Bible from cover to cover for the first time, I was bewitched by the biblical conclusion of *The Lost Symbol.* At the climax of the book, that eunuch attempts to reenact Abraham's sacrifice of Isaac, with himself as the victim. He believes, for reasons I still can't fathom, that being sacrificed will endow him with supernatural powers. (*The Lost Symbol*'s version differs from the Genesis account in other ways, too, notably in this one: Isaac is silent during the entire episode, but the eunuch never shuts up! I would have killed him just to end the crazy ranting.) After the sacrifice fails, Freemason boss Peter Solomon reveals to Langdon that the vessel containing the Ancient Mysteries is in fact . . . the Bible, buried in the cornerstone of the Washington Monument.

According to Solomon, the biblical fundamentalists who believe literally in the stories of the Bible are all wrong. Rather, concealed within that superficial Bible is another, secret Bible, and that secret Bible contains the Ancient Mysteries, the understanding that we need to realize that God is within all of us. According to Solomon, this is why so many of the great thinkers of history, from Isaac Newton to William Blake, have expended so much energy trying to unscramble the Bible, to find the codes within it. (The Bible is not unique in containing that secret, Solomon says: so do all lasting religious texts, including the Bhagavad Gita and the Koran—and presumably, the Book of Mormon, L. Ron Hubbard's *Dianetics,* etc. Incidentally, I am sure you have not failed to notice that Peter Solomon bears the name of the Old Testament and New Testament's two greatest wisdom figures.)

Of course we shouldn't make the mistake of conflating the incoherent ooga-booga spewed out by Brown's characters with his own actual theology, or anyone else's for that matter. But it did strike me that this particular kind of biblical interpretation reveals the essential mushiness of Brownian thought, which is as irritating in its own way as the stupid literalism of the Left Behind books. In one sense, Peter Solomon's insistence that we ignore the surface meaning of the Bible is appealing. After all, anyone who has actually read the whole Bible—particularly the Old Testament—can't help but notice the violence, the unlovingness of God, the absence of moral lessons, and the shortage of heroes. It's true that you can find pleasant moments—a Ten Commandments here, a gentle Psalm there—but overwhelmingly the book is about antiheroes like Jacob, meatheads like Samson, and a disturbing amount of inexplicable smiting.

Faced with this moral mess of the Bible, you can make one of five choices. First, you can take the fundamentalist approach, accept that it's all true, and tell sinners they better shape up before they're cast into the pits of hell. Second, you can reject the book as a collection of fairy tales and lies. Third, you can cherry-pick, concentrating on the most agreeable passages and reinterpreting ugly stories to make them more palatable. This is what both Judaism and Christianity have done, quite successfully. Fourth, you can focus instead on the historical context of the Bible, as James Kugel did in his magnificent book, *How to Read the Bible*. This academic interpretation ignores the Bible's divine claims, and shows how a series of ancient tribes assembled, edited, and reedited the books that would become the Bible, plagiarizing laws and stories from all over the Near East, merging at least two different Gods into a single monotheistic God, and fabricating stories about Exodus, patriarchs, and the conquest of Israel.

Brown makes the fifth and final choice: he supposes a second Bible hidden within the Bible itself. All evidence suggests that the Bible was compiled in no systematic way, but tossed together haphazardly over hundreds of years. There is absolutely nothing to suggest that there is a coherent plan behind it, or that secret laws and ideas are encoded in the text. But this fact does not deter Brown. The Bible may seem to be a book about a jealous God, a faithless people, and a struggle for belief. Actually,

Brown says, this is mere misdirection to keep superficial readers away from the real Bible, which consists of hidden knowledge about how we humans are actually gods, if we would only learn the mysteries.

It is, of course, impossible to refute this claim. If Robert Langdon were to say to Peter Solomon: "Your theory is wacky. There are no mysteries hidden in this book," Solomon could simply respond: "You don't recognize them because you're not ready for them. You're not willing to open your mind to them."

Brown isn't a religious leader, and anyone who adopts a belief system based on a reading of *The Lost Symbol* obviously needs her brain chilled in an ice bath. Even so, Brown's idea of a secret Bible is maddening to anyone who has ever grappled with the actual Bible. Rather than struggle with the messy reality of the Bible, Brown joins the all-too-many people—the Kabbalists, the Torah code seekers, etc.—who seek solace in mystical mumbo jumbo. The Bible is a complicated, morally difficult book, just as we are complicated, morally difficult people. Solomon's secret Bible invites us to reject ambiguity and embrace a purported Bible that is pure and perfect.

The message of the secret Bible, and of *The Lost Symbol*, and, indeed, of all Dan Brown's work, is that there is an order to everything, a meaning to everything, and everything happens for a reason. *Ordo ab chao*, as Brown puts it in the book, using the Latin to lend gravitas to his proposition. This is antithetical to the actual Bible—as it is to the actual Washington, D.C.—which actually shows us that life is always a mess.

Chapter
EIGHT

INTO
THE KRYPTIC . . .
ART, SYMBOLS,
AND CODES

THE CLUES HIDDEN IN CIRCLES AND SQUARES

The Art and Symbology of The Lost Symbol

by Diane Apostolos-Cappadona

In his two prior Robert Langdon novels, Dan Brown clearly wanted to let his readers know he was an aspiring and innovative art historian in addition to showing his mastery of alternate history, esoteric codes and symbols, conspiracies, and the action-adventure novel. Art has an important role in *The Lost Symbol*, to be sure. Brumidi's *The Apotheosis of Washington* plays with the theme of the divine connection between man below and god above, with the inventive power of the mind on earth blessed by the divinities. Dürer's *Melencolia I*, richly symbolic in its own right, plays a more mundane role in the novel, its offering by and large relegated to the magic square in the engraving that helps our hero on to the next challenge he will have to face. But something is different from the previous novels, Diane Apostolos-Cappadona tells us. Brown seems to back off from introducing his own interpretations of the art in *TLS*—even omitting facts about them that this time are in plain sight.

Diane Apostolos-Cappadona is adjunct professor of religious art and cultural history at Georgetown University and has been called the closest thing the academic world has to a real "sym-bologist," at least when it comes to the connections between art and the myths and traditions it conveys. We asked her to share her insights on the artworks of *The Lost Symbol*, including the Brumidi, the Dürer, and a third work that makes an appearance in the novel as well: the statue of George Washington sculpted by Horatio Greenough. A fourth work, *The Three Graces*, by the painter Michael Parkes, is discussed by the artist himself in the interview that follows.

The use of art in service to his story has been a Dan Brown trade-mark. Controversial as his interpretations may have been, he has had us look again, and in a whole new way, at Leonardo da Vinci's *The Last Supper* in *The Da Vinci Code* and Gian Lorenzo Bernini's *Ecstasy of St. Theresa* in *Angels & Demons*. Art also plays a role in *The Lost Symbol*, but it is a substantially different one, and worth puzzling over. In the earlier books, he organized his plot around "secret codes" sculpted or painted in the art of a single master. In *TLS* there is no central artwork or single artist whose symbolism must be decoded to solve the mystery, save the heroine, or preserve the world from imminent disaster. Rather, Brown utilizes the work of four diverse artists of varying reputations: Constantino Brumidi, Horatio Greenough, Albrecht Dürer, and Michael Parkes. Each expresses his art in a different medium and each plays a role in the story, some of more significance than others. What, then, might bind them together? Most likely, with Brown's clever habit of layering meanings, it is a way of underlining his theme of *E pluribus unum*, "out of the many, one."

BRUMIDI AND GREENOUGH: SYMBOLIC GESTURES

Constantino Brumidi's *The Apotheosis of Washington*, the dome fresco in the Capitol, is the one artistic work upon which *The Lost Symbol* might be said to revolve, since it is literally the alpha and omega of aesthetic and inspi-

The Apotheosis of Washington by Constantino Brumidi (1865).
(*Photograph by Julie O'Connor*)

rational value (chapter 21 and the epilogue). Like Horatio Greenough's sculpture *Washington Enthroned*, also featured in the novel, Brumidi's frescoes were heavily influenced by the neoclassical style, a mixture of Greek, Roman, and Renaissance themes adapted to the American Enlightenment ideals of justice and democracy; the updated anthropocentric universe of Athens, Rome, and Renaissance Florence; the uniting of religion and science; and the heroic stature of leaders—in this case, George Washington, honored as both first president and national "father."

Constantino Brumidi, once identified as "the Michelangelo of the Capitol," was trained in fresco, tempera, and oil. Before emigrating to America, he had gained his reputation by restoring a segment of Raphael's Loggia in the Vatican—a magnificent set of frescoes for the public diplomatic rooms of the papal apartments, including the famous *School of Athens* (symbolizing reason and the sciences) and *Disputation of the Holy Sacrament* (signifying faith and religion). Brumidi also created works for Roman palaces, giving him intimate knowledge of the great Renaissance masters.

Returning from a working trip to Mexico in 1854, Brumidi stopped in Washington, where he learned that there was need for an artist to design and execute the frescoes for the Capitol extensions and dome. What followed is a story fraught with political intrigue, conspiracy, infighting, and government red tape, highlighted by the almost daily drama of working on a government commission during the Civil War.

The Capitol's superintendent of construction, Captain Montgomery C. Meigs, had announced his desire to re-create the splendor of Raphael's Loggia for the interior of the building. Meigs had previously given Brumidi some small commissions, and knew the artist was well trained in the classical and Renaissance fresco techniques and imagery used by Raphael. So in 1862 Brumidi was formally commissioned to cover the 4,664-square-foot canopy over the eye of the Capitol Dome with a fresco glorifying George Washington.

Brumidi's first challenge was to design a scene that worked harmoniously with the earlier historical narratives on the surrounding walls. Second was the dual task of orchestrating a design whose imagery and motif were clear from all entrances and angles under the Rotunda and one that could be read from both the floor, one hundred eighty feet below, and the closer balcony.

Brumidi was an admirer of Horatio Greenough, whose neoclassical sculpture of *Washington Enthroned* had occupied center stage on the floor of the Capitol Rotunda when finished in 1849. Whatever its value as a work of inspiration, Greenough's sculpted presentation of America's national hero in the classical nude—bare-chested with his lower torso and legs covered by classical drapery—had not been well received by the public, and it was exiled to the East Capitol Lawn in 1853, and then moved again to a yet more obscure site at the National Museum of American History, where it still remains.

Brumidi went in a different artistic direction. He depicted Washington like Zeus, but dressed instead in his military uniform as leader of the Revolutionary Army, especially significant during the then-raging Civil War. He related the American national hero and first president to the heroes of classical Greece and Rome by using a lavender-hued lap rug resting across Washington's lower torso and legs to signify classical drapery. Further, Brumidi incorporated a sheathed sword in Washington's raised left hand as a gesture of authority rather than the suggestion of surrender found in Greenough's statue.

As in his earlier Langdon novels, Brown plays as much with the discrete symbolism of gestures as he does with the overt symbolism of numbers, colors, and objects. Greenough's *Washington Enthroned* originally stood on the floor of the Rotunda directly below the Dome that would be frescoed by Brumidi. The sculptor had posed Washington's right arm as upraised with an elevated right hand forming Brown's so-called pointing gesture. Cognizant of this, Brumidi positioned his Washington in a downward pointing pose just above the same spot, thereby gesturing adulation and welcome to the earlier sculpture.

The result is that the figure on the ceiling is carefully positioned by the painter to be in a form of communication with the sculpture that once occupied the floor directly below and, intriguingly, the floor below that—a space that had once been planned as the original location for Washington's burial place.

Brown adds further spice to this mix by placing Peter Solomon's severed right hand, posed in that same "pointing gesture," almost in the exact location on the Rotunda floor where Greenough's statue had been (chapter 10). This then results in a rather bizarre confluence, as Solomon's severed hand points upward to Brumidi's Washington, who in turn points downward to Greenough's Washington and further downward to Washington's empty tomb.

Whether it's Greenough or Solomon's finger pointing up, its focus is a dome fresco similar to the renowned *Apotheosis of St. Genevieve* on the dome of the Pantheon in Paris, a work that was simultaneously religious and historical in content. Brumidi was more than familiar with classical and Christian presentations of apotheosis, for which the most important visual key was to present the figures along the perimeter as if they were "anchored" in the ground, while the individual being glorified was elevated to the heavens.

Brumidi's design may seem iconographically confusing to our twenty-first-century eyes. Like Langdon's students, or Inoue Sato, the CIA director, and Trent Anderson, chief of the Capitol police, we may be taken aback by the conjoining of historical personages with deities, especially with the label "apotheosis," which Brown categorizes simplistically as a process of deification. The tradition of apotheosis, particularly well exemplified in the Capitol Dome, indicates that an individual is glorified as an ideal of patriotism, truth, and duty. In the common visual and cultural vocabulary of the mid-nineteenth century, the depiction of abstract ideas like moral courage as a recognizable person or mythological deity was commonplace, as was the custom of anchoring them solidly to the real world they had left behind—in this case, with a select group of American inventors, financiers, philosophers, and leaders, also chosen to represent the future.

In Brumidi's fresco, a central golden sky is enclosed by a slightly triangular-shaped ring of figures that includes Washington himself. The Dome's perimeter displays an outer ring of six scenes or segments—*War, Science, Marine, Commerce, Mechanics,* and *Agriculture*—connecting classical/Renaissance ideals with America in a visual marriage of the creative sciences with pragmatism.

In the center ring, Washington is surrounded by female figures. By his outstretched right hand is Liberty, wearing her red "liberty" cap and holding the fasces, a bundle of sticks from which an axe protrudes that was an emblem signifying Roman magistrates' right to pronounce sentence. Next to Washington's raised left hand is Victory/Fame, wearing a laurel wreath, holding a palm branch (the sign of peace paralleling Washington's sheathed sword), and announcing his apotheosis through her trumpet. The biblical sign of God's peace, a rainbow, curves under his feet. Positioned then between Liberty and Fame, Washington is recognized simultaneously as a military leader and a peacemaker. The rest of this inner circle consists of thirteen maidens, each with a star above her head, who represent the original thirteen colonies. Six of these ladies turn their backs to Washington, symbolizing the states that seceded from the union during the Civil War. In the very center of this inner circle is a large sun disk and a banner reading *E pluribus unum*—another indication of this fresco's connection to Dan Brown's theme.

Of the six segments on the lower perimeter, *War* is located just below Washington's feet. It depicts a figure holding an unsheathed sword in her upraised right hand and a shield emblazoned with red and white stripes in her left. She wears a helmet covered with white stars. Often identified as Columbia, she prefigures Lady Liberty. Accompanied by the eagle, the mythological companion of Zeus and avian symbol for the new nation, she tramples the symbolic figures for Tyranny and Kingly Power. Here once again Brumidi follows the Renaissance convention of depicting contemporary recognizable figures, in this case Jefferson Davis and Alexander H. Stephens, the just vanquished leaders of the Confederacy. Continuing to *Science,* we see the goddess of wisdom, war, and the arts of civilization, Minerva, with her battle helmet and spear. She is surrounded by American inventors, including Benjamin Franklin, Samuel F. B. Morse, and Robert Fulton, and by inventions such as the electric generator and printing press.

Next is *Marine,* in which the central figure Neptune, the god of the sea, can be identified by his trident and seahorse-drawn shell chariot. He is accompanied by Venus, the goddess of love, who was born of the sea foam and is here seen laying the transatlantic cable (a historical reference contemporary to this fresco). *Commerce* features Mercury, the god of commerce, recognizable by his familiar winged sandals and cap. His right hand guides men loading a box onto a dolly and his left offers a bag of money to Robert Morris, a financier of the American Revolution.

A sailor and an anchor lead us forward to *Mechanics*. Here stands Vulcan, the god of the forge, whose right hand rests on his anvil. A steam engine and war machinery surround him. The sixth and final segment, the one symbolically at "the end of the rainbow," is *Agriculture*, personified as Ceres, the goddess of agriculture, who is seated on the newly invented McCormick reaper. "Young America" stands at the bottom of the rainbow, holding the reins of energetic horses.

As the artists and philosophers of the Renaissance envisioned themselves as the leaders of a new world order that was Athens and Rome reborn, so the politicians and the philosophers of the American Enlightenment pressed forward once again as the "true heirs" of the classical and Renaissance traditions in their newest and finest expression: America and her central immortal, George Washington. Their motto became *E pluribus unum*, which is normally translated as "out of the many, one" or "one from the many," signifying the unity of the United States.

Given the disparate nature of the artworks Brown employs in *The Lost Symbol*, his growing interest in the Masons, and his quest to rebalance religion and science, he perhaps is pushing toward a revival of what philosophers, theologians, and historians identify as *philosophia perennis*. Loosely translated as "perennial philosophy," this is a concept initiated in the sixteenth century and made popular in the early twentieth century. Perennial philosophy suggests that although there are many religions, all of them are undergirded by one constant sacred or holy truth that is identified as the one god. The idea is simple and relates both to the diversity of visual imagery in need of "decoding" in *The Lost Symbol* and to the final resolution of the novel, where Katherine reminds Langdon "God is plural because the minds of man are plural" (chapter 133). "Out of the many, one."

DÜRER'S *MELENCOLIA I:* THIS TIME IT *IS* A WOMAN

In rapid succession, from chapters 66 through 70, Dan Brown incorporates into his story one of the more elusive engravings by the German Renaissance master Albrecht Dürer (1471–1528). In his *Melencolia I,* the artist examines the relationship between artistic creativity, scientific investigation, and manual skill. Unlike the more "spiritual" inspiration Langdon gets from the Brumidi, here he finds the clue that will keep him in physical motion, chasing after the Lost Word.

It is curious, however, that despite his declared knowledge of art history, Brown chooses to emphasize only the "disguised" alchemical and mathematical symbols within Dürer's engraving when, in fact, the meaning of the figure and surroundings are richly symbolic. More surprising yet is that Dan Brown, who found Mary Magdalene hidden at the right hand of Jesus in the *Last Supper* and who has been such a champion of the sacred feminine, miscues Melencolia as a *male* figure.

Dürer's *Melencolia I* incorporates a variety of classical and Renaissance traditions into the almost miniature space of this engraving (the plate impression measures only 9⅜ by 7⅜ inches). For example, he surrounds Melencolia with the then-known tools of geometry and architecture, including the four-by-four magic square interpreted by Langdon and Katherine Solomon; a truncated rhombohedrin with the faintest depiction of a human skull; an hourglass with time running out; an empty balance or scale; a purse and keys; a comet and rainbow in the sky; a despondent genius in the company of a putto; and a dog curled up in the lower-left foreground. These details have been interpreted in a variety of ways and by many people, including the great maestro of disguised symbolism, Erwin Panofsky. The engraving's rich symbolism also led to the work being featured as the pivotal image of a 2006 international exhibition on the subject of melancholy that included works by masters from Breughel to Picasso to Edward Hopper.

The presence of the rarely discussed bat in the engraving suggests a contrast between "dark" melancholy and "noble" melancholy (as represented by the dog or putto)—a contrast that reminds observers that deciphering symbolism is often treacherous work. After all, Melencolia holds the most meaningful tool in the engraving—a compass—at the very center of the composition. Although common to all architects and geometricians, this instrument signifies to all those familiar with medieval art and theology, as Dürer would have been, the ultimate creative act: God's shaping of the universe.

The multiple interpretations of this engraving have made it highly intriguing to and influential on other artists and thinkers. Another famed German Renaissance artist, Lucas Cranach the Elder, painted his own version of *The Melancholy* in 1553. It is a recognizable visual quotation from the Dürer, from her pose, her dress, her hair, and her wings to the compass she holds in both hands. Almost sixty-five years later, the Italian Baroque artist Domenico Fetti painted his own enigmatic variation of Dürer's theme, *Melancholy* (ca. 1618), in which his kneeling female figure is oft misidentified as a penitent Mary Magdalene—a figure not unknown to Brown.

In Dürer's engraving, the figure of Melencolia takes on the classical pose of contemplation and the gesture of grief as *she* broods on the "disparate and bizarre collection of objects" spread before her. There is no question that this is a female figure, but Brown arguably misidentifies Melencolia as a male figure because, as in *The Da Vinci Code*, he apparently confuses gender with sex. Gender is culturally conditioned, so that what is masculine or feminine in the sixteenth century may not be recognized the same way in the twenty-first century. Sex, however, is simpler to identify, as it is physical and biological and doesn't reflect changes in fashion, mannerisms, and hairstyles. Look at the slope of her shoulders and the softness of her face, and remember that the Graces, the Muses, and the soul were all feminine words in classical Greek and Latin. Consider further the reality that in the classical world, of which Dürer knew much, the night, with its dark potential for dreams, images, and danger, was identified as feminine and salvific.

The legendary daughter of Saturn (Cronos), Melancholia was renowned for her introspective nature, the female embodiment of gloomy contemplation in classical mythology. Dürer's Melencolia sits like an

artist in the midst of that low point in the creative process when everything looks dark, bleak, and impossible, but action will burst forth at
any moment like the infant from the womb and the roadblock will be
removed. Dan Brown suggests Dürer's figure is in despair over not being
able to get further in the process of obtaining enlightenment and secret
knowledge, like the alchemist who just can't seem to find the philosopher's stone. Others have seen Masonic, alchemical, and psychological
symbolism in the objects gathered around her.

Whether any of these hidden meanings are valid is open to speculation and interpretation, and this keeps scholars questioning and thinking.
Even Melancholy herself is endlessly fascinating; as the Danish philosopher Søren Kierkegaard mused, "My melancholy is the most faithful mis-
tress I have known, what wonder, then, that I love her in return."

VENUS, THE THREE GRACES, AND A PORTAL TO A DIVINE WORLD

an interview with Michael Parkes

Early in *The Lost Symbol*, Katherine Solomon encounters "a large canvas depicting the Three Graces, whose nude bodies were spectacularly rendered in vivid colors." She is told by Mal'akh—who is, at that moment, posing as Peter Solomon's psychiatrist, Dr. Abaddon—that this image is "the original Michael Parkes oil." We don't know it at the time, but we will later discover that the painting conceals the hidden doorway to Mal'akh's mystical—and evil—laboratory. What we also don't know at this point, and would never know without some sleuthing, is that Michael Parkes is a real living American artist. He has been called the best exponent of magical realism in painting today, and has been likened by the *London Times* art critic to a modern mix of Botticelli, Tiepolo, Dalí, and Magritte.

Parkes lives in Spain and often paints images with mystical, esoteric, dreamlike, and surreal themes. Closely identified with a growing movement in the art world to capture the power and mystique of female creativity, intuition, and spirituality, Parkes was the guest of honor at a 2007 international show, Venus and the Female Intuition, exhibited in both Denmark and Holland.

Dan Burstein reached Michael Parkes in Spain and talked to him about his unusual image, *The Three Graces*, and its role in *The Lost Symbol*. The image itself is reproduced here with the permission of Michael Parkes and his publishing company, Swan King Editions, LLC.

Dan Brown was in Spain as an art history student while in college in the 1980s, and again in the 1990s with his wife, Blythe, who is an artist. You have been living and working in Spain throughout the last forty years . . . Did you encounter Dan and Blythe back then?

No. I have never met Dan or Blythe.

There are certain obvious similarities in your work and Dan Brown's: you place a lot of emphasis on symbols in your paintings, there are many visual and psychological allusions to ancient mystical themes in your work; you are clearly interested in mythic references to Venus and the sacred feminine, as Brown is . . . So it makes sense that he would be interested in your work. But then one day in September 2009 you find out that The Three Graces is actually referenced directly in the new Dan Brown novel as "the original Michael Parkes oil." Your painting is one of a handful of specific artworks mentioned by name. One of the others is Dürer's Melencolia I. *What did you think of that?*

It was quite intriguing to find the Dürer there as well. My background was in printmaking. I didn't start painting until after graduate school. The most transformative graphic that I remember as an undergraduate was the *Melencolia I* by Albrecht Dürer. It was this incredible, wonderful, surrealistic image, full of emotion, suggesting everywhere in the image that there was so much behind it . . . So yes, it was particularly interesting to me to find my work alongside Dürer's.

Your painting is used for a particular purpose in the home of Dr. Abaddon in the Kalorama section of Washington. Dr. Abaddon turns out to be the villain Mal'akh in disguise. He admires the painting and it is obviously one of his favorite possessions. But he also uses it as the hidden doorway to the chamber of torture, death, and destruction that lies beyond. (Abaddon, by the way, is derived from a Hebrew reference meaning "place of destruction.")

The Three Graces © 2004, a painting by Michael Parkes. All Rights Reserved.
Represented exclusively by Swan King Editions, LLC.

Do you see any special symbolic significance of your image to the world of ideas that is discussed in The Lost Symbol?

I have no idea why it's in the villain's home, as opposed to being some-where else in the story. But in terms of the painting having a place in the book as a whole, it makes personal sense to me because the painting is very much a kind of a "portal"-type painting and there is a lot of discus-sion in the book about portals and passages to otherworldly places.

Tell us what was in your thought process when you originally painted The Three Graces.

The three graces are always connected to Venus (or Aphrodite, if you want to use the Greek name). Venus, throughout the history of art, takes on different levels or layers of meaning. During the Renaissance, you have paintings of Venus as a sensual nude. In those images, the three graces are shown as handmaidens to this hedonistic Venus, emphasizing themes of desire and fulfillment.

And then the next level up from that, Venus becomes a more noble figure. Venus now represents human love; love for mankind, harmony, unity, and so on. She moves away from this sensual portrayal and goes to a more humanitarian type of figure. The three graces then are often as-sociated with chastity, beauty, and harmony, or platonic love.

Plato suggested that the connections of Venus to sexual attraction are irrelevant. What's important about Venus is the way she symbolizes what he called *humanitas*, in other words, the Venus that is giving order, har-mony, and beauty to mankind. And then you have the other level, which is Venus the spiritual guide, offering divine love.

I was particularly interested in the space between the humanitarian Venus and the divine love Venus. Inhabiting this role, Venus is like the intuitive counsel, nurturing higher ideals and the beauty of the arts. The three graces then become the muses of art, literature, and music, so you're up one more rung still. If you continue on this ascending path, you arrive at what Plato called the Venus Urania, or "heavenly Venus," divine love.

This is where the idea of the portal arises in my *Three Graces* painting.

Everything that I've talked about up until now—the three different stages of interpretation of Venus and the three graces—is a normal philosophical discussion. But then you reach the point of divine love and the door is closed because you have now arrived at the level of esoteric knowledge. And so you have to go into the esoteric legend of Venus to capture what's going on behind the veil.

And if we go through that portal, what do we find?

In various esoteric texts, Venus is connected to the energy of divine creation or feminine active creation. So now you have a deity that is representing an energy that is descending from the highest planes down through the subtle physical levels, coming down to the densest of matter in the earth plane. And she is bringing beauty and order to an earth plane that was in total chaos. She is thus bringing order out of chaos.

Or as Dan Brown would have it in The Lost Symbol, *one of the most important Masonic axioms is "ordo ab chao"—order out of chaos in Latin.*

Yes. And as Venus descends through the planes, you can imagine this incredible, subtle, divine energy descending into the dense matter that's getting denser and denser and heavier and darker. In the esoteric texts that I've read, the three graces are actually guardians of the three final portals that are opened for Venus to descend to the earth.

Again, no surprise after The Da Vinci Code, *which emphasized the sacred feminine and the role in prehistory of the female goddess, that Dan Brown would find your vision of Venus and the three graces to be of interest . . . What are your thoughts, looking more generally at* The Lost Symbol? *What interests you about it, aside from seeing your own work in it?*

Dan Brown's new book arrives at a pivotal point in history. There is now a long history of humankind's physical evolution; but now we can also talk about our spiritual evolution. His basic premise is that we, as humans, also stand as gods. And I think: okay, that's a wonderful concept. The whole point is the transition between the animal human and the divine human; that's the crux. We have reached a crisis point in our evolution where we *must* evolve spiritually if we are to survive. But we can't just do it as a great Buddhist master might. Our own individual spiritual elevation is not the central issue. What's important now is our collective spiritual evolution.

That's when it really becomes interesting, frightening, exciting—all of those things all mixed in together, because it's something that has never happened in the physical plane before. Dan Brown is saying something like: yes; right here, right now. The secret is that it's here, it's now, and it's happening, so you have to know there's no turning back. You have to say okay, I have to embrace this because there's really no choice.

ART, ENCRYPTION, AND
THE PRESERVATION OF SECRETS

an interview with Jim Sanborn

Cryptic messages carved into durable materials and created to assure their longevity go back centuries. Many of these messages are readable today, such as the Egyptian hieroglyphs that finally revealed their secrets after the discovery and analysis of the Rosetta Stone in the nineteenth century. Other messages remain unsolved. Among the most famous of these is the Phaistos Disk, a circular clay tablet discovered in Crete from the second millennium B.C., and encoded with an "alphabet" of 45 different symbols and 241 signs stamped into both sides in a spiral pattern. The code has yet to be cracked on thousands of older objects from the Bronze Age, inscribed with the still-undeciphered pictographic Indus script from the Indian subcontinent. Many other examples from the ancient world continue to defy even the best linguists and code breakers working with twenty-first-century software tools.

The most famous such message in our own time was carved into the *Kryptos* sculpture. It was created by the sculptor Jim Sanborn and is comprised of copper sheets, red and green slate, white quartz, and petrified wood. Commissioned for the central courtyard of CIA Headquarters in Langley, Virginia, *Kryptos* is described by the narrator of *The Lost Symbol* as "a massive S-shaped panel of copper, set on its edge like a curling metal wall. Engraved into the expansive surface of the wall were nearly two thousand letters . . . organized into a baffling code" (see illustrations). As we will learn from Elonka Dunin's essay that concludes this chapter, *Kryptos*, too, may be among those long-kept secrets in history. Although the code has been broken for three of its passages, the fourth riddle has yet to be solved, despite copious efforts by the world's best crypto-graphic minds and their sophisticated computer programs.

Jim Sanborn is noted for his science-based installations that illuminate hidden forces. He has created artwork for major U.S. museums, the National Oceanic and Atmospheric Administra-tion, and the Massachusetts Institute of Technology, and also designed the espionage-inspired decor for the Zola restaurant, ironically enough next door to Washington, D.C.'s International Spy Museum.

Here, Sanborn is in conversation with Elonka Dunin, who, along with Jim Gillogly and a tiny handful of other cryptogra-phers, have come as close as anyone—at least anyone who has come forward—to solving a set of symbols and codes not even Robert Langdon could solve. Intriguingly and tantalizingly, San-born tells us here that even after the fourth panel of *Kryptos* is decoded, there could still be a "riddle within the riddle." Hmmm. Sounds a bit like *The Lost Symbol* itself.

Where did you get the idea for Kryptos?

When the Central Intelligence Agency was constructing the New Head-quarters Building in 1988, the General Services Administration selected artists for the CIA project as part of their Art in Architecture program. The panel reviewed the work of many artists and then chose me for the outdoor work, in part because I already had a reputation for creating public artworks, and because my work tended to deal with the hidden forces of nature, like the earth's magnetic field, and the Coriolis force.

Kryptos sculpture (1990) by Jim Sanborn at the CIA headquarters, Langley, Virginia.

The panel felt that my work with the invisible forces of nature could transfer to the invisible forces of mankind. A stretch perhaps, but I guess it worked. I spent six months doing research about the agency and decided to create a work that was encoded. My first presentation of *Kryptos* to the panel was accepted.

Was there anyone from the CIA directly involved in creating the encryption on the work?

During its development, while I was casting about for assistance with the code, the agency suggested Ed Scheidt, the retired chairman of the CIA's Cryptographic Center.

In the early stages of planning for Kryptos, *you said that you were doing it in conjunction with a "prominent fiction writer." Who did you have in mind?*

That was an idea that I entertained when I was trying to decide how I was going to write the plaintext. I considered using somebody, but that idea got scrapped early on. Why let someone else in on the secret? I decided instead to keep my project compartmentalized so that as few people as possible would know what the code was.

Have you used puzzles and encryption in other pieces that you've done?

Kryptos was the first to use actual encryption. A year after its dedication, I had an exhibition at the Corcoran Gallery in Washington called Covert Obsolescence, which included encrypted pieces. My other encrypted works include *Binary Systems* at the IRS Computing Center in West Virginia; *Circulating Capital* at Central Connecticut State University; the *Cyrillic Projector* at the University of North Carolina, Charlotte; and numerous smaller gallery works.

In Part 2 of Kryptos, *a portion of the answer says, "Who knows the exact location, only WW." You have since said that this refers to William Webster. Can you expand upon why you included his initials in the answer?*

He was the brainchild behind the commissioning of artworks for the agency, as a way to increase the agency's "openness."

Is Webster, also a former director of the FBI, necessary to solve the puzzle? Does he have information that is needed?

Only insofar as he was the progenitor of *Kryptos*.

Part 2 also has latitude and longitude coordinates. Where do those point to?

The coordinates were based on a United States Geologic Survey bench-mark that was on-site during construction (1988–1990). However, when I revisited the sculpture this year, 2009, I noticed that the marker didn't seem to be there anymore. I also noticed that the landscape around the buildings has changed quite a bit since the 1990 installation. Some areas have been excavated that weren't before, and the topography has changed.

Part 2 also has the phrase "It's buried out there somewhere." Did you bury something at the CIA?

Maybe, maybe not.

Outside the front entrance of the New Headquarters Building, you also created some pieces with large granite slabs, and Morse code messages. These say things such as "SHADOW FORCES," "T IS YOUR POSITION," and others.

Maybe, maybe not. I have almost zero recollection of the Morse code part that I wrote. I don't remember the words *Shadow Forces*.

Do the Morse messages continue under the granite slabs?

Yes, they do, for some distance.

How would researchers find out what the hidden parts of the messages say?

I have no idea.

Have you made any provisions for the full plaintext to be revealed at some future time, such as a date sometime after you are departed?

A date for it to be revealed? No.

When did you first hear about Dan Brown's use of Kryptos?

I first learned of this from a reporter for Wired.com, Kim Zetter, who wrote an article about *Kryptos* that was published in early 2005. Through her article, I learned that there were two hidden references to *Kryptos* in the book jacket of *The Da Vinci Code*. One had the latitude and longitude coordinates from Part 2, but were off by one degree. The other was the message "Only WW knows."

And what did you think about that?

All artworks should be open to interpretation. It's almost the definition of what art is. Everybody is going to look at an artwork and have their own opinions about it. To be honest though, I was a bit annoyed when I heard about the inclusion of *Kryptos* on the cover of *The Da Vinci Code*, only because I had not been contacted.

Have you read any of Dan Brown's books?

Ordinarily, I am a reader of nonfiction. But yes, once I heard there were references to *Kryptos* in the book jacket of *The Da Vinci Code*, I felt I had to, and I was advised to.

What is your opinion of The Lost Symbol?

I haven't finished reading it yet, but several people have called to tell me about it. So far, as it relates to *Kryptos*, it looks like a process of atonement.

In his novel, he implies that Kryptos *may have some Masonic messages. Are you a Freemason?*

No, I've never been a member of any fraternal organizations. I'm just not a joiner. However, in the past, I have considered myself to be a stonemason of sorts, in the original and ancient sense of the word, going back to the masons who worked on such archaic structures as the pyramids. I have made two trips to Egypt, and was deeply influenced by what I saw there. I have also created several large works in stone, including some with the pyramidal form, or truncated pyramids, such as *Elk Delta*, in Charleston, West Virginia, and *Patapsco Delta*, in Baltimore, Maryland.

As a stonemason, what do you think of the Masonic art and architecture around Washington, D.C.?

I am of course familiar with the Washington, D.C., architecture, and enjoy the monumental scale and the Egyptian elements. The Freemasons have definitely made some interesting architectural choices. The café I frequent is near the House of the Temple on Sixteenth Street, and I have frequently walked past it and admired the sphinxes.

What's your next project?

For three years I have been working on an installation called *Terrestrial Physics*, which is a working re-creation of the first particle accelerator to fission uranium. This experiment was critically important to human history, and in addition, it took place in my hometown of Washington, D.C., in 1939. The accelerator will be shown at the Biennial of the Americas Denver in summer 2010.

What has been the most surprising thing for you about creating Kryptos?

Its persistence on the stage of popular culture. I honestly believed that the game would be over by now, so I am pleased with its longevity. Of course, once the code is deciphered, I'm not convinced the true meaning will be clear. There's another deeper mystery, a riddle within a riddle, and I don't know that it will ever be totally understood. This is a good thing. I think it's important that every artwork hold a viewer's attention for as long as possible.

THE SUMMER OF THE CLUES

by David A. Shugarts

The sequel to Dan Brown's *Da Vinci Code* had been anticipated for years. But when Doubleday, Brown's publisher, finally confirmed in early 2009 that *The Lost Symbol* would be published in September, the collective blood pressure of Dan Brown watchers started to rise. Interest in *The Lost Symbol* was hyped even higher by a buzz-generating campaign by Doubleday to seed clues in cyberspace throughout the summer of 2009. The game was on for those whose interests run to code breaking and arcane bits of history.

Initially, there wasn't any prize to be won. It was a chance for Dan Brown's fans to have some fun. For mere bragging rights, people from all over the world had a chance to decrypt ciphers, grope at historical references, and soak up the deeper meaning of symbols of all cultures. Eventually, the marketing buzz coalesced into a contest to win one of thirty-three copies of *The Lost Symbol* signed by the author.

That was the outer envelope of what was going on. But, like all mysteries, including *The Lost Symbol*, there were deeper levels. What developed was a special little cyber realm of a very few people who stayed up late into the night solving the puzzles. They formed a loose affiliation, fulfilling the promise of social networking. And there were moments of intrigue.

It all started on June 23 when Facebook's page for Dan Brown, and his Twitter page for *The Lost Symbol*, posted a clue: "Codes of ethics? T 10 C; 6 P O T SOD; 12 S O T Z."

This was promptly solved by—among others—Christopher Hodapp, author of *Freemasons for Dummies* and a leading figure in Freemasonry, who hosts his own blogsite at http://www.freemasonsfordummies.blogspot .com and is writing *Deciphering the Lost Symbol: Freemasons, Myths and Mysteries of Washington, D.C.*

Hodapp decoded the clue as follows: "The 10 Commandments; 6 Points Of The Star Of David; 12 Signs Of The Zodiac."

The following day, more clues were posted by Doubleday, and thus began a steady stream, two to four clues on practically every weekday, right through the summer. Before the spigot was turned off, on the eve of *TLS*'s release on September 15, there were about 130 clues.

In short order, another Freemason and author, Mark Koltko-Rivera, cranked up a blogsite, http://lostsymboltweets.blogspot.com, and began to post the clues daily in sequence, along with decryptions and thought-provoking explications. Very soon, he commanded a following. If you were going to try to keep track of the action on *Lost Symbol* clues, you more or less had to keep tabs on Hodapp's or Koltko-Rivera's blogs. (At times, Kath-leeen Schmid Koltko-Rivera, Mark's wife, was the puzzle solver.) Koltko-Rivera is a contributor to *Secrets of The Lost Symbol*. (See page 307 for his take on the Doubleday clues and chapter 2 for his essay on Masonic rituals.)

Within days, Hodapp revealed another solution, to a puzzle posed as "MAEIETCTETAOTHPL." This turned out to be one of Dan Brown's previously used favorite coding systems, the Caesar square. If you put the letters in four rows of four, you get:

M	A	E	I
E	T	C	T
E	T	A	O
T	H	P	L

If you now read down each column in turn, you get "MEET AT THE CAPITOL." To all who were hoping to confirm that *TLS* would be set in Washington, this seemed to do the trick. As it turned out, this clue exactly presaged the plot of *TLS*, since Robert Langdon was taken directly to the Capitol building on his arrival in Washington.

Another author joined the Twitter chatter in late June: Greg Taylor, an Australian who had long studied esoterica and for years had hosted a Web site at dailygrail.com. He had authored a predictive book about the sequel to *The Da Vinci Code* in 2004 called *Da Vinci in America* that eventually was retitled to *The Guide to Dan Brown's The Lost Symbol*. Taylor also had a blog at www.thecryptex.com to keep track of news about Dan Brown and *TLS*. On his Twitter account, he logged in the answers as people solved them, and he provided encouragement and shared bits of intel.

There were now hundreds of netizens making stabs at solving the daily clues. At first it was a cacophony, with many players and many wild guesses or blurted-out half-solutions. But then a pattern began to emerge. Some of the puzzle sleuths were simply better at it than the others. Sometimes they were quicker, sometimes more accurate, and sometimes both.

One star emerged almost from the start. She was Cheryl Lynn Helm, a music scholar and choral arranger from Delaware. She showed a full complement of skills, from the ability to decode ciphers to rapidly using search engines to ferret out answers to historical riddles. Here's one:

Near the buttonwood's accord lies a field of Christ.
His marker there would make even Khafra smile.

The clue was posted on Facebook at 11:18 A.M. on July 9. Just twelve minutes later, Cheryl Helm posted the answer: the grave of Alexander Hamilton, America's first secretary of the treasury. Helm had quickly discovered that Hamilton's grave, topped with a pyramid (à la Khafra, a pharaoh entombed in Giza's second-largest pyramid), lies in Trinity Churchyard, not far from New York's Wall Street, where an agreement was signed in 1792 that established the New York Stock Exchange.

Everything began to accelerate. Now it was almost a requirement that you needed to be on Twitter continuously while also monitoring Facebook and checking in every hour or two at several other Web sites and blogs. Dan Brown's Twitter account eventually acquired more than 4,900 followers and, in turn, the Doubleday team was following more than 5,300 people on Twitter; meanwhile, Dan Brown's Facebook page acquired more than 99,000 fans.

Two other adepts began to work their way into the foreground. One was Simon Cassidy, a retired software engineer from England who divides his time between San Francisco and New Zealand. Cassidy is also an expert on Stonehenge and on the Elizabethan-era magus, John Dee. Another was Sari Valon, a writer from the Toronto area.

Enter, too, a young computer programmer from Kansas with the improbable name of Bill Gates. As one of his hobbies, Gates had taken an interest in cryptography, and had even worked out his own algorithm for deciphering codes. Gates began to solve *The Lost Symbol* puzzles like a grand master, nailing the answers quicker than others, or at times being the only one to achieve a solution.

In late July, Gates achieved an astounding solution of a two-part puzzle, one that almost defies description. (He actually published an explanation of it for those fascinated few who tried to keep up with him.)

The clue confronting Gates was an image of a series of books on a shelf, with their titles obviously Photoshopped. The titles were anagrams that, when solved, spelled out cryptic instructions: "reverse alpha," "number letter," "follow sequence," and "Vignere keyword." (The last is a misspelling that refers to the Vigenere cipher technique, a "polyalphabetic cipher" that is arcane except to cryptography buffs.)

Gates deduced that these instructions and a further line of code were to be applied to the solutions to the ten previous clues. These solutions had to be arranged in reverse alphabetical order, then the coded line could be applied by row and letter sequence, to find a single word solution: "enigma." It would be tempting to stop at that point because Enigma was the nickname of the famous encryption machine used by the Germans in World War II.

But a new image clue was posted by Doubleday, a series of apparently random letters in rows and columns, inscribed on a stone column. As Gates explained it, "At first I thought it was a columnar transcription cipher, which led me down a series of wrong paths and wasted several hours of my life." However, using letter frequency analysis, Gates came to the conclusion that his strategy wasn't going to yield an answer in English text.

"After opening my mind to other possible types of ciphers, one of the clues from the first part of the puzzle jumped out at me—'Vignere keyword,'" Gates said. "I had thought this was just a part of the first puzzle I hadn't figured out what to do with yet. Then I realized that the solution to the puzzle *was* the keyword for a Vigenere cipher. So, the letters on the column are a Vigenere cipher, and the keyword is *enigma*. With that information I could quickly decipher the column text."

Gates came up with the answer, a quote from an obscure English cleric of the eighteenth century, Robert Hall: "A religion without its mystery is a temple without a god." This well-turned phrase would later prove intellectually meaningful in the context of reading *TLS* (whereas many of the clues turned out to be red herrings), but Robert Hall was not part of the plot or otherwise directly relevant to the book.

The complexity of this particular solution began to lead some of us to wonder if Dan Brown really planned on incorporating such difficult codes into *The Lost Symbol*. As it turned out, Vigenere ciphers and the other really difficult coding methods did not appear in *TLS*. It also led to the suspicion that the unseen team at Doubleday launching the clues on the Web was not necessarily following any strict adherence to *TLS*, and they may not have seen the book's manuscript.

One clue brought this question into focus: "Mystery: Unmarked $20s. Airstair escape. Never seen again."

The answer was D. B. Cooper, the legendary airline hijacker who parachuted from the aft stairs of a Boeing 727 over Washington State in 1971 and was never caught. How did this connect with *TLS*? It didn't. No one could find any connection. And there were further daily clues that pointed to great thefts and crimes, often involving artwork, but not really related to *TLS*, as it turned out.

In other words, the Doubleday team was tossing out red herrings.

———————

It didn't much matter, because now a remarkable transformation was occurring. The top puzzle sleuths—Bill Gates, Cheryl Helm, Simon Cassidy, and Sari Valon—began to meld themselves into a team. From here on out, they began to collaborate, and they made a ferocious combination, quite like a pack of hounds with the scent of a quarry in the air.

Each day they would check the clues and begin to tweet suggestions and share discoveries. They would solve the puzzles, usually within minutes of their posting. After a while it no longer even mattered whether they got recognition, so they frequently began to skip mentioning the answers on the Facebook page. It was sufficient that their followers on Twitter could see their success. They had become a "crowd-sourcing" team—or, perhaps, a *posse*.

Gates and Helm typically led the way in solving ciphers (including a supercomplicated "Vigenere autokey cipher"), but everyone in the posse joined in for the other clues, and usually solved them in minutes. Once in a while, though, they would still be at it past midnight, and that's when Greg Taylor would chime in from Down Under, half a day ahead by time zones, with a tip or suggestion.

I also got into the fray, mainly as a kind of cheerleader, although I did offer an occasional suggestion. Simon Cassidy and Bill Gates each credit me with one instance of being useful. Most of the time, I would have barely conjured up a strategy to try, when I would see the tweet or Facebook entry from one of the others, announcing a solution.

Every conceivable symbolic coding system was thrown into the mix. There were clues in Egyptian hieroglyphics, Babylonian cuneiform, semaphore flags, Morse code, plenty of rebuses, and a healthy serving of ambigrams. In *Angels & Demons,* Dan Brown had provided a prominent display case for the exquisite ambigrams of the very talented John Langdon (a real-life friend of the Brown family whose surname was appropriated by Dan Brown in creating Robert Langdon). In the Doubleday team's ambigrams, though, it was evident that Langdon's touch was missing.

One clue used a special alphabet, the unique stick figures from the Sherlock Holmes story "The Adventure of the Dancing Men," by Sir Arthur Conan Doyle. One clue was written in Hebrew, another in Basque.

One clue was a very short snippet of written music—not even two full measures—and Cheryl Helm pounced quickly, within minutes announcing it was "Mozart: Rondo Alla Turca, from Sonata #11, K 331." Mozart was a Freemason and composed many pieces of Masonic music.

A series of clues for about a week seemed to be related to the general theme of women in history. Some of these answers included Queen Boudicca, Olympias (a snake-worshipping Greek princess), Cleopatra, Artemisia Gentileschi (an Italian Baroque painter), Emily Dickinson, and Wu Zetian (China's only empress). It appears that none of them were connected to *TLS* specifically.

Some of the puzzles were crafted in ways that required a bit of graphic skill. In one case, an image hid some letters until you changed the color balance and contrast in Photoshop, then the words "Invisible College" appeared. This is the name that the early members of the Royal Society gave themselves in seventeenth-century England. In those days, science and alchemy were essentially the same pursuits, but the Royal Society eventually came to stand for the pinnacle of scientific endeavors. Meanwhile, the coincidence that many of its members were also early Freemasons led to rumors of conspiracy. Isaac Newton was a president of the Royal Society, and later Benjamin Franklin was welcomed into its ranks. Both were connected to themes in *TLS*. Several other members of the Royal Society ended up being mentioned in the book, which also tells the story of the Invisible College and its transformation into the Royal Society.

Another puzzle offered a grid of seemingly random letters, along with a black rectangle with some holes in it. If you could superimpose the black mask onto the grid, you could discover the sequence "stormonthesea," which refers to *Storm on the Sea of Galilee,* a painting by Rembrandt that was stolen in 1990 from the Isabella Stewart Gardner Museum in Boston and has never been recovered, a heist said to be the largest art theft in history. Intriguing as the story of the museum heist is, none of it seemed to have any link to *TLS*.

In early August, Bill Gates made a startling discovery. While the Double-day team was releasing clues on Facebook and Twitter, Amazon.com had been posting the same clues on its sales page for *TLS*, apparently as a means of archiving the clues. However, Amazon had gotten out of sync, and the clues for the following day were being posted one day early!

Gates promptly solved the clues and posted the answers. He also shared this news with the posse, and now they all fell into a routine of waiting until around midday when Amazon posted the new clues (for the following day), then solving them before most of the rest of the world had even seen them. They openly tweeted about it, but Doubleday never changed the routine, right up to the last clue, which was still released a day early on the Amazon page.

But Gates and the posse had other challenges anyway. In July, Double-day had released images of the dust jackets of *TLS* on U.S. and U.K. edi-tions. On the U.S. jacket, there were lots of symbols and it was clear that some were arrayed as codes to be solved. There were two series of codes printed in red ink. One was a bunch of numbers, and Gates turned his attention to it.

In decoding ciphers, sometimes a simple "brute force" method works best. Gates had a piece of software that simply tried out all the letter com-binations that corresponded with the red numbers. It gave him a couple of dozen possible answers, but one stood out: POPES PANTHEON. It seemed the likely answer, and could apply to two different structures, both designed by John Russell Pope. One is the Scottish Rite's House of the Temple, which figures prominently in *TLS*, and might be considered a "pantheon" in the sense that the Freemasons honor all religions there. The other is the Jefferson Memorial, which was specifically patterned after the Pantheon of Rome. Gates solved this in late August, well ahead of anyone else.

The other group of red codes were scattered around the front jacket and spine; the back of *TLS* wasn't revealed (and wouldn't be until the book was released). But Gates and the posse could make a number of deduc-tions. First, they recalled that when *The Da Vinci Code* was released, there was a contest that involved calling a phone number at Random House in New York. Second, the codes that were visible were BI, C2, H5, J5, hinting that the full sequence would correspond to letter-number pairs from A through J—in other words, likely a ten-digit phone number. Not only that, but it was possible to guess the Random House (the parent publishing company that owns Doubleday) office telephone exchange in New York. Gates had it figured out down to (212) 782-?5?5 and he knew that some netizens were surely dialing all 100 of the possible number combinations, hoping to score way ahead of everyone else, but he was reluctant to disturb that many people by calling wrong numbers. (This coded number is not to be confused with Peter Solomon's phone number in Washington, published openly on page 15 of *TLS*, which many readers tried dialing—only to get a waggish Brownian message that purported to be from Peter Solomon.)

As expected, confirmation of a phone-number quest soon surfaced. At Dan Brown's official *The Lost Symbol* Web site (thelostsymbol.com) on September 8, a contest called Symbol Quest opened up, and Gates and the posse soared over this hurdle. It involved answering 33 riddles to identify 33 symbols in perfect sequence, and dropping them into a center ring. If you did that without error, you got a voice message from Dan Brown saying that the *TLS* dust jacket would contain an encoded phone number. The first thirty-three people to call that number would receive copies of *TLS* signed by Dan Brown himself.

It got down to the final week before the September 15 release of *The Lost Symbol*. At the *Today* show on NBC, Matt Lauer began to announce the last daily clues, a series of four locations that would definitely appear in *TLS*. Gates and the posse aced the first three locations (Smithsonian Support Center, U.S. Botanical Garden, House of the Temple) and only got the last one wrong because they listened to an errant journalist (me), who had been allowed into the deliberations and suggested Union Station. Otherwise, they would surely have chosen correctly, the George Washington Masonic National Memorial.

And now it was the eve of *TLS*'s release, September 14, 2009. Everyone was hoping for a peek at the back of the dust jacket, which would reveal the last two digits of the phone number. And somehow, someone got it—Gates doesn't know who. But he credits Greg Taylor for passing along the two numbers, and they were shared with the posse. For a very short window of time, each caller was instructed to send an e-mail to a specific address, with "Robert Langdon's favorite symbol" mentioned in the subject (it's the Egyptian ankh).

At press time, Bill Gates and Cheryl Helm were proud recipients of their *TLS* copies, signed in silver ink by Dan Brown. Simon Cassidy and Sari Valon were still hoping.

By late October, the posse had drifted off into their own separate lives again. The summer of the clues was over. The book was at last published, but it was a kind of anticlimax to the incredible range of the clues and codes, and the activity and interaction that went into solving them. For a certain group of people, the meaning of the experience was all about the journey. Arriving at the destination seemed not so critical in the end.

William Wirt's Skull, Albrecht Dürer's Magic Square

The Doubleday Clues and The Lost Symbol

by Mark E. Koltko-Rivera

We know Dan Brown likes red herrings—he even named a character in *The Da Vinci Code* after this plot device (Bishop Aringarosa's surname means "red herring" in Italian). In all the Robert Langdon tales, the Harvard symbologist is forever going down one road of reasoning only to reach a dead end. But along the way, Langdon has many points to make. Even when something turns out to be for naught in terms of the plot, we, the readers, have learned something new. Just before *TLS* was published, a series of official clues emerged about the then strictly guarded secret content of the new book. Mark E. Koltko-Rivera was among the first to start blogging about the possible meaning of these clues. We asked him to look back at the clues and give us a postmortem on what he found most intriguing.

Exactly twelve weeks before the publication date of *The Lost Symbol*, the book's publisher, Doubleday, began to send out clues about the content of Dan Brown's long-awaited novel. The clues went out by Twitter, with many clues being reproduced on the Dan Brown Fan page on Facebook. (A few clues just went out on Facebook.) The clues involved a wide-ranging array of puzzles: ciphered messages, anagrams, rebuses, photographs, geographical coordinates, works of art, references to historical personages from the Renaissance to the present day, and more.

Three days after Doubleday began sending out these clues, I established an Internet site (now called "Discovering *The Lost Symbol:* The Blog") where I offered answers and interpretations of the clues. I reported solutions to the puzzles; I gave historical background about the people, places, and events alluded to in the solutions; and I explained what importance any of this might have for the forthcoming novel.

In short, I had a blast. As a Freemason myself, it was fun to explain the links that many of the clues had to Freemasonry (or to myths about Freemasonry). It was intellectually stimulating to go over so much material involving so many different topics (ancient cryptography; modern double agents; Renaissance art; the American Founding Fathers; the Babington plot against Queen Elizabeth I; the temple at Chichén Itzá, and much more). I felt that I had a real handle on where the novel might go, in a tale involving dastardly double crosses and conspiracies stretching from before the American Revolution up to our own day.

And then the novel was released on September 15, 2009.

On the one hand, I was very happy to read the story that Dan Brown actually wrote. On the other hand, I was stunned to find out that most of the clues issued by Doubleday bore very little relation to anything in the novel. The Illuminati? Hardly mentioned. Double crosses dating back to the Revolution? Nothing. Ancient buildings with alignments to the stars, the sun, and the seasons? Zipperoo. American Revolution or modern-day double agents? Nary a one.

On the other hand, a small number of the clues were anything but red herrings. Freemasonry and its cryptographic systems were indeed central to the novel, as even the very first of the clues suggested. Albrecht Dürer, that master of the German Renaissance, mentioned in the solution of two of the Doubleday clues, makes an appearance through a specific mysterious detail in one of his masterpieces, *Melencolia I,* the magic square. For the most part, though, there was a real disconnect between the clues and the novel. Why? We may never know. However, the sheer brilliance of some of the clues, and their range through history and a variety of intellectual disciplines, can be appreciated in their own right. Below, I describe just two of my favorite Doubleday clues, and some of my thoughts about them.

WILLIAM WIRT AND HIS SKULL

The sixth Doubleday clue, posted to Twitter at 3:36 P.M. PDT on Wednesday, June 24:

Who stole William Wirt's skull?

The clue refers to a real person with an unusual history—somewhat peculiar during his life, and downright bizarre after his death.

Today, William Wirt (1772–1834) is mostly remembered for the work he did in helping to prosecute (unsuccessfully) Aaron Burr for treason in 1807. Largely for his distinguished work in that effort, he was appointed attorney general for the United States. He served from 1817 to 1829. However, I thought that Wirt was likely of interest to Dan Brown because of what he did after his retirement at the age of fifty-seven. To fully appreciate Wirt's place in *The Lost Symbol,* we have to consider one of the stranger aspects of American history: the anti-Masonic period. It is a story of deceit, political conspiracy, and possibly murder, with effects spanning generations—in other words, the perfect backstory for a Dan Brown novel.

In the 1820s, in upstate New York, a practicing stonemason who was not a Freemason, William Morgan, somehow blustered his way into some Masonic Lodge meetings, where he quickly learned Masonic ritual. With Morgan able to pass himself off as a Mason, his services came in demand at lodges in western New York for his ability to perform Masonic ritual with a resonant voice and an impressive delivery. On the basis of his supposed but faked membership in the Masonic fraternity, Morgan was admitted to a Masonic "high-degree" organization, the Holy Royal Arch (part of the York Rite of Freemasonry). For reasons unknown, Morgan became disaffected from Masonry, and he decided to publish publicly the rituals of the first three degrees of Freemasonry (which had been exposed to the public on several occasions before), as well as the degrees of the Holy Royal Arch (which had *not* previously been published for the public).

In September 1826, Morgan was kidnapped by several New York Masons who were offended by Morgan's plans to publish Masonic ritual. What happened next has been a mystery for almost two centuries. Some say that Morgan was murdered, drowned in the Niagara River, with his body dumped into Niagara Falls. Others say that he was released alive into Canada and told never to return. Some rumors have it that he made his way to the Caribbean and died there many years later. The only thing certain is that Morgan was never seen again.

Following Morgan's disappearance, several Masons were tried for his abduction, only to be acquitted or punished with very light sentences. The public was outraged, both by Morgan's supposed murder by Masons, and by what appeared to be Masonic collusion to avoid punishing his supposed murderers. This public outrage came to be led by religious leaders, some of whom were still in fear of the imagined power of the Illuminati. Although the Illuminati were never more than a small group that had been suppressed in Europe since 1784, several authors had written quasiparanoid accusations blaming the Illuminati for the French Revolution, and accusing the Illuminati of trying to take over American government through the Freemasons. In turn, the public and religious outrage was harnessed by political forces who were working against the policies of Andrew Jackson, a Freemason, who had been elected U.S. president in 1828.

These forces—public fury, religious outrage, and political maneuvering—combined to create the first "third party" in American politics:

the Anti-Masonic Party (also called the American Party), which declared its intent to be the destruction of all "secret" societies. Here is where William Wirt entered the picture.

In 1830, Wirt accepted the nomination for U.S. president on the sponsorship of the Anti-Masonic Party. Some might not consider Wirt to have been a likely candidate, given that he had been a Freemason. (Indeed, during his candidacy, he delivered a speech *defending* Freemasonry.) In the 1832 U.S. presidential election, the Anti-Masonic Party carried only Vermont, Wirt receiving a total of 7 electoral votes, and about 33,000 popular votes. Jackson handily won reelection. Wirt himself died just two years later, of complications due to a cold, and was interred in the vaults of the U.S. Congressional Cemetery.

Now the story takes its turn for the bizarre.

Sometime in the 1970s, well over a century after Wirt's interment, it appears that someone went into his crypt, disturbed the bones of some of the bodies that had been left there, and took Wirt's skull. (Even more creepy: either then or at another time, someone left the body of an un-identified child in this crypt.) The theft was not discovered for many years, until after an anonymous caller in 2003 offered to return the skull, which, he said, had been in the possession of a collector who had since died. Ultimately, the skull was put in the possession of a Washington, D.C., City Council member for return to the Wirt crypt, where it now resides.

Here we have a prominent nineteenth-century political figure, some-one who had known some of the American Founding Fathers in his youth, who abandoned the Masonic Order and ran for president on the Anti-Masonic Party ticket, and who then had his skull stolen right out from his crypt. Why *wouldn't* Dan Brown write about this?

Despite such a logical set of reasons for Dan Brown to be interested in him, Wirt rated only a passing mention in *The Lost Symbol*. But that is one of the pleasures of Dan Brown's books: even the most fleeting detail usually has a fascinating story behind it.

Albrecht Dürer

The ninth Doubleday clue, posted to Twitter at 2:15 P.M. PDT on Thursday, June 25:

**Albrecht Dürer, whose father was a goldsmith, was
trained as a metalworker at a young age.**

The clue refers to one of the great artists of the Renaissance in northern Europe, the German Albrecht Dürer (1471–1528). Although Dürer is known primarily for his prints made from woodcuts and, especially, his engravings on metal, the clue mentions his early training as a metalworker. The content reads like a sentence out of an art history text, nothing really provocative.

Of course, in Dan Brown's novels, many a famed artist is a member of some centuries-spanning conspiracy. As it happens, Dürer actually *has* long been rumored to have been some sort of Freemason from the era before Freemasonry became public during the formation of the first Grand Lodge, in London in 1717.

The basis of this rumor is the fact that some of Dürer's pieces contain depictions of objects that have either real or reputed symbolic significance to Freemasons. The most prominent example of this is *Melencolia I,* a copper engraving dating from 1514.

In this piece, an adult-size female angel sits in thought, holding, for no obvious reason, a set of *compasses* such as might be used by a stonemason, carpenter, or architect. (Of course, the compasses are known to be an important symbol in Freemasonry.)

Although the bottom of the etching shows the tools of a carpenter (a reference to Jesus, the carpenter's son?), the most prominent finished products appear to be stone, including a sphere and a large polyhedral prism. These are both portrayed as exquisitely finished pieces of work, smooth pieces of worked and polished stone that call to mind the *smooth or polished ashlar* that represents, in Masonic symbolism, the individual Mason after he has worked to perfect his character. (I have seen actual stones exemplifying the rough ashlar—unworked stone, and the smooth ashlar—

smoothly polished stone, in every Masonic Lodge I have ever visited. Dan Brown mentions the role of the ashlar in chapter 85 of *TLS* as a metaphor for "transformation," an important theme within *TLS*.)

Above the adult angel's wing is an *hourglass*, calling to mind the hourglass mentioned in a lecture accompanying one of the three basic Masonic degrees, or rituals of initiation. This symbolizes the brevity of life, the realization of which should encourage us to use our time well while we have it. One also sees a *pair of scales*, calling to mind *Justice*, one of the four cardinal virtues, which also occur as symbols in one of the Masonic-degree lectures (the others being Temperance, Fortitude, and Prudence). Prominent in the piece is a *ladder*. Jacob's ladder (see Genesis 28:10–22) is a symbol used in the lecture of the first degree of Freemasonry. A ladder with symbolic significance also appears in the degrees of the Scottish Rite of Freemasonry (whose real-life headquarters figure so prominently in *The Lost Symbol*).

Of course, one of the major objections to considering Dürer as some sort of secret Freemason is the fact that he died in 1528, almost two full centuries before the formation of the premier Grand Lodge of England in 1717. The earliest record of Masonic initiation in England occurs in 1641 (the initiation of Robert Moray into a traveling Scottish military lodge), although historian David Stevenson has shown that Freemason lodges were formed in Scotland as early as 1599. However, Scotland in 1599 was a long way in both time and space from Germany in 1528. How could Dürer plausibly have been a Freemason, or a member of some sort of proto-Masonic group?

Maybe the same way that Bosch was.

The late amateur historian of Freemasonry, John J. Robinson, presents a convincing case for the idea that Dürer's contemporary, the Flemish artist Hieronymous Bosch (about 1450–1516), hid Masonic symbolism in at least one of his paintings, *The Wayfarer*. (See chapter 11, pages 118–19 of Robinson's 1993 book, *A Pilgrim's Path: Freemasonry and the Religious Right*.) In Bosch's painting, Robinson finds references to Masonic initiatory ritual, as well as other Masonic symbols. I find Robinson's argument quite intriguing.

If Bosch, as a Flemish painter in the late fifteenth and early sixteenth centuries, somehow had access to Masonic initiatory symbols, then perhaps Dürer did as well in the Germany of that period, or during his extensive travels. The peculiar evidence in Bosch's *The Wayfarer* and Dürer's *Melencolia I* makes at least a plausible case for these artists being some kind of Masonic initiates.

As it happens, an element of Dürer's *Melencolia I* makes an important appearance in *The Lost Symbol*. The magic square in the engraving is the first instance of such an item in European art. Although not a specifically Masonic symbol, magic squares have been an element of ritual magic for centuries, as documented by Dürer's contemporary, Agrippa, in his famous *Three Books of Occult Philosophy*. The magic square in *Melencolia I* is the key to solving an important transposition cipher in *The Lost Symbol* (chapters 66, 68, and 70). Although Dürer's engraving is said by Robert Langdon to represent "mankind's failed attempt to transform *human* intellect into *god*like power," nothing is said in the novel about Dürer's possible Masonic membership, or the possible Masonic nature of the symbolism in his enigmatic masterpiece.

There is one other element of *Melencolia I* that may relate to *The Lost Symbol*. Within the polyhedral prism in this engraving that may symbolize the perfect ashlar, or perfected Mason, the best reproductions allow one to see variations in the "color" of the polished stone, forming the shape of an object that has resonance to William Wirt, to the prologue of *The Lost Symbol*, and to the symbols of mortality within Masonic ritual: a skull.

There were hundreds of clues, some quite fiendish, many quite clever, but very few, as it turned out, with any clear connection to the content of *The Lost Symbol*. Of course, the clues may contain the answer to one of the greatest secrets, not *within* Dan Brown's novel, but *about* it: why did he take six years to write *The Lost Symbol*? Perhaps he didn't. Perhaps he only spent two or three years writing the novel—

—and the rest of the time writing the *clues*.

KRYPTOS:
THE UNSOLVED ENIGMA

by Elonka Dunin

Well before Jim Sanborn's enigmatic sculpture of *Kryptos* outside CIA headquarters in Langley, Virginia, had attained its current level of notoriety among the general public, Elonka Dunin had emerged as the acknowledged expert on it. Before the dust jacket of *The Lost Symbol* hinted at *Kryptos* as an upcoming topic of Dan Brown's interest, Dunin had already gathered an impressive number of facts about the sculpture and the worldwide decryption effort on her Web site, elonka.com, a popular code-breakers' oasis. She is also author of *The Mammoth Book of Secret Codes and Cryptograms*.

Dan Brown himself has admired Dunin's work and paid her the stellar compliment of writing her into *The Lost Symbol* as Nola Kaye, the senior OS analyst who solves the sixteen-character Masonic cipher for CIA Director Inoue Sato and, at the end of *TLS*, comes face-to-face with the so-far unbreakable code written into the *Kryptos* sculpture. Dan Brown even gave Dunin a hint about his choice of names, sending her an e-mail two weeks before the release of *The Lost Symbol*. The e-mail contained only a cryptic message, which, deciphered, came out to NOLA KAYE SAVES DAY.

Here, our very own Nola Kaye, Elonka Dunin, tells our readers about the years of work real-life cryptographers have put into analyzing *Kryptos* and why only three of the four layers of its codes have been broken. She also comments on Dan Brown's fictional use of *Kryptos* in *TLS*.

The novel *The Lost Symbol*, as did *The Da Vinci Code*, starts with a "Fact" page:

> Fact: In 1991, a document was locked in the safe of the director of the CIA. The document is still there today. Its cryptic text includes references to an ancient portal and an unknown location underground. The document also contains the phrase "It's buried out there somewhere."

Is this indeed a fact? Well, in true Dan Brown fashion, sort of . . .

The document that is being referred to is (or at least was) in a sealed envelope, given on November 5, 1990, by artist Jim Sanborn to then CIA director William Webster. The occasion was the dedication of the *Kryptos* sculpture, an encrypted artwork installed in the courtyard of CIA headquarters in Langley, Virginia, just west of Washington.

Sanborn's artwork at the CIA comprises several pieces, the best known of which is a tall twelve-by-twenty-foot sculpture in the central courtyard, with four large copper plates that appear to be scrolling in an S shape out of a petrified tree trunk. On one side of the sculpture, two of the plates contain an enciphering table known as a Vigenère tableau. The other two plates have several hundred characters of ciphertext (codes). The envelope that Sanborn handed over during the ceremony supposedly contained the answers to the ciphers, though Sanborn has since been somewhat cagey as to whether he really put the full answer into the envelope or not. The current location of the envelope is unclear. When Webster was asked in 1999, he said he had "zero memory" of the answer, other than that it was "philosophical and obscure."

Kryptos was commissioned when the Central Intelligence Agency was outgrowing its original headquarters in the 1980s. Jim Sanborn, already a well-known artist in the area, was one of the artists selected by the General Services Administration to create artwork around the new building. Sanborn spent several months researching the CIA's history, and chose to create a sculpture with a theme of espionage and cryptography. He entitled his work *Kryptos*, the Greek word for "hidden."

He was also introduced to Ed Scheidt, a retired CIA operative who had been the chairman of the CIA's cryptographic center, who tutored Sanborn on various historical methods of encryption. Sanborn then personally chose the plaintext messages to be encrypted, and carved the ciphers into the sculpture.

Sanborn also designed several other pieces around CIA grounds, with his works being in two areas: Some in a new landscaped courtyard between the original and new headquarters buildings, and others on the opposite side of the new headquarters building, outside the main entrance. Along with the main *Kryptos* sculpture, he also placed several foot-thick granite slabs appearing to rise at a tilt from the ground. Some of the slabs have sandwiched Morse code messages on copper sheets, which Sanborn described as being like the pages of a document. Another slab has an engraved compass rose pointing at a magnetic lodestone.

In early 1992, a partial transcript of the sculpture was provided in the March/April issue of the periodical *Cryptogram*, and then a full transcript was posted on the Internet. The next major announcement came in 1999, when California computer scientist Jim Gillogly announced that he had solved the first three parts of the sculpture using a computer program he had written. When the CIA was contacted about his solution, they revealed that a CIA analyst, David Stein, had also solved those three parts in 1998, using pencil and paper techniques, but the announcement had been internal only, never released publicly. Another U.S. intelligence agency, the National Security Agency (NSA), also revealed that they had a team that had quietly solved those first three parts as well, in late 1992. But no one, in or outside the government agencies, has yet reported a solution to Part 4, which remains one of the most famous unsolved codes in the world. (The latest information on the *Kryptos* puzzle can be found at http://www.elonka.com/kryptos.)

In 2003, over a decade after the sculpture's unveiling, even more public attention came with the publication of *The Da Vinci Code*. Hidden in the artwork of the U.S. book jacket were multiple puzzles, giving hints about Brown's next novel. Two of the puzzles referred to *Kryptos*, with latitude/longitude coordinates, and the phrase "only WW knows."

THE CIPHERS

Part I of *Kryptos*

The first part of *Kryptos* (referred to as KI, that is, K-one, by those who are working on it) is made up of the top two lines on the ciphertext side of the sculpture:

EMUFPHZLRFAXYUSDJKZLDKRNSHGNFIVJ
YQTQUXQBQVYUVLLTREVJYQTMKYRDMFD

This was encrypted with a Vigenère system, or "polyalphabetic substitution cipher," a system most commonly used in the nineteenth century. There are many variants of Vigenère ciphers, which can be further complicated by which or how many key words are used, and how the deciphering tableau is formatted. In the case of KI, the keys that were used were the words KRYPTOS and PALIMPSEST (a palimpsest is a term for a scroll or manuscript that has been written on more than once, with some of the earlier writing still remaining visible). Using those two keys with the proper Vigenère system on KI, reveals the plaintext (answer):

Between subtle shading and the absence of light, lies the nuance of iqlusion.

Sanborn has said that this was an original sentence, written by him, with carefully chosen wording. The misspelling of the word "illusion" was deliberate, either as a clue, or perhaps simply as a way to make the cipher more difficult to crack.

Part 2 of *Kryptos*

The second part of *Kryptos* (K2) takes up the rest of the top ciphertext plate on the sculpture:

VFPJUDEEHZWETZYVGWHKKQETGFQJNCE
GGWHKK?DQMCPFQZDQMMIAGPFXHQRLG

TIMVMZJANQLVKQEDAGDVFRPJUNGEUNA
QZGZLECGYUXUEENJTBJLBQCRTBJDFHRR
YIZETKZEMVDUFKSJHKFWHKUWQLSZFTI
HHDDDUVH?DWKBFUFPWNTDFIYCUQZERE
EVLDKFEZMOQQJLTTUGSYQPFEUNLAVIDX
FLGGTEZ?FKZBSFDQVGOGIPUFXHHDRKF
FHQNTGPUAECNUVPDJMQCLQUMUNEDFQ
ELZZVRRGKFFVOEEXBDMVPNFQXEZLGRE
DNQFMPNZGLFLPMRJQYALMGNUVPDXVKP
DQUMEBEDMHDAFMJGZNUPLGEWJLLAETG

Similar to KI, this, too, used a Vigenère system, but with different key words, KRYPTOS and ABSCISSA (a term meaning the x-coordinate on a graph). The plaintext is:

> *It was totally invisible. How's that possible? They used the earth's magnetic field. x The information was gathered and transmitted undergruund to an unknown location. x Does Langley know about this? They should: it's buried out there somewhere. x Who knows the exact location? Only WW. This was his last message. x Thirty eight degrees fifty seven minutes six point five seconds north, seventy seven degrees eight minutes forty four seconds west. x Layer two.*

The latitude/longitude coordinates point inside CIA headquarters, to a spot in the same courtyard where *Kryptos* stands, though not to the sculpture itself. The coordinates are actually very specific, down to a tenth of a second of latitude: "6.5 seconds North." As geocache hobbyists know, a tenth of a second of latitude is a very specific location, about 10 feet across. The coordinates point about 150 feet southeast of the sculpture, in the same courtyard, along the edge of the landscaped area that Sanborn designed near the agency cafeteria. If this were a public park, doubtless tourists with shovels would have descended upon the area by now, but since the coordinates are at the center of a top secret facility, employees are of course discouraged from digging up the gardens!

Part 3 of *Kryptos*

K3 begins at the top of the second ciphertext plate:

ENDYAHROHNLSRHEOCPTEOIBIDYSHNAIA
CHTNREYULDSLLSLLNOHSNOSMRWXMNE
TPRNGATIHNRARPESLNNELEBLPIIACAE
WMTWNDITEENRAHCTENEUDRETNHAEOE
TFOLSEDTIWENHAEIOYTEYQHEENCTAYCR
EIFTBRSPAMHHEWENATAMATEGYEERLB
TEEFOASFIOTUETUAEOTOARMAEERTNRTI
BSEDDNIAAHTTMSTEWPIEROAGRIEWFEB
AECTDDHILCEIHSITEGOEAOSDDRYDLORIT
RKLMLEHAGTDHARDPNEOHMGFMFEUHE
ECDMRIPFEIMEHNLSSTTRTVDOHW

This uses a different type of cipher system, transposition rather than substitution. Transposition systems mean that all of the letters in the solution are already there, they're just rearranged via a particular method. The plaintext for Part 3 is:

> *Slowly, desparatly slowly, the remains of passage debris that encumbered the lower part of the doorway was removed. With trembling hands I made a tiny breach in the upper lefthand corner, and then widening the hole a little, I inserted the candle and peered in. The hot air escaping from the chamber caused the flame to flicker, but presently details of the room within emerged from the mist. x Can you see anything? q*

This is a paraphrased extract from the diary of archaeologist Howard Carter on November 26, 1922, the day that he discovered King Tut's tomb, in the Valley of the Kings in Egypt.

Part 4 of *Kryptos*

Then there is K4, which as of this writing remains unsolved:

?OBKR

UOXOGHULBSOLIFBBWFLRVQQPRNGKSSO

TWTQSJQSSEKZZWATJKLUDIAWINFBNYP

VTTMZFPKWGDKZXTJCDIGKUHUAUEKCAR

Why has no one been able to solve K4?

For one, because it's very short, only 97 or 98 characters (it's unknown if the leading question mark is part of K3 or K4). Generally when cryptanalysts are working on a difficult cipher, they need large amounts of ciphertext to work with. With a very short message, it becomes very difficult to find the mathematical patterns that are needed to crack a code.

Another reason it may not have been solved is because of the sculpture's inaccessibility. *Kryptos* was never intended as a public challenge, and was instead designed as a puzzle for the employees of the CIA. So it's possible that there is a needed clue on CIA grounds, which is unknown to non-CIA employees who may be working on K4.

Other reasons may include misdirection, which would fit into the theme of espionage. Both Sanborn and Scheidt have said that K4 is solvable, and Scheidt has added that the answer is in English, and will use all of the letters of K4. But this may be misdirection: it's possible that the answer isn't in English, and may even use some long-dead language. Indeed, since *Kryptos*, Sanborn has created several other encrypted sculptures, some of which do not use English. Sanborn's *Cyrillic Projector*, created after *Kryptos*, and currently at the University of North Carolina, Charlotte, uses encrypted text in the Cyrillic alphabet. Its ciphers were cracked via a joint effort of international cryptographers in 2003, revealing two Russian texts: one about psychological control of human sources, and another an extract from a 1982 classified KGB memo. Sanborn has also created sculptures that have languages in other non-Latin scripts: Greek, Amharic, Arabic, and many others.

Lastly, it's possible that Sanborn simply made a mistake in the encryption process. In fact, in 2006 he announced that he had made at least one error on the sculpture, omitting a letter from K2, which required the answer to be reworked. Previous solvers had thought that the last part of K2 said "ID by Rows," but after the error was announced, the true answer turned out to be "x Layer two." When Sanborn was then asked in an NPR interview if he was sure that the rest is correct, he said yes, that it is "safe and sound and fairly accurate." Scheidt, too, has said that he's "sure it's done right." He has also said that the fourth part uses different techniques than were used for the first three parts, and that it uses some kind of masking technique to make things even more difficult.

An ancient portal buried out there somewhere?

So is Brown's "Fact" statement true or false? Let's look at it section by section:

Fact: In 1991, a document was locked in the safe of the director of the CIA. The document is still there today.

Possibly true. Sculptor Sanborn did give an envelope with the *Kryptos* plaintext to CIA director William Webster in 1990, though what Webster did with the envelope is not clear. It's also unclear whether or not Webster even had a safe in his office, and if he did, whether the *Kryptos* envelope would be worthy of taking up space there. More likely the envelope was passed off to a historical department of some sort.

Its cryptic text includes references to an ancient portal

True. Part 3 of *Kryptos* refers to the portal of King Tut's tomb, discovered in 1922 in Egypt.

and an unknown location underground.

True. Though this is referring to a different part of the answer, in Part 2.

The document also contains the phrase "It's buried out there somewhere."

True. This phrase is from the decrypted text of Part 2. Though the question remains, just because the text says something is "buried out there," did Sanborn really bury something at the CIA, while he was installing *Kryptos*? And if he did, is it even still there?

We may never know.

Chapter
NINE

DIVINING

DAN

BROWN

THE PURSUIT OF DAN BROWN

From Secrets of the Widow's Son *to* The Lost Symbol

by David A. Shugarts

In 2005, Dave Shugarts published an amazing book: *Secrets of the Widow's Son* (*SOWS*). There has never been anything like *SOWS* before: a book-length work about a novel that had not yet been published. It was a predictive work that sought to guess what a bestselling novelist would write in the future—years before a single word of that future novel had been put on paper. It was not just any fiction writer—it was Dan Brown—world's bestselling author of adult fiction, known for the shocks, surprises, and thought provocations of *The Da Vinci Code*. Could Dave Shugarts really make educated guesses about the elements of history, philosophy, art, architecture, religion, mysticism, and science that Dan Brown would choose to use in his then-unwritten sequel to *The Da Vinci Code?*

As if writing a book about a book that has yet to be published were not a tall enough order, we gave Dave a challenge-within-the-challenge: go ahead and predict what Dan Brown will use as context and backdrop for his next novel. But do it in such a way that, whether you are right or wrong, the end product will be a fascinating, eye-opening book about Freemasons and American history, the ideas of the Enlightenment, science, ancient wisdom, myth, religion, and cosmology.

Nearly five years later, *The Lost Symbol* is here and Dave Shugarts has proven to be amazingly, uncannily, brilliantly right. In the following commentary, Shugarts sums up how he got interested in trying to predict the steps on Dan Brown's journey to a *Da Vinci Code* sequel and how his own journey into the world of these ideas unfolded.

Dan Brown writes books that compel you to turn the page and find out where the plot will take you. But for certain people—me, for instance—it's even more compelling. We wind up on a never-ending journey of discovery, in pursuit of the mind of Dan Brown.

After contributing to *Secrets of the Code* in 2004, I guessed that Dan Brown's next book in the Robert Langdon series would be a kind of treasure hunt set in Washington, D.C., and involving the Freemasons.

In 2005 I wrote *Secrets of the Widow's Son*, a book that anticipated the 2009 publication of *The Lost Symbol* by more than four years. The aim was to "reverse engineer," through certain clues and a lot of research, what Dan Brown was interested in and what he might write about in a sequel to *The Da Vinci Code*. I also sought out the more personal story of Dan Brown, the unlikely novelist from Exeter, New Hampshire, by way of Amherst College and Los Angeles. I visited his hometown, his prep school, and his college, producing an extensive biographical sketch that was published later in the paperback edition of *Secrets of the Code*.

Well, it's time to open the sealed envelope and reveal the results of my forecasts from 2005: my book, *Secrets of the Widow's Son*, scored quite a number of direct hits on the target, including some uncannily accurate details that can be found in *The Lost Symbol*. And there were some misses.

My original guesses about Washington and the Freemasons turned out to be correct. But I think more important was my belief that *The Lost Symbol* (*TLS*) would not necessarily center on a hunt for a lost treasure that was gold or had other intrinsic value. Rather, I guessed it might be a hunt for a powerful secret. This turned out to be correct. The actual secret in

TLS turned out to be anticlimactic—for me, at least. It was not what I was anticipating, but it did align exactly with the larger themes I had traced.

I think Dan Brown's real secret is that he has tapped into what I would call the "Interconnectedness of Everything."

Like the "underground stream" of the occult, this is a kind of extra dimension allowing one to travel through space and time, back to the Egyptian pyramids and then forward to the Washington Monument, or back to Isaac Newton and then forward to Einstein, or back to the prehistoric carvers of voluptuous fertility statues and then forward to Michelangelo. One of the keys to this dimension is symbolism, whether it be graphic, literary, or artistic symbolism.

No one can possibly map the entirety of this dimension, because to the mystics, cosmologists, and noeticists who inhabit this world, literally everything in the universe fits together and is interconnected in certain consequential ways. But anyone can explore this world of interconnections at any level of depth and complexity they choose, and many have. This is the voyage of discovery that Dan Brown undertook when he set out to write *Angels & Demons,* and continued in *The Da Vinci Code* and has now raised to its most explicit character in *The Lost Symbol.* It is a voyage that always entices one to a farther horizon. My task has been to pursue Dan Brown on this voyage and, at times, even sail ahead of him if I could.

THE QUEST BEGINS

It has now been more than five years since I started my quest to know all things Dan Brown. For me, it began with a couple of startling plot errors that I noticed when I read *The Da Vinci Code (DVC)* in early 2004. Naively, I actually wrote Dan Brown a letter, pointing out the flaws and suggesting ways to fix them. I never got a reply, but that's understandable, since by then, Dan Brown was avoiding interviews in the wake of the many controversies that *DVC* had started.

When Dan Burstein and Arne de Keijzer invited me to write about plot flaws for our book, *Secrets of the Code,* I began to survey the vast frontier that had been opened up via Dan Brown's allusions to art and symbolism, to history and culture, across many ages and a wide swath of the globe. I felt I had caught a glimpse of Brown's horizons.

When I learned of the clues that Brown had left in the dust jacket of *DVC*, hinting at his next book, the fun really began. The main clue was a question spelled out by putting together a series of boldface letters on the flaps of the original hardcover 2003 edition of *The Da Vinci Code:* "Is there no help for the widow's son?" This is a Freemason's cry for help when in distress, and it did indeed find a place in the plot of *TLS*.

In early 2004, our *Secrets* team announced that I had made the basic guess that Brown's next novel after *DVC* would be set in Washington, D.C., and would involve the Freemasons. It was an amazing conclusion to draw at the time, but it took less than a month to be confirmed, by Dan Brown's publishers and by Brown himself. Then Dan Brown clammed up—in a generalized silence that lasted most of the next five years—and of course, that spurred my curiosity as a journalist.

Could I anticipate the rest of what Dan Brown might cover? Maybe, but it would take a lot of digging. I would have to pursue leads and links wherever they might lead.

That one "widow's son" clue blossomed into hundreds more, because it led me to investigate the vast world of Freemasonry, from its beginnings in stonemasons' guilds and the Scottish lodges, into England and Europe, and finally to the United States.

But opening the doors to Freemasonry is also an invitation to explore dozens of other related topics, such as legends of Pythagoreans and Egyptians, and the building of the Temple of Solomon, among allegories that the Masons adopted. (In fact, for about two or three years, Dan Brown's publishers had said the title of his next novel would be *The Solomon Key*. So every conceivable meaning of "Solomon key" needed investigation—and there were many.)

My early work in the first few months of trying to see if I could figure out where Dan Brown was going took me deep into Internet searches that yielded more than seven hundred articles that seemed germane. I followed one path, pursuing the "art of memory," connecting Cicero with Giordano Bruno, thence to Scottish Freemasons. Another pathway connected Rosicrucianism, linking a resurrected set of books, the *Corpus Hermeticum* of the second or third century, with the Swiss pioneer of medicine, Paracelsus, thence to Robert Fludd, thence to Francis Bacon.

What I kept coming across was that these streams of thought all seemed to be interconnected, hopping from famous to not-so-famous people, connecting fundamental issues of philosophy and religion, and doing it all with symbols.

For instance, the Egyptian pyramid served as a symbolic connection from ancient pharaohs to the Louvre pyramid in Paris, which, in *The Da Vinci Code* was imagined as the resting place for the Holy Grail itself. Dan Brown had called attention to the use of the unfinished pyramid on the U.S. dollar bill, and the widely held belief that this signaled the influence of Freemasonry. But further, Dan Brown had made many uses of Egyptian obelisks, calling them "lofty pyramids" because of their pyramidal tops. Such obelisks are found throughout Rome (where they are referenced in the course of *Angels & Demons* numerous times), but also in other great cities like Paris or London, as Dan Brown noted.

In one fundamental interpretation of the obelisk as a symbol, it represents the connection from God to man, an imitation of a ray of light from heaven shining down on mankind. The light may be a form of energy or power or beneficence, or it may be knowledge and enlightenment. This invites many diverse religions to perceive the obelisk as symbolically appropriate, whether it be Gnostics or Kabbalists or even Christians, even though the obelisk form itself stems from "pagan" sources. Dan Brown many times has reveled in the connections of pagan symbolism to Christian art and architecture.

Back in 2005, as I was writing *Secrets of the Widow's Son* (*SOWS*), I saw this fascination with the symbolism of obelisks as a logical reason why Dan Brown would want to focus on the Washington Monument in *TLS* . . . and that's exactly what he did four years later. He even worked with the imagery of the first light from a rising sun touching the aluminum tip of the pyramid on the monument—each day's first contact with the light of heaven.

Further, I mentioned in *SOWS* that such an obelisk could be considered as part of a giant sundial, and, in the very first chapter of *TLS* Dan Brown has Langdon gaze from the plane and remark that it is a "gnomon." This is the term used for the center piece of a sundial, and it also in Greek can mean "that which reveals." The Washington Monument is "that which reveals" the secret in *TLS*.

America's Occult Heritage

But going beyond symbols to find the really deep foundations of America, it is appropriate to turn to the intellectual heritage brought to us by the great thinkers of Europe, who often held interests in both the emerging scientific tradition and the mystical, occult, and alchemical traditions. Certain historic figures provided connections that we don't generally hear about.

A good example is Francis Bacon, who studied with the great occult magus Dr. John Dee in the late 1500s. It was probably Dee who instructed him in the gematria of the Kabbalah, and Bacon went on to become a master of codes and ciphers. Bacon had a great interest in the New World and in 1623 wrote a book, *New Atlantis*, posing a utopia that governed without a king. Dan Brown mentions *New Atlantis* in *TLS* as being "the utopian vision on which the American forefathers had allegedly modeled a new world based on ancient knowledge." (*New Atlantis* was an influence on Thomas Jefferson's vision for America.)

It was Bacon who was suspected of being the founder of the Rosicrucians, an elusive movement whose members typically denied being members. Whatever the source, the Rosicrucian manifestos of around 1614 sparked an interest in the bubbling mysteries of hermeticism and the philosopher's stone. Depending on one's preferred myth, this could be the secret method to transform lead into gold, or a magic elixir granting life everlasting. It also evokes the phrase, "as above, so below," which can be construed as marking a spiritual and intellectual pathway connecting man to God.

But alchemists were also experimenters, groping for the systematic study of chemistry and medicine. Bacon wrote about a form of scientific method that was greatly revered by the Royal Society when it was founded in England in the mid-1600s as a kind of club for scientists and great thinkers. Bacon is also imagined by some to be among the first Freemasons.

Later in the seventeenth century, the great mind of Isaac Newton would turn to alchemy and to Rosicrucianism, as well as to mathematics and physics. Newton was for many years president of the Royal Society. Although Newton himself was not known to be a Freemason, a very large number of Royal Society members did join. Thus, Newton stood at the nexus of many currents of thought. One of his other passions was the study of the Bible, and he focused great attention on the Temple of Solomon. The Freemasons incorporated the Temple of Solomon into their myths.

Eventually, one of the greatest American scientists, Benjamin Franklin, would be both a Freemason and a Fellow of the Royal Society. One of the great thinkers of the age, the French philosopher Voltaire actually joined a Freemason lodge together with Franklin and also the Royal Society (of Science) in Paris. Voltaire was a great admirer of Isaac Newton. As famous as he was for his science, Franklin also maintained an interest in alchemy. He was a longtime friend of Joseph Priestley, who stood at the boundary between alchemy and modern chemistry. Priestley was an adviser to Thomas Jefferson, as well as several of the early American patriots. He was also a friend of James Smithson, who would endow the Smithsonian, which plays a significant role in *TLS*.

Thus, it became apparent that one trail Dan Brown was on was a non-traditional view of American origins that had more to do with the intellectual world of Bacon and ancient Egypt than it did with Pilgrims and traditional views of Christianity. I anticipated in *SOWS* that Brown would find a way in his next book to make the argument that you could not fully assess the American experience without looking back to Europe and its complex history, especially Freemasonry; Rosicrucianism; mysticism; and scientific, religious, philosophical, and political conceptions that may not always map neatly to what modern-day Americans believe our history to be. I thought Brown would find a story and a plot whose underlying message would be that we are deeply interconnected to one another and to the past in many ways, and that it is a surprising and "strange" past that we are so connected to.

So if you are on a treasure hunt where "It's all interconnected," is the watchword, you've got a lot of material to mine.

Not only were there endless things to find on the Internet, but there were all kinds of books to buy and borrow. To understand some of Dan Brown's allusions, you really ought to have a dictionary of symbolism. But why stop at one dictionary? Why not buy three, as I did? And be sure to make one of them the *Woman's Dictionary of Symbols & Sacred Objects*. You'll quickly understand why Dan Brown likes to say, "history is written by the victors." For instance, the symbol in *TLS* called the "circumpunct," or circle with a dot in its center, is traditionally thought of in a male context, the sign of the (male) sun, or sun god Ra. But the *Woman's Dictionary* identifies it as the "primal womb" and says the sun, in some early cultures such as the Hittites, was a goddess.

If you get one book about Freemasonry, you might as well get ten, which soon becomes dozens, since it turns out that for a secret society, the Freemasons have published an awful lot about themselves. Add another five or six about the conspiracies that Freemasons supposedly have hatched and nurtured over the centuries. To make sure you have covered the Mormon connection to Freemasonry, get about five or six books on Joseph Smith and the Church of the Latter Day Saints. Be sure to include a few books on the amazing minds that have at least a footnote in mystical/Rosicrucian/Freemason history, such as Elias Ashmole or René Descartes.

The Dan Brown novel always leads into the world of codes. Once you're attuned, you discover that practically all the famous men for the last five hundred years wrote in codes to protect their secrets. So it's a good idea to get some books about the history of codes. There are many fascinating code systems in all of Brown's books. In *TLS* Brown uses a well-known Masonic cipher, nicknamed a "pigpen" cipher, and a few relatively easy substitution ciphers. His crowning cipher is the array of symbols on the bottom of the Masonic Pyramid, which he promptly deciphers for his readers. It gathers up a gallery of Greek, alchemical, astrological, and mystic symbols.

And then there's religion. To see where Dan Brown has been and guess where he might be going, I thought it necessary to get a look at the origins of Christianity and the alternative Bible texts known as the Gnostic Gospels, which he focused on and arguably made into a household word in *The Da Vinci Code*. But in addition, you have to examine the history of Judaism, Islam, Hinduism, and Buddhism and dig still deeper, into the Egyptian religions, or Mithraism, or the beliefs of the ancient Sumerians and Babylonians. It's a good idea to trace the path of Jewish mysticism, including the Kabbalah (whose origins actually may have been Greek, I later found out).

Early on, it may have appeared a bit risky for me to devote a considerable amount of *SOWS* to a discussion of the philosophical underpinnings of the occult, hermeticism, Rosicrucianism, and the Kabbalah, but these turned out to be core building blocks in the architecture of *TLS*.

FOLLOWING DAN BROWN'S INTELLECTUAL FOOTSTEPS AND PREDICTING WHERE THEY WOULD LEAD HIM

From actually visiting Dan Brown's hometown and the schools he attended, I got a sense of a general openness to these very esoteric currents of thought. Brown is the eldest child of Richard Brown, a mathematics professor at the prestigious Exeter Academy. Brown's father authored geometry textbooks, so it is perhaps no surprise that Dan Brown would eventually develop an interest in the mystical nature of geometry so central to Freemasonry. Richard Brown was also a choir director at the Episcopal church and his wife, Connie, was the organist there, so again, it is no surprise Brown would be interested in the esoterica of music as codes, Mozart as a Freemason, etc. Dan Brown attended church and sang in the choir. He could have stuck to this single religious tradition, but it was a time when Exeter Academy itself was in flux about religion. Around the time that Dan Brown was a student there in the early 1980s, Exeter had begun allowing students to treat religious services as voluntary rather than mandatory. The school's Congregational chapel began to host diverse religious groups—Quakers, Jews, and Buddhists, as well as many different Christian strains.

What I learned at Exeter Academy was that Dan Brown was not a standout as a student, and wasn't thought of as a particularly creative person, whether it was music or writing, although he had a hand in both pursuits. But the rigors of Exeter Academy, and especially its focus on writing skills, did prepare students for distinction, if they seized the opportunity. There was a stream of Exeter alumni such as Gore Vidal, George Plimpton, and John Irving who were famous authors and gave provocative lectures when they returned to visit the school. (Think of the scene in *TLS* chapter III, when Langdon recalls Peter Solomon giving an eye-opening lecture on the Smithsonian, the Founding Fathers, and religion to Exeter students.)

Later, at Amherst College, Brown studied English and Spanish, sang in the glee club, and played squash. He found himself in classes with some major young stars, including the brilliant David Foster Wallace, and thus Brown was not considered a standout. He didn't stand out in the glee club either. Nonetheless, after graduating from Amherst in 1986, Brown pursued a music career for about six or seven years, even moving to Los Angeles and producing a studio album. This was where he met Blythe, who would become his wife and later on, his muse, his portal to mystical thought, and his most valuable research partner.

Blythe and Dan were vacationing in Tahiti in 1993 when he picked up a book by Sidney Sheldon and concluded that writing an action novel was within his grasp. It would take several years to reinvent himself, and the first efforts were not stellar successes, but soon Dan Brown the musician had been shed like an old skin, and Dan Brown the novelist had appeared. It was a transformation.

A central theme in *TLS* is the hermetic concept of transformation, which can be interpreted in several ways. Mal'akh strives to conflate all of them, whether it be physical transformation such as tattooing his entire body or castrating himself, or spiritual transformation, in the twisted expectation of being able to rise to a godlike plane of existence. Mal'akh has several chameleonlike physical changes as well, when he morphs from Zachary Solomon, to Andros Dareios, to Christopher Abaddon, then to Mal'akh.

In *SOWS*, I covered alchemical and hermetic transformation. I also devoted an appendix to the concept of death and resurrection, using mainly George Washington's deathbed scene, but also mentioning other contexts, including hermetics. A simulation of death and rebirth is at the heart of Freemasonry's central rituals. This became a major theme in *TLS*. Not only was Mal'akh hoping for a kind of rebirth, but also Robert Langdon was subjected to a deathlike experience in the liquid breathing chamber, then brought back to life.

A number of my investigations didn't pay off in directly obvious ways. In anticipation of *TLS*, I read a great deal about the men who founded America. I read biographies of Washington, Franklin, Jefferson, Adams, and various articles on George Mason, Paul Revere, Thomas Paine, and others. I was especially interested in the known Freemasons—Washington, Franklin, Revere—and anticipated that there might be plotlines that emerged from some of the less well-known features of their biographies. However, almost none of these were mentioned in *TLS* in any aspect significant to the plot. Yet it is clear from Dan Brown's interviews that he had the Founding Fathers in mind, particularly with respect to their common belief in deism. "America was not founded as a Christian nation, but became a Christian nation," he told NBC's Matt Lauer in a recent interview.

Because of certain links between Freemasonry and the Mormons, I delved deeply into the legend of Joseph Smith, founder of the Church of Latter Day Saints. Dan Brown only mentioned Smith in passing, even though Brown was seen in 2006 on a research trip to the home of the Mormon church, Salt Lake City, Utah. Some commenters have said they detect aspects of Mormon theology in *TLS*, but it is not an obvious feature of the book.

While there is plenty of focus on Freemasonry in *TLS*, one of the big surprises, for me, was that Dan Brown almost ignored the role of Freemasonry in the founding of the United States, the period surrounding the Revolution. While some have claimed it was a hydra-headed conspiracy to control the new nation and every institution in it, the real truth was that Freemasons were just one important part of the mix of influences. But *TLS* doesn't even take on this debate. The depiction in *TLS* of the 33° ritual at the opening of the book and on the MacGuffin of the videotape as a congregation of powerful government leaders is the only tangible evidence suggesting anything remotely conspiratorial about Freemasons. Like so many before him, Dan Brown could only point to this as somehow incriminating. The missing piece of the puzzle is, what are those people conspiring to do?

In *Secrets of the Widow's Son*, I think I accurately, fairly, and objectively portrayed the Freemasons. They have their interesting and complicated history, they really did have members who were prominent, in America and elsewhere—all those presidents, signers of the Declaration of Independence, astronauts, scientists, musicians—and they have endured centuries of accusations about their supposed conspiracies. With some small exceptions, I think in *TLS* Dan Brown very closely aligned with my views.

Some have already accused Dan Brown of being intimidated and co-opted by the Freemasons, but I just think he followed his own path. It appears he honestly respects the Freemasonic principles of brotherhood, equality, and religious tolerance. Also, as we have seen before in his prior novels, he always leaves an escape valve in his plot mechanism so that the larger institution, whether it be the Catholic Church, Opus Dei, or the Freemasons, can be excused. It has been more Dan Brown's style to create a rogue character and situate him within an organization so that he can misuse his position. Mal'akh was such a character, but more apparently an impostor (from page 1). This was somewhat different from the camerlengo in *A&D* or Leigh Teabing in *DVC*, who were carefully concealed as villains until the end.

I reported on the many conspiracy theories that stem from interpretations of the street layout of Washington, including the famous satanic inverted pentagram, and other symbols, often seen as signifying that Freemasonry was in control of the layout. I treated these theories with skepticism. Freemasons were certainly prominent in designing Washington and many of its key buildings. They often used good solid engineering and architectural principles that emphasized the principles of geometry, light, and alignment with nature they may have learned in Masonic lodges. But to argue that Masons were secretly trying to invoke a devil-worshipping agenda in the layout of the streets of Washington is, on its face, absurd. In *TLS*, Dan Brown's treatment of this issue was almost identical to mine in *SOWS*.

I made a point of describing the House of the Temple, which turned out to be a very important setting for *TLS*. The House of the Temple, or headquarters of Freemasonry's Supreme Council, Ancient and Accepted Scottish Rite, Southern Jurisdiction, USA, is not on the beaten path of tourist stops in Washington. But it will attract a bit more traffic now due to *TLS*. Far from being a secret place, it is open for regular public tours.

In *TLS*, Robert Langdon recognizes Albert Pike's bust in a niche at the House of the Temple, and notices a famous quote of his inscribed there. I devoted many pages to the legendary Pike, a lawyer, scholar, poet, and Confederate general who led Freemasonry's Scottish Rite in Reconstruction days. Pike wrote many of the rituals of the Scottish Rite and a famous tome, *Morals and Dogma*, amalgamating a lot of esoteric philosophies, including Egyptian, Hebrew, Babylonian, Gnostic, and Hindu legends and more. Pike, for Dan Brown, would clearly be a kindred spirit, an intellect willing to seek the connections among these seemingly disparate traditions. The Pike history is clearly in the background in *TLS*—but it is there.

MATHEMATICS AND OTHER MYSTERIES

There is a special way of arranging numbers, known as the magic square, that has fascinated mankind for millennia. This is a square array of numbers that add up in rows and columns to the same sum. Since ancient alphabets equated numbers with characters, there are magic squares of letters as well. Magic squares traditionally have been symbols of protective deities, such as Jupiter or Venus, and could be inscribed into amulets or talismans.

I correctly called attention to magic squares and devoted considerable space in *SOWS* to explaining their many instances in history. Dan Brown had often used Caesar squares in codes in his other books, so it seemed very logical to me that he would be attracted to magic squares. In particular, I mentioned both the Albrecht Dürer square (a modified Jupiter square) from *Melencolia I*, and Benjamin Franklin's mastery of magic squares, as items that might be of interest to Brown. Both of these turned out, four years later, to be integral to the plot of *TLS*.

Dürer created *Melencolia I* in 1514 and gave the engraving a wealth of hidden meaning, which has remained puzzling to scholars for the last five hundred years. Freemasons later were drawn to it because it appears to allude to ancient secrets in a veil of symbols. Masons see the stone objects and the tools of the "craft," such as a compass, as well as an hourglass (to show that time is running out on one's life). One of Dan Brown's writing quirks is to keep an hourglass on his desk, to remind him to break for exercise.

Geometric objects in the image hearken back to ancient Greek principles, as carried forward by the neo-Platonists, again of interest to Freemasons, and there are biblical allusions as well, such as Jacob's ladder (again often found in a Masonic context). While scholars have detected the influence of occult writers such as Cornelius Agrippa, the full meaning of the image remains a mystery. The apparent subject of the engraving is melancholy, which comes under the sway of Saturn, but Saturn's influence can be warded off by the sign of Jupiter in the form of the four-by-four magic square, which Dürer used in a modified way.

In *TLS*, Dan Brown made excellent use of an eight-by-eight magic square created by Ben Franklin as a decoding device for the symbols on the bottom of the Masonic Pyramid. Franklin enjoyed creating magic squares as a form of doodling while listening to the boring parts of the

Pennsylvania General Assembly deliberations. Franklin didn't ascribe a lot of magical meaning to it. He was what today would be called a "recreational mathematics" enthusiast.

While *TLS* lauds Franklin's eight-by-eight magic square, Franklin actually created a very complex sixty-four-by-sixty-four magic square and then proceeded to invent the world's first magic circle, as I mentioned in my book.

I correctly called attention to the Kabbalah, to the many correspondences between ancient alphabets and symbols, whether it be astrology or Tarot or Hebrew. Prior to our current Roman alphabet, many alphabets not only equated their letters with numbers, but sometimes with other meanings, such as deities, astrological figures, alchemical substances, even trees. By gematria, the numeral equivalents of various words and phrases can be added and then compared in order to find striking coincidences. It seemed to me that Dan Brown, by highlighting gematria in *DVC*, had already tapped into this realm of symbols and subtexts, and would explore it further in *TLS*. In explaining the numerology of the Kabbalah, I mentioned that *malakh* means "angel." Dan Brown named his villain Mal'akh in *TLS*, while relating the name also to Moloch, the Canaanite god who required child sacrifice, and who figures prominently in John Milton's *Paradise Lost*.

I called attention to myths about George Washington and especially the tendency of Americans to want to make him into a deity after his death. Triggered by the lurid passage in Mason Locke Weems's *Life of Washington*, the description of George Washington ascending into heaven eventually emerged, years later, as the painting on the ceiling of the Capitol Rotunda, the *Apotheosis of Washington*. I singled out for discussion in *SOWS* Constantino Brumidi's amazing fresco. One could write a book just on the ideas behind this artwork, and in particular, the interaction of the secular and the sacred, and what it said about Washington's transformation into a kind of American god. I was pleased but not surprised to discover Dan Brown used this artwork in important ways in *TLS*, especially toward the end, as Peter, Robert, and Katherine consider the idea that man is capable of becoming his own god.

I also pointed out that the tendency to deify Washington had been expressed in other works of art, including the Horatio Greenough statue of Washington in the odd pose of bare-chested Zeus, which had been given the central spot in the Rotunda and then was banished to other places. Robert Langdon pointed to this statue in *TLS*.

I called attention to the National Cathedral as a possible setting for the plot and this was indeed used in *TLS* by Robert Langdon and Katherine Solomon as a refuge. I mentioned the cathedral's gargoyle (or rather, grotesque) of Darth Vader, which Dan Brown also mentioned in *TLS*.

I covered the Masonic cornerstone ceremonies for the Capitol (led by George Washington in 1793) and the Washington Monument (in 1848). Freemasons carry on an ancient tradition of offering libations in these ceremonies. In American rituals they anoint the cornerstone with corn, wine, and oil, and in some European rituals, they add a fourth substance, salt. The grain represents "plenty," the wine symbolizes "joy and cheerfulness," the oil is "peace and unanimity," and the salt is "fidelity and friendship." But there's a further connection, back to times when it was crucial in such ceremonies to appease the four winds, and the four elements of earth, air, fire, and water. These are connected to the ancient principles of divination and cosmology such as astrology.

I called attention to the stories of ghosts in the Capitol, including the famous ghost cat, which Dan Brown also mentioned. I called attention to the many subterranean places in our nation's capital, including the tunnels connecting the House and Senate office buildings. Having reflected on how Dan Brown used the passetto between the Vatican and the Castel Sant'Angelo in *Angels & Demons*, I thought it a good guess that he would find similar passageways in Washington of interest. Sure enough, tunnels beneath the Capitol going to the Library of Congress proved to be important in *TLS*. Dan Brown discovered that the basements of the Capitol are riddled with hundreds of small rooms in which any number of secrets may be hidden. And there are many other tunnels and corridors lacing the underground spaces of Capitol Hill.

I related that among the very earliest plans for Washington's monument there would have been a pyramid where the obelisk now stands. I mentioned in *SOWS* that the current Washington Monument's cornerstone had disappeared somehow—a bit of trivia that becomes central to the plot of *TLS*.

I mentioned the George Washington Masonic National Memorial, in Alexandria, Virginia, which (as a diversion) ended up figuring in *TLS*, just as I had assumed. Dan Brown forgot to mention that it is 333 feet tall, another instance of the special number 33, which gets a lot of attention elsewhere in *TLS*. The significance of this number, important to Freemasons, begins with the "33" on Peter Solomon's ring, a mark of his ascent to the thirty-third degree of the Scottish Rite and continues throughout *TLS*, which itself has 133 chapters.

Due to very specific clues left by Dan Brown on the cover of *The Da Vinci Code*, I gave an account in *Secrets of the Widow's Son* of the sculpture of *Kryptos*, the enigmatic coded collection of objects that stands outside the CIA headquarters. It has stood in mute challenge to the world's best code breakers since 1990, when it was created by sculptor Jim Sanborn. Several of its secrets have been revealed, but one part of the coded message remains unbroken even today. *TLS* hints at an "ancient portal," and part of the known *Kryptos* message relates to the 1922 description by archaeologist Howard Carter when he first peered into King Tut's tomb through a small opening. This is apparently the "portal."

But *TLS* also plays around with *Kryptos* references. Dan Brown notes that part of the decoded message says, "It's buried out there somewhere. Who knows the exact location? Only WW." As I reported in my book, the "WW" in question has been confirmed by Sanborn as being William Webster, director of the CIA at the time the sculpture was commissioned. As part of his agreement, Sanborn handed Webster an envelope containing the decryption. (However, Sanborn later revealed that he had not given the entire solution to Webster.)

In *TLS*, Dan Brown tosses in a different idea about who "WW" is, obliquely suggesting William Whiston, whom he calls "a Royal Society theologian." It could be a mere red herring, but it also could be a clue to the next Dan Brown novel. Whiston is famous for his translation of the works of the Jewish historian Josephus, and for a dispute over theological matters with Isaac Newton, the president of the Royal Society in the early 1700s. Whiston also had a theory that comets were responsible for certain cataclysms on earth.

Further, *TLS* has a weird addendum on the "*Kryptos* forum" that says, "Jim and Dave had better decipher this ENGRAVED SYMBOLON to unveil its final secret before the world ends in 2012." This at first blush would seem to refer to the well-known urban legend that the ancient Mayan calendar predicts an apocalypse on December 21, 2012. In *TLS*, Brown mentions but debunks this idea, suggesting that Peter Solomon had correctly predicted that there would be considerable public and media attention devoted to the presumed 2012 end of the world but that it would be for the wrong reasons. Like the Christian sense of apocalypse and revelation, Solomon and Langdon seem to think the Mayan calendar, too, references only the end of the world *as we know it*, and the beginning of a new era of enlightenment. However, I wonder if Dan Brown has something different in mind as a plot device for his next book.

My research has already begun.

Caught Between Dan Brown and Umberto Eco

Mysteries of Science and Religion, Secret Societies, and the Battle for Priority over New Literary Genres

by Amir D. Aczel

Amir Aczel, scientist and mathematician, is the rare science writer who combines a mastery of his subject with a lightness of touch that make his books at once compelling and accessible. He also never separates scientific accomplishment from the innovative ideas and forceful personalities behind them, which is why we asked him to share his thoughts on *The Lost Symbol*.

The result was vintage Aczel: not so much an analysis of the book as a virtual encounter with its author. Along the way, Aczel introduces us to Teilhard de Chardin, the French Jesuit priest who invented the discipline of noetics; the Vatican's often touchy relationship with scientists going back to the days of Bruno, Galileo, Descartes, and others; the thought-to-be-missing Rosicrucian texts; and Umberto Eco, professor of semiotics and author of *Foucault's Pendulum*, who feels Dan Brown has taken his ideas and stripped them of their cultural and intellectual value in order to "squeeze money out of fools"—the same charge he once leveled against Aczel (they have since become good friends).

Amir Aczel has written fifteen books, of which *Fermat's Last Theorem* became an international bestseller. His most recent book is *Uranium Wars: The Scientific Rivalry that Created the Nuclear Age*. He was also a contributor to *Secrets of Angels & Demons*, where he untangled entanglement theory. The prolific Aczel shows no signs of slowing down. "I've got quite a few more ideas that beg exploration," he told us. We can't wait. In the meantime, we have his journey into the mind of Dan Brown.

I'm a science writer. But everywhere I go, every book I write, every research project I undertake, I find that Dan Brown and his ideas are there, too. My first encounter with Brown's ubiquity took place in Italy.

In the summer of 2006, I flew to Rome. I had a meeting with the director of the Jesuit Archives, as part of my research for my book *The Jesuit and the Skull*, about Pierre Teilhard de Chardin (1881–1955), a fabulously prodigious French paleontologist, a deep mystic, and an ordained Jesuit priest who happened to believe in evolution and whose ultimate punishment for this belief was twenty years of exile in China. Teilhard was also the inventor of the concept of the noosphere—the sphere of ideas, which he believed to surround our early biosphere—and the discipline of noetics.

I was thinking of Teilhard, who in 1947 came to Rome to plead his case with the Jesuits, as I walked down the Via della Conciliazione, the wide, elegant avenue, flanked by marble statues, leading from the Tiber right into Saint Peter's Square. This was clearly Dan Brown territory. The very landscape had been the setting for his book *Angels & Demons*.

I continued onto a stately bridge over the Tiber, and a block after I crossed it, I passed by a bookstore. In its window I noticed a prominent display of books by Dan Brown. This was no surprise given that some of Dan Brown's topics have revolved around the Vatican. But what I saw next made me stop dead in my tracks: framed by Dan Brown's novels I recognized the Italian edition of my own book of nonfiction, *Descartes' Secret*

Notebook. This was certainly a pleasant surprise—but I found it puzzling. Why would my mathematical-scientific biography of Descartes be displayed right between Dan Brown's novels? I would not have considered my book to have much appeal here. But I smiled and continued on my way.

I didn't have an easy time at the Jesuit Archives. Father Thomas K. Reddy, the head archivist of the Society of Jesus, was evasive. My visit had been arranged months in advance, and I had been led to believe that I would be able to see any document I wanted.

At the end of our interview, Father Reddy said, "You know, he was very controversial . . . I have some material here on Teilhard de Chardin."

"May I see it?" I asked.

"No," he said, "it is confidential." Then he added, "But you can see other things. My assistant will take you into the stacks now."

Pondering this setback, I proceeded to the reading room, and ordered the first Teilhard item from the archive's catalog. A short time later, a dusty pile of documents, bound with faded string, was placed on my table. I untied the knot—clearly no one had looked at this collection in many years—and began to examine the contents. These were Teilhard's manuscripts, which I knew had been typed in China in the 1930s by his intimate friend the American sculptor Lucile Swan, and which he sent here in hopes of gaining approval from the Jesuits to publish. But as I lifted the untied pile of manuscripts, what looked like a folded letter of several pages fell out.

I picked it up, opened it, and scrutinized the yellowing sheets. What I held in my hands was a curious ten-page document, carefully handwritten in Latin, and dated March 23, 1944. I was engrossed in reading it when I suddenly looked up to see Father Reddy standing right in front of my table, looking at me intently. "What is that?" he demanded, "What is the date?" I told him. He turned pale and said: "This is exactly what I didn't want you to see."

I knew that in 1925 Teilhard had been forced to sign six confidential propositions demanded by Rome and aimed at curtailing his freedoms of speech and expression, and that these documents were kept locked in a vault somewhere in the city. Teilhard scholars—even those within the

Society of Jesus—have been barred from seeing them. But the document now in front of me dated from 1944. What was contained in these pages that the Jesuits considered so important to hide?

In his frustration that I had now inadvertently seen the document, Father Reddy decided to seek an immediate meeting with the Jesuit father general, Peter-Hans Kolvenbach, to discuss what could be done about my discovery. The Jesuit headquarters, the Curia Generalizia, was next door, at 4 Borgo Santo Spirito, and as Reddy left the room in a hurry to go there, he turned to me and said: "You are a writer: be careful with what you write! Don't get us in trouble with the Vatican."

Teilhard de Chardin was a reformer. He believed that science and spirituality were equally valid attempts to reveal to us the work of God. His thought was like a breath of fresh air within a stagnant religious establishment: here was a devout priest who actually believed in science, and many of the younger Jesuits in his native France flocked to learn from him. But Teilhard's ideas were flatly rejected by the Catholic Church, and when he refused to recant them, he was punished.

Three centuries earlier, Galileo, who was one of Teilhard's heroes and whose picture the priest kept by his bedside throughout his life, had desired a similar revision of Catholic thinking by urging the church to accept the Copernican theory that the earth and the other planets revolved around the sun. And Galileo, too, was punished severely for his belief. But two decades before Galileo's infamous 1633 trial by the Roman Inquisition, a series of books that no one had expected—for they dealt with science and its relation to religion—suddenly appeared in print in Germany.

These curious manifestos were purportedly written by a secret society of scientists and scholars who also wanted to reform the Catholic Church. These people believed in science, and one of their stated goals was to distribute free medicines to all and to heal the sick. They pursued the study of mathematics and physics—and an inevitable part of physics was the conclusion that the earth revolves around the sun. This alone would have gotten them in trouble. They were hated by the Holy Office and searched for by the Inquisition. But they could never be found because membership in their society was secret. They were said to make themselves "invisible." These people, authors of the new books and their associates, were called "Rosicrucians"—members of the secret Order of the Rosy Cross. Dan Brown has been fascinated by the Rosicrucians, as well as by Freemasons and other secret societies, because they are surrounded with mystery and mystery is what Dan Brown does so well. But many people believe that the Rosicrucians never existed.

Others who pursued scientific ideas in the open, such as the philosopher Giordano Bruno, paid a heavy price for their convictions: in 1600 Bruno was burned at the stake by the Inquisition at the Campo dei Fiori, in the heart of Rome, for professing his belief in the Copernican system and for proposing that life might exist elsewhere in the universe. If the seventeenth-century Rosicrucians indeed existed, they had very good reasons to remain in hiding.

I crossed the bridge over the Tiber and continued to the secular center of the city of Rome. On my way, I passed two more bookstores, and both had my book in their windows—again right next to Dan Brown's novels. Something weird was going on with my book here in Rome, I thought; it made no sense at all. Finally, I arrived at a mall in the heart of the city, and entered one of the largest chain bookstores in Italy. My book, next to Dan Brown's *Crypto* (the title of the Italian edition of *Digital Fortress*), was in the window. And there were large stacks of both our books, one next to the other, on the table at the entrance to the store. I went to the counter, and talked to the bookstore manager.

"Ah, you are Mr. Aczel? Wonderful! Would you like to sign your books?" the manager said with a big smile.

I did, and when I finished, I asked him why the book was selling so unexpectedly well, and why it was always placed next to Dan Brown's books.

"You don't know?" he asked, looking at me incredulously.

"No . . . ," I had to admit.

"So you haven't seen what Umberto Eco has said about you? . . . These were terrible things. Absolutely terrible. And he published them in *L'Espresso*—the most important magazine in Italy. Since then, the book has been selling like crazy."

I asked him if he could show me Eco's article, or tell me where I might find it, but he mumbled something and quickly disappeared to take care of a customer.

When I arrived back home in Boston, two letters were waiting for me. One was from the Jesuit father general, and it informed me in very polite language that I had been denied retroactive permission to see the document I had already seen. The other letter was from a friend who had come back from South America, and it contained a clipping from a newspaper in Santiago, Chile, which was a translation into Spanish of the terrible things Umberto Eco had said about me in Italy. As I later learned, newspapers all over the world—those published in romance languages from Spanish to Romanian—had republished Eco's article about me.

In 1614, the first of the so-called Rosicrucian texts appeared in Kassel, Germany. It was titled, in Latin, *Fama Fraternitatis*—the "Statement of the Fraternity." The book told the fantastic story of a German man of humble origins named Christian Rosenkreutz (German for "Rosy Cross"), who was born in 1378. As a five-year-old boy, Rosenkreutz's parents sent him to a monastery where he learned Greek and Latin. At the age of sixteen, he left the monastery and joined a group of magicians, learning their art and traveling with them for five years. When he left them, Rosenkreutz continued to travel on his own, to Turkey, Damascus, and farther into the Arabian Desert. He reached an oasis, a mystical city named Damcar, whose inhabitants were all philosophers and scholars. The people of Damcar appeared to have been expecting his arrival, for he was welcomed in the city with great honor. He taught them the magic he had learned from the magicians, and in turn they instructed him in philosophy, science, and mathematics. After three years of absorbing the wisdom of the East in Damcar, Rosenkreutz returned to Western Europe, bringing with him his new knowledge.

Rosenkreutz followed a route from Arabia to Palestine and present-day Israel, crossed the Sinai Desert, and continued along the North African coast. He sailed across the Strait of Gibraltar and entered the Iberian Peninsula, and then crossed the high Pyrenees and continued into the heart of Christian Europe. He brought with him the knowledge of the ancients, as transmitted through the Arab scholars of his day, and he tried to impart this information about science and mathematics and nature to the Europeans. But everywhere he went, he encountered only hostility to his ideas and a rejection of science.

Upon his return to Germany, by now discouraged with the state of society on his native continent, Rosenkreutz built a large house and filled it with scientific instruments and continued to study mathematics, physics, chemistry, medicine, and astronomy on his own. He died at the age of 106 and was buried in a cave. Exactly 120 years later, in 1604, his burial place was discovered by four scholars. When they entered the cave, they found golden vessels sparkling in light that emanated from inside the cave. They found books on science, and a chalice inscribed with the letters RC. This became their emblem and their secret code, and they decided to form the Brotherhood of the Rosy Cross and to continue the work of Christian Rosenkreutz, bringing knowledge to the people and wedding science with religion. So the story goes.

While of course this tale is fictional, any historian of science would recognize in it a germ of truth. For we know that the science, mathematics, and philosophy of the ancient Greeks declined quickly at the end of the Classical Age as the West entered the Dark Ages with the fall of Rome in the fifth century. This knowledge was then passed on to Arabia, and science and ideas thrived there during the caliphate in Baghdad. Science and philosophy, firmly based on Greek ideas, flourished in Arabia and the Fertile Crescent during the ninth and tenth centuries. Three hundred years later, this knowledge was injected into a reawakening Europe. We know, for example, that Euclid's *Elements* traveled into Europe following the same route as did the mythical Christian Rosenkreutz: from Arabia to North Africa and Spain, and then across the Pyrenees into Christian Europe (eventually to become one of the first books printed on the new presses in Venice). So the Rosicrucian myth actually contains the story of the transfer of ancient knowledge from East to West during the end of the Middle Ages—including its exact route. The European Renaissance is based on this ancient Greek cultural essence, kept alive in the East during the Dark Ages, and reimported into the West.

Once science, philosophy, and artistic ideas arrived in Europe, they faced a staunch religious establishment that by its conservative nature was resistant to change. Painters and sculptors had to pay homage to the church by concentrating on religious themes, as did writers and philosophers. Scientists had a much harder time because science had been discovering truths that were unpalatable to the church and contrary to traditional interpretations of Scripture. The resulting conflict between science and faith that erupted in sixteenth- and seventeenth-century Europe created an atmosphere of secrecy, intrigue, and mysticism. Science was seen as possessing hidden powers, and its information content had to be coded to hide it from the church. The mythical Brotherhood of the Rosy Cross was founded on such secrecy and hidden codes, but real scientists such as Galileo, Da Vinci, Leibniz, and Descartes also relied on cloak-and-dagger methods to hide their scientific findings. Descartes, for one, was the inventor of an intricate code that he used to hide his scientific findings about the rotation of the earth from possible discovery by the Inquisition. His letters to his friends show that he was very worried about meeting a fate similar to Galileo's, and this concern drove him to resort to secrets and codes, which he felt were necessary for his protection.

But intrigue and codes are the stuff of legends, and soon enough, modern writers would seize the opportunity to capitalize on these promising themes.

While Dan Brown's *The Da Vinci Code* is a work of fiction, he says the following in a note before his story begins:

> FACT:
> The Priory of Sion—a European secret society founded in 1099—is a real organization. . . . All descriptions of artwork, architecture, documents, and secret rituals in this novel are accurate.

And the new *The Lost Symbol* claims in its opening page, under "Fact":

> All organizations in this novel exist, including the Freemasons, the Invisible College, the Office of Security, the SMSC, and the Institute of

Noetic Sciences. All rituals, science, artwork, and monuments in this novel are real.

What Dan Brown did with *The Da Vinci Code* and then with *The Lost Symbol* was to use the mystery and intrigue (real or imagined) resulting from the historical clash between science and religion within works of fiction. And the claims made in the novels were presented in a way that implied they carried real historical value: namely the author's theories, based on some historical research. I must take issue with Brown's statement that the "science" in *The Lost Symbol* is true. In chapter 15 of his novel, Brown says: " 'Well . . . like *entanglement theory*, for one!' Subatomic research had now proven categorically that all matter was interconnected . . . entangled in a single unified mesh." As I show in my book, *Entanglement* (Plume Publishing, 2002), and as every physicist knows, entanglement is a very complicated phenomenon that is difficult to obtain in practice. We are certainly *not* all entangled in a mesh—far from it—in any physical way. But science had nothing to do with Eco's objections to Dan Brown's work.

Umberto Eco was born in 1932 in the northern Italian city of Alessandria, located between Turin and Genoa. He earned a doctorate from the University of Turin, took up a professorship of semiotics—the philosophical study of signs and symbols—at the University of Bologna, and within a few years, publishing prodigiously, became Italy's leading intellectual.

In 1980, Eco published a novel in Italy, *The Name of the Rose* (as it was titled in English, published in translation in 1983)—a mystery set in a fourteenth-century monastery. The book became an international bestseller, and eight years later, Eco followed it with another very successful book, *Foucault's Pendulum*. This novel dealt with science, Kabbalah, mysticism, and the Brotherhood of the Rosy Cross. With this book, Eco indeed founded a new genre: a historical mystery novel about science and religion. Both of these immensely successful and innovative novels, especially the latter, bear an uncanny resemblance to Dan Brown's novels.

Eco was not pleased with Dan Brown's earlier work, *The Da Vinci Code*, appearing fifteen years after *Foucault's Pendulum*. It wasn't that he was envious—his own books had been huge commercial successes. It was simply that he felt that Brown had taken his idea, shed the philosophical-intellectual milieu of his novels, stripped them of their cultural value, and run away with a good story. Now, of course, Brown had done the same with *The Lost Symbol*. Eco retaliated against Brown right after the appearance of *The Da Vinci Code* by using his Web site. Visiting the page, umbertoeco.com, one can find Eco's books as well as some biographical and other information. But a place of honor in Eco's home in cyberspace was reserved for an essay entitled: "About God and Dan Brown," which ends with the following bizarre statement.

> The "death of God," or at least the dying of the Christian God, has been accompanied by the birth of a plethora of new idols. They have multiplied like bacteria on the corpse of the Christian Church—from strange pagan cults and sects to the silly, sub-Christian superstitions of *The Da Vinci Code*.

Eco also reportedly refused to attend an international meeting in the town of Vinci in Tuscany some time ago because he knew that Dan Brown was also invited to speak there. But he couldn't do much more to show his anger and frustration, and nothing could stop Dan Brown's juggernaut.

I had been oblivious to the conflict brewing between Eco and Brown, and while I had read their books, I'd never found anything in the works of either author of relevance to my own. But on July 6, 2006, three weeks before my arrival in Rome, Umberto Eco struck at me. He devoted his entire weekly column in the influential Italian magazine *L'Espresso* to my book *Descartes' Secret Notebook*. Eco tried to destroy my thesis that Descartes used secrets and codes to hide his scientific work from the Inquisition by attacking my descriptions of putative connections between Descartes and the Rosicrucians, which were secondary to the main thrust of my book. He ended his essay with the following (my translation from the Italian):

Aczel . . . comments on his various suggestions by saying, "A coincidence? Perhaps." This is the typical method of such writers trying to exploit casual coincidences to squeeze money out of fools. Pure Dan Brown.

I responded to the article once I found out about it, and *L'Espresso* published my response. I pointed out that my book simply quoted Descartes' biographers, including the contemporary Baillet, that the Rosicrucians were not the key to my thesis, and that I never did claim that they existed. The magazine then published Eco's answer to my response. Umberto Eco did not give in. He admitted that he had criticized me with "excessive polemical force," but maintained that because the Rosicrucians did not exist, there could not have been any connection with Descartes.

But did the Rosicrucians exist? This remains an open question. Scientists and reformers living during the time of the Inquisition had to hide in order to remain alive. They also felt the need to write and disseminate their ideas to others. So the people who wrote the Rosicrucian texts must have existed in one way or another since *someone* did develop the science described in these books, and someone did write the books. Was it all a hoax? We simply don't know. But Descartes' early biography makes it clear that he was influenced by a certain kind of mathematics—much of it done by a mysterious German mathematician named Johann Faulhaber, who most sources claim was indeed a Rosicrucian. And we know that Descartes had read some of the Rosicrucian texts, so at least from this point of view, there were connections between him and Rosicrucian ideas.

In an effort to understand Eco's rage, I picked up *Foucault's Pendulum*. On page 167, I read:

Descartes—that's right, Descartes himself—had, several years before, gone looking for them in Germany, but he never found them, because, as his biographer says, they deliberately disguised themselves. By the time he got back to Paris, the manifestos had appeared, and he learned that everybody considered him a Rosicrucian.

So that was what was bothering Umberto Eco. My book had the same stories he had in *Foucault's Pendulum* about Descartes and the Rosicrucians—taken from the same source: Baillet's 1691 biography of Descartes. Eco was upset because he believed that I (and Dan Brown before me) had taken over his genre. But did I? I wrote strictly nonfiction. And the historical events themselves did not need any fictional embellishments, as I see it. There is more than enough intrigue, secrets, and codes to be found whenever science and religion clash—be it four centuries ago or today. My vindication came in February 2007. That month, the French literary magazine *Lire* published a review of the French edition of my book on Descartes. It described my book as: "a 'philosophico-historical thriller'—a new genre." What made me even happier was a sentence toward the end of the review: "The book respects historical truth (nothing in common with the fantasies of *The Da Vinci Code*)."

Two and a half years later, Dan Brown's much anticipated next book, *The Lost Symbol*, was published. I was not surprised by the book's increased resemblance to Eco's *Foucault's Pendulum*, which is dense in symbolism, since this is the kind of writing Brown always does. I was surprised, however, by the reference to noetics—an area championed by Pierre Teilhard de Chardin. I hadn't expected Brown to move in this direction. But this innovation delighted me. Teilhard de Chardin's work has all but been forgotten by modern readers, and I compliment Brown for bringing his work to the fore. We need to hear more about the powerful ideas of this progressive Jesuit thinker who was decades ahead of his time.

On September 15, 2009, the official publication day of *The Lost Symbol*, Dan Brown gave a radio interview in which he was asked about the profession of his protagonist Robert Langdon. In this book, as in previous ones such as *The Da Vinci Code*, Langdon is identified as a Harvard professor of symbology. Brown explained that there is no department of symbology at Harvard. What he meant by "symbology," he said, was the science of *semiotics*, but he said that he felt the public would not understand what semiotics means. Perhaps Brown had another reason for not using this term. Brown is fully aware that Umberto Eco is, in fact, a professor of semiotics at the University of Bologna.

Chapter

TEN

BROWNIAN

LOGIC

Not All Is Hope

Reading the Novel's Dark Side

an interview with Michael Barkun

Dan Brown's first two Langdon novels were thrillers involving vast, potentially world-changing conspiracies. *The Lost Symbol*, however, has no massive conspiracy to propel it, and the "terrible secret" the lone villain threatens to release would likely rate little more than an embarrassing titter on YouTube. Ordinarily a favorite shadow organization for film, TV, and book plots, the Masons are instead portrayed in *TLS* as a rather benign brotherhood bent on nothing more than enlightenment for themselves and the sharing of knowledge and insight for the benefit of others. But take a second look, suggests Michael Barkun in the interview here, because below the novel's beatific veneer conspiracy theorists will find plenty to feed their fears.

Michael Barkun is a professor of political science in the Maxwell School at Syracuse University. Barkun is an expert on conspiracy thinking, a respected scholar, and a former FBI consultant. He has written extensively about marginalized groups and their cultural and historical roots. He is the author of *A Culture of Conspiracy: Apocalyptic Visions in Contemporary America*.

Before we start talking specifically about The Lost Symbol, *could you give us a quick overview on conspiracy theory as it might relate to this novel?*

For those who already believe in conspiracies, the novel can be read within the generic theory that some secret cabal is planning to seize power in the U.S.—and ultimately the world—and completely dismantle the institutions of democratic governance. It's the so-called New World Order theory that has been around since at least the early 1970s. It takes different forms. Sometimes it involves UN troops moving into the U.S. to establish concentration camps, run by FEMA, to hold dissenters and gun holders. Sometimes it involves the Trilateral Commission, a cabal of industrialists and other people in the highest levels of government in several countries with the professed, dangerous aim of fostering world cooperation. The conspiracy scenarios often involve the Federal Reserve and Jewish international bankers. The personnel tend to vary depending on whose version of the theory one is looking at.

Most directly relevant to the novel is the conspiracists' fear that there is a plot to substitute a New Age religion for Christianity. Versions of this among evangelicals usually involve the rise of the Antichrist, but secular versions have also risen among militia circles.

The Lost Symbol doesn't appear to be a conspiracy novel and it has a very upbeat ending. What are most of us missing?

Some people will make the case that there is a conspiracy hidden in plain sight in a couple of respects. One is that in at least two points in the novel, characters speak about circles within circles, and you're left with the feeling that, regardless of the sense of closure at the end of the story, there's still the possibility that some kind of hidden plot has yet to be revealed, one that the characters themselves might be unaware of. Plus, of course, the novel is largely structured as a succession of puzzles that have to be solved and messages that have to be decoded. The subtext is that there may be meanings that remain unrevealed in the book and that have to be supplied by the reader (or, perhaps, in a sequel?).

The other interesting element is the strange role of the CIA. They're running around Washington in a law enforcement capacity, which is in direct contravention of the statutes that govern them. And they're showing up in black helicopters. Conspiracy theorists often speak of black helicopters hovering over America as a sign of an imminent military takeover, and it's hard to believe Dan Brown included this symbol accidentally. Black heli-copters occupy a conspicuous role in virtually every iteration of New World Order conspiracy theories. Their placement in *The Lost Symbol* looks like a message from Brown that New World Order conspirators are involved, even though he says nothing explicit about it. In addition, we never learn how the CIA knows about the video that Mal'akh has taken of Masonic rites, which suggests there's another conspiracy out there that hasn't yet been revealed.

Another plot element that points to the darker side for conspiracy theorists is Brown's focus on the Great Seal: the pyramid with the eye on top, and particularly the words *"novus ordo seclorum"* there, which in contemporary conspiracy theory is always mistranslated as "new world order" but that more accurately translates as "new order of the ages."

All of this makes *The Lost Symbol* enormous grist for the mill for any conspiracy theorist. They would pay absolutely no attention to the New Age message at the end of the book. That would be utterly meaningless to them, a diversion from what really matters. They would zero in on all of the earlier material: the Washington street map, the Great Seal, the notion of circles within circles and brotherhoods within brotherhoods, the role of the CIA, and so on.

And on top of that you never quite know what motivates the CIA to take up the chase.

Right. The CIA's surface story is that they're acting on a matter of na-tional security, that if the public were to see government officials partici-pating in Masonic rites it would somehow be enormously destabilizing. But then there's the other possibility: if the New Age knowledge that Brown suggests the Masons possess were somehow to be revealed, this, too, would threaten the holders of power.

All of which suggest that there is a lot more going on here than most readers might suspect.

Yes, it's got the Masonic conspiracy element that you can read as confirming the conspiracy or debunking it. It's also got a kind of New Age millenarian element that is somewhat tied to the Masonic part and somewhat independent of it. Which part is be emphasized varies by the audience. This plays off of the expectation of an apocalyptic event at the end of 2012. So there's a lot going on here, a lot that he's trying to synthesize.

It seems Dan Brown is also throwing in an extra curve that helps feed suspicion. His other books involve conspiracies centered around plots and organizations with which the vast majority of readers are likely to have been previously unfamiliar—for example, Opus Dei and the Illuminati. Therefore, readers don't have preconceived notions about the character of the alleged conspirators. *The Lost Symbol* is different because the conspiracy is so familiar. Even today when you mention "Mason," people are likely to associate the word with secret rites and nefarious activities. We're not talking about a group like the Illuminati in *Angels & Demons*. Readers of *The Lost Symbol* may already be programmed with a set of attitudes.

I've found that even though Brown gives a very positive spin to the Masons at the end of the book, conspiracy theorists read this book and say, "This isn't a positive book at all. This is a book about Masonic conspiracy."

To cite one example, if you go to the Web site of major American conspiracy theorist Alex Jones (www.infowars.com), Jones claims that the book confirms everything that has always been claimed about the Masons: their blood-soaked oaths, their street plans for Washington, the obsession with ancient mysteries, and the raising of political figures to the level of demigods as represented by the painting *The Apotheosis of Washington*. There's a whole list of these things on the Web site, accompanied by page references to *The Lost Symbol*.

In my book *A Culture of Conspiracy*, I talk about what I call fact-fiction reversal, in which conspiracy theorists will often say that what purports to be nonfictional accounts are untrue, and what purports to be fiction is actually veiled fact. What they're saying about the Dan Brown book is that while it claims to be just a story, if you decode it the right way, it is in fact a true account of Masonic conspiracy. Whether it has to do with the CIA or the substitution of a New Age religion for Christianity, they will read this book and say, "Ah-ha! This is another proof that we were right," because they're going to read this book as fact rather than fiction.

Perhaps the most controversial aspect of the novel is that Brown seems to be lobbying us to embrace noetics as a legitimate science and embrace the notion that ancient wisdom has given us everything we need to know.

Interestingly, even though that's a very strong New Age motif, it is also a motif that a lot of conspiracy theorists accept. The reason is that they tend to reject mainstream sources of authority. They reject the authority of government, obviously, but they also tend to reject the authority of mainstream science, mainstream medicine, mainstream universities, and so on. Therefore, much conspiracy literature shows them to be very receptive to the notion that the ancients had made extraordinary scientific discoveries that have been lost, ignored, or suppressed and can somehow be rediscovered. So, oddly, conspiracy theorists, who may be talking about plots by the Masons, the Trilateral Commission, or international bankers, will often also talk about the scientific feats that were accomplished by ancient people. So there's a funny link between conspiracy theorists and New Age followers. The link is a rejection of authority.

Then there is Dan Brown's inclusion of references to 2012.

The 2012 business started some years ago, based on Jose Arguelles's claim that his study of the ancient Mayan calendar had led him to the conclusion that there would be a great transformative event on December 21, 2012. For quite a while, the interest in 2012 was limited to New Age circles. And then there was a point where it began to go mainstream. For me, the indicator was the publication of *The Idiot's Guide to 2012*. Then there is the movie *2012* released this year by Sony. When you get a book or a movie like that, these kinds of conspiracies have gone mainstream.

Believers are convinced that something tremendous is going to happen but, depending on the perspective, this will either be something immensely positive or something absolutely horrible. This gets picked up in *The Lost Symbol* in a scene where Peter Solomon is with students. One student links December 21, 2012, with his notion of world enlightenment, presenting it with a positive spin. But then there's mention that Langdon has correctly predicted the spate of television specials connecting 2012 with the end of the world. I take it that the point Brown is making is that whatever secrets the Masons and Katherine Solomon have access to are the same secrets of enlightenment that are somehow linked to 2012. Brown is coy and indirect when he talks about 2012, but fundamentally I think he sees it in very positive terms, just as New Age writers tend to.

The conclusion of The Da Vinci Code *shocked people with its interpretations about one of our deeply held cultural beliefs. What about* The Lost Symbol? *Do you think the ideas expressed—such as noetics and other New Age concepts—which look ahead instead of backward, will have a similar impact?*

It depends on who reads it and what they bring to it. I think conspiracy theorists are going to read this book as a confirmation of the views they already hold. They're going to see all kinds of concealed meaning. However, I think for people who don't already hold those views, it's possible that some of them are going to be introduced to a kind of New Age mythology.

I've been wondering ever since Dan Brown became a cultural phenomenon if his popularity makes the subjects he writes about become legitimate and important or if it ends up trivializing them because he uses these subjects as elements in popular novels. I'm inclined to believe the former rather than the latter. I think that even though at one level people will just read *The Lost Symbol* as a story, they will absorb some content. In this case, it leaves readers questioning whether they've understood everything that is there, a sense heightened by Dan Brown's clever use of puzzles, esoteric symbols, and hidden messages. It certainly legitimizes the conspiracy novel.

It is fascinating that a thriller writer can have such a profound impact on the discourse.

I wonder if in this case it may unintentionally be heightened by the release date of the novel. It is widely reported that *The Lost Symbol* was supposed to come out in 2006. Instead it comes out in 2009 at the tail end of the greatest economic collapse since the Great Depression, a period of greatly heightened anxiety when people are far more disturbed emotionally and intellectually, far more confused about how the world is organized than they were in 2006. They want to know where the power lies and who makes the decisions. Again, I think that affects the way you read a book like this. The suggestion that some kind of inner circle of the powerful meets in secret always has resonance. But it surely will resonate even more in this environment. A perfect climate for conspiracy theories.

—*Interviewed by Lou Aronica*

THE POLITICS OF
THE LOST SYMBOL

by Paul Berger

Within days of *The Lost Symbol*'s release, conservative readers began to complain that Dan Brown's latest novel was anti-CIA, anti-Bush, and pro-Obama. Those charges quickly melted into the background as Brown's tribute to Freemasonry and his popularization of noetic science came to the fore. But is it possible that their view of *The Lost Symbol* as a liberal-leaning book is correct? Certainly, it would be almost impossible for a book set in Washington not to have a political slant. And if a reader was inclined toward hidden meanings, subtexts, codes, and ciphers, he or she wouldn't have far to look for evidence:

I. *Negative portrayal of the CIA.* Langdon solves the mystery of *The Lost Symbol* and rescues Peter Solomon despite the intervention of the CIA's Inoue Sato rather than because of her. Indeed, far from being an efficient, evil-fighting organization, the Agency, as personified by Sato, is stubborn, authoritarian, and always two steps behind Langdon. Brown chooses his historical terms carefully. So it is notable that in chapter 48, after Langdon and architect Warren Bellamy escape, Sato threatens Capitol police chief Trent Anderson and security guard Alfonso Nuñez with a "CIA inquisition."

2. *Torture.* Torture was on the minds of Americans during a significant portion of the Bush administration and will forever be entangled with America's controversial interrogation techniques following the invasions of Afghanistan and, particularly, Iraq. Torture plays a significant role in *The Lost Symbol* as well. Katherine Solomon's assistant, Trish Dunne, is tortured to reveal her PIN code. Robert Langdon is tortured to force him to translate the symbols on the bottom of a pyramid. And Katherine endures the gruesome torture of being slowly bled to death to force her brother, Peter, to help Mal'akh complete his quest. Unlike other pop-culture tales of this decade—such as the TV series *24*—there is no ambiguity here about the evil of torture.

3. *Water as a means of torture.* Mal'akh's method of securing information from Robert Langdon—nearly drowning him in a sensory-deprivation tank filled with a watery liquid—immediately suggests the years of recent debate over waterboarding. The standard American waterboarding technique involves laying a hooded prisoner on a board with his head slightly lower than his heart, covering his face with towels, and slowly pouring water over the towels to simulate drowning. Mal'akh's props may be different—a glass crate slowly filled with (unknown to Langdon at the time) "breathable" water—but the effect is almost the same.

4. *Religious fundamentalism.* Mal'akh is clearly his own uniquely mad character, not part of any known group or movement. But he is certainly a religious fundamentalist and in his literal reading of the Ancient Mysteries, he is remarkably similar to what a liberal might describe as a biblical literalist.

5. *"Rush to war."* When Langdon, Sato, and Anderson discover the Masonic Chamber of Reflection hidden in the subbasement of the Capitol building, Langdon explains that it could be a room where a powerful lawmaker might "reflect before making decisions that affect his fellow man." He then imagines "how different a world it might be if more leaders took time to ponder the finality of death before racing off to war." This might easily be read as Brown implying a lack of such re-

flection when it came to the Bush administration's war plans for Iraq and Afghanistan.

6. *Hope.* Dan Brown ends his novel with a one-word paragraph: *Hope.* In a book that has been devoted throughout to a discussion about "the Word," the very last word just happens to match Barack Obama's campaign slogan and the single word that will forever be associated with Shepard Fairey's iconic poster. Given the usual six- to nine-month gap between the submission of a manuscript and publication, it's a fair guess that Brown was tweaking, and perhaps even writing, the conclusion to *The Lost Symbol* while the 2008 presidential election was reaching its peak. Was "Hope" sitting at the end of the manuscript before Barack Obama's campaign began? Did it find its way, subconsciously, into Dan Brown's brain during the campaign? Or did he place it there on purpose, one final, powerful message for our times?

Secret Fundamentalism
at the Heart
of American Power

an interview with Jeff Sharlet

At the climax of *The Lost Symbol* plot, Dan Brown asks readers to believe that the dissemination of a video showing Washington power brokers performing Masonic initiation rites would create chaos. "The government would be thrown into upheaval," Langdon fears. "The airwaves would be filled with the voice of anti-Masonic groups, fundamentalists, and conspiracy theorists spewing hatred and fear . . ." The jeopardy is so great that Langdon could "barely get his mind around" how bad things might become. The very future of the American government would be in doubt.

Really? One of Dan Brown's biggest plot problems in *TLS* may be that most readers don't get the sense that exposure of the secret videotape Mal'akh has made is likely to bring the government down or have any dire consequences at all. The days of anti-Masonic hysteria are history. Today, it would take a lot more than learning that politicians belonged to a secret brotherhood with weird practices to galvanize Americans into bringing the government down.

Jeff Sharlet, a contributing editor for *Harper's* and *Rolling Stone* knows this all too well from recent firsthand experience. In 2001, Sharlet briefly moved in with the Family, one of the oldest and most influential religious conservative organizations in the United States. His 2008 exposé, *The Family: Secret Fundamentalism at the Heart of American Power*, revealed senators, congressmen, and governors motivated by a cultlike zeal to spread a particularly strange version of Jesus' gospel, emphasizing an extreme form of capitalism, and a cultlike reverence for men in power. The Family's leader, Doug Coe, points to Hitler, Stalin, and Mao as models for how a small group of men can effect enormous change. This group is involved in organizing the National Prayer Breakfast at which every president since Eisenhower has spoken.

Yet it wasn't until Family members became embroiled in sex scandals in the summer of 2009 that Americans finally started to take note. Even then, faced with the obvious hypocrisy of these men who were allegedly committed to strong Christian family values, no one seriously questioned the ongoing world of the Family. As of this writing, the most scandal-plagued officials associated with the Family—Nevada senator John Ensign and South Carolina governor Mark Sanford—haven't even seen a need to resign.

In the following interview, Jeff Sharlet discusses a real-life story of a shadowy organization that operates at the highest levels of Washington power—and where the exposure of cult-like activities and loyalties has scarcely moved the needle of public outrage.

Washington is full of political action groups and special interests. How does the Family differ from, say, conventional Christian-right groups?

First, it doesn't seek publicity. They have a religious idea that God works through elites, not through ordinary people. Their leader, Doug Coe, says "the more invisible you can make your organization, the more influence it will have."

Second, they're not concerned with the typical Christian-right issues of abortion or same sex marriage. Their focus is on economics, what some in the group call "biblical capitalism," and on foreign affairs, by which they mean the extension of U.S. power and, by association in their minds, the Kingdom of God.

So what is their vision?

The Family began as a union-busting group in 1935. They were wealthy businessmen who didn't like Franklin Roosevelt and the New Deal and who started backing politicians in the Northwest. On the strength of their successes, they moved to Washington where they began organizing congressmen and supporting anti–New Deal legislation.

Their idea was that God will decide who's wealthy and everyone should accept that. It's sort of a trickle-down fundamentalism. They wanted legislation that would radically deregulate the economy so that God-chosen wealthy businessmen could do their work unfettered by things like minimum wage laws and health insurance.

Why did they also become involved in foreign affairs?

As the Cold War progressed, they began exporting their ideas overseas, seeking out foreign dictators who exhibited what they saw as strength. When the Family looked at Jesus and read the New Testament, they didn't see a story about mercy, love, justice, or forgiveness. They saw it as a story about power. In that context, during the 1930s, many were partial admirers of Hitler. They were not Nazis, but they liked his model of strength. They still speak in those terms to this day, saying that the best way to understand Jesus is to look at guys like Hitler, Stalin, and Mao. They recognize that these are evil men, but they exemplify the model of power that they're interested in.

That sounds evil.

They express their vision in very benign terms. They say the reason they're reaching out to these people is because they're trying to build a worldwide family of two hundred world leaders who are bound together through invisible bonds—they speak of themselves as an "invisible organization"—and when they are successful, there will be no more war, no more strife, no more conflict, because everyone will be on the same team: their team.

They even use this pretentious Latin phrase, *beyond the din of the vox populi,* "beyond the voice of the people." They're thinking of a worldwide order, an establishment along religious lines.

How much power do these people actually have?

That's a really important question. And I want to emphasize that the Family are not some sort of secret puppet masters controlling everything. There are multiple power bases. The Family is just one of them.

But you have to look at the guys who are involved today. They run a house on Capitol Hill called the C Street House, which is a former convent they registered as a church where they provide below-market-cost housing for congressmen. Senator John Ensign and Senator Tom Coburn live there. Senator Sam Brownback has lived there, as has Senator Jim DeMint, Congressman Zach Wamp, Congressman Heath Shuler, and Congressman Jerry Moran.

What do they use the house for?

Some live there. Others use it for meetings. Senator Inhofe says he conducts foreign policy meetings there. He travels around the world representing the U.S. as a senator, but, according to him, also promoting "the political philosophy of Jesus" as taught to him by Doug Coe.

Can you give an example of foreign policy initiatives favored by the Family members?

Senator Brownback volunteered an example to me once of something he had been working toward called the Silk Road Act with another Family member, Representative Joe Pitts of Pennsylvania. If the act is passed it will funnel a lot of U.S. foreign aid to various Central Asian republics, most of which are dictatorial regimes.

Brownback explained that the act benefits us threefold. First, he says we're going to stop radical Islam by buying off dictatorial regimes. Second, we're going to open up these countries to U.S. investment. And third, where U.S.-style capitalism goes, the gospel follows. Now, whether or not that's true, the gospel is not a U.S. foreign policy interest. That's not why we put these guys in office.

What about the Family's domestic influence?

David Kuo, a special assistant to President Bush during his first term and a supporter of the Family, has written of it as "the most powerful group in Washington that nobody knows." This is a group that sponsors the National Prayer Breakfast every year. Now, if you ask a lot of congressmen, they'll tell you that the National Prayer Breakfast is an old tradition going back to the founding of the republic. It's not. It's a private, sectarian event invented by the Family in 1953. I don't think they're setting policy, but I do think that their senators and representatives are able to move things legislatively. They are not the single decisive factor, but they are probably one of the largest unknown factors in American foreign and economic policy.

Before your book came out, how widely known was the Family?

Before the 1960s, the Family wasn't really all that secretive. But after Doug Coe became leader of the group in 1969 he sent a memo to various associates around the world, saying the time had come "to submerge" the Family's public profile.

Reporters did investigate the Family in the 1970s and 1980s, but their stories didn't gain traction. In 2002, Pulitzer Prize–winning reporter Lisa Getter uncovered some amazing things, including the fact that the Family acted as the middleman between the Reagan administration and Central American despots. The *Los Angeles Times* put the story on page one. They thought they had a big scoop. But there was very little response.

Even when my book came out, *NBC Nightly News* got hold of it and found a video of Doug Coe talking about Hitler, Himmler, and Goebbels and that model of leadership. They, too, thought they had a major scoop. But no one in the rest of the media followed the story.

Most of the press really didn't start paying attention until the sex scandals in the summer of 2009, involving Senator John Ensign and Governor Mark Sanford.

Why did no one act earlier?

Frankly, I think we have a religiously illiterate press.

If a politician says he is guided by prayer, and that he has a prayer group that guides him in his decisions, it is respectful and appropriate to ask him more about that. But, generally, the press does not. They don't say, well, what do you pray for? Who do you pray to? Who do you pray with? What are your beliefs on the nature of prayer? When you start asking these questions of the Family, you get some answers that I think are frightening.

The Lost Symbol *plot is predicated on the idea that it is vital to stop a videotape showing Washington power brokers involved in secret Masonic ceremonies from leaking onto the Internet. Do you think there would be a scandal if that were to happen?*

When *NBC Nightly News* found a video of Doug Coe talking about the Family's power model of Hitler, Himmler, and Goebbels, we thought, boy, this is going to blow the lid off everything. But nobody cared. So, not to steal the thunder from Mal'akh, but it's very hard to convince people that there may be something deeply problematic going on.

We did notice one parallel between one of the ideas in The Lost Symbol *and your research into the Family. And that was the idea, from noetics, that human thought has the power to change matter. The Family appears to have a very similar idea about the power of prayer.*

This is one of the interesting connections between the Family and *The Lost Symbol.* One of the big financial backers of the Institute for Noetic Sciences is a former oil executive named Paul Temple, who is also a longtime participant in the Family. This idea that you can have a direct impact on things through prayer is very important. But one of the things that the members of the Family emphasized to me is that it's not so much belief that matters, it's obedience. You obey God and things work.

So is the Family a conspiracy?

It is not really a conspiracy. It's an idea of how power should work.

People will say they loved my book and then compare me to Dan

Brown, saying they learned all about Opus Dei from *The Da Vinci Code* and all about the Family from my book. I think fictional conspiracy theories are great entertainment. But the people who read Dan Brown's books and mistake fiction for fact distract from the real work of open democracy and holding politicians accountable.

The truth is that they didn't learn about Opus Dei from *The Da Vinci Code*, they read an entertaining novel. If you want to understand how Opus Dei or the Family really works, if you want to push back against invisible power structures in our society, that's a different project altogether.

GEOGRAPHY, HOLOGRAPHY, ANATOMY

Plot Flaws *in* The Lost Symbol

by David A. Shugarts

Dave Shugarts was the first to perform a detailed analysis of plot flaws and factual errors in *The Da Vinci Code*, in an essay that appeared in our 2004 book, *Secrets of the Code*. He reprised this type of analysis for *Angels & Demons* in our 2005 book, *Secrets of Angels & Demons*. Shugarts ended up practically creating a whole new cottage industry, one that was in full flower for *The Lost Symbol*. He was invited back for the hat trick, taking his Sherlock Holmesian magnifying glass to Dan Brown's latest novel.

In keeping with his tradition of leaving errors strewn throughout his books, Dan Brown has delivered plenty of them in *The Lost Symbol*. Since Brown has had ample time for news of the errors in *Angels & Demons* or *The Da Vinci Code* to percolate up to him, not to mention the funds to hire an army of research assistants, it's beginning to look as though he either just doesn't care, or is deliberately making mistakes to see how many of them people will catch. Since many, many bloggers, critics, and others have now joined the hunt for flaws in Dan Brown's books, there surely will be dozens and dozens of them unearthed in *TLS*. Here, we will just cover some of the highlights:

SCIENCE AND TECHNOLOGY

One of the really glaring blunders comes early in the book, as Brown describes Katherine Solomon's laboratory, saying it enjoys "full radio-frequency separation from the rest of the building" and that it is "isolated from any extraneous radiation or 'white noise.' This include[s] interference as subtle as 'brain radiation' or 'thought emissions' generated by people nearby." It is also intended to block eavesdropping by would-be spies.

Yet, only a few pages later, Katherine is making and receiving cell phone calls and text messages inside the lab! This may be because the room's shielding is constructed with "a stiff mesh of titanium-coated lead fiber," apparently a complete invention of Dan Brown's that isn't used in actual shielded rooms. Most shielded rooms today are made of copper or steel, combined with specially shaped foam insulation panels, depending on the frequencies of the different kinds of radiation being blocked.

When Mal'akh prepares to destroy Katherine Solomon's lab, the *TLS* narrator tells us he retrieves a "Pyrex jug of Bunsen-burner fuel—a viscous, highly flammable, yet noncombustible oil."

There are several things wrong with this description. First and foremost, a Bunsen burner does not use liquid fuel. It uses gas, such as natural gas (e.g., methane), that is usually piped into a lab. And there is not much point to a fuel oil that is noncombustible. But further, a Pyrex jug would be made of glass, which would be considered very unsafe for storing a fuel, and certainly wouldn't be used in a laboratory. However, it's not totally clear that Dan Brown knows Pyrex is a type of glass, since only a few pages later, the perimeter security guard sees not a glass jug, but "what appeared to be a metal can of some sort. The can's label said it was fuel oil for a Bunsen burner."

When lab assistant Trish Dunne can't trace an Internet protocol (IP) address, she calls in a computer network hacker. He comes back with a quick assessment: "This IP has a funky format. It's written in a protocol that isn't even publicly available yet. It's probably gov intel or military." This makes no sense, since an IP address that did not conform to the IP format would not even be visible on the Internet. If it really had a "funky" format, Trish Dunne would have immediately detected it, and even her merest attempt to trace it would have been rejected by her own software.

In general, it looks as though Dan Brown is mixing terms and concepts of the Internet that were current circa 1999, with other terms and concepts that applied in 2009. Trish's use of "traceroutes" and "spiders" and "delegators" is relatively old, while mention of an iPhone or Twitter is relatively new. Twitter was founded in 2006 and the iPhone went on sale in 2007. This may be a sign that much of *TLS* was written by 2005 or 2006, but certain passages and later chapters may have been written in the past two years.

There are some similar telltale chronological fingerprints on other subjects. Brown mentions two real-life entities doing noetics-related research (besides Katherine Solomon's lab). One of them—the Institute of Noetic Sciences (IONS)—is still in operation, and has been deluged with new interest since the publication of *TLS*. But the other—Princeton Engineering Anomalies Research (PEAR)—was shut down in early 2007.

Further, when Brown wants to sound leading-edge, he describes Katherine's laboratory early in the book as using "redundant holographic backup units" for data storage, enclosed behind "three-inch-thick shatterproof glass" within a "temperature-controlled vault." There are two units that are said to be "synchronized and identical." There were some expectations by 2004 that holographic discs would emerge as a leading technology. In reality, the long-heralded advent of holographic data storage has never quite materialized. Although some of these devices have been developed, there has been no real market for them, since conventional magnetic hard drives have constantly dropped in cost and increased in capacity. Also, although most high-tech storage rooms are temperature and humidity controlled, there is nothing about holographic storage that would call for three-inch-thick glass.

Late in the book, after Katherine's lab is blown up and her data presumably lost, her brother, Peter Solomon, reveals that he has been keeping backups of her data—apparently not needing the special holographic drives. "I wanted to follow your progress without disturbing you," he explains. If her research is so data-intensive (nothing in the description tells us why the data storage needs of noetics research are so much greater than any other kind of lab work), why doesn't Peter need climate-controlled holographic storage media as well?

This brings up a list of ethical issues that surround Peter Solomon. Not only did he keep sneaky watch over his sister, but also, she will eventually realize that Peter refused to acknowledge the secret that resulted in the death of their mother. For years, he has failed to admit to Katherine that he knew what "pyramid" the intruder was seeking. Further, Peter Solomon has surely committed a number of breaches of standard government ethics and conflict-of-interest policies, as well as downright criminal acts, by misusing the Smithsonian's facilities for Katherine's secret lab, even if he used his own private money to fund it.

GEOGRAPHY

In his prior books, Dan Brown often has Robert Langdon rushing in the wrong direction in Paris, Rome, or London. The tradition continues in Washington with *TLS*.

Early in the tale, Langdon looks up at the change of road noise as his limo crosses Memorial Bridge into Washington. As Dan Brown describes it, "Langdon gazed left, across the Tidal Basin, toward the gracefully rounded silhouette of the Jefferson Memorial." In the real world, when you are on the [Arlington] Memorial Bridge and headed directly at the Lincoln Memorial, as the book recounts, the Jefferson Memorial is on the right, not the left.

In chapter 92, Langdon finds himself racing "northward" from the National Cathedral on the way to Kalorama Heights. This is quite a trick since Kalorama lies to the southeast of the cathedral. At another point, as Langdon and CIA agents approach the House of the Temple along S Street, which runs along the north side of the building, Dan Brown calls it the east side.

But one passage reveals just how confused Dan Brown is about geography. Apparently, he doesn't even have a basic grasp of how longitude works. The clue calls for Langdon and Solomon to go due south from the House of the Temple. Langdon says that's too ambiguous, because "due south of this building could be anywhere on a longitude that's over twenty-four thousand miles long."

From this comment we can infer that Dan Brown believes that a line of longitude, also known as a meridian, circles the globe at the poles. But that's not how it works. A distinction is made between an east and west meridian, the former running through the U.S., the latter through Asia. This means a single line of longitude runs from the North to the South Pole, a distance of about 12,430 miles (not 24,000). The distance from the House of the Temple to the South Pole is about 8,890 miles and that's the farthest south they could possibly travel on that longitude. (The distance to their actual destination, as it turns out, is less than two miles, making the reference to a longitudinal line 24,000 miles long wrong but moot.)

HISTORY

Dan Brown says there are 896 steps in the famous stairs of the Washington Monument. Most sources and guides say there are 897; there were originally 898 but one step was covered by a wheelchair ramp.

Langdon says of the Washington Monument, "There's a very old law decreeing that nothing taller can be built in our capital city. *Ever.*" The Height of Buildings Act, passed in 1899, said that nothing taller than the *Capitol* could be built (not the Washington Monument). The law was superseded in 1910.

In speaking of the engraving by Albrecht Dürer, *Melencolia I,* Langdon recognizes the symbol combining an *A* and *D*. Dan Brown notes that this symbol, "as any scholar of medieval art would recognize, is a symbature—a symbol used in place of a signature." In fact, however, art scholars typically call it a "monogram" and sometimes it is considered a "logo." It appears that "symbature" is Dan Brown's own creation, since we couldn't find it in any dictionary. Perhaps Langdon, our symbolist— another made-up word—will include a lesson on symbature for his next Harvard seminar.

Admiring his tattoos, Mal'akh contemplates the undecorated space on the top of his head, which Dan Brown calls the "fontanel . . . the one area of the human skull that remained open at birth. *An oculus to the brain.*" However, basic anatomical texts tell us that there isn't just one fontanel, but six fontanels at birth: the anterior, posterior, and on each side of the head, the sphenoidal and mastoid fontanels.

Masonic Legends

There's a fundamental plot point that bears a lot of pondering, since it's disguised by a lot of different allusions and clues. But it readily explains why none of the real action in *TLS* is connected to the Founding Fathers, despite all the anticipation that the book's secrets would involve Freemasonry's putative great conspiracy among men like Washington and Franklin to mold the nation's destiny.

Despite all the uses of the word "ancient" and the other descriptions that imply a long, hoary history of the secret hiding place and the clues to find it, the secret cannot be very old at all. The fact is that if the "secret" book containing the "Ancient Mysteries" was put into the cornerstone of the Washington Monument, that event occurred on July 4, 1848. This was long after the Founding Fathers were dead. This also was a period when the popularity of Freemasonry was recovering from a severe setback that had caused many lodges to go dark. It was certainly not a time when the Masons could be considered a powerful organization.

This also was two years before the legendary Albert Pike, a huge force in the Scottish Rite, even joined the Freemasons. It was under Pike's leadership that the Scottish Rite's Southern Jurisdiction came to Washington around 1870. During Pike's era, the Supreme Council had quarters on Third Street, not far from the Capitol, but miles from its location today.

In *TLS*, the Masonic Pyramid references the House of the Temple as the starting point for a two-mile journey due south along Sixteenth Street to the Washington Monument. Logically, the coded pyramid itself would not have been created until after the Scottish Rite's current House of the Temple at 1733 Sixteenth Street was completed, which occurred in 1915. Thus, the Masonic Pyramid is less than one hundred years old.

After all of that, what is the "secret" information that was so carefully guarded for so long? Merely a book that was published many centuries ago, has many millions of copies in print, and which the Freemasons neither created nor kept hidden. We call it the Bible.

Finally, Dan Brown mixes up a quote that is at the center of the legends of Freemasonry, the plea, "Is there no help for the widow's son?"

As Brown depicts it in *TLS*, "These same words had been uttered centuries ago . . . by King Solomon as he mourned a murdered friend." But, according to Masonic legend, these words were actually uttered by Hiram Abiff, the master craftsman who was the builder of Solomon's Temple, as he was being murdered for not divulging certain secrets hidden in the temple. Whether he was a "friend" of the king's isn't specified. The full quote is, "Oh Lord, my God, is there no help for the widow's son?" and it is the signal of distress that one Mason conveys to another in a time of need.

Hiram Abiff is said in some traditions to be the first Mason. Whether he is or isn't the first Mason, there's no question that this important quote is always attributed to him, not to King Solomon. It is further interesting to note that both Kings and Chronicles reference the idea that Solomon called on Hiram to help him build his temple. Both passages refer to Hiram himself as a "widow's son." Dan Brown knows all this perfectly well.

Indeed, Brown made this phrase semifamous when he encoded it in boldface letters on the jacket flaps for the original hardcover of *The Da Vinci Code* in 2003, thus silently communicating to us and others that his next book would be about the Freemasons. So why the misattribution of this incredibly important phrase? That's just one of the many modern mysteries of *The Lost Symbol*.

DAN BROWN'S GREAT WORK

An Exercise in Maybe Logic

by Ron Hogan

Going down the rabbit hole of "maybe logic," Ron Hogan engages in a series of fascinating speculations in the following piece. He wonders about the motivations of Dan Brown in writing *The Lost Symbol*, he shares some intriguing ideas about the book's structure, and he imagines some of the potential impacts this novel will have on readers. "Allegorical page-turner, postmodern sorcery, or just a clever yarn?" Hogan asks. After you read his piece, you will at least know how you feel about those three possible ways to summarize what *The Lost Symbol* is in its essence. Hogan is senior editor of GalleyCat, a Web site devoted to the book publishing world, where an earlier version of this commentary first appeared.

In January 2008, Stephen Rubin, then president of the Doubleday Broadway Publishing Group and Dan Brown's publisher, was confronted by the question publishing industry observers had been asking for several years: Where was the sequel to *The Da Vinci Code*? "Dan Brown has a very specific release date for the publication of his new book," Rubin assured Jeffrey Trachtenberg, a reporter for the *Wall Street Journal*, "and when the book is published, his readers will see why."

Trachtenberg suggested possible dates. Would the release of *The Solomon Key* (as it was then known) commemorate the laying of the cornerstones at the Washington Monument (July 4) or the Capitol Building (September 18) or the White House (October 13), all of which involved public Freemason rituals?

Nearly two years passed between Rubin's statement and the publication of what had since been retitled *The Lost Symbol* on September 15, 2009—by which time that declaration about the significance of the release date had apparently been forgotten by the journalists covering the event. The statement was still out there, however, waiting for an explanation.

If you've read *Secrets of Angels & Demons*, you may recall the interview with Robert Anton Wilson, especially his explanation of *maybe logic*, "in which I consider ideas not simply true or false, but in degrees of probabilities." It was in this spirit, shortly after reading *The Lost Symbol*, that I began to consider the mysteries of September 15.

A preliminary Google search didn't turn up anything linking the date to Masonic history, and a Wikipedia page listing all the births, deaths, and major events occurring on September 15 throughout recorded history didn't seem to offer anything that would fit with the novel's narrative or themes. It *was* the birthday of the Italian king Umberto II and the American filmmaker Oliver Stone; could Dan Brown be announcing himself as the second Umberto Eco or paying tribute to a man who'd done as much as he had to popularize conspiracy theory? Those possibilities were amusing, but utterly improbable.

At the bottom of the page, however, I found one intriguing entry: in ancient Greece, September 15 marked "the second day of the Eleusinian Mysteries, when the priests of Demeter declared the public start of the rites." The Eleusinian Mysteries were an annual celebration of the cult of Demeter and Persephone, going back nearly three and a half millennia until they were forcibly ended in the fourth century C.E. by Christians working in tandem with Gothic armies attacking the Roman Empire. To this day, we don't know the full extent of what took place during this multiday celebration, largely because initiates were forbidden to reveal what they witnessed and learned during the ceremonies—which were divided into "lesser" and "greater" mysteries—upon pain of death.

The obvious superficial similarities have inspired speculation that these ceremonies served as a template for Masonic initiation rites, though whether it's a matter of direct lineage or a historical appropriation depends on who you're reading. It's highly probable Dan Brown came across the Eleusinian/Masonic connection during his research, and an enthusiasm for suppressed alternatives to contemporary religious institutions permeates his writing: as Peter Solomon tells Robert Langdon near the end of *The Lost Symbol*, "you and I both know the ancients would be horrified if they saw how their teachings had been perverted." So how likely is it that Brown would select the publication date of his most anticipated novel as a subtle invitation to readers of the world to take part in an initiation ritual based upon an ancient template?

And what, exactly, would be the revelation he was attempting to impart?

To answer those questions, let's make a brief digression into the field of twentieth-century occultism. It's a subject with which we can assume Dan Brown has some familiarity, given a casual reference to the infamous ceremonial magician Aleister Crowley as one of Mal'akh's inspirations. One of Crowley's more widely known contributions to occult literature was a cotranslation of a seventeenth-century grimoire, or magical handbook, called *The Lesser Key of Solomon* (a possible source of inspiration for the original title of *The Lost Symbol*?) that describes how to summon and control seventy-two demons through a combination of ritualistic language and magical symbols known as "sigils" (from the Latin word for "seal," because they were designed to hold the demon within a magical container). These sigils often draw upon the imagery of established mystical and alchemical traditions, such as the Hebrew alphabet or astrological notations. We can be sure Dan Brown knows this, too, because Robert Langdon notices the sigils Mal'akh has tattooed onto his flesh when they finally meet.

(As an aside, Mal'akh's self-designed tattoo "masterpiece" is a rich symbolic field. Chapter 2 contains an extended description of how his legs have been inked to resemble two pillars supporting an arch defined by his groin and abdomen, while his chest bears a double-headed phoenix. The relevance of the phoenix in Masonic iconography becomes obvious later on, when the same icon—the symbol of Freemasonry's Ancient and Accepted Scottish Rite—appears on Peter Solomon's ring. The meaning of the pillars is left obscure in the novel, but because Mal'akh refers to them by name—"Boaz and Jachin"—we know they represent the two pillars of the entrance to the biblical Temple of Solomon, which in turn became the foundation of much Masonic lore. Given Mal'akh's true identity, his quest to transform himself into "Solomon's Temple" is a particularly clever piece of the novel's symbolic infrastructure.)

For centuries, aspiring magicians would use the classical sigils of *The Lesser Key of Solomon* and other grimoires when attempting to invoke supernatural forces. In the early twentieth century, however, a British artist named Austin Osman Spare began to experiment with designing his own "alphabet of desire," creating abstract designs that would serve an individuated set of sigils keyed to his unique magical intentions. Spare believed every magician should create his or her own sigils, which would be more potent because of the subconscious imprints from the magician's mental and emotional energies.

His ideas remained somewhat marginal even within occult circles until the late 1970s, when a new generation of British "chaos magicians" began to develop a more individualized style of sorcery. The chaos magicians took one aspect of Aleister Crowley's teachings—the idea that ceremonial magic was a form of applied psychology—and pushed it to the next level. If the beings invoked in such rituals were projections of the magician's own psychological state, they reasoned, why limit oneself to the angels and demons described in the historical grimoires when you could invoke H. P. Lovecraft's Cthulhu, or the Marvel Comics version of Thor (or any other fictional character, for that matter)? Spare's concept of personalized sigil design became one of the most popular planks in the chaos magic platform, with various techniques available. (The most common consists of writing one's desire out as a sentence, then rearranging the letters to create a unique design.)

As the body of literature on chaos magic grew, the concept of the sigil took on additional complexity. Grant Morrison is a writer who has spoken openly of the influence of chaos magic on his work, particularly a comic book series published in the 1990s called *The Invisibles* which chronicled, in part, the recruitment and training of a young man by a secret magical society fighting to liberate humanity from extradimensional aliens who are keeping us from recognizing the true nature of reality. Morrison has described that multivolume work as a *hypersigil*, a complex work of art crafted to achieve a magical purpose, charged not by the magician's attention but by the audience's. In an essay called "The Palimpsest," the anarchist philosopher Hakim Bey elaborates on the concept, describing "a consciously-devised 'seduction machine' or magical engine meant to awaken true desires, anger at the repression of those desires, [and] belief in the non-impossibility of those desires."

The goals Bey identifies are similar to those of many initiation rites: opening the initiate's eyes to hitherto secret knowledge, which results in a new, fuller understanding of reality. Grant Morrison's descriptions of his own work give us a verified example of a creative artist producing a hypersigil and releasing it for public consumption. We wouldn't necessarily know about that layer of intentionality, however, if Morrison himself didn't speak about it publicly. That raises the question: How many other creative artists are creating hypersigils and *not* letting readers in on their plans?

And: could Dan Brown be one of them?

A mega-bestselling author trying to transform the consciousness of millions of readers through a complex framework of magical symbolism? It hardly seems possible. But what would a careful examination of the narrative structure of *The Lost Symbol* tell us?

We don't even have to look that hard. Robert Langdon himself tells us at the end of chapter 17: The severed hand of Peter Solomon on the floor of the Capitol Rotunda is "an invitation to receive secret knowledge— protected wisdom known only to an elite few."

After receiving that invitation, Langdon remembers how Solomon, the Worshipful Master of a Masonic Lodge, came to him earlier bearing a box the contents of which, he said, "imbue its possessor with the ability to bring order from chaos." Giving the box to Langdon, Solomon charges him with a mission: "I would like you to keep it safe for me for a while. Can you do that?"

"Peter Solomon would be horrified to know how badly Langdon had failed him," Brown writes, but that's just the beginning. Warren Bellamy, the Architect of the Capitol, Peter Solomon's close friend, and a 33° Mason, rescues Langdon and brings him to the Library of Congress, where he elaborates upon the nature of the Masonic Pyramid ("a map that unveils the hiding place of mankind's greatest treasure") and then warns Langdon, "[I]t is our duty to ensure this pyramid is not assembled." Langdon, who brought the base of the pyramid with him from the Capitol basement, wants to save Solomon, but Bellamy insists "the great secret our brotherhood protects for all mankind" cannot be surrendered "even in exchange for Peter Solomon's life."

So what's the first thing Langdon does once he's separated from Bellamy? He stands by helplessly while Katherine Solomon opens the box her brother entrusted to him and reads the inscription on the golden capstone.

The significance of this act is underscored when Langdon and Katherine encounter another 33° Mason, the Reverend Dr. Colin Galloway, dean of the Washington National Cathedral. When they share what they have discovered, Galloway does not praise them for their resourcefulness. "The package containing the capstone was sealed," he reminds them. "Mr. Bellamy told you *not* to open it, and yet you did. In addition, Peter Solomon told you *not* to open it. And yet you did." The consequences for their failure to protect the secret are grave: "[W]hen you broke the seal on that box, you set in motion a series of events from which there will be no return. There are forces at work tonight that you do not yet comprehend. There is no turning back."

After they leave Galloway and extract another layer of meaning from the pyramid, Langdon and Katherine are lured into a trap. Mal'akh places Langdon in a sensory deprivation tank which he then begins to fill with water. Faced with the threat of drowning, desperate to survive, "with his last few seconds of air, Robert Langdon shared the secret of how to decipher the Masonic Pyramid."

To recap: as three high-ranking Masons—a Worshipful Master, an Architect, and a "High Priest"—use highly charged language to impart secret knowledge to Robert Langdon and urge him to protect that knowledge at all cost, he fails in that duty over and over again until he is confronted by a magical adversary who (unknown to Langdon, and possibly forgotten or unrecognized by readers) has used deception to assume the status of an equal degree to the other Masons encountered along this journey— and whose body is, as discussed above, a grotesque parody of the Masonic temple. The consequences of Langdon's compounded failures is death.

Or, rather, a very convincing simulation of death, after which Langdon, even though he is little more than a spectator at the climax, manages to redeem himself sufficiently for Peter Solomon to reveal the final truth about the Lost Word with "the power to transform humankind by unlocking the Ancient Mysteries."

So, the narrative of *The Lost Symbol* is built upon a structural framework resembling Freemason initiation rites, down to the symbolic death and rebirth of the initiate. (Brown gives us a purposefully lurid version of the "death ritual" of the third Masonic degree in chapter 117.) Symbolic death permeates the novel from its very first line—"*The secret is how to die*"—and even Langdon's own near-death experience is foreshadowed as far back as his escape from the Library of Congress in chapter 59: "Robert Langdon felt like a corpse."

At the very least, then, I would feel comfortable asserting that *The Lost Symbol* is intended as a Masonic allegory much like Mozart's *The Magic Flute*. (Dan Brown confirms his familiarity with Mozart's connection to the Freemasons through a veiled reference in an interview reprinted in *Secrets of the Code*.) An allegorical novel, however, is not necessarily the same thing as a hypersigil; Langdon's initiation may simply be an elaborate literary device rather than an attempt to spark a similar awakening within the reader's consciousness.

Is there anything in *The Lost Symbol* to persuade us to take that extra step in how we perceive it?

I would suggest this is a good time to consider the other major theme of *The Lost Symbol*, the one we've ignored up to now: Katherine Solomon's preoccupation with noetics. "We have barely scratched the surface of our mental and spiritual capabilities," Katherine thinks to herself early on. "Human thought, if properly focused, [has] the ability to affect and change physical mass . . . Human thought can literally transform the physical world . . . We are the masters of our own universe . . . This is the missing link between modern science and ancient mysticism."

Similar celebratory references to noetic science, like Katherine's far-out claim that she's successfully established the weight of a human soul, crop up throughout the novel, and though some critics have called Katherine's field of research an annoying distraction from the "real" story of the action-packed thriller plot, perhaps it's more integral to Dan Brown's intended effect than they recognize. After all, Peter Solomon's final revelation to Robert Langdon is immediately followed by a similar presentation from Katherine—a speech that both complements and completes the wisdom passed on by her brother. "I have witnessed human minds affecting the physical world in myriad ways," she tells Langdon. "We have scientifically proven that the power of human thought grows exponentially with the number of minds that share that thought . . . The idea of *universal consciousness* is no ethereal New Age concept. It's a hard-core scientific reality."

This alludes to the real-life research described in Lynne McTaggart's *The Intention Experiment*, which Katherine (and thus Dan Brown) name-checked much earlier in the novel. It's at this point that Brown reveals his own "intention experiment," when Katherine tells Langdon: "I guarantee you, as soon as I publish my work, the Twitterati will all be sending tweets that say, '*learning about noetics*,' and interest in this science will explode exponentially."

Can we take this to be Dan Brown's "mission statement" for *The Lost Symbol*—and is it possible Brown wrote this novel in order to put readers through an overwhelming experience specifically designed to make them receptive, through both esoteric and scientific arguments, to the possibility of human consciousness obtaining godlike powers, the "Great Work" of alchemical lore? And can those tweets, which began appearing shortly after the book was released to the public, be taken as evidence of the hypersigil's successful activation?

Remember, I am dealing strictly in maybe logic here, unconcerned with what is true or false, only with what appears plausible based on the evidence seen. Allegorical page-turner, postmodern sorcery, or just a clever yarn? You'll have to decide for yourself what to believe.

I should make one confession, though: not everybody forgot Stephen Rubin's claims about the importance of the novel's release date. I e-mailed Doubleday asking if September 15 was the date Rubin had been hinting at back in 2008 and, if so, what significance it held. A spokesperson replied with a simple explanation: the publication date was nothing more than "classic Dan Brown fun." September 15, 2009, was 9/15/09; the sum of those three numbers was 33. (It's a shame he didn't get the novel completed closer to his original schedule, as he could have achieved the same effect on September 18, 2006, *and* worked in that reference to the laying of the Capitol's cornerstone.)

As far as the public is concerned, then, the publication date of *The Lost Symbol* was just an opportunity for Dan Brown to make another Freemason in-joke, and has nothing to do with his intention of opening our minds to the ancient mysteries, at least not the ancient mysteries of the Eleusinians.

As far as the public is concerned, anyway.

The Critics Speak—Loudly

by Hannah de Keijzer

After a six-year wait, Dan Brown's follow-up to *The Da Vinci Code* was never going to slip unnoticed into stores. But rarely has a book received the sort of attention showered on *The Lost Symbol*, fed by a relentless and, for the book industry, an unprecedented marketing campaign.

The release of the cipher- and symbol-bedecked cover in July 2009, followed later by a daily release of clues to its contents on Facebook and Twitter, set off a flurry of blog posts and tweets. Newspapers, magazines, and television fed the anticipation, offering speculation and commentary. Not only was *The Lost Symbol* the story, the security surrounding *The Lost Symbol* was the story, the decision to publish a Kindle edition was the story, the *New York Times*'s breaking of Doubleday's embargo was the story, and an unauthorized early review of the book—in Norway!—was the story.

The effort had its intended result. The book sold a record one million copies on its first day. The number reached two million the first week. The *Guardian* (UK) heralded it as the "fastest-selling book of all time."

Predictably, *The Lost Symbol* also propelled critics to their keyboards to see who could compose the most acerbic prose. "Didactic . . . repetitive . . . clumsy," was Maureen Dowd's snarky verdict in the *New York Times*. "In the next opus," she continued, "Langdon will probably be wearing a red Shriner's fez with his Burberry turtleneck and Harris tweed." Lev Grossman, of *Time* magazine, said Brown introduced characters with "a kind of electric breathlessness that borders on the inadvertently hilarious." Reviews by readers were hardly kinder: *The Lost Symbol* received a decidedly tepid three stars on both the Amazon and Barnes & Noble Web sites. Comments ranged from "the ending sucked" to "fire your editor."

Other piquant critiques included:

- " . . . lumpen, witless, adjectivally-promiscuous and addicted to using italics to convey excitement where more adept thriller writers generally prefer to use words." (Jeremy Jehu of the UK *Telegraph*)
- Like "riding pillion on a jetbike driven by a demented architectural historian screaming conspiratorial travelogue descriptions into your ears via a radiomike." (blogger Nick Pelling)
- "It is not the theological message of the Bible that 'ye shall be gods,' despite Dan Brown's wishing it to be so. That would be the message of the serpent, not the message of the Savior." (Ben Witherington on Beliefnet.com)
- Langdon is "the most irritating Harvard-educated, mullet-wearing sexless pedant of all time." (Matt Taibi in *Rolling Stone*)

The book also inspired parody and satire. The online magazine *Slate* released a "Dan Brown Sequel Generator" inviting readers to select a city (Philadelphia, Ottawa, Chicago), a nefarious cult (Major League Baseball, Daughters of the American Revolution, the Shriners), and out popped a three-paragraph dust-jacket summary that looked shockingly similar to a real Dan Brown synopsis. *At least a dozen writers mimicked Brown's penchant for thinking aloud in italics.* Meanwhile, blogger Phil Terrett said a simple "hello" to Robert Langdon might elicit the following response:

"Hello, now let me see, Hello is a word that originally was invented by devil worshipers for a new pudding they invented in Abyssinia in 1283, it was red, invoked hell and contained jello, hence hell-o. They began to take the pudding to food parties at each other's houses and greeted their brethren with Hell-o. . . ."

And what was Dan Brown's response to the torrent of negative criticism that has followed all his novels? "Some critics say I don't write like William Shakespeare or William Faulkner, and they're right. I write in a modern, efficient style that serves only the story."

Indeed, Brown is an excellent storyteller despite stylistic flaws and a tendency toward information overload. He knows how to string the reader along: protagonists appear to die when there are two hundred pages left! How can you not want to find out how *that's* explained? And since the next chapter is only three pages away, who cares if it's already one o'clock in the morning? We *have* to keep reading.

Many of mainstream America's newspapers lauded Brown's ability to keep readers on the edge of their seats. "Call it Brownian motion: a comet-tail ride of short paragraphs, short chapters, beautifully spaced reveals and, in the case of *The Lost Symbol,* a socko unveiling of the killer's true identity," wrote Louis Bayard in the *Washington Post.* "Dan Brown spins a good yarn, plain and simple. When did that become something not deserving of respect?" demanded Reed Tucker of the *New York Post.* Or, as Katie Crocker of the University of South Carolina's student newspaper, the *Daily Gamecock,* admitted somewhat guiltily, *The Lost Symbol* is "a read you curl up to, at home, when you feel your own drab life needs excitement."

Janet Maslin, the reviewer for the *New York Times,* summed it up well. Dan Brown's "authorial shortcomings," she wrote, "were outweighed by his craft as a quizmaster and a storyteller." And "within this book's hermetically sealed universe, characters' motivations don't really have to make sense," she argued, "they just have to generate the nonstop momentum that makes *The Lost Symbol* impossible to put down." Dan Brown, she declared, had brought "sexy back to a genre that had been left for dead." Just because many critics panned it, said Reed Tucker of the *New York Post,* "enjoying it doesn't make us stupid. That's TV's job."

The novel was also an unexpected boon for Masons, many of whom had anticipated the same evil conspiracy-within-a-conspiracy treatment from Brown as the Illuminati received in *Angels & Demons.* Arturo de Hoyos, Grand Archivist and Grand Historian of the Scottish Rite in America and a top-ranked 33° Mason, found *The Lost Symbol* "respectful" of the brotherhood. *The Masonic Traveler* was downright effusive, noting that "Brown's treatment of Masonry was very tender, almost too much so . . . in parts [Brown was] almost writing as if he were creating one of our own brochures."

A few critics also found intellectual heft in Brown's latest offering. They understood that Brown's appeal came not just from the story, but also from the way he wrestled with big ideas not usually associated with action-adventure tales. As Stephen Amidon in the *Sunday Times* (London) put it: "Brown's big breakthrough is to understand that most fiction readers these days are really looking for nonfiction books in disguise." Steven Waldman of Beliefnet credited it with renewing interest in deism, the faith of our Founding Fathers. (Dan Brown has himself reminded his audience that America was not founded as a Christian country, but became one.)

Perhaps the most intriguing theme to emerge from among the reviewers of *The Lost Symbol* was that it was very much an "American" story.

First, there's the childlike, innocent fun of Langdon's puzzles, which reflects Dan Brown's own childhood. "On Christmas morning, when we were little kids, [my father] would create treasure hunts through the house with different limericks or mathematical puzzles that led us to the next clue. And so, for me, at a young age, treasure hunts were always exciting," the novelist told one interviewer. Adam Gopnik, of *The New Yorker*, highlighted this theme in his review: "Tom Swift and the Hardy Boys were always in the midst of compelling conspiracies; there was always a code that had to be cracked, and ancient Asian priests and ancient Asian cults invading their cozy American worlds."

Second, the novel "comes home" to America after Langdon's adventures in Paris and Rome. Brown imbues Washington with the same sense of intrigue he'd already bestowed upon his European settings. This note, from Lev Grossman of *Time*, may not be exactly a welcome home for a hero, but it resonates:

What he did for Christianity in *Angels & Demons* and *The Da Vinci Code*, Brown is now trying to do for America: reclaim its richness, its darkness,

its weirdness. It's probably a quixotic effort, but it is nevertheless touchingly valiant. We're not just overweight tourists in T-shirts and fanny
packs, he says. Our history is as sick and weird as anybody's! There's . . .
order in the chaos! It just takes a degree from a nonexistent Harvard
department to see it.

Dan Brown himself appraised his choice of settings this way: "Washington, D.C., has everything that Rome, Paris, and London have in the
way of great architecture—great power bases," he told NBC. "Washington has obelisks and pyramids and underground tunnels and great art
and a whole shadow world that we really don't see."

Third, what could be more American than our drive toward self-
improvement and self-realization? The message of hope and moral uplift
that is most often found in talk shows and Hollywood movies? "Ye *are*
gods," Brown (selectively) quotes the Scriptures, as he suggests that you,
too, can elevate your consciousness to the point where you will understand "The Word."

Adam Gopnik saw it this way: "Brown's secret turns out to be the same
as Oprah's beloved 'Secret'—you can have it all." Or, as Janet Maslin put
it: "In the end it is Mr. Brown's sweet optimism, even more than Langdon's sleuthing and explicating, that may amaze his readers most."

Perhaps Dan Brown's own review of his novels says it best. As he told
Matt Lauer of NBC News, "One thing I love to do is to get people to see
things through a slightly different lens. . . . I think my books contain a lot
of meat, but it tastes like dessert."

Acknowledgments

This book has been a fascinating journey among the many layers of plot, puzzles, and ideas to be found in *The Lost Symbol*. Many people have helped us see it to completion.

As ever, the people to whom we owe the greatest debt are our families: Julie and David, Helen and Hannah. We imposed upon them the side effects of a pressure-filled deadline; their understanding never flagged. The importance of their wisdom, love, and support cannot be overstated.

The book owes its existence in the first place to Danny Baror, agent extraordinaire, who had the vision and turned it into reality. Thanks as well to Heather Baror, who has joined her father's team.

We also want to thank our contributing editors. First and foremost, David A. Shugarts, extraordinary investigative journalist, invaluable contributor to the entire *Secrets* series, and great storyteller. His singular insights into the mind and methods of Dan Brown has allowed him time and again to predict, with remarkable accuracy, the ideas and plotting of *The Lost Symbol*, as evidenced by his groundbreaking *Secrets of the Widow's Son*, written in 2005.

Paul Berger, who has served as a researcher, writer, and editor on our previous *Secrets* books, was once again a reliable and cheerful aide-de-camp, ready at all hours to fill in the hole or find the missing piece of a puzzle. We wish him well as a new father, and express our thanks to Sofie for lending so much of Paul's time to us. Lou Aronica is the newest member of our team. Lou is a richly experienced publisher, editor, and author, and his interviewing and writing skills proved of great benefit to this book.

Our network of expert contributors are the heart and soul of this book. They responded generously when asked for their hard-won insights on very short notice. We thank them all for very special contributions: Amir Aczel, Diane Apostolos-Cappadona, Karen Armstrong, William Arntz, Lou Aronica, Michael Barkun, Paul Berger, Steven C. Bullock, David D. Burstein, Richard Dawkins, Arturo de Hoyos, Hannah de Keijzer, Elonka Dunin, Glenn W. Erickson, Heather Ewing, Jack Fruchtman Jr., Warren Getler, Marcelo Gleiser, Deirdre Good, Ron Hogan, Mitch Horowitz, Eamon Javers, George Johnson, Steven Johnson, Mark Koltko-Rivera, Irwin Kula, Thomas Levenson, Lynne McTaggart, Michael Parkes, David Plotz, Ingrid Rowland, Jim Sanborn, Marilyn Mandala Schlitz, Jeff Sharlet, Mark Tabbert, and James Wasserman.

We were also fortunate to work with the able team at William Morrow, led by our editor, Peter Hubbard. Peter's own fascination with science, cosmology, and new paradigms of thought made him an ideal partner for this project. We also want to thank Liate Stehlik, publisher; Lynn Grady, associate publisher; Tavia Kowalchuk and Shawn Nicholls from marketing; Shelby Meizlik and Seale Ballenger from publicity; art director Mary Schuck; and the rest of the Morrow team.

Personal acknowledgments from Arne de Keijzer: Warmest of thanks for the understanding and support given by family and friends, including Dan Burstein, Julie O'Connor, and their son, David; Steve de Keijzer and Marni Virtue; Bob and Carolyn Reiss; Jelmer and Rosa Dorreboom; Brian and Joan Weiss; Clem and Ann Malin; Lynn Northrup; Sandy West; Ben Blout and Marit Abrams and all my other forbearing friends. Hannah de Keijzer, whose contribution can be found in chapter 10, was not just a fine editor and researcher, but of great moral support. Elonka

Dunin, our friendly dean of sleuths, wrote the cipher found in my dedication. I also thank all those who helped us, in large ways and small, to develop this amazing run of *Secrets* books.

Personal acknowledgments from Dan Burstein: My wife, Julie O'Connor, and my son, David D. Burstein, have not only put up with a lot to make these books happen but have contributed a great deal as well. As a family, we have spent countless hours trying to decode artworks, mysteries, clues, and connections in the Dan Brown novels. We have traveled in the footsteps of Robert Langdon to Paris, Rome, and now Washington, D.C., as well. As tangible indications of our rich family collaboration on these pursuits, *Secrets of The Lost Symbol* features an essay by David D. Burstein (see chapter 2) and photographs of notable buildings in Washington by Julie O'Connor. My partnership with Arne de Keijzer to create and write these books is a family affair, too, and I deeply appreciate the love and support from Helen and Hannah de Keijzer. Special thanks to family, friends, and business partners for all their ideas, practical help, moral support, and patience while I have been occupied trying to finish this book: Jean Aires, Dan Borok, Craig and Karina Buck, Bonnie Burstein, Max Chee, Betsy DeTurk and her family, Marty Edelston, Judy Friedberg, Adam Guha, Joe Kao, Barbara O'Connell, Cynthia O'Connor and her family, Joan Aires O'Connor, Maureen O'Connor, Peter G. Peterson, Angeles and Sergio Sanchez, Sam Schwerin, and Brian Waterhouse. As I think about the forces that have shaped my life, my ideas, and all my creative works, including this book, there is perhaps no more important acknowledgment due than the one to my parents. If ever there were immortal souls in this world, they belong to Dorothy and Leon Burstein, who died in 1983 and 1991, but whose gifts of wisdom and values remain accessible to me every single day of my life.

And last but far from least, we raise in thanks a glass, or perhaps a skull, to Dan Brown. His groundbreaking efforts to wrap some of the great ideas from the history of Western culture—complete with its controversies, "hidden history," and ties to ancient wisdom—within the genre of the action-adventure story set us off on our quest to know more, and to share the results with our readers. It has been a rich intellectual journey for us, and deeply satisfying, no matter how much remains "buried out there."

Dan Burstein

Arne de Keijzer

DECEMBER 2009

Contributors

Dan Burstein is the co-author and co-editor, with Arne de Keijzer, of *Secrets of The Lost Symbol*. This is the sixth title in the *Secrets* series, which was launched in 2004 with Burstein's *Secrets of the Code: The Unauthorized Guide to the Mysteries Behind The Da Vinci Code*. On its way to becoming the world's bestselling guidebook to *The Da Vinci Code*, *Secrets of the Code* spent more than twenty weeks on the *New York Times* bestseller list, appeared in more than thirty languages, and landed on more than a dozen notable bestseller lists around the world. The *Secrets* series, developed by Burstein and de Keijzer, includes *Secrets of the Code*, *Secrets of Angels & Demons/Inside Angels & Demons*, *Secrets of the Widow's Son*, *Secrets of Mary Magdalene*, and *Secrets of "24."* The series has led to two special collector's editions of *U.S. News & World Report* and three documentary films now available on DVD, including Sony's *Secrets of the Code* (narrated by Susan Sarandon). Currently, some four million copies of *Secrets* books are in print in more than fifty publishing markets around the world.

An investor in innovative new technology companies since his first experiences in Silicon Valley in the 1980s, Burstein founded in 2000 Millennium Technology Ventures, a New York–based family of venture capital and private equity funds. Since then, Burstein has served on the boards of more than a dozen technology companies. Prior to Millennium, he served as senior adviser for more than a decade at the Blackstone Group, one of Wall Street's leading private equity firms. He is also a prominent corporate strategy consultant and has served as an adviser to CEOs and senior management teams of Sony, Toyota, Microsoft, and Sun Microsystems.

Dan Burstein is an award-winning journalist and author of numerous books on global economics, politics, technology, and culture, including *Blog!* an in-depth analysis of the emergence of the blogosphere and new social media in the first decade of the twenty-first century. Burstein's first bestseller, *Yen!*, focused on the rise of Japanese financial power in the late 1980s and was a bestseller in more than twenty countries, achieving recognition as the number one business book in Japan in 1989. His 1995 book, *Road Warriors*, was one of the first books to analyze the impact of the Internet and digital technology on business and society. *Big Dragon*, written with Arne de Keijzer in 1998, outlined a long-term view of China's role in the twenty-first century. The book was read by both U.S. President Bill Clinton and Chinese Prime Minister Zhu Rongji prior to their first summit. As a freelance journalist in the 1980s and early '90s, Burstein wrote more than one thousand print articles for more than one hundred different global publications. His leading-edge journalism has been recognized with Sigma Delta Chi and Overseas Press Club awards. Burstein has appeared on talk shows that span the gamut from *Oprah* to *Charlie Rose*, with dozens of appearances on CNN, MSNBC, and CNBC.

Arne de Keijzer is co-creator, with Dan Burstein, of the *Secrets* series. He has written or contributed to a wide variety of publications and books on topics ranging from international business guides to new technologies. Early in his career he was directly involved with the development of cultural, educational, and business exchanges with China, which led him to form his own business consultancy in the China trade. During that period he also wrote the bestselling *China Guidebook* and two editions of *China: Business Strategies for the '90s*.

He turned to writing full-time in the mid-1990s and, together with Dan Burstein, wrote *Big Dragon*, an innovative look at China's economic and political future and its impact on the world. The team subsequently formed Squibnocket Partners LLC, a creative content development company whose first book was *The Best Things Ever Said About the Rise, Fall, and Future of the Internet Economy* (2002). Most recently, he helped launch the *Secrets* series, which now includes the bestselling *Secrets of the Code*, *Secrets of Mary Magdalene*, *Secrets of the Widow's Son*, *Secrets of "24,"* and *Inside Angels & Demons*.

Amir Aczel is a mathematician and historian of science known for numerous nontechnical books, including several *New York Times* and international bestsellers. Among his best-known works are *Fermat's Last Theorem*, which was nominated for a Los Angeles Times Book Award, and *The Jesuit and the Skull*. Aczel is a frequent guest on television and radio programs for CNN, CNBC, NPR, and others. He is a fellow of the John Simon Guggenheim Memorial Foundation.

Diane Apostolos-Cappadona, adjunct professor of religious art and cultural history at Georgetown University, has been called the closest thing the academic world has to a real "symbologist." Her research focuses on the interconnections of art, gender, and religion. Her books include the *Encyclopedia of Women in Religious Art*. She currently serves as a guest curator for the international exhibit The Seventh Veil: Salome Unveiled, Re-veiled, and Revealed.

Karen Armstrong is an international bestselling author who writes and comments frequently on comparative religion and the search for religious traditions suited to modern times. She was awarded the TED prize in 2008 and is working on an international project to launch an online Charter of Compassion, crafted by leading thinkers in Judaism, Islam, Hinduism, and Buddhism. Her many books include *The Great Transformation: The Beginning of Our Religious Traditions* and, most recently, *The Case for God*.

William Arntz is a physicist, software developer, and practicing Buddhist. As producer, writer, and director of the award-winning documentary *What the Bleep Do We Know!?* he explored the interconnectedness of all things, from quantum physics to New Age thinking. He has recently completed a new film on similar themes, *GhettoPhysics*. A *Bleep* study guide created with the Institute for Noetic Sciences can be found at www.whatthebleep.com/guide.

Lou Aronica is a contributing editor to *Secrets of The Lost Symbol*. His successful career includes serving as head of several publishing houses, where he acquired notable bestsellers, as well as writing successful fiction and nonfiction himself. His latest book is *The Element* (written with Sir Ken Robinson), which is a *New York Times* bestseller.

Michael Barkun has written widely on conspiracy theories, terrorism, and millennial and apocalyptic movements. A professor of political science at Syracuse University, he has served as a consultant to the FBI and has held grants and fellowships from the Harry Frank Guggenheim Foundation, among others. His books include *A Culture of Conspiracy: Apocalyptic Visions in Contemporary American Society* and *Religion and the Racist Right: The Origins of the Christian Identity Movement*.

Paul Berger is a British freelance writer living in New York. He is the author/ contributing editor of seven books, including *All the Money in the World: How the Forbes 400 Make—and Spend—Their Fortunes, Secrets of the Code*, and *Secrets of The Lost Symbol*. His writing has appeared in the *New York Times*, the *Guardian*, the *London Times*, *Wired*, and *Forbes*, among others. He is author of the blog Englishman in New York (www.pdberger.com).

Steven C. Bullock is a specialist in American social and cultural history. His bestselling book, *Revolutionary Brotherhood*, is recognized as the classic work about Freemasonry and its connections to the Colonial period, the American Revolution, and the Founding Fathers. A professor of history at Worcester Polytechnic Institute, Bullock has commented on Masonry in documentaries and is a frequent media guest.

David D. Burstein is the founder and executive director of 18 in '08, the nation's largest youth-run nonpartisan not-for-profit young voter engagement organization. He is the winner of a 2009 Do Something Award and writes regular commentaries on media, youth, and politics for the *Huffington Post*. He is currently a junior at New York University and at work on a book about the Millennial generation.

Richard Dawkins, a British zoologist, neo-Darwinian evolutionary biologist, and outspoken atheist, established the Richard Dawkins Foundation for Reason and Science to promote rationalism over religion. The Charles Simonyi Professor Emeritus for the Understanding of Science at Oxford University, he has authored numerous books, including *The Greatest Show on Earth* and the worldwide bestselling *The God Delusion.*

Arturo de Hoyos is a 33° Mason and holder of the Grand Cross of the Court of Honor in the Supreme Council of Scottish Rite Masonry. Considered America's leading Masonic scholar, his most popular book, *Is It True What They Say About Freemasonry? The Methods of Anti-Masons,* co-authored with S. Brent Morris, is now in its fourth enlarged edition. De Hoyos is also author of *The Scottish Rite Ritual Monitor and Guide.*

Hannah de Keijzer is a writer, researcher, dancer, massage therapist, and paper artist living in Philadelphia. She was a contributing writer and editor for *Secrets of Angels & Demons,* and has worked as an editorial associate at the publisher David R. Godine. Hannah continues to explore the intersections of religion, cognitive science, and culture.

Elonka Dunin is an expert on the CIA's *Kryptos* sculpture and author of *The Mammoth Book of Secret Codes and Cryptograms.* She helped crack the ciphers on the *Cyrillic Projector* and maintains a popular cryptography-related Web site at www.elonka.com. She is a game developer at Simutronics, the developers of CyberStrike and HeroEngine, among others. She is cofounder and chairperson of the International Game Developers Association's Online Games Group.

Glenn W. Erickson, professor of philosophy at the Universidade Federal do Rio Grande do Norte, Brazil, has written extensively on the interstices of philosophy, mathematics, and the arts. He is a prior contributor to *Secrets of the Code* and *Secrets of Angels & Demons.*

Heather Ewing is a former curator and architectural historian at the Smithsonian Institution, and the author of a biography of its founding benefactor, *The Lost World of James Smithson: Science, Revolution, and the Birth of the Smithsonian.*

Jack Fruchtman Jr., professor of political science at Towson University, is the author of, among other works, *Atlantic Cousins,* which traces the extraordinary influence of Enlightenment thinking on all areas—science, politics, faith, and the mystery traditions—for Ben Franklin and the other Founding Fathers. He is also author of *Thomas Paine: Apostle of Freedom.*

Warren Getler, a Washington, D.C.–based former investigative reporter with the *Wall Street Journal* and the *International Herald Tribune,* is co-author of *Rebel Gold.* He served as historical consultant for Disney's *National Treasure: Book of Secrets* and has given lectures on the theme of the Knights of the Golden Circle at the National Archives, Ford's Theater, and other locations in the nation's capital.

Marcelo Gleiser is the Appleton Professor of Natural Philosophy and professor of physics and astronomy at Dartmouth College. He has written several popular science books, and is also author of more than eighty peer-reviewed papers in cosmology and astrobiology. Gleiser is the recipient of many awards, including the Faculty Fellows Awards from the White House. His forthcoming book is *A Tear at the Edge of Creation: Searching for the Meaning of Life in an Imperfect Cosmos.*

Deirdre Good is professor of the New Testament at the General Theological Seminary in New York. A widely respected scholar of religion, her work centers on the Gospels, noncanonical writings, and the origins of Christianity. She has served as a consultant to A&E, the History Channel, and others for programs and publications relating to *The Da Vinci Code.*

Ron Hogan is the founding curator of Beatrice.com, one of the Internet's first literary Web sites, and the author of *The Stewardess Is Flying the Plane!: American Films of the 1970s.* The ideas in his article were first developed in posts to the publishing industry news blog GalleyCat.

Mitch Horowitz is the editor in chief of Tarcher/Penguin and the author of *Occult America: The Secret History of How Mysticism Shaped Our Nation*. A widely known proponent of metaphysical and esoteric ideas, Horowitz has written for *U.S. News & World Report, Parabola*, the Religion News Service, and the popular Weblog BoingBoing and has numerous media appearances to his credit. His Web site is: www.MitchHorowitz.com.

Eamon Javers is a White House correspondent for *Politico* (www.politico.com). He has also served as a Washington correspondent for *BusinessWeek* and an on-air reporter for CNBC.

George Johnson is winner of the AAAS Science Journalism Award and co-founder of the Santa Fe Science Writing Workshop. He writes about science for the *New York Times, Scientific American*, the *Atlantic*, and other publications. In addition to several books on science (including, most recently, *The Ten Most Beautiful Experiments*) he has also written *Architects of Fear: Conspiracy Theories and Paranoia in American Politics*.

Steven Johnson has worked as a columnist for *Discover* magazine, *Slate*, and *Wired*, and founded the news-aggregator outside.in. He is an expert on the interconnection between technology and culture and author of *Everything Bad Is Good for You: How Today's Popular Culture Is Actually Making Us Smarter*. His most recent book is *The Invention of Air: A Story of Science, Faith, Revolution, and the Birth of America*.

Mark E. Koltko-Rivera is a 32° Freemason, Masonic Knight Templar, and Masonic scholar who holds awards for research in humanistic psychology and the psychology of religion. He is the author of *Freemasonry: An Introduction* and the forthcoming *Discovering The Lost Symbol: Magic, Masons, Noetic Science, and the Idea That We Can Become Gods*. Koltko-Rivera also maintains several blogs on Freemasonry at www.google.com/profiles/markkoltkorivera.

Irwin Kula is a sought-after speaker, writer, and commentator. Rabbi Kula has inspired millions by using Jewish wisdom to speak to all aspects of modern life. *Newsweek* ranked him in the Top 10 of its "Top 50 Rabbis in America." His book, *Yearnings: Embracing the Sacred Messiness of Life*, won several awards, and he regularly blogs for the *Huffington Post* and the *Washington Post* and *Newsweek*'s On Faith section. Kula is president of CLAL, a leadership-training institute, think tank, and resource center in New York City.

Thomas Levenson is a professor and the director of the graduate program in writing and humanistic studies at the Massachusetts Institute of Technology. The winner of a Peabody Award (shared), New York Chapter Emmy, and AAAS/Westinghouse Award, his articles and reviews have appeared in the *Atlantic Monthly,* the *Boston Globe,* and *Discover.* His most recent book, *Newton and the Counterfeiter,* was published in 2009.

Lynne McTaggart is a researcher, lecturer, and an authority on the science of spirituality. She publishes health newsletters and is editor of an online course called Living the Field. McTaggart has written five books, including the bestsellers *The Intention Experiment* and *The Field.* She is also the architect of the Intention Experiment, a Web-based "global laboratory" that tests the power of group intention to change the world.

Michael Parkes studied graphic art and painting at the University of Kansas and then traveled for three years throughout Asia and Europe. An American, he settled in Spain in 1975, where he still lives. He has had numerous international exhibitions of his work, in which metaphysical and spiritual elements are joined to reality. His work evokes a mysterious atmosphere that can often only be deciphered with the help of ancient mythology and Eastern philosophy.

David Plotz is editor of the online magazine *Slate* and author of *Good Book: The Bizarre, Hilarious, Disturbing, Marvelous, and Inspiring Things I Learned When I Read Every Single Word of the Bible.* The recipient of the National Press Club's Hume Award for Political Reporting and other awards, Plotz has written for the *New York Times Magazine, Harper's, Rolling Stone, New Republic, Washington Post, GQ,* and other publications.

Ingrid Rowland is a professor at the University of Notre Dame School of Architecture, based in Rome. An expert on the history of ideas, she is a regular contributor to the *New York Review of Books.* She has written several books, including *The Scarith of Scornello: A Tale of Renaissance Forgery, From Heaven to Arcadia: The Sacred and the Profane in the Renaissance,* and, most recently, *Giordano Bruno: Philosopher Heretic.*

Jim Sanborn is the Washington, D.C.–based sculptor of *Kryptos.* Noted for his science-based installations that illuminate hidden forces, he has created artwork for locations such as the Massachusetts Institute of Technology and major U.S. museums. He received a Bachelor of Arts degree in art history and sociology from Randolph-Macon College, and a Master of Fine Arts degree in sculpture from Pratt Institute in 1971.

Marilyn Mandala Schlitz serves as the CEO and president of the Institute of Noetic Sciences (IONS) and has pioneered clinical and field-based research in the areas of human consciousness, transformation, and healing. Her books include *Living Deeply: The Art and Science of Transformation in Everyday Life* and *Consciousness and Healing: Integral Approaches to Mind Body Medicine*. She is also senior scientist at the California Pacific Medical Center.

Jeff Sharlet is a Pulitzer Prize–winning writer and investigative journalist who stirred up the Washington, D.C., establishment with his book *The Family: The Secret Fundamentalism at the Heart of American Power,* for which he reported from within the oldest and most influential religious right organization in the United States. He is co-author of *Killing the Buddha, A Heretic's Bible* and is also a visiting research scholar at New York University's Center for Religion and Media.

David A. Shugarts, the senior contributing editor for *Secrets of The Lost Symbol,* is an investigative reporter and core member of the *Secrets* team. He has been a journalist for more than thirty-five years, and his profile of Dan Brown and the predictions he made about the content of *The Lost Symbol,* detailed in his book *Secrets of the Widow's Son* (2005), proved remarkably prescient and won him national acclaim. Additionally, he is a songwriter, beekeeper, sailor, aviation expert, and marketing and communications consultant.

Mark A. Tabbert is director of collections at the George Washington Masonic National Memorial in Alexandria, Virginia. A Masonic brother, leading Masonic historian, and former director of collections at the Scottish Rite National Heritage Museum, he wrote the definitive work, *American Freemasons: Three Centuries of Building Communities.*

James Wasserman is the founder of TAHUTI Lodge, now the second oldest continuous Ordo Templi Orientis Lodge in the world. His several books include *The Secrets of Masonic Washington* and *The Mystery Traditions: Secret Symbols and Sacred Art.* He is currently at work on *An Illustrated History of Solomon's Temple.* Wasserman's Web site is www.studio31.com.

PLAN
of the City of Washington
in the Territory of Columbia.
ceded by the States of
VIRGINIA and MARYLAND
to the United States of America,
and by them established as the
SEAT of their GOVERNMENT,
after the Year
MDCCC.

Engrav'd by Sam.l Hill, Boston.

GEORGE TOWN.

Rock Creek.

Road leading from the Canal at the Lower Falls, distant 3½ miles.

President's House.

Mouth of Tiber Creek.

PART OF VIRGINIA WITHIN THE TERRITORY OF COLUMBIA.

POTOMAK RIVER.

Observations
explanatory of the Plan.

I. THE positions for the different Edifices,
and for the several Squares or Areas of different
shapes, as they are laid down, were first determined on the most advantageous ground, com-
manding the most extensive prospects, and the
better susceptible of such improvements as either use or
Ornament may hereafter call for.

II. LINES or Avenues of direct communication have
been devised, to connect the separate and most distant
objects with the principal, and to preserve through the whole
a reciprocity of sight at the same time. Attention has been
paid to the passing of those leading Avenues over the most favorable ground for prospect and convenience.

III. NORTH and South lines, intersected by others running
due East and West, make the distribution of the City into Streets,
Squares, &c. and those lines have been so combined as to meet at certain given points with those divergent Avenues, so as to form on the
spaces first determined, the different Squares or Areas.

SCALE OF POLES.

100   200   300   400   500   600 Poles

2.   3.   4.   5.   6. Inches